COPYRIGHT © 2003
CROWN OF LIFE MINISTRIES, INC.
P.O. BOX 306
JASPER, AR 72641

*THE MYSTERY OF ISLAM* ISBN 0-972-49700-5

Unless otherwise noted, all scripture quotations are taken from the KJV Bible. Koranic references are selected from *The Meaning of the Glorious Koran* by Mohammed M. Pickthall.

Cover photograph: Sherwood Burton  Two Arab men going up to Abraham's tomb in Hebron to pray.  Daystar Images 400 Bath Road, Brunswick ME 04011, USA.  Copyright 1995, All rights reserved.

Cover Design: Joy Little and Isaac Rudolph
Interior Design: Alysa Little

Greatful acknowledgement is also given to:
DAYSTAR INTERNATIONAL INC., Orlando, FL. for permission to print excerpts from *The Jesus Visions*.

*Mountain Movers,* Springfield, MO. for permission to print *"I Saw Jesus".*

Keith Wheeler Ministries, Tulsa, OK. for permission to quote portions of the June '95 and October '96 newsletters.

TO THE MISSIONARIES AND MARTYRS
WHO HAVE SO FAITHFULLY LABORED
AND SACRIFICED FOR THE GOSPEL IN MUSLIM LANDS

AND TO THE MULTITUDES
WHO WILL YET DEDICATE THEMSELVES TO CHRIST
TO BRING IN THE LAST GREAT HARVEST OF SOULS:
THE SONS AND DAUGHTERS OF ISHMAEL

# The

# Mystery

# of

# Islam

## A CHRISTIAN PERSPECTIVE ON ISLAM

GENE LITTLE TH.D.

# Acknowledgments

I would like to thank the following "saints" without whose prayers and encouragement this book could not have been completed: to Marylois, my loving wife and fellow co-laborer in the Lord, "Mom" Hilley, "Auntie" Milly, Sister Gwen, and June Lewis. *May the Lord richly bless you.*

# "The Mystery of Islam"

FOREWORD
    BY JUNE LEWIS         1
PREFACE         5

CHAPTER ONE:
    A SON TO LOVE         10

CHAPTER TWO:
    THE WORLD OF ISLAM         14

CHAPTER THREE:
    THE TENTS OF ISHMAEL         29

CHAPTER FOUR:
    MUHAMMAD, PROPHET OF THE SWORD         50

CHAPTER FIVE:
    QUALITIES OF A PERFECT MAN         57

CHAPTER SIX:
    *"WHO IS LIKE UNTO THEE, O LORD..."*         74

CHAPTER SEVEN:
    *"THE TRUTH MADE PLAIN"*         82

CHAPTER EIGHT:
    THE SWORD OF THE GIANT         89

CHAPTER NINE:
    *"THE SCRIPTURES SPEAK OF ME..."*         109

CHAPTER TEN:
    THE TRADITIONS OF ISLAM         120

CHAPTER ELEVEN:
    THE SPIRIT OF TRUTH         131

**CHAPTER TWELVE:**
    THE SON OF GOD        149

**CHAPTER THIRTEEN:**
    *"AT THE CROSS"*        160

**CHAPTER FOURTEEN:**
    *"IF ALLAH WILLS"*        180

**CHAPTER FIFTEEN:**
    THE HAND OF FATIMA        190

**CHAPTER SIXTEEN:**
    SETTING THE CAPTIVES FREE        212

**CHAPTER SEVENTEEN:**
    HAGAR'S LEGACY        226

**CHAPTER EIGHTEEN:**
    DAUGHTERS OF THE KING        240

**CHAPTER NINETEEN:**
    *"YE SHALL FIND"*        254

**APPENDICES**

| | | |
|---|---|---|
| A. | ISLAMIC ARTICLES OF FAITH | 282 |
| B. | THE PILLARS OF ISLAM | 285 |
| C. | THE HISTORY OF MUHAMMAD'S SUCCESSORS | 288 |
| D. | ISLAM, ONE FAITH: MANY SECTS | 291 |
| E. | NAMES GIVEN TO MUSLIM MEN AND WOMEN | 297 |
| F. | "THE POWER OF THE PRINTED PAGE" | 300 |
| G. | "I SAW JESUS" | 305 |
| H. | SEVEN STEPS FOR WINNING MUSLIMS TO CHRIST | 309 |
| I. | THE WORTH OF A SOUL | 311 |

GLOSSARY        315
SELECTED BIBLIOGRAPHY        324
AN APPEAL TO MUSLIMS        331

# Explanatory Notes

Throughout this manuscript, the more phonetically correct English spellings for Muhammad and Muslim are used. Other translations, such as Mohammed and Moslem are correct and appear in various quotations and references. I have chosen to retain the more traditional English form of spelling for Koran. The word Quran is also correct and gaining wide acceptance in the English language

Koranic references in English are in many cases an approximation. The numbering of verses may differ by some two or three *ayas* in various English versions, depending on what Koran the reader is using. The letter *S.* (*Surah, Sura, Surrat*) is used to identify particular chapters in the Koran. I have also chosen to insert Koranic chapter titles after many of the *Surahs* that are cited, so as to assist the reader.

# THE MYSTERY OF ISLAM

*L*ET THE WILDERNESS AND THE CITIES
THEREOF LIFT UP THEIR VOICE,
THE VILLAGES THAT KEDAR DOTH INHABIT:
LET THE INHABITANTS OF THE ROCK SING,
LET THEM SHOUT FROM THE TOP OF THE MOUNTAINS.

LET THEM GIVE GLORY UNTO THE LORD
AND DECLARE HIS PRAISE IN THE ISLANDS.

ISAIAH 42:11-12

# FOREWORD

"*The Mystery of Islam*" began not as a book, but as a Bible School Course taught by its author, Gene Little, at the International School of Ministry (I.S.O.M.), located near Jasper, Arkansas. I sat in those classes, hungrily devouring the wealth of information that this course offered.

Abraham's prayer in Genesis 17:18, "*O that Ishmael Might Live before thee*" had also been my frequent prayer for several years as I interceded for the forgotten sons and daughters of Abraham and Hagar. My intercession began when God gave me a supernatural burden for the Arab nations, and the Islamic peoples over three years earlier. God had also spoken to me, that I must make space in my teaching schedule on several continents, yearly, for the nations of the Mid-East. Soon, the Lord said, He would move mightily amongst these people.

It was only after that I had begun praying for Muslims that supernatural things began to occur concerning these nations and my life. I began to receive fax's from people I didn't know, who lived in nations I'd almost never heard of —nations that were reportedly "closed" to the Gospel. These messages were from hidden groups of Christians within these countries. They were urging me to come to them. These secret believers wanted teachings on prayer, spiritual warfare, high praises and worship. They wanted to know also, how God would use them to open the heavens over their nations. I knew at once, I was to go to them. The inner witness that I had already received from the Lord had already moved me in this direction.

1

It was at this point that Gene Little taught his course on on Islam. We learned how to build bridges of trust and friendship with Muslims; an essential undertaking if they are ever to be open to us, and to hear, really hear our words of life. The course also informed us about what Muslims believe, and how they practiced their faith. It taught us which of the Old Testament truths Christians and Muslims agreed upon, and also what parts of the New Testament were accepted by Islam. I knew this study was a provision of God for me, for I was planning even then, to make a trip into an Islamic nation. This Muslim country was one of the nations, where a hidden group had asked for me to minister. I cannot reveal more than this, without endangering the people there, and the work for Christ that they are doing.

I left the United States, having only the name of the group's leader and his telephone/fax number; a single number. Other than this information, I had no other way to contact or communicate with them. Just before leaving, though, I sent them my arrival date and time by fax. However, I did not realize that this information never reached them, as the telephone number had been disconnected (Afraid of discovery, this group had moved suddenly to a new and safer location. The old number was disconnected while they awaited a new number).

As I sat in an airport somewhere in the Middle East awaiting my final connection, which would carry me to my destination, the Holy Spirit whispered softly: *"No one will meet you at the Airport when you arrive, but do not be afraid, for I am with you."* God spoke so peacefully to me, that I did not become afraid. I knew I was in His Hands.

After boarding the aircraft, I was surprised to see at the last possible moment, a veiled Muslim woman come aboard the plane, and with many seats available, she came straight to me, even squeezing between me and another passenger. I felt a shiver of fear. Could she be a spy sent to discover my full purpose in visiting this nation? As

2

I was prayerfully pondering this possibility, the Holy Spirit brought to memory all the things I had learned in Brother Gene's course, only a few weeks earlier. I then decided I would use this new knowledge to make this veiled woman my friend, instead of my enemy.

At first we chatted freely, but then we began to talk earnestly about God. It was easy for me, since I already knew what she believed. I was able to ask questions to which I could then happily respond, *"That's what we Christians also believe!"* We shared about our faiths with each other. She was not threatened, and so this happy exchange went on for several hours. This beautiful Arab woman enjoyed talking about her faith with me, and soon bonds of fellowship were forged between us, during this four-hour flight.

We arrived, yet the plane was so late in getting in that even the money changers were closed. I did not even have a local coin to phone my only contact. Even as the Lord had forewarned me, there was no one there to meet me. I was alone late at night in a hostile nation and without any local currency.

As we proceeded through customs, I was horrified to see that all the luggage was being opened and then thoroughly searched. This was NOT SUPPOSED TO HAPPEN! The underground church had assured me that luggage was never opened in this small airport, and so they'd asked me to bring in as many Bibles, Christian books, tapes and studies as possible. I had done this!

Later I was to learn what happened. There had been riots in the days preceding my arrival, between two Islamic sects. Foreign agitators were coming in, and as a precaution against admitting terrorists, all luggage was now being searched. What could I do?

Just then, my friend from the flight, seeing the long lines of people being searched, turned to me and said, *"Come with me."*

I fell in behind her and her carts of luggage, with my own cart. To my amazement, when the custom officials saw her, they nodded respectfully, smiled, and then waved her, and me (since I was with her) through customs; without even opening one suitcase. I praise God who sees so far ahead, and who makes provision for every kind of situation and circumstance.

This precious lady would not leave me alone in the airport. It was she who called the number I had, and discovered the phone had been recently disconnected.

*"Tomorrow"* she said, *"I will find out the new number for you and I will call your friends to let them know where you are, but tonight I will put you in a hotel. I insist!"*

She did all these things for me, and by noon the next day I was united with my friends. We had many days of teachings and praying together.

But that night, alone in the hotel, I thanked God for His great mercy and care for me. I praised Him for providing me with such a kind and powerful friend in this time of crisis. It was this devoted Muslim lady that God had used to deliver me out of a situation so potentially dangerous.

I also thanked God for my Brother Gene, who had taught me such precious and valuable things about Islam. Things that had enable me to make friends with a Muslim woman who had blessed me so richly.


Dr. June Lewis, ThD
Missionary, Author, Bible Professor
Jackonville, Florida

# PREFACE

# "In Perils of Deep Waters"

My first exposure to the Muslim world came as a shock. It was precipitated by a collision between two ships. Late at night, while undergoing refueling operations our aircraft carrier the USS Saratoga was struck on the starboard side by a tanker, which had suffered a "steering casualty." Some of our "catwalks" were crushed and the aft elevator was damaged, but God was good to us. It was only a glancing blow and damage was minimal. No one was hurt. We soon dropped anchor in Alexandria, Egypt for scheduled port visit and damage assessment. Here we stayed for five days.

Leaving the ship, I found myself walking the streets of Alexandria and then Cairo. I saw the land of Egypt, the Nile, the villages, and the ever-present desert. As a new Christian, my eyes were opened to the influence of Islam. I saw the mosques, and even ventured into the great Mosque of Cairo, humbly taking off my shoes to walk upon the "holy ground." In the marketplace, I heard the call for prayer go forth. Some of the people I saw ignored it, while others placed their prayer mats to the ground. I spent a few days among these people, yet barely got to know them. I was a light for Christ, but unfocused.

Since that time, my journey in life has taken me to many nations of the world. My love for the Muslim people has grown, overcoming earlier fears and ignorance. I want to see them joyfully embrace Jesus Christ. As a missionary to these people, I look for "heaven sent" opportunities to witness and lead them to salvation. I now live within sight of a mosque. Long before dawn I hear the cry of the *Muezzin*, calling the faithful to prayer. I have seen on Arabic television, hundreds of thousands pilgrims circling the *Kaba*. I have been in the midst of faithful Muslims streaming towards the *Al-Aksa* mosque to worship. I have felt the concussions of Islamic terrorist bomb blasts. I have also known the love extended towards my family from Muslims who have opened up their homes and hearts.

For those who have chosen not to embrace its ways, Islam is a mystery, an enigma, a puzzle. It has been described as a simple faith, a religion of the times adhered to by more than a billion followers. A popular faith, Islam is a religion of the people. It lacks a central leadership thus having, no ecclesiastical offices. Guidance is received from its holy book, the Koran, and from the recorded traditions of its prophet Muhammad. Approval is found through meritorious acts, fasting, prayer, pilgrimages and obedience to God.

Islam is a religion which speaks of peace, yet urges its followers to wage *jihad* or holy war against non-believers. It is a study in contrasts. The Koran, declares *"there shall be no compulsion in religion"*(S. 2:256). Then this divine guidebook mysteriously reverses its earlier thoughts and issues forth an edict *"He who chooses a religion other than Islam will not be accepted in this world and in the world to come"* (S. 3:86). The only true faith in *Allah's* sight is Islam (S. 3:19). It is a faith, which identifies itself as the last great revelation from God. The fact that many of its theological revelations run counter to what God had disclosed in His words to the Jewish and Christian people is no matter for Islam. It is always right. This religion declares that its followers are the most noble. Islam views God as being mysterious, incomprehensible and removed from His creation. He cannot be approached or known. Christianity though teaches its followers that they can enjoy a personal relationship with the Creator, calling Him Father. Paradise in Islam is ordained by fate or martyrdom. Salvation for Christianity is by faith.

Islam is declared to be an easy religion by *Allah*, but to many outside the faith, it is rigid, inflexible and smothering. Muslims are counseled by the Koran to view Christians as being the best of all friends (S. 5:83), then mysteriously warned by their Book to make no friends with anyone but their own people (S. 3:118, S. 4:145). Islam is also abrupt and direct in its mandates. The Koran states that those who deny its revelations will burn in everlasting fire and torment (S. 4:56).

Islam is a mysterious faith; a belief system which accepts converts on the strength of a simple declaration. It is religion though which does not allow defections. Anyone who leaves this faith risks losing his life. Muslims are commanded by the Koran to murder those who renounce the faith or seek after another religion (S. 4:89). The *Allah* god, who issues this mandate, is described by the Koran as being merciful and full of grace. Even so, this same god mysteriously abstains from forgiveness and approves of stoning, amputations, crucifixions and beheadings. Islam is mystery, an enigma that begs for an understanding in these times.

Today, Islam is also a social-political system, currently in an epic impact with Western cultural values and Judeo-Christian beliefs. The horrific events of September 11, 2001 perpetuated by Muslim extremists: the hijacking of four airliners, and their subsequent disintegrations, the total destruction of the World Trade Center, the damage to the Pentagon, the loss of countless thousands of lives, followed by deadly anthrax attacks have undeniably focused the world's attention on Islam. These tragedies have engendered calls for retribution, hardened opinions against Muslims, implemented new security measures and generated a war against the *Taliban* regime in Afghanistan.

On the other hand, we now have a President of the United States who willingly enters mosques, hosts Ramadan dinners in the White House and praises Islam for inspiring *"countless individuals to lead lives of honesty, integrity, and morality."*[1] Challenging these declarations is religious broadcaster Pat Robertson. He criticizes these actions, and states President Bush is ignoring history by not acknowledging that Islam is *"violent at its core."* [2] Who then is speaking the truth? Does Islam have an agenda to destroy Western world or is it really a just moral religion? Undoubtedly, this religion is a mystery, an enigma to which most Christians and Western inhabitants of the world are ignorant.

As Christians we no longer have the leisure of ignoring Islam's presence or of avoiding its recognition. Yet, it is imperative that Christians realize that despite world events, we are not at war with Muslims. The Bible says that we war not against flesh and blood, but against powers and principalities. This war against Islamic terrorism is also a war against the kingdom of darkness. A battle though in which we as Christ-believers will emerge victorious if we faint not.

I have endeavored to be like the Gospel Evangelist Luke in the writing of this book, *"to write unto thee"* (dear reader), *"that thou mightest know the certainty of those things wherein thou hast been instructed"* (Lk. 1:4). I have tried to set forth in order *"those things"* which Muslims surely believe, and unravel the mysteries of Islam. I have also sought to include reports from eyewitnesses and ministers of the Word relating as to how the Lord is bringing Ishmael's sons and daughters into His glorious Kingdom.

This is also an hour for intercessors to arise and pray. It is a time to seek the Lord and ask that the veil of hatred and blindness which cover the eyes of Muslims be removed. This is a *kairos* moment to intercede that the demonic strongholds, which hold it together, be shattered. Plead with God that the Holy Spirit be loosed in power throughout the Islamic world, so that the captives of this religion would be set free to find the true path: Jesus Christ, the way, the truth and the light.

My prayer is that Christians will also in these last days reach out to these people. This is a journey that will not be without risks.

There will be perils as we step out in faith to declare the word of God to Muslims. The greatest danger through would be to disobey the Lord's command wand not heed his call to *"Go ye therefore and teach all nations."* The rewards though will be greater than any hazards we will grace. Jesus has promised that *"I am with you always even unto the end of the world."* Hear His call today, and bring them the good news of Salvation.

---

1  *The Washington Times*, Bush praises Islam for its 'morality' 12/6/02, pg. A1.

2  Ibid, Mr. Robertson is also quoted in this article as saying *"Any student of history knows that it's not a peaceful religion. There is absolute virulent hatred of Jews, and the idea that every Jew has got to be killed before the culmination of the age. That what Islam teaches, and I think that's violent."*

# ONE

## *A Son To Love*

Oh, how Abraham must have loved Ishmael. For sixteen years the boy had walked in his shadow, lived in his tent and listened to his words. A precious son, an answer to a old man's wish. A son to teach, to train, to love, to pass an inheritance on to.

Ishmael surely must have loved his father as well. His presence in the household brought Abraham much gladness, but gave the patriarch no peace. Ishmael was a child born of a love divided. The result of a fleshly union long ago between his father and his mother Hagar, a lowly Egyptian maid. She became his second wife, conceiving Ishmael and yet despising the barren Sarai. This root of pride and disrespect gave way to arguments and conflicts within the home. Ishmael as a young boy must have surely witnessed the strife between the two women. As Hagar's child, he was undoubtedly trained by her to be rude and insolent towards Sarai. Ishmael became as *"a wild man,"* spoiled, stubborn, rebellious, untamed. Isaac, the promised son and heir was then born to Sarah (formerly Sarai). This event probably gave Ishmael even more reason to become a thorn in the side to Sarah. The day Isaac was weaned, Ishmael, who was now a young man, mocked her and the babe. The Hebrew verb *tsachaq* is used to interpret his actions. It means scornful laughter: insulting words coupled with shrieks of hateful venomous laughter. Perhaps, in his derision to this miraculous event, Ishmael may have even spit on the boy, since Isaac is a type of Christ. It was all too much for Sarah. She called

Abraham into this, and told him to cast the troublemakers out. A separation ensued. Hagar and Ishmael were permanently banished. Instead of a time of rejoicing, Abraham became deeply grieved.

When Abraham had first heard from the LORD God of Isaac's forthcoming birth, he had earnestly prayed that Ishmael might live before God. The Hebrew word for "live" is *chayah*. It can be interpreted as: to be nourished, to live, to quicken, to restore and to be made whole. Abraham's first thoughts were for God to bless Ishmael. Now abandoned in the desert, he was without water and with no hope of living. The young man's cries were seemingly unanswered. Even his own name: Ishmael, seemed to be a mockery of God's attentiveness to him. Ishmael in the Hebrew language literally means "*God hears.*"

At this very moment of deepest despair, when death seemed near, "*God heard the voice of the lad*" (Gen. 21:17). In an Hebraic play on words, Ishmael heard the voice of Ishmael (the lad). An angel attracted Hagar's attention "*and God opened her eyes...*" to see a well of water. She then went and filled the empty water skin and gave her son a life-giving drink. Scripture then informs us that "*God was with the lad,*" despite all his faults, imperfections, rebelliousness and deep roots of rejection. "*God was with the lad*" (Gen. 21:20).

Today, Ishmael's descendants are the princes of Arabia, the Arabs of Africa, and the Muslims of the world. These "children of Ishmael" honor and revere this man, as well as Abraham. The son of the bondwoman has become a great nation, a multitude of souls. God though still wants to bless Ishmael. He wants to draw all of these children to His side. The LORD God wants to reveal to these lost sons and daughters how much He truly loves them. The Eternal LORD wants these precious children to be *chayah*: restored, made whole again and nourished in His everlasting love. As Creator, He desires that these children know that they are "*...accepted in the beloved*" (Eph. 1:6). They are not cast off or rejected by a distant god who cannot feel their infirmities. Our loving Father God wants to establish a personal relationship with each one of these sons and daughters.

Ishmael's sons and daughters are very thirsty. They are all inwardly crying for a drink of the pure life-giving water, which only God can provide. This water is not found in the well of *Zamzam* for *"...whosoever drinketh of this water will thirst again"* (Jn. 4:13).[1] The real fountain for all of Ishmael's descendants issues forth from the side of Christ crucified. Jesus has said that *"If any man thirst, let him come unto me, and drink"* (Jn. 7:37). This is the true water and hope for Islam: loving submission at the foot of the cross and at the feet of Jesus Christ.

*The Mystery of Islam* is a book written for believers of Jesus Christ. It is a call to more fully know who Muslims are. This writing, is a guidebook for understanding Ishmael: his needs, weaknesses, superstitions, strength and cries. It is a look at Ishmael's world today: Islam, the Koran, *Allah* and Muhammad. It is a call for Christ's people to **LOVE** those who have spit upon and persecuted our Savior unknowingly. It is a plea to hear the advice of our Lord who said, *"Father, forgive them; for they know not what they do"* (Lk. 23:34). Most of all, this book is a call from the minaret of Christianity, for laborers to go forth into the deserts of Islam and give these thirsty sons and daughters of Ishmael a joyful drink from the waters of salvation (Isa. 12:3). They are waiting for you.

---

1.  According to Muslims, the actual well that Ishmael drank is in Mecca. It is located near the sacred *Ka'ba*. This was the well that was revealed to Hagar by an angel (Gen. 21:19). It does not matter to them, that the Bible says she *"...wandered in the wilderness of Beersheba"* (Gen. 21:14). Pilgrims flock to this fount to drink of its life-giving waters. Muhammad, the prophet drank here. Tradition has it that anyone who drinks from the waters of *Zamzam* (Ishmael's well) will find healing, restoration and endued strength. These mineral waters have become highly desired throughout the entire Islamic

**12**

world. Folktales and superstitions abound as to its magical curative effects. Lucrative businesses revolve around the distribution rights ot this water source.

An Arabian legend relates how, Hagar and Ishmael wandered far into the wilderness until they came to the valley where Mecca is located today. It was here, as they were perishing from thirst, that the angel appeared to them and revealed the spring of *Zamzam*. As they lay by the water, the Black Stone (now embedded in the *Ka'ba*) fell from heaven and landed at Ishmael's feet.

Mecca, before being renamed, was originally called *Bakkah*. Some Islamic "scholars" seek to prove the truth of this tale from a portion of scripture found in Psalm 84:6 which says *"Who passing through the valley of Baca make it a well."* The true Baca valley is nowhere near Mecca. It is in Israel near Jerusalem. Here the spring of Gihon is located outside the gates of the city. The valley to the spring is a site for funerals, for it is a graveyard. Hence, the oblique reference to the valley of weeping. *Baca* in Hebrew is translated "weeping."

# TWO

## *The World of Islam*

*T*he faith of Muhammad is experiencing a phenomenal growth in the world today, surpassing all standards and expectations. The crescent shadow of Islam encompasses over forty-four nations. Its presence greatly influences some forty other countries where sizable populations of believers exist (50%). Significant numbers of followers are also found in sixty more homelands (10%). Over **one billion people** claim to adhere to Islam's traditions and rule. This is a faith which has more than doubled in size in the last forty years. It will double again to two billion believers by the year 2020. These Muslim adherents exert a major influence upon the affairs of all humankind. Presently one out of every five persons on the earth is a Muslim (20%). This statistic will again change to one out of four in a quarter century. The vast majority of these Muslims though are not Arabs, but practicing disciples from every race, tribe and nation (80%). The "heart" of Islam is found in the continent of Asia. Here over 60% of the world's Muslim community lives. The four largest Muslim nations in terms of believers are: Indonesia, Pakistan, India, and Bangladesh.

Much of this increase in religious belief, has come quickly, quietly and nonviolently. Fueled by massive injections of petro dollars, Islam is aggressively reaching out into every corner of the world. Mosques appear in every major Western city, and the call to prayer resounds in the ears of the inhabitants. Large Muslim communities are being established within the borders of nations

**14**

once opposed to it. A missionary faith with a worldwide vision, Islam is prospering because of new immigration patterns, inter-marriages and a high birth rate. New converts also add to its explosive increase, as whole people groups reach out to embrace this faith. Islam has awakened from the slumber of centuries, and is now eagerly vying to make disciples from all nations. The Muslim world is experiencing a revival.

Many find themselves attracted to Islam because of its simplicity, legalism, and high moral standards. A spirit of triumphalism has also invaded this faith. Victory without compromise is seen in the attitudes of many who profess its tenets. Islam is also a religion of the sword. *"Submit or perish"* has always been the cry of its militants. Terrorism, fanaticism, and violence help keep its ordinances in effect. The zeal and purity of its members have gained the admiration of many. A strong warlike faith seems infinitely better than the weaknesses of Christianity and other "corrupted beliefs." The Christian concept of humility, lowliness, and turning the other cheek, is just one more sign of how despicably weak it really is. The Muslim believer avows with all his heart that God is on his side. His duty is to be the guardian of the last revelation of God. Those who refuse to accept Islam are heretics: to spill their blood is a privilege meriting the gardens of paradise.

The Koran, Islam's "Bible" has many commands ordering Muslims to carry arms so as to bring the unbelievers into submission. Muslims take these "divine commands" seriously and seek ways to implement them. Those who believe and submit to Islam are of the House of Peace: *Dar al-Islam*. This Arabic term defines the territories in which Islam and Islamic religious laws prevail. The vision of Islam is to include all realms which fall outside of this domain also. These places are considered *Dar al-Harb*: the Abode of War. Muslims therefore, believe that their faith has a Koranic mandate to capture these lands and bring them into the will of *Allah*.

Strategies for winning these territories are being developed and implemented. The most powerful radio transmitter in the world is in Saudi Arabia: *"The Voice of Islam."* Satellite systems are now being used to make this Islamic appeal global. The world's largest printing company is also found in this land. It prints and distributes some 28 million Koran's a year. Saudi Arabia also selectively funds numerous Islamic fundamentalist and reformist movements. Focusing on the Western nations, Islam is making a concerted effort to evangelize and win these countries.

## Europe

In Europe, Islam is making great strides to normalize it presence in society. Denmark now has the first Islamic bank, while Switzerland is home to an Islamic university.[1] Muslims all across the continent, are petitioning authorities for the recognition of their faith as an official religion. Mosques are now established in London, Rome, Paris and Berlin. Germany has some three million believers of Islam within its borders.[2] France has even more. Recently this country has had to ban the recognition of Muslim polygamous marriages, since the net effect of all these "extra" people was harmful to it social/welfare system. *Newsweek* states that France is in serious danger of becoming an Islamic republic unless the tide of North African immigration is soon turned back.[3] Islam is also making tremendous inroads in the United Kingdom.[4] Muslims are now the largest minority religious group in this nation, representing 11% of the total population. Muhammad is the most popular name given for infant boys in the British Isles. The first official Muslim political party has been established. The Islamic Council of Europe is also located in London. Here, Islamic expansion and evangelistic programs are planned and coordinated for the continent. Muslims see England as being the gateway to all of Europe. Hence, if London and the British Isles can be converted, the rest of the Western world will follow.

## Latin America

Latin America beckons the crescent of Muhammad. New mosques are rapidly appearing in Peru, Bolivia and Brazil. Venezuela is home to an $8.5 million dollar Islamic Center and mosque. Panama, Mexico, Chile and Argentina have all had substantial numbers of Muslims move into these nations within the past ten years. The majority of these immigrants who arrive in these lands are Islamic missionaries, sent in by wealthy Arab nations. Their goal is to *"change the religious landscape"* of this area.[5]

## North America

North America is also not immune to this Islamic wave of expansion and revival. The United States is now home to some 1500 mosques. Muslims, with an estimated six million members in this nation, now outnumber those of the Presbyterian faith and the Episcopalian Church.[6] By the year 2015, the number of adherents to Islam is expected to surpass those of the Jewish faith. Islamic chaplains have been accepted within our armed forces. Islamic radio stations beam their messages across every principle city. Arabic television programs are also making an entry into this marketplace. New Mexico is home to an entire Islamic community: the Dar al-Islam. Sizable Islamic populations are found within each one of our continent's major cities. New York City holds over 400,000 Muslims, while Toronto hosts an estimated 200,000. Los Angeles is now, the second largest Iranian city in the world.[7] New mosques have been built in Chicago, Toledo and Washington D.C. Abandoned churches in the ghettos of our country are being rapidly purchased and converted into mosques. The Black community is rushing to embrace Islam. Muhammad's idea of a universal brotherhood, a strict moral code and ethical conduct appeals to many. Eighty-Five percent of all Islamic converts in the United States come from the Afro-American community. Nationwide Muslim students have become more active, organizing over 200

17

chapters of Islamic student associations on university and college campuses. This limited success has encouraged Muslims to exercise more of their Constitutional freedoms. They are now seeking to become more involved in the political and educational processes governing this nation. Political Action Committees have been formed to lobby Congress. The American Muslim Council is one of Islam's most politically active groups in Washington, D.C. This lobbying organization presses government officials for special quotas for Muslim immigrants, as well as the inclusion of Muslims in affirmative-action plans. It also seeks to compel corporations to make special allowances for Muslim employees. Other aims of Islamic groups, include public financial support for Islamic schools, mosques and other institutions, the national recognition of Muslim holidays, and the issuance of commemorative stamps. Appearing to answer these pleas, the U.S. Postal Service released a stamp September 1st, 2001 honoring *Id Al-Adha* (Abraham's offering of his son) and *Id Al-Fitr* (the end of the Ramadan fast). A few weeks later it found itself under attack, from anthrax tainted envelopes presumably sent by Islamic terrorists.

Many of these groups have hidden agendas, a militant outlook and want to pursue a political agenda that advocates a total Islamic United States.[8] Siraj Wahaj, who in 1991 was the first Muslim to deliver the daily prayer in the U.S. House of Representatives, told an Islamic audience in New Jersey that *"If we were united and strong, we'd elect our own emir* (leader) *and give allegiance to him...Take my word, if the six to eight million Muslims unite in America, the country will come to us."*[9] Zaid Shakir, a former Muslim chaplain at Yale University has also stated that Muslims cannot accept the legitmacy of the American secular system which *"is against the orders and ordainments of Allah."*[10] Other Muslim leaders are more conservative, believing the goal of Islam in the new millineum is to elect a president of the United States who will be a Muslim. Shamin A Siddiqi, an influential commentator on American Muslim issues sees Isalmists in power in Washington before 2020. An Assembly of God home missionary to Detroit, the most populous city for Muslims in America, warns that *"We are seeing the thin edge of a large wedge penetrating our cities, and that wedge is Islam."*[11]

## A Change of Allegiance

Despite these sobering facts, Christians should feel encouraged. Jesus said that the gates of hell would not prevail against his church. The fields of Islam are also indeed white unto harvest. Muslims are people who are bonded together by tradition, legalism and fear. God is allowing these barriers to be shaken. Many Muslims are rejecting the idea of Islamic terrorism and reaching out for stability and peace. They are desperately searching for a true God of Love. Surveys prove that only 5 to 10% of all Muslims living in America, are active and affiliated with local mosques or Islamic centers. The rest of these Muslims in the United States are not overtly practicing their faith. Many are in a state of flux, attracted by our relaxed secular lifestyle, yet drawn to the old acceptable ways and folk customs of the past. This change of allegiance has not gone unnoticed by the Islamic nations. Sheik Abdul-Aziz bin Baz, Saudi Arabia's head cleric, issued a warning to parents not to send their children abroad for study or to live with foreign families to learn a Western language. He cited a plot by *"the enemies of Islam"* to corrupt young Muslims as evidence.[12]

The myth of an impregnable Islam is no longer valid. Muslims can, will and are coming into the Kingdom of God. Many have accepted Jesus as their Savior, and have willingly endured persecution and rejection to bring others to Christ. Thousands of African Muslims now believe in Jesus Christ as their Savior, and now meet in "Jesus" mosques. They recite chants in Arabic, worship on Friday, not Sunday and pray five times a day. When they pray, they turn towards Jerusalem instead of Mecca. These "Muslims" have added baptism, communion and foot washing to their practices. They are learning to love instead of hate, and to trust Christ for salvation, rather then their own works. These new believers daily read the New Testament so as to find the guidance they need. Most of these groups have to meet in secret.[13]

## Fallow Fields Ready for Seed

Yes, Islam is experiencing a revival, but all Christianity is on the verge of a greater breakthrough in winning the souls of Ishmael. The last ten years have seen more Muslims come to Christ, than all who have found him in the past 15 centuries. In 1871, the church in Iran had but just nine converts. Robert Bruce, an Irish missionary to this area, summed up his many years of dedicated service to the Muslims by writing this statement: *"I am not reaping the harvest; I can scarcely claim to be sowing the seed; I am hardly ploughing the soil, but I am gathering out the stones. That too is missionary work; let it be supported by loving sympathy and fervent prayer."*[14] Paul Harrison, an early missionary to Arabia, reported winning just five converts to Christ in 50 years. His closing remarks to the Tambaram Missionary conference in 1938, reflected his future vision and mustard seed faith: *"The Church in Arabia salutes you."*[15] These early efforts to evangelize Muslims were small, but sure and steadfast. They were a beginning, from whence a mighty church could flourish. There is still much work to do, but the fields are ready for seed. This seed that we sow is costly, for it has been paid for in blood; the blood of Christ and of the martyrs, who have sacrificed all to prepare the ground (the hearts of men) to receive salvation. Islam is not a religion that will yield it territories easily. Many have died proclaiming Christ to Muslims. God though is not a God who would forget this sacrifice. The spirit of Islam, despite the daily cries from the minarets and the roars from all its fiery fundamentalists is quivering in fear. The time for its dominion is short, for the Last Days are upon us. The LORD in response to this challenge is pouring out His Spirit upon all flesh (Acts 2:17). Today, there is a new openness among Muslims worldwide, to hear and receive the Good News of Jesus Christ. The Spirit of God is indeed moving among these people, in a strong and mighty way.

## Albania

The tiny nation of Albania, which was once declared to be an atheistic state by its former Communistic ruler, Enver Hoxha, is now experiencing a tremendous growth in Christianity. A Muslim nation of nominal believers (65%), Albania is opening up it doors to the good news of Jesus Christ. Some 300 new churches have been established in the country in the past few years. Oil rich Saudi Arabia is frantically trying to turn this nation back to Islam, and has elected to spend a fortune distributing the Koran, as well as rebuilding many mosques. Even so, Islam is not deeply rooted in the country. The people, after decades of communism, are not very sure about their religion. They are though, truly seeking to know God.

## Uzbekistan

Many of the former republics of the Soviet Union, which are now independent such as Uzbekistan have large numbers of Muslims. The church is steadily growing in these areas. This increase in Christian believers has brought persecution, but also has united them and given them a boldness in their witness . There are now over twenty indigenous Uzbek congregations.

## Iran

Iran, hosts a growing church, which has endured much persecution. More than 1000 converts have been baptized in water over the past four years.[16] Some of these converts have never seen a pastor, a Bible nor a church. The Lord though has sovereignly appeared to them and has manifested his love to these little lambs, through healings and miracles.

## Bangladesh

Bangladesh is a fertile field for Christianity. Many Muslims have also seen visions of Jesus and are coming to Christ. The

21

churches in Dhaka, the capital city, have grown from 10 to over 40 places of worship in the last five years.

## Indonesia

A new emerging church is developing in Indonesia. Despite oppression, Christianity has increased 300% in the last 25 years. The U.S. Center for World Missions reports that there are now some 3,000 new village churches with 50,000 converts (90% from a Muslim background).

## Africa

Africa is another fertile field of souls for Christianity. It can no longer be labeled *"the dark continent"* as it is becoming filled with the light of Christ. It once was a continent that was only 3% Christian (1900). Now, more than 40% of the population professes to be Christian. More than 20,000 people a day are coming into Christ's arms.[17] At present the continent is evenly divided between Muslim and Christian believers. The remainder of the populace are tribal animists and/or followers of syncretistic practices. An invisible line though, can be drawn across the middle of this land, separating Islam in the North from Christianity in the South.

Islam is also energetically seeking to evangelize Africa. The sword of persecution is effectively being used in Sudan, in an effort to impose Islam on all the inhabitants. Since 1956, over one million Christians and non-Muslims have been either abducted or murdered by the hands of the country's Muslim majority.[18] The Christian captives who are mostly young boys, are forced to convert to Islam then sold as slaves.[19] Financial enticements are also being used on a national and singular level to add more nations into the fold of Islam and to "recruit" believers into the brotherhood. Malawi, a Christian nation, was offered $640 million dollars by Kuwait, if it would declare itself a Muslim state, and agree to install an Islamic government.[20] On an individual level, non-

Muslims have been promised wives, jobs, money, as well as tax and military exemptions if they convert to Islam. South Africa has also been targeted to be the next Islamic state. Muslim representatives met in October of 1995 in Libya, to discuss ways to Islamize this nation. Yousef Deedat, a spokesman for the South African Muslim delegation, boasted that *"We are going to turn South Africa into a Muslim state. We have the money to do it"*[21] Libyan leader, Muamar Gaddafi, is helping subsidize this plan. Muslim evangelists are also training locals in many nations across the continent, teaching them to refute Christian beliefs with dishonest arguments and half truths, thereby discrediting the Christian faith.

Even so, the church in Africa continues to grow at a prodigious rate. African Evangelist Reinhard Bonke's ministry reported large numbers of people accepting Jesus Christ in a series of revival meetings held in 1995, in Cairo, Egypt. Over 12,000 people attended four nights of services. Pastor William Kamui, of Nigeria, ministers to a mega-church with 150,000 members.[22] The nation of Mozambique, recovering from a 15 year civil war, is in the midst of what can only be termed "supernatural church growth." Zambezoa Province alone has some 300,000 Christian believers. Missionaries state that this area had 380 congregations 10 years ago, but now has 600, and some 2,000 are projected to be established in the next ten years.[23] Nampula Province records a new church being started every month. Steve Hardy, a missionary with the United Baptist Church states that, *"Suffering may be one of the keys as to why so many Mozambicans are turning to Christ."*[24]

Millions of Africans are encountering Christ through cinematic presentations. Two films have had an enormous evangelistical impact on this continent. A movie entitled, *"Sabrina's Encounter"* has been most effective among Muslims. It presents a story of a childless woman's discovery of peace in Christ. To reach the vast audience of African tribes and peoples, the Evangelical Lutheran Church of Tanzania distributes this motion picture via "cinema vans." Already, more than 8 million people have viewed the movie.[25] The *Jesus* film, based on the Gospel of Luke, is also helping to bring millions of souls into the Kingdom of God. Despite the threat of persecution, over 1.6 million citizens of the nation of Sudan have chosen to watch this picture. After just three weeks of showing this movie, 120,000 people indicated that they wanted to follow Jesus. This one outreach saw the establishment of five new churches and hundreds of Bible study groups throughout the country.[26]

### "An Open Door"

Many other "closed" Islamic countries are open to the Gospel. Christian literature, radio and satellite television programs are penetrating these areas with seeds of the Word. A former Soviet radio transmitter on Mt. Ararat is now being used to broadcast Christian programs into the Arab world. Saudi Arabia in an effort to regulate what is being watched inside its kingdom, has banned satellite dishes which pick up international channels. Instead, it has tasked the Ministry of Information with the responsibility of selecting what programs are acceptable from the international networks. These "approved choices," are then distributed by cable, so as to ensure what is seen truly conforms to the country's religious and social values. Even so, Christian television is being broadcast from satellites and onto videos, reaching those who dwell in darkness. Several Christian organizations have recently united together to successfully televise a series of Arabic programs incorporating the Gospel through personal testimonies. These *Oasis* broadcasts have drawn responses from over twenty countries. Letters have been received asking for Bibles and for additional information about the teachings of Christianity[27]. The Voice of Russia radio network is also presenting the Good News to a potential audience of 260 million Arabic-speaking people.[28] This outreach touches listeners as far away as Morocco and Algeria.

The World-Wide Web as well as e-mail, has also penetrated Islam. Christian information, correspondence courses, Bible scriptures and ministry are now available to those who are seeking after Jesus Christ in secret. The International Bible Society has just added onto its web site, a complete version of the Bible translated into the Arabic language.[29] Much more prayer though is needed, before these areas can truly bear fruit. The yearly efforts by the body of Christ to pray for Muslims and others in the 10/40 window are an encouraging start. In addition many Christians are choosing to fast and pray for Muslims during Islam's holy month of Ramadan. This is a time when Muslims unite to seek *Allah* for dreams and visions. Many reports have been received of Jesus appearing to Muslims and revealing himself as their Savior, during this prayer focus.

The fields are indeed white with souls, but the laborers are few. Please, dear reader, pray to the Lord of the Harvest to send Spirit-filled workers into this field. Ask Him to give you a burden to go. It could be as near as your doorstep, the Internet, or your work place. Christian, take the initiative today. **Be Bold!** The Lord will open doors for you. The rewards are eternal!

---

1    Islam has become the fastest growing religion in Denmark. There are at least 25 mosques in Copenhagen alone, as well as Islamic "mission" centers whose task is to spread this faith all over Europe. *Intercede*, Nov. 1994, pg. 8.

2    The largest mosque in Germany with a capacity of 2,500 was dedicated in March of 1995. Lutheran leader Gerherd Ziegler presented the leaders of the mosque with a large check in the name of the city's Protestants, Catholics and Jews: *"To help cover the cost of the DM 10 million building."* *Middle East Digest*, Mar/Apr 1995, pg. 3.

3    May 9, 1989.

4    There are more than 300 former churches in England which have been converted into mosques. The Baptist church that was once attended by William Carey is now a mosque. Carey founded the modern Christian missionary movement, in 1792.

5    "Islamic Leaders Focus On Latin America" *Intercede*, Jan. 1995, pgs. 1, 7.

6    The U.S. Census Bureau cannot ask questions in its surveys about a citizen's religion. Hence, Muslim organizations have be asked to furnish their own estimates on numbers of Islamic believers in the United States. They have arbitrarily come up with the figure of six million Muslims. This estimate was raised in 2001 to seven million. An independent survey conducted in 2001 by the Graduate Center of the City University of New York polled 50,000 Muslims in the United States and submitted an estimate of 1.8 million Muslim believers in the United States. The University of Chicago also held a survey of Muslims and arrived at the figure of two million. The large discrepancy in estimates concerning Muslim believers in the U.S. suggests that Islamic groups are using inflated statistics and phony numbers to influence their political clout in the United States

7    "Mosques on Main Street," Elisabeth Farrell, *Charisma*, Oct. 1997, pgs. 1, 6-7.
8    *"Eighty percent of all mosques, websites and Islamic organizations in the United States are dominated by militant Islam"* Comments by Daniel Pipes, address to University of Washington School of International Studies, Apr. 12, 2002.
9    Daniel Pipes "The Danger Within: Militant Islam in America", Commentary Nov. 2001, www.danielpipes.org
10    Ibid.
11    Joseph Daniels, "Rebuilding The Walls," *Pentecostal Evangel*, Dec. 26, 1993, pgs. 20-21.
12    Akhbar Al Khaaleeji, Dubai, United Arab Emirates, cites by *Arkansas Democrat-Gazette*, Little Rock, AR Aug. 19, 1996, pg. 1.
13    "Of Jesus Mosques and Muslim Christians", Erich Bridges *Mission Frontiers* Jul-Oct 97, pgs. 19-21.
14    Quoted by E. Stock, *History of the Church Missionary Society,* Vol. III, pg. 125.
15    S. Neil, *History of Christian Missions,* pg. 368.
16.    *Herald of His Coming,* July 1996, pg. 11.
17.    Countdown to A.D. 2000, ed. Thomas Wang. 1989.
18.    *Signposts,* Vol. 15 #6, Nov. 1996, Arcadia, South Africa, pg. 15.

19.    Muslim fanatics have crucified hundreds of Christian men and sold thousands of young believers into slavery. A group of doctors traveling in the Sudan on behalf of *The Voice of the Martyrs* ministry, purchased 15 Christian children from Muslim slave traders for $1000. *The Voice of the Martyrs*, Dec. 1996, pg 3.

Two *Baltimore Sun* reporters also bought two slaves for $500 apiece and returned the young men to their families. They used this experience to write a series of front page articles in the summer of 1996 exposing the slave trade in Sudan. See also: Mindy Belz , "Faces in the Cloud" *World*, Vol. 11 #28, Nov. 30/Dec. 7, 1996, pgs. 12-15.

20. *The Malawi Times*, June 6, 1995 pg. 1; cited by *Midnight Call*, Sept. 1995.
21. *Middle East Digest*, Sept/Oct 1996, pg. 2.
22. "Introducing Signs, Miracles & Wonders" Che Ann, *Spread the Fire* Toronto Airport Christian Fellowship, Dec. 96, pg. 10.
23. *Herald of His Coming*, Sept 1991, pg. 11.
24. Ibid.
25. Ibid. Jul. 1996, pg. 11.
26. *Intercede*, Jan/Feb 1997, pg. 3.

"Bishop Nathaniel Garang of the Episcopal Church of Sudan estimates that before the civil war in Sudan, about 15 percent of the southerners were Christian. Now he believes as much as three-fourths of the population has turned to Christ. *'The church is the only institution offering hope to Sudan'* explains Joseph Ikalur, a worker with the New Sudan Council of Churches.

The threat of martyrdom has drawn believers of all denominations closer together and strengthened their resolve. In January (1996), News Network International reported 32,000 people baptized around the Nile town of Bor within two weeks after government troops killed the Rev. Paul Kon Agilti at Bor's Makuac Episcopal church.

Renato Kizito Sedana, a Roman Catholic priest who teaches at Tangaza College in Naairim, Kenya, and has traveled through southern Sudan, tells of Bible teachers trudging on foot from village to village. Tattered record books list hundreds of newly baptized adults in areas where 10 years ago only Islam and spirit-worship were practiced.

*"We visited chapels deep in the bush where people from nearby villages would congregate,"* Sesana recounts, describing undernourished villagers in rags worshipping outdoors by moonlight. *"Their faith and love for Jesus were utterly serious and unquestionable.*

*People long for the healing power of Jesus, the power to restore love and community where there is hatred and division"* World Vision Jun/Jul. 1996, pg. 4.

27. "Oasis Broadcasts Present The Gospel In Arabic" *Intercede* Nov/Dec 1996, pg. 1,6.
28. Ibid., pg. 6.
29. www.gospelcom.net/ibs/bibles/arabic

# THREE

# The Tents of Ishmael

"*These are the sons of Ishmael, and these are their names, by their villages and by their encampments; twelve princes according to their tribes.*" The sons of Ishmael are angry. Many of their tents echo with the sounds of rage and hostility. Chants of *"Death to America"* and calls for *"holy war"* ring out from their dwellings. The nations of Islam are in a ferment. Acts of violence against the West and Israel are rising in popularity. The Third World non-aligned nations are not immune to this outrage either. Algeria, Nigeria, the Philippines and Indonesia are just some of many countries where Islam is in collision with forces that appear to resist its advance. It is a hostility manifested in part through rioting, kidnappings, slavery, assassinations, bombings and church burnings.

The new heroes of Islam are not the rich oil sheiks of Arabia, but terrorists, suicide bombers, and fiery mullahs.[1] The horrendous destruction of the World Trade Center in New York, coupled with the ruin of the Pentagon was brought about by Muslim extremists. Their victory was celebrated with shouts of joy and spontaneous dancing throughout the Islamic world. "The great Satan" had been struck a death blow.

This successful act of terroristic warfare appeared to herald the coming downfall of Islam's enemies. The aftermath of these acts engendered a different reaction from what was originally envisioned by the militants. Nations and world agencies banded

29

together to banish Muslim fanaticism. Success though in this venture must be judged in doing something more than stopping a few terrorist leaders, for the sons of Ishmael are drinking wine from the cup of violence. Triumph over rage must be seen in the light of changing the hearts and minds of all Muslims. Only the Prince of Peace can do it. For it is only through his merciful kindness that he will serve them from the cup of salvation, ere they fall victim to a sword of their own making.

Islam is in the midst of a movement called Islamic extremism. Known also as radical Islam, fundamentalism and Islamism, it is the single most important trend within this faith today. Its cause has existed since the Second World War and is expanding in acceptance. Fundamentalism gained strength during the Iranian revolution of the 1970's. Its message spread during the decade of the 80's and now influences most of the world's forty-four Muslim countries, particularly Egypt, Syria, Lebanon, Iran, Afghanistan, Saudi Arabia and the Palestine Authority. Radical Islam is also widespread within the Muslim community living outside the *Dar al Islam*: Britain, Canada, the United States and other Western Countries host militant Islamists. Its followers advocate a return to pure Islam, such as was practiced by Muhammad in the seventh century. These disciples of rage speak of Islamic world dominion. This form of extremism has inspired more violence and led to greater acts of terror, persecutions, bloodshed and wars in this modern age than any other movement. [2] Driven by fanatical legalism, these Islamic fundamentalists seek to impose a literal Koranic obedience upon their wives, children, neighbors, countrymen and everyone else who stands in their way. They endeavor to stir up the uneducated masses and naïve individuals with slogans and passionate speeches. Those who lead this movement also freely make use of its religious legalisms and fanaticisms as a "cover" so as achieve political aspirations. These radicals also use this movement to obtain money and power.

Muslim fanaticism is a zealous undertaking that strives to live by the sword, choosing to impose its rule by force. Believers adhere to the Koranic command of *Allah*: *"Fighting is obligatory for you"* (S. 2:216, The Cow). Highly intolerant and angry, Muslim radicalism is profoundly hostile to Christians and Jews.[3] Its roots are fed through oil revenues but fertilized by the kingdom of darkness. Muslim fundamentalism is also a generational fury, which affects Ishmael's descendants. It draws its strength from ages past, finding support through a romanticism of terrorism. Martyrdom is glorified, inspiring young children, students and even women to sacrifice themselves for *Allah's* wishes and his offer of a sensual paradise.

## The Spirit of Ishmael

The Lord God promised Abraham that he would bless Ishmael, the son of the bondwoman (Gen. 17:20). He would be great, but the covenant would be established with Isaac, the chosen son. Ishmael, who had grown up at his father's side must have been bitter. He had thought the inheritance of the first-born son would have been given to him. The jealousy and contempt that he had towards Isaac slowly turned into bitterness, resentment and hatred. Ishmael became as God had spoken: a wild man....hostile to every man.

Muslims have chosen their identity with Ishmael. Their traditions are rich with the mighty works of their forefather. They state that it was Ishmael that Abraham offered to God and not Isaac. It was Abraham and Ishmael who rebuilt the sacred *Ka'ba* in Mecca (S. 2:124). Ishmael is their hero. Muhammad in writing the Koran ensured a place of adulation for Ishmael. He cited Ishmael as being an apostle and a prophet to the Arabs. Yet, Ishmael's spirit, that of an untamed hostility, came with this acceptance. Whether all Muslim people physically have Ishmael's blood in their genes is no matter. Through, their love of this man and their rejection of Isaac, they have spiritually tied themselves to Ishmael's heritage. Muslims have unconsciously embraced his spirit of anger, revenge, and hatred towards Isaac (the Jewish race). It is a hatred that is

**31**

manifested throughout the Koran. Numerous *ayas* condemn the Jews: *"Allah has cursed them for their unbelief"* and *"the Jews say: Allah's hand is chained...May they be cursed for what they say!"* serve as just two sterling examples. (S. 4:46, Women; S. 5:64, The Table). Other Koranic passages speak of *Allah* casting the Jews aside and wrathfully turning some of them into *"apes and pigs"* (S. 2:65, S. 5:60, S. 7:166). These particular *ayas* are frequently used by Islamic radicals to further incite hatred against the Jewish race. Sheikh Muhammad Sayyid Al-Tantawi, the highest authority in the Sunni Muslim world described the Jews in his weekly sermon, as being *"the enemies of Allah, sons of pigs and apes."* 4

Christians are affected in this ancient rivalry too, for we are adopted into Isaac's line. Paul writes in Galatians *"We brethren as Isaac was, are the children of promise. But as then he that was born after the flesh persecuted him that was born after the Spirit, even so it is now."* It is Ishmael's spiritual nature to oppress Christianity. The body of Christ has been harassed and vexed for centuries by Islam. It is repressive faith intolerant of other religions. Those who profess Christianity today find themselves persecuted in Lebanon, Egypt, Turkey, Sudan, Saudi Arabia and Pakistan as well as other Islamic nations. The Koran curses those who believe in the Son of God. *"Unbelievers are those who say God is the Messiah, the son of Mary...God will deny him Paradise and the fire shall be his home"* and *"The Christians say Messiah is the son of God...God confound them! How perverse they are!"* (S. 5:72, The Table; S. 9:3, Repentance). Christians are to bless those who persecute them and pray for those who despitefully use them, thus allowing God to use the situation for His glory (Mt. 5:44-45). Christians must also rejoice, for *"We are not children of the bondwoman, but of the free."* Muhammad in condemning the Christian and Jew brings down God's denunciation upon Islam. In Genesis 12:3, the LORD while speaking to Abraham states, *"Whoever curses you, I will curse."* Islam will never succeed in its quest for world dominion, while cursing what God has blessed.

## Ishmael's Rage Against the West

Ishmael's rage knows no bounds. Islamic fundamentalists demonstrate a vile hatred of West. The West represents to these defenders of Islam, all that is wrong with the world outside of Islam. Islamists reject the West's secularism, pop-music, Hollywood films, and fashions. This hatred is further compounded by denouncing Western technologies, laws and governments and society's love for modern life (i.e., fast foods, styles, satellite television, free speech). Often these hatreds are excuses fundamentalists use to gloss over the failures of Islam. The Islamic world in its rigidity disallows free speech, the right to assembly, and a free press. Life is hard in many Muslim nations with slums, poverty, and corruption rampant. Many of Islam's nations have problems controlling a growing population that is youthful, zealous and restricted[5]. The West provides a handy target to deflect criticism of regimes at home mired in totalitarianism.

Much of this Muslim fundamentalist hatred is focused on America, *"the great Satan."* For many radicals, the United States is the premier enemy of Islam. This animosity towards America stems not from its wealth, cultural influence or large population (more crime, corruption, and conspiracies). Islamic radicals target America, because of its preventative actions in halting the creation of Muslim nations. *"America is the tyrant, a global dictatorship that robs hundreds of millions of Arabs and Muslims of their right to freely elect their governments and rulers because corporate America dreads the outcome of democracy in the Muslim world."*[6] A Palestinian journalist's comments typify this rancor: *"America is the tormentor of my people...America is the all powerful devil that spreads oppression and death in my neighborhood..."*[7] They rage against the USA because it also represents *"an infidel occupation force propping up corrupt, repressive and un-Islamic governments."*[8] Islamic governments, which are friendly to the United States, are not acceptable to Muslim radicals for they are *"all in the pockets of the Western powers"*[9]

Islamists rant against the United States because it represents the last stronghold of Christianity. A triumph over America would signal the collapse of Christianity and all that constitutes contemporary Western civilization. Lastly, Islamic fundamentalists desire to convert this nation into an Islamic state, thus ending the rule of liberal democracy and establishing a powerful Muslim government.

## The Most Noblest People

Among other lies that the Koran, espouses is that the Arab people are the most noblest nation that has ever been raised up (S. 3:110, The Imrans). Ishmael's descendants have taken this declaration by *Allah* to their hearts. Thus Islam pronounces through its mullahs that the Muslims are God's chosen people, and not the Jews. Ishmael is ever trying to steal back the blessing of being first-born, even though he never had title to it. This lie is further compounded in the Koran. *Allah* reveals that the Jewish people lost their inheritance *"Because they broke their covenant We laid on them Our curse and hardened their hearts"* (S. 5:12-13, The Table). Therefore *Allah* denies his blessing, *"Because of their sins We forbade the Jews good things which were formally allowed them"* (S. 4:159, Women). This "god" also tells Abraham *"My covenant does not apply to the evil doers"*(S. 2:124, The Cow). According to the Koran, God gave the Jews only two chances to follow him. They were defeated by the Assyrians but later restored by Him to the land. It was when the Roman Armies conquered Jerusalem, and destroyed the Temple, that God decreed their covenant with Him was eternally broken. It could never be restored (S. 17:1-8, The Night Journey). Perhaps, the spirit who brought the revelations of "god" to Muhammad was ignorant of the Biblical prophetic Word. The LORD *Sabaoth* through the prophet Ezekiel promises to His people the Jews, that despite these expulsions from the land, they would be restored.

*I will open your graves, and cause you to come up out of your graves and bring you into the land of Israel...And*

34

*shall put my spirit in you and ye shall live, and I shall place you in your own land: then shall ye know that I the LORD have spoken it, and performed it, saith the LORD* (Eze 37:1-14).

*Allah* after he rejects the children of Israel in the Koran supposedly decides to link up with the followers of Islam, as they were reputably more worthy and faithful. The god of the Koran though is either a little forgetful or very confused for he also reminds the *"Children of Israel to remember the favor I bestowed upon you and how I exalted you above all nations"* (S. 2:47, The Cow). Then in another *Surah* called The Night Journey, *Allah* decrees to the Israelites: *"Dwell in the Land. When the promise of the hereafter comes to be fulfilled, We shall assemble you all together"* (S:17:103). These are two *ayas* that Muslims chose to forget, lest they be Koranicly required to observe them.

Using other selected verses in the Koran, many Muslim radicals affirm that all the land currently known as Israel must be returned to its rightful owners. This lie which Ishmael's children declare, is truly off the tree of evil for there is not a single verse in the Bible where God says He will revoke His promise to His chosen people, the Jews. Instead, the LORD declares *"I will give unto thee and to thy seed after thee the land...for an everlasting possession"* (Gen 17:8). This eternal promise is spoken again in Psalms 105 where David declares:

*He hath remembered his covenant forever the word which he commanded to a thousand generations. Which covenant he made with Abraham, and his oath to Isaac; And confirmed the same unto Jacob for a law, and to Israel for an everlasting covenant. Saying unto thee will I give the land of Canaan, the lot of your inheritance* (Ps. 105:8-11).

Ishmael through Muhammad has given his prodigy a deafness to the promises of the Bible. He has usurped the blessings of God over Isaac's children and ignored the Word of Lord to Abraham: *"But my covenant, I will establish with Isaac"* (Gen. 17:21). Much to Ishmael's shame, the Jewish people are still, and will always be God's most noblest people.

## Contending with Israel

Fundamentalism targets Israel. This land of promise is coveted by Ishmael's seed. It represents the one single factor, which unites the Arab world. Israel must be destroyed. Every year since the establishment of the state of Israel, the call for waging a holy against it has gone out from leading Islamic nations

For 1300 years this territory was under Muslim rule. What was known as the kingdom of Israel had ceased to exist by then. The Roman destruction of Jerusalem and the Temple in 70 AD ensured that. The few Jews that remained in the land eventually became subjects to Islam after the Caliphs established their rule. These Jewish subjects were called *dhimmi* or "protected ones." They were essentially protected from the wrath of Islam, and allowed to practice their faith, if certain rules were adhered to. These limitations included: incurring the death penalty if they criticized the iman, Islam, Muhammad in any way, being forbidden from marrying Muslim women, paying a *jiyza* tax of servitude (S. 9:29), being prohibited from riding horses, and camels or building a house higher than a Muslim, the necessity of bowing before passing Muslims and speaking to Muslims only when authorized to do so.

Israel's rebirth as a nation came as a tremendous shock to Islam. For the Arabs the Jews were a *dhimmi* people, second-class citizens who were not supposed to rule, let also be masters over Muslims. This is a Arab mindset which is still carried over even today, for one hears this even on the Palestinian television: *"We welcome the Jews to live as dhimmis, but the rule of this land and in all Muslim countries must be the rule of Allah"*[10]

For the first time in modern history, a subjugated territory was liberated from Islamic government and laws. This territory was located in the heart of Arab and Muslim lands. The children of Israel took a land considered by many to be a wasteland, and transformed it into a garden. Once again the children of Ishmael felt humiliated and inferior because the children of Isaac excelled. Islamists cry out for vengeance, and teach that the Jews future aligns with the judgments pronounced against them in the Koran. *"Shame and misery were stamped upon them and they incurred the wrath of God* (S. 2:63). Islam also has declared a "holy war" on Israel to resolve their own theologies. The Koran states that *"It is ordained that no nation We have destroyed shall ever rise again"* (S.. 21:96, the Prophets). Israel's continued presence reveals to Muslims the lies of their "holy book." The numerous defeats that the Arab nations have suffered at Israel's hands also counters their word which says: *"Make war on them: God will chastise them at your hands and humble them. He will grant you victory over them"* (S. 9:14, Repentance). These defeats have caused trouble in Ishmael's tents, and have engendered unanswerable questions, such as: *"How can Israel shame righteous Islam and still have continued success?"* or *"Does this mean that God is blessing the Jews in these matters?"* Fundamentalists conclude that they must retake this Holy Land for Islam, so as to reestablish Islam's superiority over the Jews, and confirm the truth in the Koran. Ishmael needs to hear and believe the eternal word of the Lord: Psalms says, *"He who touches Israel, touches the apple of God's eye."*

## Defaming Zion

Islamists in their quest for world dominion often bring up the threat of Jewish Zionism. Radical Muslims blame this Jewish movement as being the root of all their troubles. These defenders of *Allah*, freely use "International Zionism" as a primary source for rampant conspiracy theories, imagined plans, and endless Jewish schemes. These devious plots are played constantly in the media, mentioned frequently in political diatribes, and spoken by fundamental Islamic clerics in threatening sermons.[11]

Zionism originated in the 19th century when Theodor Herzl and other Jewish leaders called for the establishment of a Jewish homeland. The First Zionist Congress was held in Basel Switzerland in 1897. The goal of Zionism then and now was to instill a love of the land (Israel) within the Jewish people. Zionists since the creation of the State of Israel have promoted immigration, settlement within Israel and education. Islamic fundamentalists though have perverted this movement and equated it with racism, Nazism and even Western colonialism. So successfully have their efforts been, that even the United Nations passed a resolution in 1975 equating Zionism with racism. The UN then rescinded this travesty in 1991.

Islamic radicals though have never relinquished the task of promoting the perceived threat of worldwide Zionism. Loath even to identify the nation of Israel by that name, they have instead chosen to label it "the Zionist entity." The Saudi Government Daily Al-Riyadh has claimed that hatred of the Zionist enemy is found even in babies. *"For this reason, Arab infants are nursed with hatred of the Zionist enemy from their mother's milk, and this hatred cannot be uprooted despite all the talk about false peace agreements."*[12] The Saudi Editorial then declared, *"These are our enemies, our hatred towards them* (Zionism) *is rooted in our souls and the only thing that can remove it is their departure from our lands and the purification of their defilement of our holy places!"*[13]

Zionism has become to the Arab world a convenient "whipping boy" for allegations, rumors, and blame. Even Islamic governmental mistakes, crimes, natural disasters, and plane crashes are seen to be the result of Zionist plots. The Arab media, as well as major Islamic leaders have even transferred the fault for the 9/11 disaster over to Zionism. Columnist Ahmad Al-Musallah of Jordan's Al-Dustor wrote: *"What happened is the work of Jewish-Israeli-American Zionism, and the act of the large Zionist Jewish mind controlling the world economically, politically, and through the media."*[14] The Saudi Minister of the Interior, Prince Nayef Ibn Abd Al-Aziz stated in an interview: *"I think the Zionists were behind these events."*[15] The Prince's thinking simply reflects the common opinions of the Arab world in relation to the 9/11 terrorist attacks in the United States. This is despite overwhelming evidence to the contrary that 19 Muslims, including 17 Saudis carried out this attack.

One of the most blatant forms of anti-Semitism that Islamists employ is the distribution of *"The Protocols of the Elders of Zion."* This notorious forgery is promoted throughout the Arab world. It has been serialized on television in Egypt, lauded as fact in Iran and become a best seller in the PA. None other than Adolf Hitler endorsed and used it justify his murder of 6 million Jews. "The Protocol's" premise is one of Jewish leaders banding together to create a global empire. Its vagueness, including a scarcity of names, lack of dates and unspecified issues contributes to its popularity. "The Protocols" has been proven to be a forgery created by the tsarist secret police in 1898. Even so, it draws many Muslims to justify their hatred of what they think is Zionism.

Many Islamic controversies against Zionism also border on the ridiculous. Reports from Cairo have cited unnamed Egyptian authorities finding that Zionists were distributing animal shaped chewing gum throughout the country. Such gum was found to cause sterility in children and sexual lusts in students. Other plots condemn Zionism for contaminating Egyptian soil. One story held business interests from the Zionist entity liable for sending ten of thousands of tons of defective crop seeds to Egypt. These seeds rendered the soil infertile. Another fantastic news article condemned the Jews for using the Internet to falsify Egypt's history.[16] Even the heavens are not safe from the apparent threat of Zionism.

The launching of Israel's first astronaut aboard the space shuttle *Columbia* in January of 2003 drew Islamic accusations. The Arab League condemned NASA's inclusion of Col. Ilan Ramon as being *"the first step in an illegal Zionist occupation of space."*[17] The tragic destruction of the *Columbia* upon its re-entry provoked another flurry of Islamic anti-Zionistic comments. Muslim fundamentalist Abu Hamza Al-Masri stated *"This is a divine message to the Israelis, saying that they are not welcome in space"*[18].

Much of what the Arab world reads/sees through their media or hears from their Islamic leaders is rhetoric, meant for public consumption. Often Muslims, will say the exact opposite to you in private. Nonie, the daughter of an Islamic "martyr" is one example. Years ago, Israeli soldiers had killed her father for his violent actions against them. Many Muslims then praised her for being the child of a martyr. Yet, despite these accolades, Nonie knew she was still an orphan. Her father's absence caused Nonie to resent the idea of martyrdom. *"The Middle East culture deprived me of my father."* Then Nonie's mother placed her daughter in a Catholic school. Here she felt peace and love among the people. *"It was a different kind of love, a peaceful love that wants nothing in return."* She knew that Islam's god was always angry. Later, as Nonie grew up, and her education was completed, she realized that she could no longer stay in her society any longer. She had to leave her country. Nonie could not adjust to a Middle East culture that orphaned its own children and glorified an endless cycle of hate. She is now a naturalized citizen of the United States. Nonie hopefully envisions *"A day in which all Muslims welcome and celebrate the Jewish existence in the Middle East and realize that the Jewish religion is not a threat to them and that it is the origin of both Christianity and Islam."*[19]

Islamists in their quest to rid the world of Zionism, miss the fact that God is the ultimate Zionist. The word is used over 150 times in the Bible. It has been used to represent Jerusalem, the Temple Mount, Judah as well as the people of Israel. Zion is primarily a word that figuratively describes Israel as the people of God. Those that attack Zion and defame its people should pay heed to what the LORD God says in His Word. He is a God who has engraved Zion upon His hands. Those that mock Zion and slay her inhabitants will face a severe judgment. God is a righteous Judge. Three Biblical promises about Zion will suffice.

> *Therefore all they that devour thee shall be devoured; and all thine adversaries, every one of them, shall go into captivity. and they that spoil thee shall be a spoil, and all that prey upon thee will I give for a prey. For I will restore health unto thee, and I will heal thee of thy wounds, saith the LORD; because they called thee an Outcast, saying This is Zion, whom no man seeketh after* (Jer. 30:16-17)

> *For it is the day of the LORD's vengeance, and the year of recompenses for the controversy of Zion* (Is. 34:8)

> *The sons also of them that afflicted thee shall come bending unto thee; and all they that despised thee shall bow themselves down at the soles of thy feet; and they shall call thee, the city of the LORD, The Zion of the Holy One of Israel. Where thou hast been forsaken and hated, so that no man went through thee, I will make thee an eternal excellency, a joy of many generations* (Is. 60:14-15).

The savior of Zion is Jesus Christ, the Messiah. Out of his mouth will go a sharp sword to smite the nations; and he shall rule them with a rod of iron. Scripture says: "*Rejoice greatly, O daughter of Zion; shout O daughter of Jerusalem: behold thy King cometh unto thee: he is just and having salvation...*" (Zec. 9:9).

### Regaining *Al-Quds*

Muslim radicals have made the defense of their holy sites a

paramount issue. The liberation of Jerusalem and the establishment of it as the capital city of Palestine is their goal. Jerusalem is called *Al-Quds* or "the holy" in the Arab world. It is considered an Islamic holy city, although it is not even mentioned once in the Koran. Central to this city is the Temple Mount or the Noble Sanctuary, as Muslims know it. The Dome of the Rock and the *Al-Aksa* mosques are located there. Here, legend has it was where Muhammad flew from Mecca on his mystical horse to visit heaven (S. 17:1, The Night Journey). Muslims have made *Al-Quds* (Jerusalem) their third holiest site after Mecca and Medina. Frequent appeals go out from this temple mount complex inciting Muslims to rise up and protect it from the Jews. The Mufti of Jerusalem, Akrama Sabri, declared to 130,000 Ramadan worshipers that *"The residents of Jerusalem are temporary, we will get rid of them and conquer all of holy Palestine."*[20] This vision of a pure Muslim land has been Islam's holy grail, even before Israel's creation.

Two important Biblical prophecies speak against Islam's designs for Jerusalem. The LORD revealed to Zechariah that He *"will make Jerusalem a cup of trembling* (poison) *unto all the people round about, when they shall be in the siege both against Judah and against Jerusalem."* The LORD also declares that *"I will make Jerusalem a burdensome stone for all people: all that burden themselves with it shall be cut in pieces, through all the people of the earth be gathered together against it."* (Zec. 12:2-3). Islam has laid a siege against Jerusalem, but in doing so has drunk the cup of God's trembling. It will also be cut to pieces for coveting Zion. The LORD states that He will *"defend the inhabitants of Jerusalem"* and *"destroy the nations that come against Jerusalem"* (Zec 12:8-9).

### Signs of the End-Times

Islam's rage against the Jew and Jerusalem will eventually lead to an end-time war. Muslims speak of many signs which portent the last hour. Two of these signs are found in Muhammad's Hadith or sayings. There will be final war against the Jews and the appearance of a beast, which destroys Mecca![21] Palestine Authority Chairman Yasser Arafat comments seem to foreshadow this conflict. He regularly incites his people with such remarks as:

*We will all redeem the holy Christian and Muslim sites, we will defend them and will strengthen them since this is our destiny, to live on the frontline until judgment day. One martyr for these is worth seventy* (namely, one martyr on the front line in Jerusalem is worth seventy martyrs on any other front of *Jihad*). *Why? Because we are in the holy land. We shall fight on this blessed land, on this blessed land, this is our message.*[22]

The intent of Islam's heart was revealed long ago by Abd al-Rahman Azzam, the Secretary General of the Arab League in a conversation he had with Abba Eban and David Horovitz, Jewish Agency liaison officers with the United Nations Special Commission on Palestine in 1947. *"You achieve nothing with talk of compromise and peace...You speak of the Middle East. For us there is no such concept; for us there is only concept of the Arab world...For us there is only one test, the test of strength."*[23] There is indeed a test of strength coming, the arm of the flesh (Ishmael) against the mighty arm of the Lord.

Zechariah speaks of a day coming when the LORD will *"gather all nations against Jerusalem to battle: and the city shall be taken and the houses rifled...then shall the LORD go forth and fight against those nations, as when he fought in the day of battle"* (Zec. 14:2-3). This will be day like no other. Islam will bow the knee and submit to the Lion of Judah. The LORD will judge and then rule as king over the earth. Jerusalem shall once again be safely inhabited, with nations going up to it to worship the king.

### "Is There Not A Cause"

Fanaticism, radicalism and zealousness are not new movements in the history of mankind. The Bible is replete with examples. David said, *"Is there not a cause?"* The actions of the great prophets may have been labeled fanaticism by some, but they were ordained by God. Moses called down the LORD's judgments upon Egypt. David was crazy about worshipping God. Isaiah walked around naked. John the Baptist wore clothes made from camel's hair and ate locusts. None of these men were "lukewarm." Jesus cleansed the temple with a whip and fulfilled the scripture where David declared, *"the zeal of thine house has eaten me up."* Such courses are not wrong, but when these actions incorporate hatred, rage, terrorism and murder, God is not pleased. He warns man that His face is against those who do evil. Proverbs reveals that the LORD hates, hands, which shed innocent blood, hearts that deviseth wicked imaginations, feet, which run to mischief, and men who sow discord among the brethren. Proverbs also counsels that an angry man stirs up strife, and a furious man abounds in sin.

Jesus Christ proclaimed *"Think not that I am coming to send peace on earth: I came not to send peace but a sword"* (Mt. 10:34). This was a stunning announcement, a spiritual declaration of war against the kingdom of darkness, and the religious traditions of man. To become a disciple would require a commitment greater than loving one's family, friends and own life. It was an appeal to his followers to dedicate themselves to a cause guaranteed to bring conflict. They would be entering into a spiritual battle, which would invite persecution, but reap great rewards. Christ was proclaiming the entrance of new government of God. Its motto would be *"not by might, nor by power, but by my spirit says the Lord."*

Nowhere though in the Gospels did Jesus Christ call for his followers to wage war by an armed crusade. He disavowed the use of violence and adjured his disciples that *"all they who take the sword, shall perish with the sword"* (Mt. 26:52). They were to

**44**

embark on missionary journeys, without weapons. Jesus counseled his disciples to depend on Spirit of God who would give them wisdom and deliverance in their hour of need. Christ even set forth an example by not calling forth twelve legions of angels to rescue him. He instead submitted himself to the Father's perfect will.

## A Brand Pulled from the Fire

The LORD extends his love to terrorists, but abhors their atrocities. He hates all sin but loves sinners. The Apostle Paul was a terrorist, until he was apprehended by Jesus Christ. Luke writes, *"As for Saul, he made havoc of the church"* (Acts. 8:3). Jesus though appeared to Saul on the Damascus road and asked him: *"Saul, Saul, why persecutest thou me?"* Saul was so smitten that his heart of hatred was changed in an instant. He cried out to the Lord, *"What wilt thou have me to do?"* Saul changed his name and life and after Ananias's visit *"straightway he preached Christ in the synagogues"* Jesus Christ still wants to pull terrorists from the fires of their fanaticism, before they are consumed in their own burnings. There is a potential harvest of souls among Muslim fanatics today, if Christians would but pray.

The following reports illustrate how God still intervenes in the lives of men:

"Nassim" was a Hezbollah fighter in the hills of Lebanon. He was on a mission to kill Israelis when he heard the voice of the Lord say: *"Islam is a lie."* Stunned, his one thought was, *"If Islam is a lie, then why am I fighting for it?"* He dropped his weapon and fled from the battle zone. He eventually found himself in a church. There the pastor counseled him and led him to Christ. "Nassim" was discipled and now seeks to lead others to the Savior.[24]

Tazir also was a radical Islamist, hating Jews and consumed with rage. He became a strong supporter of Islamic fundamentalism, ran away from home and trained to become a terrorist. His parents though discovered where he was and brought him home. Later they sent him to the United States where "Taz" entered business, married and accepted Jesus Christ as his Savior. Two weeks after his salvation, Tazir found that God was cleansing his heart of his hatred towards the Jews. Later, he was invited to speak at a Christian day of prayer. His co-speaker was a Messianic Rabbi. Tazir spoke to the audience but couldn't walk away when he had finished. God spoke to him to ask forgiveness from the Jews. Tazir wanted to do it privately, but found himself asking the Rabbi out loud *"Will you, in the name of the Jews forgive me for all the pain I have caused your people."* The Rabbi jumped up and hugged him. The crowd went crazy with joy.[25]

The Lord is not limited in this harvest. Others Muslims, who live among those who practice violence and hatred, find themselves rejecting their faith. A Tehran taxi driver startled two Christians who were passengers in his car, by declaring the day after Bishop Haik was murdered by Islamic radicals, *"I've always have been a strong Muslim, but since I have heard this news on the BBC, of what they have done to this Christian pastor, I don't want to be a Muslim anymore."*[26]

### Heart Surgery

Only Jesus can work a "heart change" among those who are consumed with hatred. The future will see more attacks and violence stemming from Islamic fanaticism, yet it is the Lord's desire to pull as many souls as possible from its burning fires. The Savior wants to redeem these "brands" from violence before they perish. The LORD God is clear that He will punish those who wage terrorism and violence according to the fruit of their doings (Eze. 21:14). He will also redeem souls from deceit and violence, if they cry unto Him. He who loves them wants to wash them from their sins in his own blood. The Father's ring, robe and shoes await even now all of the prodigal sons of Ishmael. The LORD God wants to make merry and slay the fatted calf, for those who were once considered dead but now live again.

1. Living in Jerusalem, after the 9/11 attacks and while the Palestinean *intifada* war against Israel, was being waged, I had many opportunities to observe this Islamic "admiration" for fundamentalism One instance happened when I had stopped at a local PAZ service station in the city to purchase diesel fuel for our ministry's van. During my brief time there, I decided to try out my primitive Arabic on the young Arab attendants. I greeted them and then asked each one of them *"Shu Ismak?"* or *"What is your name?"* The first one said *"Islamic Jihad!"* while his buddy announced that he was *"Osama bin Laden!"* I knew they were "joking," but I also saw that this radical movement and this man had become in their eyes, something to be proud of Arabs admire people who exhibit power and might. These are their "mighty ones". Islam declares itself to be a religion of peace, but teaches its people to practice violence and wage war. It is a religion which glorifies battles thus promoting a warrior mentality. The result is a militant population ready to sacrifice their lives and that of their children to *jihad*.

2. Today, there are some 30 conflicts that are currently being waged throughout the world. Twenty eight of these wars involve Muslim governments, communities and terroristic separatist groups. *"Jihad devolved from ancient religious decrees"* Arnaud de Borchgrave, www.washingtontimes.com Jan. 2, 2003.

3. One small example of this hatred is found in the murder of Missionary nurse Bonnie Witherall who was shot dead in Oct. 2002 by Islamic murderers at the age of 31. Witherall was accosted while opening a clinic that she and her husband operated for the poor in Southern Lebanon. Commenting on the news of her death, "The Pulpit of the Calling" an influential Muslim publication in Lebanon, denounced the Christian and Missionary Alliance in which Mrs.

Witherall participated as "a Zionist organization. They destroy the fighting spirit of the children, especially of the Palestinian youth, by teaching them not to fight the Jews, and for the Palestinians to forgive the Jews." Commentator Michael Medved responds, "Imagine… a Christian organization that actually teaches peace and forgiveness. No wonder that the Arab terrorists felt the need to assassinate Bonnie Witherall." See "Blaming the victim for murderous Muslim rampages" Michael Medved Dec. 2, 2002. www.worldnetdaily.com

4.   www. palestine-info.info/arabic/palestoday/4/22/02

5.   The Arab world is currently facing a substantial youth explosion Of Saudi Arabia's 15 million citizens 62%, are under age 25. Yemen has 68%, while Syria has 63%, Iraq 62%, Jordan 61%, Iran 59%, Libya 58%, Algeria 57%, and Egypt 56%. United Nations statistics, cited by *Newsweek* "The Arab World" Oct. 15, 2001, pg. 31. This population bulge is susceptible to Islamic idealism. It also serves as a rich recruitment base for Islamic radicals.

6.   "Why I Hate America" Khalid Amayred, *Palestine Times*, London, Nov. 2001 cited by Middle East Research Institute www.memri.org, Nov. 27, 2001.
7.   Ibid.
8.   "Danger Within: Militant Islam in America" Daniel Pipes, *New York Post*, cited by Independent Media Review Analysis Nov. 1, 2001; www.danielpipes.org or www.imra.org.il
9.   Ibid.
10.  "Too Late for a Peaceable Solution" Editorial by Boris Shusteff citing sermon on Palestinian Television July 6, 2001; www.israelnationalnews.com"
11.  See "Friday sermons in Saudi Mosques" www.memri.org Jan. 26, 2002
12   Excepts taken from an article in the Saudi daily '*Al-Riyadh*' by Abdallah Al Ka'id titled "The Culture of Hatred" www.memri.org, Jan. 8, 2002
13   Ibid
14   "A New Anti-Semitic Myth in the Arab Press: The September 11 Attacks Were Perpetrated by the Jews" by Yael Yehoshua, www.imra.org.il

15  Interview by '*Ain-Al-Yaqeen*', a weekly news magazine published online by the Saudi royal family. Cited by www.memri.org #446, Dec. 3, 2002.

16  "International Jewish Conspiracies" www.memri.org #67 and #79 Jan. 6, 2000 and Mar. 20, 2000.

17  Newsflashes www.haaretz.com Jan. 20, 2003

18.  Al-Sharq Al-Awsat, Feb 4, 2003 cited in "Arab Media Reactions to the Columbia Space Shuttle Disaster" www.memri.org; Feb. 7, 2003

19  "Rejecting Martyrdom" www.noniedarwish.com, also cited in www.aish.com Jan. 12, 2003

20.  Israel Broadcasting Network, *Arutz Sheva* July 18, 2001.

21.  Abu Huraira reported *Allah's* Messenger as saying: *"The last hour would not come unless the Muslims will fight against the Jews"*, *Sahih Muslim*, Vol. 4, Ch. MCCV #6985; *Abdullah b. 'Amr reported...that after the sacred house* (the *Ka'ba*) *would be burnt, Allah's Messenger said the Dajjai* (the beast) *would appear and he would stay forty months"*, *Sahih Muslim*, Vol. 4. Ch. MCCX, #7023

22.  "Recent Statements by Yasser Arafat" (An address to Jerusalemites given in Ramallah, Dec. 18, 2001); Special Dispatch - PA Dec. 20, 2001 No. 317; Middle East Media Research Institute, www.memri.org"

23.  "Too Late for a Peaceable Solution, " Editorial by Boris Shusteff, Ibid.

24.  Personal testimony given to author

25.  Personal testimony given to author

26.  *Intercede*, Oct. 1994, Vol. X. No. 9.

# Four

# Muhammad - Prophet of the Sword

According to Muslims, the greatest man who ever lived was their prophet. To them, he is no less than *al Insan al Kamil*: the perfect man. A knight of the sands who brought light into the darkness of their lives. As their supreme role model, he is seen as: *"a devoted husband, father and grandfather, a kind and responsible kinsman, a faithful affectionate friend, a leader alike in worship and battle and statesman par excellence."*[1] Spiritually, Muhammad is even more emulated by his followers, than any other man. He has become their teacher, guide, leader and the only connecting link with God. Muhammad was the visible proof of God's approval. His name means *"The Praised One."* This man so revered by the Arab world is their apostle (*rasul*), their messenger from Heaven, and their prophet (*nabi*).

Muhammad, the founder of Islam (submission to God), was born in the city of Mecca, during the year of the Elephant, 570 A.D. This event marked the campaign of the Christian viceroy, Abrahah the Abyssinian, to capture Mecca. The Koran declares that this army from Yemen was miraculously defeated by *"birds in flight"* which carried stones in their beaks (S. 105, The Elephant).[2] The *Ka'ba* was safe once more, and a great prophet had been born on June 8th of that year.

The prophet's early life was filled with tragedy and loss. Orphaned at the age of six, he was first raised by his grandfather

Abn Muttalib, then brought up by his uncle, Abu Talib, a merchant along the great camel trade routes.[3] Muhammad spent much of his youth working the caravans, traveling to Syria, Persia and Yemen. Here, was opportunity to meet with Jews, Christians, heretical believers, monks, and animistic worshipers. Tales were told and portents interpreted. As a young man, Muhammad would have absorbed stories from the Old and New Testaments, as well as apocryphal legends. He was strongly impressed that the Jews and the Christians possessed their own scriptures.

Muhammad was married at age 25 to Khadijah. She was a wealthy Jewish widow who was forty years old.[4] She had allowed him to manage her caravans. Between them they had seven children. Four daughters of this union survived into adulthood. During this period Muhammad was known as *al-Amin*, or *"The Trustworthy One."* He helped rebuild the *Ka'ba* by setting the Black Stone back into its place.

As was his custom, Muhammad would go to the hills near Mecca to meditate during the Arabic month of Ramadan.[5] On one of these occasions, he became frightened by a mystical being who commanded him to:

> *Recite in the name of thy Lord, who has created all things; who has created man of congealed blood. Recite! Thy Lord is the most beneficent, who taught by the pen, taught that which they knew not unto men* (S. 96, Congealed Blood).

After this vision, no more revelations came to Muhammad for two years. He passed off this initial experience as being the work of *jinns*, but was led by his wife and friends to believe that it was *Allah*, whom he had encountered. Later, he came to believe that it was none other than Gabriel the Angel, who had accosted him with the divine message and the news that he had been selected to be God's prophet. Suddenly these revelations came to him again.

**51**

This time, the prophet dictated the words to his followers. He started to preach this message to the city of Mecca. Persecutions and threats of murder soon followed. Muhammad's wife then died and he chose to marry again. First Sawda, a widow, then A'isha who was six years old. This was the time of the *hijra* or emigration.[6] Muhammad slipped off to Yathrib where he was welcomed. The city was renamed *Medinat al nabi* or "city of the prophet," in his honor.[7] Here he was allowed to organize this new religion and establish a mosque. The prophet then called for everyone to *"Submit to God."* This revolutionary obedience was called Islam. The revelations continued. Muhammad soon turned against the Christians and the Jews, who had refused to accept his divine prophetic mantle of authority.[8] The followers of Islam were also divinely instructed to no longer bow towards Jerusalem, but instead face Mecca, home of the sacred *Ka'ba*.

Battles were waged and Muhammad found his sword. He was wounded in the mouth in one raid and left for dead, but recovered and rallied his believers to win. Neighboring tribes were overpowered, and forced to submit to *Allah* or the sword. A total of 76 campaigns were fought. His own tribe vowed to crush him and his religion. Muhammad also continued to marry, taking 14 more wives and numerous concubines. Mary the Copt, Muhammad's slave, gave birth to his son Ibrahim.[9]

Towards the end of his life, Muhammad was able to regain Mecca. Triumphantly, he entered this city and went to the *Ka'ba*. Here, he destroyed the idols and worshipped *Allah*. The sacred Black Stone was preserved. The prophet then participated in the pilgrimage, dedicating it to *Allah*. Near Mount Arafat (Mecca), Muhammad preached what was to be his last sermon. His followers were to deal justly with one another, treat women kindly, and abandon the practice of blood feuds. The *umma* (community) was to be one. They were to *"Know that every Muslim is a Muslim's brother and that Muslims are brethren."* No longer were they to be members of separate tribes. Muhammad then returned to Medina where he fell ill and died on the 8th of June 632. He was 62.[10]

The prophet died without appointing a successor or leaving an heir. Abu Bakr (A'isha's father) a trusted friend, warrior, and an early companion of the prophet, was set in place as the first Caliph or Deputy to the prophet. Rebellion and strife broke out though, as the neighboring tribes renounced their loyalty and attempted to separate from the community of believers. This brief insurrection was quickly quelled in a brilliant series of battles. Abu Bakr then forged these desert tribes into a disciplined army of followers, who went forth to conquer an empire for Islam.

The realm of "submission" swiftly expanded. Damascus fell in 635, Jerusalem in 636, Persia by 637, and then Egypt in 640. In one hundred years, all of North Africa and Spain was under the shadow of Islam.[11] Only Charles Martel's victory at the Battle of Tours, France, in 732, held check on the soldiers of Islam. The year 1000 saw most of India within the folds of Islam. A long period of decline then set in. Islam's rule was supreme, but decadence and lethargy helped moved this faith into a period of slumber.

The rise of the Turkish Ottoman empire in 1362 marked the second period of Islamic growth. The Balkan states, North Africa and the Near East came under its control. The great city of Constantinople fell to Muslim armies in 1453. Traders and merchants also continued to spread this new religion by peacefully bringing it into Indonesia and to the southern most islands of the Philippines. It was the ascendancy of European colonialism that brought an end to the rule of the Ottomans (1918). Yet, even this defeat did not hinder Islam. The faith continued to spread in numbers and in power. The post World War II, creation of sovereign Islamic nations in the Middle East and Africa, coupled with a new-found oil wealth, further propelled Muhammad's faith into even greater waves of expansion.

1.   *Haneef*, 1979, pg. 25
2.   Scholars speculate that possibly a smallpox epidemic, may have actually struck down the Christian forces.

3.   Muhammad's grandfather Abu Muttalib ibn Hashim, was no ordinary man.  He was custodian of the sacred *Ka'ba* in Mecca. Arab tradition also credits him with rediscovering the sacred well of *Zamzam*.  The location of the fount had been lost in times long past. It had been filled in during one of the frequent tribal disputes and forgotten.  Abu Muttalib found this well and restored it.  For this good deed, Abu Muttalib was given the lucrative rights to distribute its life-giving waters.

Muslim lore states that at the time of this discovery, he had only one son.  Therefore, he prayed to the lord of the *Ka'ba* to grant him ten sons, and in return, he would sacrifice one of them.  His prayers were answered and when the time came, the youngest Abn Allah was chosen for sacrifice.  The family protested, so Abn Muttalib consulted a witch as to whether the god of the *Ka'ba* would accept a substitute. The soothsayer's informing spirit confirmed this approach.  Abn Muttalib then cast divining arrows at Mecca to learn how many camels would merit an acceptable sacrifice.  The answer was 100 camels to spare the boy's life.  These animals were slaughtered and Muhammad's father was spared.

Abn Allah died a few months before Kutam's birth (Muhammad's original birth name).  His mother Amina gave the child to a Bedouin mother named Halima to nurse.  Amina died before Muhammad was six.  Muhammad's grandfather, Abn Muttalib, assumed responsibility for the boy.  This care lasted only two years, then he died also.  The orphan boy was left once more in the care of one of Abn Muttalib's many sons, Abu Talib, uncle of Muhammad and later head of the Hashimite clan.

4   Some say that he married Khadijah around 595 AD, when she was thirty.
5.   Ramadam during this period, was already the traditional Arabic month of retreat.  Muhammed though, expanded this ritual by decreeing that fasting should be observed from before dawn to after sunset.

6.     Muslims date their era from that year 622 A.D.  This time (622-623 A.D.) on the Christian calendar corresponds to the year 1 A. H. or *Anno Hijra* (the year of the flight) on the Islamic register.

7.     Later shortened to Medina or city in Arabic.

8.     A prayer distributed by the Episcopal Church for All Saints' Day 2001, may herald a new era of acceptability for Muhammad's revelations!  The petiton was written by the Rev. Charles T.A. Todd, a Philadelphia pastor and member of an Episcopal disaster response team.  The faithful are required to remember saints who *"managed to raise up our faith in God and in one another."* Among them, Flood includes biblical heroes like Abraham, Joshua and the Virgin Mary, as well as *"Budda and Muhammad and all the prophets of old.  They led God's people to God's light."* It was promoted and distributed by the Right Rev. George Packard, the church's bishop for the armed serviccs, health care and prison ministries.  This prayer sadly illustrates the degree of spiritual blindness found in certain church leaders today (*Ark. Democratic Gazette,* Nov. 11, 2001, pg. 2H.)

9.     All of Muhammad's sons died in infancy.  This child perished as a toddler.

10.   The Hadith (the sacred writings of Islam), say that Muhammad died (four years!), after suffering from the effects of a meal prepared by Zainab, a Jewish slave.  She had served the prophet dinner, prepared from poisoned goat meat, following the beheading of hcr father, husband and brother by his army.  Other hadith have Muhammad afflicted by a headache (probably, from the effects of pleurisy), and dying on A'isha's lap.  During his final sickness, Muhammad repeatedly asked *Allah* to *"curse the Jews and Christians because they took the graves of their prophets as places of worship" Sahih al-Bukhari,* Vol. 7 #706.

Interesting enough, piligrimages are now made by Muslims to Muhammad's grave and prayers are offered there for his intercession!  Devotees also throw "presents" into the enclosure.  A space also has been reserved within the tomb's confines for Jesus.  This lesser pilgrimage or *ziyarat* to Medina is thought by believers to be meritorious.  Many pilgrims base their visit here on the words of the prophet himself:  *"Who goes on Hajj and does not visit me has insulted me!"*

The Wahhabis though, consider such pilgrimages an infidelity that honors the creature more than the Creator.

The hadith proclaim that *"the son of Mary"* will be buried there, after he supposedly returns a second time to preach Islam and then die!  Medina is also called *al-Munowera*, or "the illuminated."  On approaching this city, devoted Muslims have claimed to see a luminous haze suspsended over its mosques and houses.  See Samuel M. Zwemer *"Al Haramain," The Moslem World*, Jan. 1947, pgs. 7-15.

11.  Historians estimate that during this period of conquest, 3,200 Christian churches were either destroyed or converted over into mosques.  90% of the population became Muslim.

# FIVE

# Qualities of a Perfect Man

## *"A Good Name..."*

T he Book of Ecclesiastes declares that *"A good name is better than precious ointment..."* (Eccl. 7:1). Muhammad, for the followers of Islam, has a very good name. In the eyes of all Muslims, Muhammad is identified as being the greatest of all human beings. He is portrayed as being the most God-conscious, pious individual among all created mortals, including all the prophets before him. According to his words, he will be the one who will be pre-eminent among the descendants of Adam on the Day of Resurrection. Muhammad further proclaimed to his brotherhood of believers, that he will be the first intercessor, and the first whose intercession will be accepted by *Allah*.[1] Muslims also believe that he is the keeper of the gates of paradise. Muhammad is in the light of their knowledge, **the perfect man.**

The Koran encourages Muslims to pattern their lives and behavior after this man with the words: *"Verily in the messenger of Allah ye have a good example for everyone who looks forward towards Allah and the Last Day of Judgment"* (S. 33:21, The Clans). Tradition ascribes some two hundred names to Muhammad, including:

| | |
|---|---|
| *Ahmad* | The Most Praised |
| *Ajmal Khalq Allah* | The Most Beautiful of God's Creation |

57

| | |
|---|---|
| *Al-Ghawth* | The Redeemer |
| *'Ayn an-Na'im* | The Fount of all Blessings |
| *Al Ma'sum* | The Infallible |
| *Al-Hashir* | The Gatherer (the Day of Judgment) |
| *Ruh al-Haqq* | The Spirit of Truth |
| *Ruh al-Quddus* | The Holy Spirit |
| *Ash-Shams* | The Sun |
| *Shafi'al-Mudhnibin* | The Intercessor for Sinners |

Most Muslims will readily admit, that their prophet was a man, but not like other men. Muhammad is seen as a jewel among stones. As a man, he could err, but the nature of this error would be minor and insignificant, since *Allah* safeguarded him from major sins.[2] The followers of Islam have elevated this man to such a degree, that they have come close to deifying him.[3] Samuel Zwemer, a latter day apostle to Muslims minces no words with his comments: *"The sin and guilt of the Muslim world is that they have given Christ's glory to another, and that for practical purposes, Mohammad is the Moslem Christ"*[4] The heart of the true Muslim is consumed with Muhammad. The Hadith decrees that the true proof of a believer's faith is found in the measure of how great his love is for the prophet.[5]

As a leader, he defended the cause of the poor, the orphan and the widow. The messenger of *Allah* prescribed an alms tax, prohibited female infanticide and permitted widows to have inheritance rights. Marriages were restricted. No longer could men take more than four wives into their family. The prostitution of slaves was forbidden. The tormenting and beating of animals was also disallowed, although a man could still freely "scourge" his wife (S. 4:34, Women).

The man socially transformed Arabia. He caused the desert tribes and warring clans to become united under one common government: Islam. Religiously, Muhammad presented a new faith that was acceptable to a paganistic people. He gave them a monotheistic belief, ethical doctrines and a revealed book of scriptures to follow. His own words and behavior became as a guide for generations to emulate in thought and conduct. As a self proclaimed prophet, Muhammad aroused a people who were desirous of a new revelation. He gave these seekers a vision and hope for the future. His presence encouraged men and brought revival to all of Arabia. A great warrior and a general, Muhammad fearlessly entered into combat and defeated clans and infidels who opposed this new faith. He was courageous, generous to the poor, and compassionate to those he loved. The Hadith proclaim that his most sublime qualities were his humility, mercy, and the tenderness that he demonstrated towards children, as well as to the members of his family.[6] A'isha, the prophet's favorite wife after Khadijah, once summed up his desires by saying that Muhammad loved three things: *"women, perfume and food, and that he had his heart's desire of the first two but not of the last."*

## A Few Dead Flies

The wisdom of Ecclesiastes also states that *"Dead flies cause the ointment of the apothecary to send forth a stinking savor"* (Ecc.10:1). Muhammad's character is not entirely sweet smelling. The man has a few dead flies in his perfume. In his lifetime, he married sixteen different wives. In addition, the man found it necessary to have numerous concubines, slaves and free women. Muslim scholars defend this behavior by comparing their prophet to the pattern set by the Biblical Kings David and Solomon. These men who had been approved by God had possessed an even greater number of women. However, it is easy to ignore and forget that the LORD did not approve of their marital actions. David and Solomon's multiple marriages and relationships caused heartache and grief for all of Israel (II Sam. 12:14; I Kgs. 11:1-8). These same Islamic theologians state that only through Muhammad's polygamous marriages could a group of women be trained in Islamic ideals. *"It was not an ordinary work, but an important task of vast magnitude which required the sweat and labor of so many pious souls, and these were the noble wives of the Holy Prophet."*[7]  Other arguments in favor of Muhammad's marital practices include the need to form political alliances and to preserve the community by marrying widows whose husbands had perished in battles.

Muhammad's revelation, the Koran, permits multiple marriages for men. A man can take up to four wives if equality among them is maintained. Muhammad as the prophet of God was able to marry without limits, *"A privilege being granted to no other believer"* (S. 33:50). Two verses later into this disclosure, the Creator apparently changed His mind. Muhammad is instructed that *"It shall be unlawful for you to take more wives or to change your present wives for other women, though their beauty please you, except where slave-girls are concerned. God takes cognizance of all things"* (S. 33:52, The Clans).

A'isha was engaged to the prophet when he was fifty years old and she was six. On the day of her marriage three years later, she was outside playing on a swing with her friends and had to be called into the ceremony. The girl had no idea she was becoming Muhammad's third wife. After this marriage, she was taken to his house as a bride and *"her dolls were with her."*[8]

Muslim apologists try to justify this match citing that this difference in age was needful to bridge the generation gap. *"Thus the marriage of the Prophet with A'isha at an age when she was at the threshold of puberty was a great necessity, as it was through her that instructions could successfully be imparted to the young ladies who had newly entered the fold of Islam."*[9] Early marriage to children is still an accepted practice in Islam. In considering such a practice, perhaps the words of Jesus should be recalled:

> *And whoso shall receive one such little child in my name receiveth me. But whoso shall offend one of these little ones which believe in me, it were better for him that a*

*millstone were hanged about his neck, and that he were drowned in the depths of the sea* (Mt. 18: 5-6).

Muhammad also chose to marry his adopted son's wife. He informed Zayd of his desire and persuaded him to divorce Zainab. This incident cause a great scandal in the community. Muhammad though was able to get a special revelation from God to justify this action.

*And when Zayd divorced his wife, we gave her to you in marriage, so that it should become legitimate for true believers to wed the wives of their adopted sons if they divorced them. God's will must needs be done. No blame shall be attached to the Prophet for doing what is sanctioned for him by God* (S. 33:37-38, The Clans).

A'isha was overheard to remark to Muhammad upon hearing of this new marriage: *"Truly thy Lord makes haste to do thy bidding."*

The prophet of God was cruel and vicious in spirit. He cursed those he did not love. When seventy men who were his "reciters" were killed in the battle of Bi'r Ma'uma, Muhammad invoked a curse for one full month upon their murderers: *"O Allah! curse the tribes of Lihyan, Ri'l, Dhakwan, and 'Usayya for they disobeyed Allah and His Messenger."*[10] However, if the person(s) that Muhammad cursed was (were) by some chance Muslim(s), the prophet would repent and pray *"O Allah, I am a human being and for any person among Muslims, upon whom I curse or hurl malediction make it a source of purity and reward."*[11] Jesus set a better example, by forgiving his enemies. He did not choose to curse Judas who betrayed him, or even those who had spit on him and nailed him to the cross.

Muhammad was quick to ensure that those who deviated from Islam's rule were punished. Vengeance was a part of his nature as he exceeded the Old Testament decree: *"eye for eye and tooth for tooth."* The prophet approved of and ordered crucifixions, amputations, whippings, beheadings, and stonings as methods of punishment. The Koran reinforces these deeds:

> *The only reward for those who make war upon Allah and His messenger and strive after corruption in the land will be that they will be killed or crucified, or have their hands and feet on alternate sides cut off, or will be expelled out of the land. Such will be their degradation in the world, and in the Hereafter theirs will be an awful doom* (S. 5:33, The Table).

These practices are still in force today, throughout the Muslim world.

A woman who was accused of committing theft was once brought before Muhammad. He commanded that this woman's hand be cut off. Later A'isha commented that she had a good repentance, as there was a wonderful change in her soul afterwards because of this punishment. Jesus demonstrated His goodness the night He was betrayed, by choosing to heal Malchus' right ear before the eyes of his enemies, after Peter had severed it. An act so gracious and loving that Luke the physician mentions it in his Gospel (Lk. 22:50-51).

Mercy was not one of Muhammad's foremost qualities. A thief once stole a sheet from one of Muhammad's followers, Safwal-b-Umayyah. The prophet gave the order for the thief's hand to be cut off. Safwal protested this judgment and said, *"I do not wish it. I give it* (the sheet) *to him as charity."* The messenger of *Allah* asked him, *"Why didn't you tell him that before you came with him?"* Muhammad would not retract his order, and the man's hand had to be cut off. Jesus counsels his followers in the Sermon on the Mount that *"Blessed are the merciful: for they shall obtain mercy"* (Mt. 5:7). Muhammad also apparently had never heard the words of the prophet Zechariah: *"Thus speaketh the LORD of hosts saying, Execute true judgment, and show mercy and compassions every man to his brother"*(Zec. 7:9).

In another instance, a woman who had become pregnant through adultery came before Muhammad. She said to the prophet: *"Messenger, I have wronged myself, I have committed adultery and I earnestly desire that you purify me."* Muhammad permitted her to birth and wean the child, then had her stoned to death. She too was judged to have made a good repentance. Jesus was confronted with an adulterous woman who had been caught in the very act. He also had every right to stone her, yet showed mercy, telling her to *"go, and sin no more"* (Jn. 8:11). Isaiah earlier had reaffirmed the godliness of Jesus' actions through his proclamation of the LORD's words; *"And in mercy shall the throne be established..."* (Isa. 16:5).

The messenger of *Allah* hated poets. More than once he condoned and participated in their murder. Poetry was a skill valued by the Arabs. These reciters sang of the glories of each tribe, past battles, and achievements. They interpreted the times through their verse. Often the people viewed these poets as having magical powers. Muhammad had the poet Ka'b assassinated in response to his demeaning poetry about him. His very words reveal the magnitude of his temper: *"Who will kill Ka'b Ashraf? He has maligned Allah, the Exalted and His Messenger."* When the opportunity to murder this man came, the prophet said this indicting statement to his companions: *"As he comes close, I will extend my hands toward his head and when I hold him fast you should do your job."*[12] A spear was then driven into the man's side. The Hadith record the extent of this man's hatred: *"It is better for the belly of any one of you to be stuffed with pus rather than to stuff ones mind with poetry."*[13] Even today, hate and revenge serve as strong motivating forces within Muslim society. Jesus revealed to all mankind a better way of behavior when he rebuked his disciples for wanting to call down fire on a Samaritan village.

He said, *"Ye know not what manner of spirit ye are of. For the Son of man is not come to destroy men's lives, but to save them"* (Lk. 9:55-56).

Muhammad did not hesitate to order bloodshed. When asked about the days ahead, he spoke of different evils making their appearance in the near future. Yet to his listeners, he gave this command: *"Anyone who tries to disrupt the affairs of the umma* (brotherhood of Islam) *while they are united, you should strike them with the sword and kill them."*[14]

The messenger of God, participated in the wholesale slaughter of the Jewish tribe of Quraiza. The tribe surrendered their city after a prolonged siege by Muhammad's army, and asked for mercy. None was given; 700 men and one woman were beheaded in the marketplace. The remaining women and children were then sold into slavery. Islamic historians defend this behavior as being completely in line with the Jewish Old Testament law. These people were traitors and had plotted to overthrow Islam. They cite the rule where the children of Israel were given permission to besiege cities that did not make peace with them. When the city was taken, then every male was to be smitten with the sword, and the rest of the inhabitants taken captive (Deut. 20:10-14). To condone the actions of their prophet, Muslims will also remind the Christian of Jesus' words where he said: *"Think not that I am come to send peace on earth: I came not to send peace, but a sword"* (Mt. 10:34). They fail to see that this was a spiritual sword, separating light from darkness, good from evil and the kingdom of God from the kingdom of self. Christ never preached a gospel of warfare, but one of love and forgiveness. He proclaimed that *"...all they that take the sword shall perish with the sword"* (Mt. 26:52). Yes, He will return with a sharp two-edge sword. but one that issues forth from out of His mouth, to judge the nations (Rev. 1:16, 19:15). Even so, Jesus came that we might have life, and *"have it more abundantly"*

## An Alabaster Box

Muhammad never knew the joy of forgiveness. His revelations speak constantly of the need to have his past and future sins purged (S. 40:55; 47:19; 48:1-2; 49:1-3). He said to his companions, *"There is some sort of shade upon my heart, and I seek forgiveness from Allah a hundred times a day."*[15] Muhammad, like all men, had to ask for forgiveness for his transgressions. Only Jesus Christ possessed the power to forgive sin, for He was sinless. In the Gospel of Luke there is a precious story, where the Lord allowed a woman who was a known sinner to wash His feet with her tears and then kiss and anoint them with a costly ointment. This perfume came from her alabaster box, which she was saving for her wedding day. Jesus saw how great the woman's sacrifice was, felt her desire for forgiveness and accepted this true repentance. The Savior then said unto her, *"Thy sins are forgiven...Thy faith hath saved thee; go in peace"* (Lk. 7:36-50).

## *"What think ye of"*

Muslims will frequently ask Westerners and Christians the question: *"What do you think of our prophet?"* One should answer this query with great wisdom. **To slander and insult the prophet is a great sin in Islam.**[16] **In some countries, it is a capital offense worthy of imprisonment and death.**[17] A Chinese proverb states that *"Words are the sounds of the heart."* There could be many negative things said about Muhammad, but to what avail? Muhammad is only a memory. He left a great legacy to his disciples, but even so his body lies buried in the prophet's mosque in Medina. It serves no useful purpose to inflame the hearts of those you wish to speak Christ's gospel of love to. Avoid arguments and controversies. At the very least, derogatory comments by Christians about the character of Muhammad will needlessly close the door to any witnessing opportunities that the Lord would give. The Koran warns all Muslims; *"O ye who believe! Take not the Jews and Christians for your friends and protectors...take not*

65

*for friends and protectors those who take our religion for a mockery or sport"* (S. 5:51, 57, The Table). A missionary to the Muslim people advises Christians *"to apologize to Muslims on behalf of other Christians who have intentionally or unintentionally insulted their religion and their prophet."* This act of love on our part does not mean that we are in agreement with their teachings. It just witnesses to Muslims that you are one of the true followers of Jesus who loves the Muslim people, that the Koran speaks about (S. 5:82,). This act of humility on our part, reveals our heart to them and helps win theirs to the God of LOVE.

One hundred prayer marchers on a reconciliation walk from Germany to Jerusalem, demonstrated this fact in 1996. On the first leg of their trip, they stopped at a Turkish mosque in Cologne. Here, they read an apology for Christian crimes done against Muslims during the Crusades, to the *Iman* and some 200 men and boys.[18] The *Iman,* they reported was amazed that anyone would do this. He said to them, that *"Whoever had this idea, must have had a visit from God Himself."*[19] The Turkish religious leader announced that he would distribute this apology to 250 other mosques in Europe.[20] Six months later, one team member of this walk was in a park in Vienna, Austria, where between 3,000 and 4,000 Muslims were meeting. She heard a speaker saying, *"On the first Sunday in April, Christians visited our mosque in Cologne to ask forgiveness for the Crusades. The time has come for us to also admit and ask forgiveness for our historical mistakes."*[21] This one act of remittance, prompted many Muslims to examine their own sins against Christians and Jews.

### *"His Name is as Ointment Poured forth..."*

If you as a Christian are confronted by Muslims and asked to comment about their prophet, trust in Jesus, and if possible **change the issue**. Speak the truth in love, from a pure heart, knowing that in that hour the Holy Spirit shall give you what to say. Answer your audience as Jesus did to the Pharisees: *"What think ye of Christ?"* (Mt. 22:42).

Speak to these sons and daughters of Ishmael. Tell them about the character of the one you are devoted to. Proclaim His presence as the writer does in the Song of Solomon: *"I am my beloved's, and my beloved is mine"* (6:3). Introduce them to His humility, generosity, kindness, courage, compassion, righteousness and holiness. JESUS is His name and *"Because of the savor of thy good ointments thy name is as ointment poured forth..."* (Song of Sol. 1:3).

Declare His sincerity. This son of man came to reveal all truth. Jesus was incapable of a lie. Tell them His words: *"I am the way, the truth, and the life"* (Jn. 14:6). He came to show men truth. An ancient proverb holds that *"Truth is God's daughter."* Perhaps, your listeners could also understand this saying in a better way: *"Truth is God's Son"*

Illuminate your friends as to the love of Christ. Open their hearts to His sayings. Speak to Muslims as to how Christ told men to *"Love your enemies, bless them that curse you, and to do good to them that hate you, and pray for them which despitefully use you, and persecute you"* (Mt. 5:44). Tell them what it means to love an enemy and to bless those that persecute you. Remark to your listeners about Christ being a brother to all. He came to the rich and to the poor; to sinner and saint alike. He ate with tax collectors and in the presence of Pharisees. Tell them about Zacchaeus, or the Roman Centurion whose servant He healed. Perhaps, they would even like to know about the thief He forgave, and then promised heaven. Advise them on how Jesus wants to be their brother also.

Tell every Muslim you meet who speaks to you on the greatness of Muhammad, about the achievements of Jesus. He never wrote a book, chiseled a statue or led an army, but He will return to judge the living and the dead. Speak of His coming on a white horse with eyes of fire, and a head adorned with many crowns. Ask your audience what they would do if Muhammad came into the room? Would they stand up? Then inquire to them, what their actions might be if Jesus would then enter in. Would they not see Him in His true glory and fall to their knees? Jesus is the **perfect man.** *"His name is as ointment poured forth."*

## "A Sweet Savor of Christ"

Evangelist Dwight L. Moody once said that *"Character is what you are in the dark."* It is the sum of one's qualities that distinguishes you from all other men. Christian, the attitude we demonstrate towards others reflects our inner man. If we choose to ignore and hate Muslims and their magnificent prophet, then we shall be no better than the words the Apostle John wrote in His Epistle: *"He that saith he is in the light, and hated his brother, is in darkness even until now"* (I Jn. 2:9). *"God is light, and in him is no darkness at all. If we say that we have fellowship with him and walk in darkness, we lie, and do not the truth"*(1:5-6). Paul informs us that *"We are unto God a sweet savor of Christ, in them that are saved, and in them that perish"* (II Cor. 2:15). The anointing of Jesus' presence in us; His Love, His Light, His Wisdom, makes us a sweet incense unto God and to those we witness to. As believers we can reflect the qualities of Christ's perfection in our spirit. Our Christ-like behavior will show Muslims the true essence of what a perfect man is.

## A Witness From Kurdistan

A missionary to Kurdistan writes of Nahida and Chinar, two young girls who have recently become believers in Jesus, and have been healed through a miracle of surgery:

*They have suffered persecution from their families and neighbors because of their witness, but the Lord has kept them strong. When Nahida was threatened she told her mother, 'Even if you kill me, I won't do the Muslim thing (prayers). I belong to Jesus! Who do you think did all this for me?' Her mother replied, 'Muhammad.' Nahida said, 'Muhammad is dead! Jesus is alive! He is the one who healed me and saved me. I belong to Him!'*

The woman missionary adds to this testimony writing that:

*I invited both the girl's mothers to my house for tea one morning and explained the whole Gospel to them. They received it very well, and after that they didn't persecute their daughters any more. They had done it because they had never heard the Gospel and didn't know who Jesus really is.[22]*

Paul pens these striking words in Romans 10:14: *"How then shall they call on him in whom they have not believed? and how shall they believe in him of whom they have not heard? and how shall they hear without a preacher?"* Nahida and Chinar believe in Jesus today because of a preacher. Let our feet be beautiful as we preach the gospel of peace and bring glad tidings of good things. Jesus said that He would draw all men unto him. Ask the Muslims you meet in love, ***"What think ye of Christ?"***

---

1.  Vol. 4, *Al Fada'il* CMLIII, #5655.

2.  Vol. 4, *Al-Birr* MLXXV, See interpreter's comments pg. 1373.

3.  Muhammad's visage is regarded by Islam as being so sacred, that no portrayal of his person is permitted. All depiction's of the prophet whether drawings, artwork or other images are considered highly blasphemous. Taking the name of the prophet Muhammad "in vain" under a 1985 Pakistani law is also considered blasphemy. Ghudam Akbar Khan, a member of Pakistan's Shiite Muslim minority was convicted of this crime and sentenced to death for it, in 1998 (*Arkansas Democrat-Gazette* "In The News" Sept. 11, 1998 pg. 1A)

4.    Zwemer, *The Moslem Christ*, 1912, pg. 157.

5.    Anas b. Malik declared that the Messenger of *Allah* said: *"None of you is a believer until I am dearer to him than his child, his father and the whole of mankind"* Vol. 1, Al-Iman XVII, #71.

6.    Vol. 4, *Al-Fada'il* CMLXVI, #5356.

7.    Vol. 4, *Fada'il Al-Sahabah* MV, See interpreters comments #2728, pgs. 1298-1299.

8.    Vol. 2, *Al-Nikah* DXLVIII, #3311.

9.    Vol. 4, *Fada'il Al-Sahabah* MV, See interpreters comments #2728, pgs. 1298-1299.

As if in answer to the Hadith's pious explanation of Muhammad's marriage to the child A'isha, the former president of the 16 million member southern Baptist Convention, Rev. Jerry Vines, presented another viewpoint. His opinion, *"Islam was founded by a demon-possessed pedophile who had 12 wives —and his last one was a 9 year old girl,"* was voiced at a pre-convention pastors conference in St. Louis. It ignited a firestorm of controversy.

Episcopal Bishop George Wayne Smith of St. Louis responded: *"We condemn the hateful statement made in our city about Islam and the prophet Muhammad and we express our solidarity with our Muslim brothers and sisters."* The Council on American-Islamic Relations or CAIR denounced Vines statement as *"Outrageous."* Perhaps Vines could have tempered his bold words somewhat in public, although he was correct in his statement. The Hadith reports that Muhammad married A'isha at age 6 and consummated their marriage when she was 9 years old. Today under U.S. laws, Muhammad would have been sentenced to life imprisonment for committing such perverse acts. See "Muhammad's child wife" Les Kinsolving, June 18, 2002 www.worldnetdaily.com

10.   Vol. 1, *Al-Salat* CCXLIV, #1438.
11.   Vol. 4, *Al-Birr Wa's-Silat-I-Wa'l-Adab* MLXXV, #6285.
12.   Vol. 3, *Al Jihad Wa'l Siyar* DCCLXVII, #4436.
13.   Vol. 4, *Al-Shi'r* CMXLV, #5609-5611.

14. Vol. 3, *Al-Imara* DCCLXVII, #1031, #4565, #9566.
15. Vol. 4, *Al-Dhikr* MCXXVII, #6523.

16. Sometimes the most innocuous comment about the prophet can inflame the defenders of Islam into committing violent acts of rage, and revenge. Islamists use such purported insults to advance their cause, politically, religiously and culturally. This agenda was particularly in evidence during the Miss World Pageant held in Nigeria in November 2002.

During this time, the popular Nigerian newspaper *This Day* published a commentary by one of its reporters, Isioma Daniel. She was attempting to defend the Miss World Competition from opposition by local Islamic authorities. In her article, Daniel ventured to say: *"The Muslims thought it was immoral to bring 92 women to Nigeria and ask them to revel in vanity. What would Muhammad think? In all honesty, he would probably have chosen a wife from one of them."*

This small comment was judged by Muslims to be blasphemous to their prophet. Islamic fundamentalists then incited the faithful to riot, burning down the newspaper office despite its apologies. A death *fatwa* (religious decree) was issued against the 22 year old Daniel, who fled the country. The Deputy Governor of the Nigerian Zamfara State, then announced on national television: *"Any true Muslim would make sure that this woman's blood is spilled wherever she is"*

Angry mobs continued to riot, looting and burning churches. Christians responded back, burning mosques. The Pageant was moved to London. In the aftermath, over 250 people perished and some 1000 were injured. Later, not one of Nigeria's leading Muslims would condemn these acts. They chose to blame cause of the incitement on the journalist. It was her fault for daring to insult the prophet's holiness. See "Understand Nigeria and you understand the Islamic threat," Dennis Prager. Dec. 22, 2002. www.worldnetdaily.com

17. The Rev. Jerry Falwell infuriated Muslims worldwide by telling reporter Bob Simon on CBS's 60 Minutes: *"I think Muhammad was a terrorist. I read enough, by both Muslims and non-Muslims to decide that he was a violent man, a man of war. Today he would probably be associated with Arafat and Saddam Hussein as a terrorist. Killing people didn't bother him. Muhammad is not a good example for most*

*Muslim people. Jesus set the example for love.*" Upon hearing this statement Muslims worldwide reacted in rage. Falwell later said that his characterization of Islam's prophet Muhammad as a terrorist was not intended to antagonize Muslim people. See "Falwell: Intent not to attack Muhammad," Art Moore Oct.14, 2002. www.worldnetdaily.com

The Farsi language daily *Abrar* reported that Iranian cleric Mohsen Shabestari called for Falwell's death during weekly prayers in Tabriz , declaring that he was a "*mercenary who must be killed*". In Lebanon, Grand Ayatollah Mohammed Hussein Fadlallah called on Muslim countries to respond to Falwell who, he said had "*infringed on the prophet's dignity.*" A third Ayatollah Hussein Nouri Hamedani, accused Falwell of implementing "*a Zionist plan*" to cause a clash between Islam and Christianity. Freedom of speech in Islam especially in regards to criticizing the prophet Muhammad, does not exist. See "Muslims Irate over Falwell Slur of Muhammad" *Jerusalem Post*, Oct. 13,2002, pg. 4.

18. The text of the apology:

*Nine hundred years ago, our forefathers carried the name of Jesus Christ in battle across the Middle East. Fueled by fear, greed and hatred, they betrayed the name of Christ by conducting themselves in a manner contrary to His wishes and character. The Crusaders lifted the banner of the Cross above your people. By this act, they corrupted its true meaning of reconciliation, forgiveness and selfless love.*

*On the anniversary of the first Crusade we also carry the name of Christ. We wish to retrace the footsteps of the Crusaders in apology for theirs and in demonstration of the true meaning of the Cross. We deeply regret the atrocities committed in the name of Christ by our predecessors. We renounce greed, hatred and fear, and condemn all violence done in the name of Jesus Christ.*

*Where they were motivated by hatred and prejudice, we offer love and brotherhood. Jesus the Messiah came to give life. Forgive us for allowing His name to be associated with death. Please accept again the true meaning of the Messiah's words: 'The Spirit of the Lord is upon me, because He has anointed me to bring good news to the poor. He has sent me to proclaim release to the captives and recov-*

*ery of sight to the blind, to let the oppressed go free, to proclaim the year of the Lord's favor'* (Isa. 61:1-2). *As we go, we bless you in the name of the Lord Jesus Christ.*

19. *National & International Religion Report*, Roanoke, VA; May 13, 1996, pg. 2.
20. *Friends of Turkey* reports that this Iman in fact sent this message to some 600 mosques, *Call to Prayer*, Oct. 96, pg. 2.
21. Ibid, pg. 2.
22. J. Johnston, Aug. 1996.

# SIX

## "Who is like unto thee, O LORD...?"
### (Ex. 15:11)

*T*he first step in evangelizing Muslims for the Christian is to settle the issue as to who their god is. Christianity is divided in its theology about who *Allah* is. Traditionalists accord *Allah* the same respect as given to the God of the Christian and of the Jews.[1] They are one and the same; the true God of the Patriarchs. Christian conservatives dispute this position and deny that *Allah* is anything more than a high demonic prince, and a pagan god.

The name *Allah* itself, offers little help in determining who Muslim's worship. It is made of the definite article *Al* and the root *ilh* meaning "the god." It appears to be an Arabic rendering of the Hebrew *El* for the name of God. The word *Allah* is similar to the Hebrew *Eloah*, which is the lengthened form of *El*, but it is not etymologically related to it.[2] The Aramaic word for God, *Elah* is also found in the Old Testament: thirty-seven times in Ezra, and forty-six occasions in Daniel.[3] There is no plural in Arabic for the name of *Allah*. The word both designates the One True God, and is used to label pagan gods. The Sirwah inscription, an early Christian monument in Yemen (est. 547 AD), records the name of *Allah* as God. Etymologists also debate the origin of the Arabic *'ilaha*,

74

meaning "the eternal" and whether it could be derived from the Hebrew verb *'illaha* which means: to fear, to be perplexed and to adore. For the Christian, *Allah* is a mystery. His name is "The God," yet he is never personalized like the LORD God of the Bible who revealed His name to Moses as *Yahweh* or "I Am." The god of the Koran is aloof, sterile and hidden. He cannot be the same God that Christians and Jews worship.[4]

Historically, *Allah* was worshipped in pre-Islamic Arabia. Some desert tribes acknowledged the sun as their high god. Other clans in ancient Arabia venerated a moon god, and called the sun a goddess. Three shrines close to Mecca were dedicated to the daughters of *Allah*. In the city of Taif, the Bedouin worshipped, *Allat* the sun goddess who was also called *Al-Rabba* "the Sovereign."[5] Near Nakhlah, *Al-Uzza* "the mighty one," the goddess of the morning star was adored. The seaside village of Qudayd revered *Manat* the goddess of fate and fortune. These goddesses were related to the ancient fertility goddesses *Anat* and *Istar*. Lesser gods were found in sacred trees, stones, mountains, and in the elements. *Quzah* was the rainbow god, *Nasr* the eagle deity, *Wudd* the goddess of love, and *Awf* served as the great Bird. A whole host of demons, and *jinns* were also recognized. Their presence was seen and feared in the shrieking desert winds, the shifting dunes, and within the mysterious depths of wells. Above all these gods, it was *Allah* who reigned supreme.

The cube-shaped stone walled *Ka'ba* in Mecca was *Allah*'s house. The primitive tribes through their folklore had always identified this location as being the *beit Allah*, or the house of God. This house was never called *beit el-Alihet*, or home of the gods, although by Muhammad's era some 360 idols were kept inside and worshipped there.[6]

Early Arabia was polytheistic, yet also monotheistic, as Jewish and Christian tribes inhabited the same area. Over time their beliefs became intermingled with the desert community. The

Nestorean church was established in the area, as were monks and Jewish traders. Certain religious seekers, called *Hanifs*, were also present in Mecca. These people were neither Christian nor Jews. They rejected the practice of idolatry and sought freedom from sin by resigning themselves to the will of *Allah*. Muhammad apparently learned a great deal from his own cousin Waraqa, who was one of these individuals. The Koran reflects this influence, as well as Jewish and Christan adaptations.

Some similarities in the essence of *Allah* are found in the Koran that Christians could unhesitatingly accept as being aspects of the true God. The Koran identifies *Allah* as being the Creator. He is also titled as the Holy One, the Guardian of Peace, and the First and the Last. He is called as well, the Absolute, the Owner of Prase (S. 31:26, Lukman), the True (S. 31:30), and the Lord of Kindness (S. 2:251, The Cow). For the Muslim, *Allah* is terribly near, closer than the artery of his neck (S. 50:15, The True Believer). One of Muhammad's early *Surah's* speaks of the Creator: *"Say: God is One, the eternal God. He begot none, nor was begotten. None is equal to him"* (S. 112:1-4, Oneness). *Allah* is presented positively in some parts of the Koran, and is called Beneficent, Merciful and Compassionate. This god is labeled *"all powerful and mighty."* Most of these titles correctly identify the outward qualities of the LORD God's character.

Christians who disown the name of *Allah* as representing the One True God, reject the idea that this Arab god is equal to the Creator *Yahweh*. Rather, *Allah* is a strong Satanic prince with a stranglehold over the Muslim people. He is an evil presence dwelling within the *Ka'ba*, and the source of all the Antichrist venom of hell. This entity is a fallen angel, masquerading as the true God ( II Cor. 11:14). *Allah* is never identified in the Koran as a God of LOVE. He is a cold and angry god. He is never found there as *Abba* Father either, but only as a distant despot. This god refuses to love the prodigal: *"O children of Adam, look to your dress at every place of worship, and eat and drink, but be not*

*prodigal. Lo! He loveth not the prodigals"* (S. 7:31, The Heights).
The backslider receives no mercy either: *"Lo!, those who believe
then disbelieve, and then increase in disbelief, Allah will never pardon them, nor will he guide them unto a way"* (S. 4:137, Women).

Among the ninety-nine names that *Allah* is reverently called by
Muslims are the titles: **the Master Deceiver, the Supreme
Plotter,** and **the One Who Leads Astray.** This god also has no
mercy for sinners, neither is there a suggestion of holiness. Love
is conditional and is accepted from only those who believe on the
revelations of the apostle Muhammad. *"Whoso opposeth Allah
and His messenger, for him lo! Allah is severe in punishment. That
is the reward, so taste it and know that for disbelievers is the torment of fire"* (S. 8:13-14, The Spoils). The culminating evidence
lies in how this god views Jews and Christians:

> *You to who the Scriptures were given! Believe in that
> which We have revealed, confirming your own Scripture
> before We obliterate your faces and turn them backward,
> or lay Our curse on you as We laid it on the Sabbath-
> breakers* (S. 4:47, Women).

This message is repeated again, in *Surah* 98:6: *"Those who
disbelieve among the People of the Scripture, they are the worst of
the created beings."* Another divine admonition chastises the faithful for finding friendship outside the umbrella of Islam: *"O You
who believe! Take not the Jews and Christians for friends. They
are friends one to another. He among you that taketh them for
friends is one of them. Lo! Allah guideth not wrongdoing folk"*
(S. 5:51, The Table).

The assumption is that, since no Christian can rightfully accept
Muhammad's revelation of the Koran as truth, then Islam is founded on a false gospel promulgated by a beguiling angel of light
called *Allah*.[7] Paul's warning to the Galatians is paramount for all
believers in Christ: *"...there be some that trouble you and would*

77

*pervert the gospel of Christ. But though we, or an angel from heaven, preach any other gospel unto you than that which we have preached unto you, let him be accursed"* (Gal.1:7-8).

### The Koran, a work of the flesh

Perhaps a case could be made that Muhammad cleverly composed these revelations from God. Hence, his theology would be a mixture of what he had heard and experienced. Thus the deity that is revealed in the Koran would be only what Muhammad's mind could have conceived, a god with the name *Allah*, but without a heart of love. The Apostle Paul perceived in the Athenians the same problem Muhammad experienced: Ignorance. *"For as I passed by, and beheld your devotions, I found an altar with this inscription, TO THE UNKNOWN GOD. Whom therefore ye ignorantly worship, him I declare unto you"* (Acts 17:23).

Samuel Zwemer writes:

> *The Moslem idea of God is wholly inadequate and distorted from a New Testament standpoint; it may even be called anti-Christian. But it is not therefore, anti-theistic. No one is to be called a theist who does not believe in a personal God. Theism assumes a living relation to God such as Moslems feel and exercise in their prayers and meditations, such as Mohammed himself experienced. One may be a theist and not be a Christian; but he cannot be a Christian and not be a theist.*[8]

One should certainly bind the Antichrist spirit when witnessing to Muslims. Yet, one must also realize that there are Muslims who are truly seeking God. They will have an awareness of the Creator in their heart's. Psalms declare that *"The fool hath said in his heart, There is no God"* (14:1). The Muslim is not a fool, for he recognizes that there is a God. He is not an atheist. Proverbs declares that *"The fear of the LORD is the beginning of knowledge"*

(Pr. 1:7). The Muslim in his primitive faith fully believes in the One True God. He fears the Creator's presence, and practices righteous deeds to gain His acceptance. Muslims reject vehemently any notion of idols or false worship. The problem is that they do not have a relationship with God, nor can they conceive of a personal loving God who can be a Father to them. The Muslim fears God, yet desperately needs to know how to approach his Creator. Paul in his letter to Timothy reveals how Muslims can come to God: *"For there is one God, and one mediator between God and man, the man Christ Jesus"* (I Tim. 2:5).

Yes, the god of the Koran is an impostor but the problem Christians face when witnessing to Arabs is that the Arabic Bible uses the name of *Allah* for God. The original Bible translators had no other choice. There was no alternative linguistical term to use for the LORD God in Arabic than *Allah*. Arab Christians today, who live in Syria, Iraq, Egypt, and Lebanon, as well as in other Arabic speaking nations, recognize the name of *Allah* as referring to the One True God. Christian, our mision is not to debate with one another over who *Allah* is. Our task is to reveal the Word of God to the Muslim. Place a Bible is his/her hands and let them find a relationship with the One True God who can and will deliver them from all demonic strongholds and superstitions.[9] Let this Muslim discover his or her acceptance in the beloved. Let them find the true gift of God for them: Jesus Christ (Rom. 6:23). He is the bridge between man and God.

---

1    The Second Vatican Council on November 20th, 1964 approved the following declaration concerning Muslims. The declaration says in part:

*The Church is filled with esteem for Muslims. They adore the one God who exists in himself and wields all power; they adore the Creator of heaven and earth who has spoken to them; they strive to obey wholeheartedly even His incomprehensible decrees just as Abraham did, to whose faith they like to link their own. Though they*

*do not acknowledge Jesus as God, they revere him as a prophet.*
*They also honor Mary, his virgin mother, at times they even call upon*
*her with devotion. Also, they await the day of judgment when God*
*will reward all those who have been resurrected. Furthermore, as*
*they worship God through prayer, almsgiving, and fasting, so they*
*seek to lead the moral life--be it that of the individual or that of the*
*family and society--and conform to his will. In the course of cen-*
*turies, however, not a few quarrels and hostilities have arisen*
*between Christians and Muslims. Hence this sacred synod urges all*
*not only to forget the past but also to work honestly for mutual under-*
*standing and to further as well as guard together social justice, all*
*moral goods, especially peace and freedom, so that the whole of*
*mankind may benefit from their endeavor.*

2.   *Eloah* occurs in the Book of Job, forty times.
3.   *Synonyms of the Old Testament,* Griddlestone pg. 31; *The*
*Christian Approach to Islam*, Barton, pg. 133.

4.   The author while living in Jerusalem once employed a Muslim
to paint the interior of our house. When the job was completed, it
was near the time for afternoon prayer. He knelt down on the living
room rug and faced Mecca. I begin to pray quietly in tongues against
his words. The moment he finished his prayers to *Allah*, a ceramic
plate with the Hebrew word *Shalom* (Peace), fell from the wall and
crashed into the sink. Coincidence? Highly unlikely!

5.   Remnants of this early pagan worship can still be seen in Islam.
The crescent moon decorates the flags of many Islamic countries
today. It is also placed on the tops of mosques, minerets, and identifies the Islamic Red Crescent Society. The horns of the crescent
symbolize to Muslims good fortune and happiness . Originally, the
crescent symbol represented worship of the goddess *Al-Uzza*. Later,
the Ottoman Rulers adopted this emblem.

6.   *The Moslem Doctrine of God,* Samuel M. Zwemer, pg. 26.
7.   English versions of the Koran, now use the word God, instead
of *Allah*.
8.   *The Allah of Islam and the God Revealed in Jesus Christ,*
Samuel M. Zwemer, pgs. 309-310.

9.   A Christian man from Malaysia, who formerly was a Muslim,
testified to Don McCurry (missionary, author, professor), how the

Word of God changed his life. The man was given a Bible by a Christian. He began to read from it, starting in the book of Genesis, Chapter One. The story of Adam's creation greatly impressed him. The idea that God created man in His own image, persuaded him to accept Christianity. Islam states that God is unknowable, neither can He be understood.

# SEVEN

# "The Truth Made Plain"

The Koran is the very heart and soul of Islam. Its message and words are revered by all Muslims as being *"the truth made plain."* This holy book is spoken of as being eternally present before creation (S. 5:59, The Table). Its revelations are declared to be written *"on a guarded table"* placed near the throne of God (S. 85:22, The Stars). Every word, letter, form, as well as its entire content and meaning, is considered to be inerrant.

The Koran is spoken of as the final revelation from God, the culmination of all other sources. *"He hath revealed unto thee, the Scripture with truth, confirming that which was before it, even as He revealed the Torah and the Gospel"* (S. 3:3-4, Imran). The Koran's purpose is to guard the soundness of all previous revelations by restoring the eternal truth of *Allah*. As a holy book, the Koran declares that it contains all knowledge, through which humanity can supposedly attain salvation and paradise. Mankind then, is brought out of darkness and into the light, by obedience to its decrees. These instructions of *Allah*, guide men *"unto a straight path."* It is *"a plain Scripture"* whereby this god of Mecca is able to *"guideth him who seeketh His good pleasure unto paths of peace"* (S. 5:16, The Table).

The sacred book of *Allah* is relatively short, and can be compared to the size of the New Testament. It consists of 114 *Surahs* or chapters, each one comprising of a single revelation. Tradition

82

accords that Muhammad dictated it to attendants while in a trance or shortly thereafter.[1]   Materials to record these sayings were scarce, so bits of leather, palm leaves, stones, ribs of animals and the shoulder blades of camels were used.  A select group of men who could recite these revelations from memory were later called upon to retain them.  The Koran is arranged in order of length rather than in chronological order.  Each *Surah* is composed of verses called *ayats* (signs or proofs).  There are a total of 6,236 of these signs in the Koran.

From the different chapters and verses one may perceive a dim resemblance to familiar Bible stories.  Both books relate of the creation of Adam and Eve, their expulsion from the garden, the great flood over the earth and the witness of Noah.  The traditional heroes of the Jewish-Christian faith are also found in the Koran. Abraham, Joseph and Moses, as well as David and Solomon, are mentioned.  The major prophets like Jeremiah and Isaiah are conspicuous by their absence.  This holy book neglects to recognize the Divine Christ.  It also omits any reference to the Pauline Epistles of the Christian Bible.  The Koran speaks little of the lostness of man.  The reader will find though, even in the most cursory reading of this record that a great emphasis has been placed on the outward qualities of submission.  Hence, the Koran details prayers, washings, and prohibitions as to eating.  Man's role in this book is limited to one of strict obedience to God.  The penalty for disobedience is eternal doom and hellfire.

Jesus Christ appears some 93 times in various scattered verses. He is called "*Isa,*" a mighty prophet, born of a virgin (Mary).[2]  His birth is a miracle, yet not one Old Testament scripture is cited to justify the reason for it.  It just happens.  Jesus is spoken of healing the blind and the leper, as well as raising the dead, yet He is not recognized as "*the Son of God.*"  There is no crucifixion of Jesus either in the Koran.  It instead, infers that "*Isa*" was rescued by God and then taken up to heaven (S. 4:157-158, Women).

**83**

The star of this heavenly book is Muhammad. The man's name appears only four times in the Koran, but allusions to his presence, and his selection as a prophet, radiate throughout this work. He is the warner, the final prophet, and the seal of the plain truth. Above all though, Muhammad is God's messenger, a man who must be obeyed.

Islam believes that the Koran is Muhammad's greatest miracle. It authenticates Muhammad's claim as a prophet of God. He who could not read nor write, heard this document and was obedient to the divine command to transmit it to mankind. The word "Koran" means "recitation." The book supposedly was revealed to Muhammad by the Archangel Gabriel over a 22 year period. Muslims believe by faith, that it is the actual word of God. The text for the Koran is at times incomprehensible, confused and difficult. Muslims scholars justify this awkwardness as being the divine effect on the language of man, which being under the *"formidable pressure of the Heavenly Word, is broken into a thousand fragments."* Islam believes that the very recitation of its words in Arabic brings one blessing, and will place that person in the presence of God. Muslims hold that the meaning of the Koran is inseparable from the language in which it was revealed. Thus, while the Koran is available in other languages than Arabic, these are considered to be approximations and not exact translations. Therefore all Muslims, whatever their native tongue, must recite the Koran in its original Arabic, whether they understand it or not!

The Arabic language and prose in the Koran has been called, *"striking, soaring, vivid, terrible, tender and breathtaking."*[3] The majority of the *Surahs* are written in rhymed verse. Each one has its own rhythm and cadence, a beauty of words. The book possesses an overwhelming richness of flashing images, and poetic measures which have a hypnotic effect on listeners. Skilled reciters of the Koran have been known to reduce an Arabic-speaking audience to helpless tears.

The pious man venerates the Koran with an intensity beyond what most Jews and Christians exert for the Scriptures. Many Muslims have memorized the entire Koran by heart. They can recite large portions of it. Some, never leave their home without a copy. The Koran is treated by Muslims with great reverence.[4] No other book is allowed to be placed over it, nor is it to be carried below the waist.

A missionary to Bangladesh told me of how he was once invited into a Muslim's home. The Koran was displayed in a prominent place in the house. All other books were beneath it. The missionary left the Muslim a small thank-you gift for his hospitality: a Bible. Over the months, he visited the man three more times. On his subsequent visit, he observed that the Bible was placed on the shelf, below the Koran. Returning again, the missionary chanced to see that the Bible was located alongside the Koran. The third visit was even more surprising. The Bible now held the most honored position in the home, and the Koran was nowhere in sight!

Muslims speak of the Koran's fragrance, of its eloquence, poetry and rhythm. It is a revelation to them, which gives forth a sweeter scent than that of rose watered perfume. Yet if a traveler is dry and thirsty and in a desert, he does not ask for rose water. Thirst can only be satisfied by water.[5] It is God alone who can satisfy the thirsty soul. The River of Life (God's Spirit) inhabits the Word of God. The Bible is a wellspring of life which can freely and liberally provide refreshing waters to the Muslim's soul.

Samuel Zwemer once wrote about the Koran and the waters it possessed:

> *Wherever the water of life goes, life comes and everything blossoms and bursts into fruitage. The water that goes forth from the springs of Arabic literature (the Koran & Hadith), and of Islam is bitter water, a Dead sea of thought. It is true that the desert is the garden of Allah,*

*but the desert is not the garden of Jehovah. Where Jehovah walks is paradise, and where Allah walks there is the desert, even as in "the Garden of Allah" you find three great elements—sensuousness, fanaticism, intolerance, coupled with the great propagating force—so wherever Islam has extended, the influence of that religion is found producing four similar results.*[6]

Jesus once stood and declared to the people: *"If any man thirst, let him come unto me, and drink."*[7] He also promised that *"He that believeth on me, as the Scripture hath said, out of his belly shall flow rivers of living water"* (Jn. 7:37-38). Christian, take courage. Drink daily of His Word, knowing that he is fashioning you to become his end-time vessel of living water. You have the Lord's promise to be that vessel of living water to those who are parched and dry. Ask God to let you be part of that bridal company in Revelation that links up with the Spirit and says, *"Come. And let him that heareth say, Come. And let him that is athirst come. And whosoever will, let him take of the water of life freely"* (Rev. 22:17). Volunteer today in prayer to the Lord. Tell Him that you are willing to be a water bearer of His word to the Muslims; in whatever capacity and place, He can use you. The Savior will not disappoint you, nor will He ignore the cries of those who are thirsting for a drink. Your efforts will also not be in vain as the Lord has said: *"And whosoever shall give to drink unto one of these little ones a cup of cold water only in the name of a disciple...he shall in no wise lose his reward"* (Mt. 10:42).

---

1.   His close disciples observed that when the messenger of *Allah* felt a *"burden the color of his face underwent a change."* A'isha reported that he would begin to perspire profusely. Muhammad said that the inspiration came to him like *"the ringing of a bell and that is most severe for me, and when it is over I retain what I have received."* In other incidents, the prophet spoke of an angel in the form of a human being coming to meet with him. Muhammad then recited the words that he had heard from this entity (Vol. 4, *Al-*

*Fada'il*, CMLXXIII, #5764-5767). Sometimes the prophet would speak of a revelation which had come to him while he was asleep. On other occassions, he would arbitrarily cancel what verses he had already dictated to his writers, since a greater revelation would be forthcoming.

The reports of these revelations lead to five conclusions:

1. Muhammad, actually heard from God. The Koran therefore is the truth of heaven brought down to men. All Muslims ascribe to this position. This conclusion is impossible for a Christian to accept.
2. Muhammad artificially produced these symptoms, thereby putting on an act to convince people of his callings and claims.
3. He was possessed by a familiar spirit, "demons."
4. Muhammad suffered from epilepsy and masked his seizures as "revelations."
5. The prophet was able to induce a trance upon himself (self-hypnosis)

2.    The name *"Isa"* has caused problems among Christians in witnessing to Muslims, converting them and in the translation of the Bible. Etymologists suggest that perhaps this "name" was purposly given to Muhammad by Arabian Jews to mislead him into thinking Essau and Jesus were the same. To the Jew, Essau was symbolic of evil. Jesus was also hated for being a "false" messiah. Still, other scholars propose that *"Isa"* is an Arabized form of *"Ishu,"* which is derived from the Syriac name for Jesus: *"Yeshu."* A third camp sees similarities in the name of *"Isa"* to the Greek name for Jesus in the Gospels *"Iesous."*

Many Christians in lands where Muslims reside, prefer to use the name *"Yasua"* when speaking about Jesus. Muslims though, may not recognize "who" you are talking about. For further discussion, see "A case of Mistaken Identity" J. Ellington, *The Bible Translator*, Vol. 44 #4, Oct. 1993, pgs 401-405.

3.    Islam, edited by J.A. Williams pg. 16.

4.    This reverence for the Koran, sometimes goes beyond all human reasoning. Muslim extremists in Kano, a city in Northern Nigeria,

killed a truck driver for allegedly desecrating the Koran. The man, Uche Nwama was seen unloading fruit from his truck which was parked near an open air meeting. Hundreds of Muslims descended on Nwama and clubbed him to death. He had "sinned" by allowing the exhaust fumes from his truck to pollute the air, thus desecrating the Koran (*Intercede*, May/June 2002 pg. 3)

5.    "*When one is thirsty, one thousand pearls are not worth one drop of water,*" Persian Proverb.

6.    "The Arabic Language and Islam";  Samuel Zwemer, *The Missionary Review of the World,* Oct. 1910, pg. 776.

7.    "*The thirsty person goes to the well, not the well to him.  The thirsty is most eager for water*" Urdu Proverb.

# EIGHT

# The Sword of the Giant

The Koran is the glittering sword of Islam. It shines forth with the oil of men's praises, yet is soaked with the innocent blood of those it has slain. The book is a powerful weapon in the hands of its defenders, but is no contest against the Bible. For the Koran is a coarse saber, while *"the word of God is quick and powerful, and sharper than any two-edged sword, piercing even to the dividing asunder of soul and spirit..."* The Koran is a weapon that is scarred by omissions, dulled by changes, scratched with errors, pitted with paganistic beliefs and rusted throughout with an abysmal lack of moral principles. The writer of Ecclesiastes declares that *"If the iron be blunt, and he do not whet the edge, then must he put forth more strength"* (Ecc.10:10). In these last days, as Islam has grown, Muslim leaders have had to increasingly resort to using hyper-legalism and fanaticism to enforce this religious abomination upon greater numbers of unwilling and fearful adherents. The Koran has but one edge: judgment. It is the spiritless, untempered and fearful god of this world and man. The book of Muhammad is deficient in that it will never be like the true word of God and be *"a discerner of the thoughts and intents of the heart."* The Scripture that has been given to Christians and Jews breathes with the Spirit of God. It holds the manifested Word, the Logos eternally present with the Father. This honed weapon possesses a double edge: God's Mercy and that of His Judgment. The Greek term used in scripture for the word "double edged" is *diastoma:* which means "double mouthed" (Heb. 4:12; Rev. 19:15). The Word of God is powerful. It came

**89**

forth from the LORD's mouth with might and authority, and will also exit our very mouths in the same way; doubling the effect. God's Word does not come back void!

## A Perfect Work

Islam claims that the Koran is perfect: *"A book sent down to thee."* Thus this work is a direct revelation of God and not the labor of any human.[1] The idea that the Koran was influenced by monks and rabbis whom Muhammad met in the desert, or by their scripture, is anathema to Muslims.[2] The book is above all criticism. To disbelieve, the Koran's revelations merits the ownership of hellfire. The gates of heaven are shut to the unbeliever and a painful doom is authorized by their god (S. 16:104, The Slanderer). This god curses these unbelievers saying:

> But as for those who disbelieve, garments of fire will be cut out for them. Boiling fluid will be poured down on their heads, whereby that which is in their bellies, and their skins too will be melted; and for them are hooked rods of iron, whenever in their anguish...it is said unto them: Taste the doom of burning (S. 22:19-22, The Pilgrimage).

Again, the words of judgment come forth: *"And whoso disobeyeth Allah and His messenger and transgresseth his limits, he will make him enter Fire, where such will dwell forever; his will be a shameful doom"* (S. 4:14, Women).

This vengeful god also strikes out against those beings which dare to follow after another faith. *"Whoever seeks a religion other than Islam, it will not be accepted of him"* (S. 3:85, Imran). The Koran, declares itself an instrument of *"good tidings for those who have surrendered to Allah"* (S. 16:89, The Bee). Yet it clearly instructs its followers to strive against all disbelievers with great endeavor, and to *"kill them wherever you find them"* (S. 4:89,

Women). There is no second chance to reconsider in Islam. Believe in Muhammad's revelations or perish by the sword.

## A Heavenly Inspired Document?

Is the Koran truly inspired by God according to Islamic conceptions? If this supposition were true, we would expect to find a perfect document written in Arabic without any problems. This is just not the case, as difficulties occur which cannot be explained away as just being the results of faulty translations. Errors, contradictions, legends and changed verses, all arise to confront those who dare examine this word. Consider the following arguments:

## The Original Manuscripts are Missing

The Koran that Muslims follow today has no original manuscript or documents to draw from. There is no recorded proof of what Muhammad actually said. The Hadith informs us that the prophet's revelations were first copied unto broken pieces of pottery, palm leaves and pieces of leather and on *"the hearts of men."* These external writings were haphazardly stored. Some were kept in a bag, while others were placed in tents, homes, and in areas near the prophet. A'isha, Muhammad's youngest wife, reported that after the prophet's death, a goat ate a whole chapter of the Koran that had been recorded on a piece of cloth and which she had placed under her pillow. Major portions of this revelatory work have been accepted by Muslims as being "lost." *Surah* 33 called "The Clans," contains only 73 verses. A'isha stated that this *Surah* once numbered 200 verses, and when Othman assembled the Koran, these missing verses could not be found. John of Damascus, an early Christian apologist (690-770 A.D.), writing on the heresies of the Ishmaelites, comments on a section of the Koran called, "The Camel," which is no longer in existence.[3] Umar speaking on the Koran, once advised *"Say not I possess the whole Koran, but of it what is extant."* [4]

The first two Caliphs that followed after Muhammad, endeavored to assemble the Koran. Four variant versions were accepted. When Othman assumed the role of Caliph in 644, he ordered that all versions except the one he approved of, be destroyed. Even so, unauthorized editions of the Koran still appear. The Ryland's Library in England contains a Koran with a text that is considerably different from the present source used today. The Koran was also originally inscribed on the interiors of men's hearts. Muhammad sought to assemble an oral record of his revelations, and recruited "reciters." Seventy of these oracles were slain in the battle of Bir Ma'uma. Under the Caliphs scores more were slain in further hostilities. The Koran, they possessed, died with them.[5]

## The Answer is Blowing in the Wind

Muhammad's word of god shifts like the desert winds, where he once lived. What the prophet previously revealed in one verse or during a revelation, often becomes "abrogated" in the interest of greater revelations.[6] The Koran approves of this sleigh of hand act with the "divine" words: *"Such of our Revelation as we abrogate or cause to be forgotten, we bring in place one better or the like thereof. Knoweth not that Allah is Able to do all things?"* (S 2:106, The Cow). Again, this god justifies this smoke screen with the words: *"And when we put a revelation in place of another revelation and Allah knoweth best what he revealeth. They say Lo; Thou art but inventing. Most of them know not!"* (S. 3:85, Imran).

The most famous cancellation occurred in *Surah* 53 "The Star." The Hadith and early histories preserve the story.[7] When Muhammad first recited this chapter in Mecca, as he was meditating before the *Ka'ba*, he swore by three pagan Arab goddesses, praised them and approved of their intercession saying:

*Did you consider Al Lat and Al'Uzza and Al Manat, the Third, the other? Those are the cranes exalted* (female goddesses) *between heaven and earth like angels. Their intercession is expected. Their likes are not neglected.*

It is thought that Muhammad when he spoke these verses may have been trying to effect a compromise with the Quraysh tribe that worshipped these ancestral goddesses. Hence, he was seeking to establish a peace between his group of believers and those in Mecca that rejected this path. The Quraysh were delighted with this new revelation and spread the news that Muhammad was approving of their gods. Islam was no longer a threat to the faith of their fathers, or their way of life.

The story continues, in that Gabriel the angel, allegedly appeared one night before Muhammad and rebuked him intensely for his actions. The angel accused the prophet of reciting to the Quraysh, verses that did not come from God. The prophet was informed that Satan had entered into his mind and caused him to err. Muhammad though, was not to worry for this very thing had happened to other godly prophets. Gabriel had also "earlier" given the prophet other verses to prove this matter to him: *"Never have we sent a single prophet or apostle before you with whose wishes Satan did not tamper. But God abrogates the interjections of Satan and confirms His own revelations"* (S. 22:51, The Pilgrimage).[8] God therefore, would improve matters by sending him new verses.

Muhammad later announced that Satan had given him these evil verses, hence the name *"the Satanic verses."*[9] He then declared a new revelation to replace the old:

> *Have you though upon Al-Lat and Al-Uzza, and Mannaat, the other third goddess? Have you male chil-dren and Allah female? This is indeed an unfair division! They are no other than empty names which you and your fathers have named goddesses. Allah has not revealed concerning them anything to authorize their worship* (S. 53:19-23, The Star).[10]

The former "mistake" was quickly "erased" out of the Koran, but the story was remembered by Ibn Sa'd, and is recorded in his Hadith. Scripture says: *"Be sure your sin will find you out"* (Num. 32:23).

## The Sword Verse

The greatest "change" in the Koran is the infamous Sword *ayat:*

> *Then when the sacred months have passed, slay the idol-aters wherever you find them, and take them prisioner, and besiege them, and prepare for them each ambush. But if they repent and establish worship and pay the legal tax, then leave their way free. Lo! Allah is Forgiving, Merciful* (S. 9:5, Repentance).

In revealing this verse, Muhammad canceled out no less than 119 other divine *ayas* in the Koran! Then as a further evidence of this book's bi-polarism, the first clause of this Sword verse is abrogated by the second part.

Muhammad in his continuing series of revelations "nullified" the direction of prayer, changing it first from a freedom to turn either East or West (S. 2:115), to Jerusalem (S. 2:142), and finally towards Mecca (S. 2:144). The drinking of wine is forbidden by *Surah* 5:90, and yet *Surah* 16:11, implies that permission is granted. The Koran further muddles this abrogation, by revealing that heaven is full of *"rivers of wine, delicious to the drinkers"* (S. 47:15). J. Windrow Sweetman in his study of *Islam and Christian Theology* documents more than 260 abrogated verses in the Koran!

Christian, abrogation does not exist in the Bible. Our God, the LORD is not a God that He should lie, or be double minded, or change His word every chapter. There is a continuity in the Word, a security of knowing that the truth which is revealed to Christians *"is settled in heaven"* (Ps. 119:89). The LORD may correctly say,

"*Behold I make all things new,*" but His Word is established forever. Jesus Christ came not to destroy the law or abrogate it, but to fulfill it (Mt. 5:17-18). The Old Covenant of the Law was not done away with or changed, but fulfilled in the New Testament through the New Covenant, as Jeremiah correctly prophesied:

> *Behold, the days come, saith the LORD, that I will make a new covenant with the house of Israel, and with the house of Judah: Not according to the covenant that I made with their fathers But this shall be the covenant that I will make with the house of Israel; after those days, saith the LORD, I will put my law in their inward parts, and write it in their hearts; and will be their God, and they shall be my people* (Jer. 31:31-34).

The writer of Hebrew's speaks of "*Jesus, the mediator of the new covenant*" (Heb. 12:24). It is an "*everlasting covenant*" fulfilled through His shed blood (Heb. 13:20).

### Pure Arabic?

The Koran conceitedly speaks to its hearers that it is a word prepared in heaven and transmitted in "pure Arabic." In case one might forget the beauty of this dialect or turn to read this revelation in a lesser noble tongue, the Koran repeats this wondrous disclosure in eight other *Surahs*. "*And lo! it is a revelation of the Lord of the worlds which the true Spirit has brought down upon thy heart, that thou mayest be one of the warners in plain Arabic speech*" (S. 26:191-196, The Poets).

Apparently though, whatever entity in the heavens or under the earth, which made this confession to Muhammad, must have been greatly misinformed. Scholars have identified over one hundred foreign words which are contained in the Koran. The book abounds with Hebrew, Greek, Syrian, Persian, Coptic, Assyrian, and even Egyptian terms. The word *Jinn* comes from the Persian language.

**95**

The name *Ibis* represents Satan in the Koran and is derived from the Greek. *Gehannam*, the abode of fire, is clearly Hebrew, as well as *Tawrah* (Torah). The very word *Koran* in Arabic is traceable to the Syriac *qeryana* which refers to "readings."

## Koranic Errors

Muslims accuse Christians of tampering with the Bible, and of polluting the scriptures. Yet, the Koran as the last revelation of God, reflects a grave heavenly confusion as to what is really the genuine Word of God. Muhammad's "true word" speaks of *Allah* creating the world in two days (S. 41:9-12), then reminds it's hearers that God completed this task in six days (S. 7:54; 10:4). Yes, God truly did create the earth in six days, but the Bible further reveals that, He *"blessed the seventh day, and sanctified it"* and then *"rested from all his work"* (Gen. 2:3). The Koran neglects to show the LORD blessing this final day, nor mentions the sanctifying of it. *Allah* is also a god that does not appreciate rest either. No reference to this act, occurs in the Koran.

Noah, finds safety in the ark, but one of his son's *"a disbeliever"* drowns in the flood (S.11:41-43). This statement contradicts the story in Genesis where Noah and all three of his sons went into the ark with him (Gen. 7:1,7,13). After the flood, the Koran has the ark landing on Mt. Judah (S. 11:44) and not Mt. Ararat (Gen. 8:4). Haman, the evil adviser in the book of Esther, is found in this book to be a helper to Pharaoh, as well as the builder of the tower of Babel (S. 28:38). A Samaritan is credited with making the golden calf for the Israelites (S. 20:88), when in fact the Bible reveals that Aaron initiated this act (Ex. 32:2-4, 24). The Samaritans did not exist as a people until the Israelites later came into the promised land. This mixed race of people and Jewish believers came into being during the reign of Omri, King of Israel. The King of Assyria moved these people into the Northern Kingdom of Israel (8th century B.C.).

The story of Jesus is also inaccurate. He is said to be born in a desert area under a date palm tree (S.19:23), not in a manger in Bethlehem (Lk. 2:15-16) Miriam (Mary) His mother is declared to be *"the wife of Imran"* (the father of Moses) and the *"sister of Aaron,"* the brother to Moses (S. 19:28).[11] Jesus speaks from the cradle and declares that He is *"the slave of Allah,"* hence a Muslim! (S. 19:30). The boy also wondrously creates live birds out of clay (S. 5:110). These tales are obviously drawn from the early apocryphal writings such as the Proto-evangel of James the Less, the Gospel of Nicodemous, and certain Infancy Gospel's rejected by Christianity as being outright fables. The next incredible unveiling of the Koran, occurs when Jesus declares to his disciples to *"Believe in me and My messenger"* (Muhammad). Of course, they believe, and in doing so, ask him to bear witness that they have surrendered or *"are Muslims"* (S. 5:111). The worst omission is the total rejection of the crucifixion of Jesus, and His resurrection (S. 4:157-158). The Koran and Muhammad just cannot accept the idea of being upstaged by a greater and mightier Prophet: Jesus, the Son of God!

## Paganistic Practices

One of the pillars of Islam is its requirement to make a pilgrimage to Mecca.[12] This "holy city" with its sacred *Ka'ba*, and Black Stone is nothing more than an ancient worship site for paganistic gods. Muhammad, incorporated the ritual's of pre-Islamic *Allah* worship into his religion. Rites include kissing the Black Stone, circling the *Ka'ba* seven times and stoning the devil.[13] Three pillars at Mina represent the devil. The pilgrim approaches each one and then throws seven pebbles at these idols and says, *"In the name of Allah and Allah is mighty, in hatred of the devil and his shame, I do this"*[14] The pilgrimage is concluded with a sacrifice. A sheep, goat, cow or camel is offered, depending on the wealth of the visiting.[15] The animal is placed facing the *Ka'ba* and then sacrificed with a knife being plunged into its throat. The cry *"Allah akbar"* or "God is great!" is then shouted.

In idolatrous days, the Arabs worshipped sacred stones and made a circuit seven times in imitation of the planets. This rotation around the *Ka'ba* therefore, is a throwback to the Arab's pre-Islamic Sabean homage, as is the adoration of the sacred stones, and the blood sacrifices. In the early eighth century, John of Damacus recorded that *"This stone that they talk about is a head of that Aphrodite whom they used to worship and whom they called Khabar. Even to the present day, traces of the carving are visible on it to careful observers."*[16] A second lesser known stone is also set in the *Ka'ba* and worshipped.[17] It is called *Rakn-el-Yemeni*, or the Yemen pillar, and is frequently kissed by pilgrims.

## Lunar Nonsense

The greatest miracle that Muhammad performed, which the Koran records, is when *"the hour drew nigh and the moon was split in two"* (S. 54:1, The Moon). A "sign" was requested of Muhammad by the Meccans to prove that he was a prophet. Accordingly, he stood on the hill overlooking the *Ka'ba* and split the moon into two parts with his sword. These pieces then moved around the *Ka'ba*. The Hadith reaffirms this false miracle by commenting that *"...one part was behind the mountain and the other one was on this side of the mountain." Allah's* messenger then said, *"Bear witness to this."*[18] Afterwards the moon, was supposedly restored to its original form, with both of its parts being integrated together. Yet, neither the Koran nor the Hadith confirm this reassembly. The Meccans did not believe this miracle and neither should Christians. Most Muslims will affirm that this "sign" really happened, but it is a natural impossibility. The laws of physics would cause the moon to break apart if such an event actually happened. Cyril Glase saves face over this, and states that the Koran *"...is speaking allegorically of a sign of the Last Day, rather than a miracle."*[19]

## A Koran of Immorality

The worst "sin" in the Koran is its lack of moral precepts. The Ten Commandments which were given to Israel are omitted. The wisdom and commandments of Jesus are also missing. The Sermon of the Mount, the two great Commandments of Love (Mt. 22:34-40; Mk. 12:29-31; Lk. 10:25-28), the parables, and the wise sayings of the Savior are absent as well. Muhammad's view of godly morality is curiously warped to justify: lying, swearing, vengeance, killing, violence, and murder. Adultery and thievery are forbidden, but divorce and conditional forgiveness is allowed.

The god of the Koran commands bloodshed. Murder is the approved punishment for unbelievers. *Allah* declares, "*I will throw fear into the hearts of those who disbelieve.*" and then, orders his slaves to "*smite the necks and smite of them each finger*" (S. 8:12, The Spoils). Muslims are counseled to fight disbelievers "*...who are near to you, and let them find harshness in you*" (S. 9:123, Repentance). The follower of Islam who turns from his faith and embraces another religion is to be killed. "*If they turn back, then take them and kill them whenever ye find them, and choose no friend nor helper from them*" (S. 4:89, Women). These are divine orders from *Allah*, "*the Lord of Kindness*" to his creatures (S. 2:251). *Jihad* or holy war, is obligated upon every true Muslim:

*Warfare is ordained for you, though it is hateful unto you; but it may happen that you hate a thing which, is good for you, and it may happen that you he love a thing which is bad for you. Allah knoweth, you know not* (S. 2:216, The Cow).[20]

Blood feuds and revenge are warranted for the faithful:

*O you who believe, retaliation is prescribed for you in the matter of the murdered; the freeman, and the slave for the slave and the female for the female...This is an allevia-*

**99**

*tion and mercy from our Lord. ...And there is life for you in retaliation, O men of understanding that you may ward off evil* (S. 2:178-180, 5:45).

Jesus' words contradict this final revelation: *"Ye have heard that it hath been said, An eye for an eye, and a tooth for a tooth: But I say unto you, that ye resist not evil; but whosoever shall smite thee on thy right cheek, turn to him the other side also"*(Mt. 5:38-39; Lk. 6:29-30). The Christian's Gospel of peace leaves no room for holy wars, blood feuds, unforgiveness, hate, and murder.

Speaking falsehood is a grievous sin to the Christian, but the Koran absolves the Muslim who takes an oath or vow then reneges and declares that it was unintentional (S. 5:89). The Hadith reinforces this practice by decreeing that lying is a grave sin but is permissible, especially in three instances: 1). In case of battle (holy war), 2). To bring about reconciliation among hostile Muslims, 3). *"And in the narration of the words of the husband to the wife, and the narration of the words of a wife to her husband, in a twisted form in order to bring about reconciliation between them."*[21] Al-Tabari (839-923 AD), an Islamic fundamentalist who is highly respected by Muslims today, declared that *"Lies are permitted if they are for the good of a Muslim."*[22] The LORD God countermands this opinion in His Law to Moses. *"Thou shall not bear false witness against thy neighbor"*(Ex. 20:16). This rule of God is reaffirmed throughout the Gospels (Mt. 19:18; Mk. 10:19; Lk. 18:20).

Swearing is also permitted. Expressions abound in the Koran where such declarations as, *"By the fig,"* and *"By the olive,"* as well as, *"By the heaven and the morning star,"* or *"By the Koran"* are made by *Allah*. These epithets may have been written to impute a greater forcefulness of speech into the Koran, or perhaps the god of Islam needs to swear. The Bible though, exhibits none of these pointless expressions. Jesus said to:

*...Swear not at all; neither by heaven; for it is God's throne: Nor by the earth; for it is his footstool: neither by Jerusalem; for it is the city of the great King...But let your communications be, Yea, yea; Nay, nay: for whatsoever is more than these cometh of evil* (Mt. 5:33-37).

The Koran is curiously silent as to the sacredness of the name of the LORD God. A name so holy, that the Jewish people would not even pronounce it. Substitute names like *Ha Shem* (The Name) were used. The name *Allah* in Muslim lands, has never had a sacredness to its use. It is often incorporated into everyday expressions such as: *"If Allah wills."*

The Book of Proverbs advises that *"There is a way which seemeth right unto a man, but the end there of are the ways of death. Even in laughter the heart is sorrowful; and the end of that mirth is heaviness"* (Pr. 14:12-13). The Koran masquerades as life, but quickly ministers a spiritual demise to the Muslim. It is a "straight path" unto death. What little laughter and mirth that occurs in Islam, rapidly perishes under the all-consuming weight of legalism. The writer of Hebrew's confirms this truth stating that:

*...the law made nothing perfect, but the bringing in of a better hope did; by the which we draw nigh unto God ...By so much was Jesus made a surety of a better testament...wherefore he is able also to save them to the uttermost that come to God by him, seeing he ever liveth to make intercession for them* (Heb. 7:19-25).

### The Faithful Witness

Our Lord, Jesus Christ is called *"the faithful witness."* He stands at the door of Islam and knocks at the hearts of those who reject Him. Many Muslims have reported Jesus (*Isa*) witnessing to them, through the "deadness" of the Koran. As they read this corrupt book, with a heart that is seeking to know God, Jesus manifests Himself unto them. There is a wealth of Koranic verses that can create a hunger to know more of Jesus and of His truth. A solitary *ayat* in the fifth *Surah*, "The Table Spread" has drawn many Muslims to read the Bible:

> *And We caused Jesus son of Mary to follow in their footsteps, confirming that which was revealed before him, and we bestowed on him the Gospel wherein is guidance and a light, confirming that which was revealed before it in the Torah, a guidance and an admonition unto those who ward off evil* (S. 5:46, The Table).

Another witness to Muslims is found in the *Surah* called "Mary." Here, two verses declare a hidden Gospel: *"Peace on me the day I was born, and the day I die, and the day I shall be raised alive. Such was Jesus son of Mary..."* (S. 19:33-34, Mary). These verses have led many Muslims to ponder on who Jesus really is. They have also served as a springboard for Christians to witness about the Savior.

## A Mystery

The Koran for many Christians is a mystery. Many have never seen a copy, or even bothered to page through the text. To open its pages, and read the revelations makes one wonder: What is there in this little book that so infatuates Muslims? The Koran on the surface is contradictory, repetitious, confusing and yes, boring. Yet, this book full of damnable heresies, is Goliath's sword. David used the giant's sword to sever the man's head. Can we as Christians not profit from a knowledge of this work? **A familiarization with the Koran can be beneficial, but not to sever heads in arguments over it, nor to prove Jesus from its pages.** We are to be ambassadors of God's love. Jesus cautioned us to be as wise as serpents, and as harmless as doves. One should be acquainted with it in order to build bridges of evangelization, and to find ways of bringing Muslims to *"the straight path."*

A Nigerian evangelist related to me, how he used the familiar opening verses of the Koran to witness to a Muslim village in the North of his country:

*Praise be to Allah, Lord of the worlds. The Beneficent, the Merciful Owner of the day of Judgment. Thee we worship; Thee we ask for help. Show us the straight path. The path of those whom Thou hast favored; Not the path of those who earn Thine anger nor of those who go astray* (S. 1:1-7, Preface).

Brother Abu, began with these words, speaking on each verse; telling his listeners about the true nature of God and the soon coming day of judgment. Then he focused on showing his listeners that *"the straight path"* could be none other than Jesus! He declared with all boldness, the Lord's words: *"I am the way, the truth, and the life: no man cometh unto the Father, but by me"* (Jn. 14:6). Abu then, spoke even more verses from the Bible. His anointed preaching drew many to make a decision for Christ. He ministered to these new believers and then decided to stay on for their hospitality, bypassing the still soft voice of the Holy Spirit, which was prompting him to immediately leave. Abu did tell his ministry team to go. A little while later, brother Abu left, but it was too late. As he was crossing a field outside of the village, an angry mob of Muslims from the local mosque, set upon him. They proceeded to beat him with sticks, clubs, and fists. As he lay near death; bleeding and unconscious, he was rescued and dragged under the field's wire fence by the two Christian brothers who had accompanied him. They picked up his body and swiftly drove away in their car.

Brother Abu's beating sparked religious riots all over this part of Nigeria. The disturbance, made the papers and numerous people came to Christ as a result. Many believed that God had literally raised Abu up from the dead, and desired to know more of Jesus, because of this incident. Abu states that he cannot say if he was, or was not dead, only that Jesus was with him. Brother Abu recov-

**103**

ered, but can no longer return to that area of his country.[23]  God though, is still using this evangelist as an apostle to the Muslims. He needs your prayers.

Christians, you may say: *"I would not have done it that way."* But brother Abu was invited.  Some of the villagers wanted to hear the Word of God.  He was willing to hazard his life *"for the name of our Lord Jesus Christ"* (Acts 15:26).  Revival does not always come in the fashion we desire it to, nor according to our plans. Paul's presence in Ephesus caused *"no small stir about that way"*(Acts 19:23).  We have been called to *"receive power, after the Holy Ghost is come upon you..."* and to be *"witnesses unto the Lord in Jerusalem...and unto the uttermost part of the earth."*  The word *"power"* in the Greek is *dunamos*.  It literally means the dynamiting, explosive kind of power that God will bestow on us, to perform His mighty miracles and to stand strong in the Lord's strength as His witnesses.  The term in the Greek language for witnesses is *martureo*: "martyrs."  Christian, what price are you willing to pay, so as to be a witness for Christ?  Is He not worth living for and worth dying for?

---

1.   The Koran declares that *"Verily if men and jinns were assembled together with a purpose of producing this (book), they could not do it, even though they helped one another"* (S. 17:88, The Night Journey).

2.   Many of the divine Surahs in the Koran are prefaced by the Arabic letters: **Alif, Lam,** and **Min.**  These mysterious headings have puzzled Muslim scholars, since this is a book of clear revelations. Some feel they are allegorical and search for a meaning, while others state that *"Allah has not made their meaning clear."*  Therefore it is of no use in trying to know their exact meanings.  Abdul Siddiqi in his English translation of Iman Muslim's Hadith cites an opinion by Iman Ghazali to the effect that since these verses *"pertain to the Attributes of God and are allegorical in the sense that it is not possible for the finite beings to know exactly the implications of the words and phrases which have been used to express the Divine attributes."* The full comprehension of these letters is beyond the power of man

**104**

and "*thus much is left which is incomprehensible and nothing can be said with certainty about that.*" Siddiqi further advises that it is a waste of time to seek after what *Allah* has made allegorical. If one persists, then this is evidence of a "*diseased mind,*" as this research will "*create doubts in the minds of Muslims and sow the seed of dissension in the Muslim society,*" (Vol. 4, *Al'Ilm* MCX, interpreters comments #2906-2907). This remark represents one of the best educated opinions of the Muslim world, about the content of their book of clear revelations!

Mohammad Pickthall in his English translation of the Koran states that "*the prevalent view is that they indicate some mystic words.*" He himself believes that they are nothing more than the initals of the scribe that wrote Muhammad's revelations. "*They are always included in the text and recited as part of it*" (S. 2, "The Cow," pg. 34). Pickthall also voices a "second opinion" in that such Arabic letters were "*generally used instead of titles by the early Muslims*" (*The Meaning of the Glorious Koran,* comments S. 19 "Mary," pg. 221).

Victor Mordecai in his book "*Is Fanatic Islam, A Global Threat?*" speaks of these mysterious Arabic letters which translate into Hebrew as **Alef, Lamed** and **Mem**. He cites a Jewish traditon spoken by Jews who originate from Islamic lands:

> A great rabbi of Babylon, from whence the Talmud was concurrently being compiled, was kidnapped by certain bedouin Muslims who "*were illiterate and needed someone literate, a man of God to write them a holy book.*" This rabbi was placed in a deep pit and commanded to write this holy book or else be executed. These successors of Muhammad promised the rabbi that if his work was acceptable, he would be set free. This man who was an expert in the laws and gematrias of the Jewish faith "*wrote the Koran under great duress, obviously and wanting to remain loyal to God, placed all kind of loopholes that would make any sophisticated reader of the Koran find inconsistencies and satanic verses*" Part of the code which he placed in the Koran, were these opening alphabetical letters which, are now found at the beginning of some of the *Surahs*.

These letters which no Muslim understands, are in reality abbreviations in Hebrew for ***Ani Lo Ma'amin*** which is translated "I don't believe." The rabbi was trying to weave into the Koran a hidden message that his captors would overlook, but those who would be educated in the Talmud would quickly observe. Having completed this task, the rabbi was then stoned to death, despite the promises of his kidnappers to give him freedom for writing the Koran (pgs. 181-182).

3.    John of Damacus, *The Fountain of Wisdom, Part II* "The Camel of God" *The Fathers of the Church*, Vol. 37, pg. 158.
4.    John Burton, *The Collection of the Qur'an,* pg. 117.
5.    *Sahih Al-Bukhari,* Vol. 6 #509.
6.    J. Sweetman, *Islam and Christian Theology* Vol. 2, pgs. 238-239.
7.    *Sahih Muslim* Vol. 1 *Al-Salat* CCXLV, #1438.
8.    *The Koran,* translated by N. J. Dawood.
9.    These are the same "*Satanic Verses*" that author Saliman Rushdie wrote about. A death *fatwah* or religious order was then issued against his life, for writing a satirical novel about Muhammad.

10.  George Sale's translation of the Koran.
11.  Muslims justify this aberration of Biblical Scripture with the excuse, that the authority of the Koran reveals that the grandfather of Jesus was really named Imram, which was also the name of the father of Moses. As for Miriam (Mary) being the brother of Aaron, those that uphold the Koran, state that this *ayat* proves the Virgin Mary had a brother named Aaron, or else Aaron was her ancestor, therefore she was of the tribe of Levi!

12.  An estimated 2.3 million Muslims from 100 countries participated in the 2002 *hajj.* Fifty years before this date, the *hajj* drew only an estimated 10,000 people annually. The rapid increase of pilgrims to Mecca has forced the Saudi Arabian government to limit participants from each given country to 1000 per 1 million population. Some Muslim's complain that they must wait years for permits to fulfill their religious obligation.

13.  Samuel Zwemer cites assertions by the ancient Persians (the Guebars) that the Black Stone was "*an emblem of Saturn and was left in the Ka'ba by Muhabad.*" More likely, the origin of this stone (possibly a meteorite) may stem from altar of Dushrat, the Sun god of Petra (Seir), the ancient rock city located in Jordan. His symbol/shrine was a black stone, which the inhabitants smeared with

blood taken from their sacrifices. Later this stone may have been taken by Bedouin tribesmen who offered it for trade to the Meccans. These city dwellers placed it in the side of the *Ka'ba*. Muslims prefer to believe that this stone came down from heaven, snow-white in color but was blackened by the touch of sin. One tradition speaks that an impure woman touched it and caused it to immediately darken! *"Al-Haramain," The Moslem World,* Jan. 1947, pg. 9.

14. Ibid, pg. 11. Some 180 people lost their lives in this ritual in 1998, when thousands of surging pilgrims, that were seeking to *"stone the devil"* stampeded on the bridge to this site. A similar occurance led to the deaths of 270 worshipers in 1994.

15. Saudi officials estimated that more than one million sheep, goats, cows, and camels were sacrificed by pilgrims to fulfill the 1998 *hajj* obligation. *Arkansas Democrat-Gazette* 4/7/98, pg. 7A.

16. John of Damacus, *The Fountain of Wisdom*, Part II *"Heresies," The Fathers of the Church,* Vol. 37, pg. 157.

17. Muslims justify this behavior as acts of reverence, not worship. The Black Stone *"is to be revered since it is the only remnant of Abraham's original building; and because the lips of Muhammad touched it on his farewell pilgrimage."* Comments by Abdul H. Siddiqi, English translator of *Sahih Muslim* (Vol. 2 *Al-Hajj* CDLXXXIV, pg. 642). This interpretation is also subject to a wide latitude, as other pilgrims kiss the stone so as *"to embrace the prophet."*

This "reverence" for a piece of rock borders on the fanatical. Some years ago, a Iranian pilgrim attempted to kiss the Black Stone. The man, in the act of doing so, instead found himself vomiting on it. His throat had suddenly tickled him, causing this unfortunate incident to happen. The royal guardian of the shrine, promptly apprehended this desecrater and had the pilgrim taken to the chopping block. There he was summarily beheaded for his sin! This outrage led to a diplomatic disagreement between Iran and Saudi Arabia. Reparations and apologies were demanded, but Saudi Arabia remained firm. The man had by his obscene actions, defiled the holiness of the *Ka'ba,* thus the matter was closed (*The Moslem World,* Vol. XXXIV #1, Jan. 1944, pg. 184, citing *New York Press* reports).

18. *Sahih Muslim*, Vol. 4 *Sifat Al-Qiyama Wa'l-Jamma Wa'n-Nar* MCLXI, #6724-6730.

19. Author of: *The Concise Encyclopedia of Islam,* pg. 274.

20. *"Narrated A'isha* (Muhammad favorite wife), *the mother of the faithful believers: The Prophet was asked by his wives about the Jihad and he replied the best Jihad for you is the performance of the Hajj"* (*Sahih Al-Bukhari,* Vol. 4 Jihad, #128). A'isha later disobeyed these instructions and led an army into battle against Ali, her son- in-law. Muslim women have participated in Jihad in the past and do so today, despite the esteemed words of the prophet.

21. *Sahih Muslim,* Vol. 4 *Al-Birr Wa's Silat-I-Adab* MLXXVII. See commentator's note #2865.

22. "Will Europe and America Become Islamic?" *Israel Today,* Mar. 2002, pg. 18.

23. Personal testimony given by Abu B. to author, Jerusalem, Israel Sept 1996.

# NINE

## "The Scriptures Speak of Me..."

*T*he Koran with all of its divine revelatory bluster proclaims that Muhammad's advent was foretold in both the Penateuch and the Gospel: *"Those who follow the messenger, the prophet who can neither read nor write, whom they will find described in the Torah and the Gospel"* (S. 7:157, The Heights). On the authority of this *ayat*, Muslims have diligently scrutinized both the Old and the New Testaments to verify *Allah's* prediction. The Koran seems to suggest that these particular passages can be found without difficulty. Every one of these attempts though, by Islamic theologians has been futile. When Muslims have applied their "best" exegesis to the Bible, they have discovered to their dismay, that it is Jesus who is the subject of many prophecies, and not the messenger of *Allah*. Islam has been unable to prove Muhammad's coming and thus establish the truth of the Koran.

This fruitless search has caused this "religion" to level multiple unjust accusations against the Jewish and Christian faiths, for allegedly corrupting their own scriptures. Muslims feel that they have a divine right to do this, as the Koran repeatedly affirms these spurious claims:

> *O people of the Scripture: Why do you confound the truth with falsehoods and knowing conceal the truth?* (S. 3:71, Imran).

**109**

*O people of the Scripture!  Do not exaggerate in your religion* (S. 4:171, Women).

*O people of the Scripture!  Stress not in your religion other than the truth and follow not the vain desires of folk who erred of old and led many astray and erred from a plain road* (S. 5:77, The Table).

Muslims in their vain quest to find Muhammad in the scriptures have "adopted" certain passages in the Testaments as "proof" of his coming.  Christians who witness to Muslims may be confronted with these "prophetical" scriptures.  Muslim evangelists also will not hestitate to show them to new Christians in attempts to sway or convert them to Islam.  Most of these scriptures are either taken out of context or painfully twisted to "fit" into an acceptable Islamic exegesis.  An Arab proverb advises one to: *"Shut the window from which the bad smell comes."*  Perhaps Peter says it better:

*But sanctify the Lord God in your hearts:  and be ready always to give an answer to every man that asketh you a reason of the hope that is in you with meekness and fear: Having a good conscience; that, whereas they speak evil of you, as of evildoers, they may be ashamed that falsely accuse your good conversation in Christ*  (I Pet. 3:15-16).

A sampling of these favorite scriptures which are used by Muslims, to authenticate Muhammad's forthcoming is listed so you may *"Shut the window"* to the devil's manipulations and to answer *"every man that asketh you..."*

### Purported Old Testament prophecies announcing Muhammad's advent

1.  A future prophet (Deut. 18:15,18)

*I will raise them up a Prophet from among their brethren,*
*like unto thee, and will put my words in his mouth; and*
*he shall speak unto them all that I shall command him.*

This passage is one that is classically selected by Muslims to support their claims as to Muhammad being found in the Torah. They justify this travesty with three arguments.

A. The Word of God

The Koran is supposedly the Word of God. Therefore, Muslims believe that these Words in the Koran were placed in Muhammad's mouth by God, in fullfillment of this prophecy.

The Koran is not the Word of God, even if *Allah,* Muhammad and *"all the kings men"* (Islam) declare that it is so. It is a poor counterfeit of the real Word of God. Even if Muhammad was a prophet, the scripture does not automatically prove that he was one. All true prophets speak the Word of God (Jer. 1:9; Jn.12:49-50; Jn. 17:8). The real identity of a forthcoming prophet cannot be established from just possessing an ability to proclaim the Word of God.

B. The "prophet" would come from *"among the brethren."*

The Israelites in this prophecy have brethren: Ishmaelites. Muslims assume that since Jacob (Israel) and Ishmael both descend from Abraham, this lineage includes all their descendants. Hence the sons of the twelve tribes of Israel are related to twelve sons of Ishmael. They are "brethren." Muhammad as an Ishmaelite supposedly can rightfully claim the prophethood which is spoken of here. Therefore, Muslims reason that this prophecy must refer to Muhammad.

**111**

The mystery of this passage is easily resolved, if one reads it in its context. The chapter begins by referring to the tribes of Levi (Deut. 18:1-2). The word "brethren" then, can only pertain to the tribes of Israel. Ishmael is not in the picture. Any other interpretation of this scripture is error.

Muhammad is in fact disqualified from being the predicted prophet of this passage. He was an Ishmaelite. Who then is this future prophet? JESUS! He is the only one who is descended from the tribe of Judah (Mt. 1:2; Heb. 7:14). It is the Lord who is uniquely qualified to be the Prophet raised up from among the brethren of the Levites.

C. A Prophet equal to Moses

Muslims have made many comparisons between Moses and Muhammad, identifying similarities so as to prove his prophetic credentials.[1] Some of these ridiculous efforts, which have been advanced to verify this passage include:

1). Moses and Muhammad were both married.
2). Moses and the "prophet of *Allah*" were both great warriors.
3). Moses and the "messenger" were Lawgivers.
4). Moses and Muhammad were liberators of their people.

Jesus though is the real fulfillment of this prophecy.[2]

1). Moses and Jesus were Israelites; Muhammad was an Ishmaelite.
2). Moses and Jesus were both mediators between God and man. Muhammad never saw God.

3). Moses introduced the Old Covenant (the Mosaic Law). Jesus brought forth the New Convenant (Salvation through the Cross).

4). Jesus and Moses both performed extensive signs and miracles. Muhammad never demonstrated any miraculous works (*Surahs* 6:57, 28, 48).[3]

2. The Chariots of Camels (Isa. 21:7).

*"And he saw a chariot with a couple of horsemen, a chariot of asses, and a chariot of camels..."*

This isolated passage represents another ludicrous attempt by Muslims to herald their prophet's coming. Islamic reasoning justified this "prophetic illumination" by stating that Jesus is the one picture here riding the ass (Mt. 21:1-11; Mk. 11:1-11; Lk. 19:28-40; Jn. 12:14-15). The "logical" assumption then in Muslim thinking is to place Muhammad next in prophetical order riding into history on a chariot of camels. Chariot in this case is interpreted as being "a troop." Muslims, of course, ignore the first point about the chariot with a couple of horsemen. Who is this? Apparently that little matter is overlooked in the rush to document Muhammad's advent. The complete passage correctly interpreted refers to the coming fall of Babylon (519-513 B.C.)

3. The Witness of the Servant (Isa. 43:10).

*Ye are my witnesses, saith the LORD, and my servant whom I have chosen: that ye may know and believe me, and understand that I am he: before me there was no God formed, neither shall be after me.*

Muslims have adapted this text to serve their purposes. They identify the servant in this text as

**113**

Muhammad, since he is the one who has made the declaration: *"There is no god but Allah and Muhammad is his servant."* The prophecy though pertains to Israel. The servant is Jesus Christ, not Muhammad.

4. The Man with the Sword (Ps. 45:3-5)

*Gird thy sword upon thy thigh, O most mighty, with thy glory and thy majesty...*

Another preposterous claim of Muhammad's forthcoming which Muslims delight inshowing is this Psalm. Muhammad was a warrior, just as this portion of the Psalm declares. Thus, in their eyes, it was he that David prophesied of, who girded his sword upon his thigh before riding out to battle. The truth is that, this Royal Wedding Psalm refers to the LORD girding His sword upon His thigh. Muslims neglect also to consider the following verse in this Psalm. Verse six is a prophetic reference to Jesus Christ's future reign: *"Thy throne O God is forever and ever: the scepter of thy kingdom is a right scepter."*

## The Fraudulent Testimony of Surah Sixty-One (Battle Ranks)

*And when Jesus son of Mary said: O children of Israel! Lo! I am the messenger of Allah unto you, confirming that which was revealed before me in the Torah, and bringing good tidings of a messenger who will come after me, and whose name is Ahmed* (The Praised One), (S. 61:6).

Muslims on the basis of this *ayat* attempt to certify that Jesus prophesied the coming of Muhammad. One should remember that this verse has all the authority of *Allah* behind it. Muslims have thoroughly searched the Gospels, in an effort to locate Jesus' words announcing Muhammad's advent. The Scriptures were curiously silent to their efforts. Not willing to accept defeat though, Islamic apologists became more creative. They then ascertained that perhaps the fulfillment of *Surah's* 61's prophecy and its relation to scripture lay in the very name of Muhammad. The word for praise in Arabic is *Ahmed*. The name Muhammad is drawn from a variant of this Arabic root, "**h-m-d**" and means "the Praised One." Reviewing the Gospels again, Islamic search parties "found" passages in John where Jesus speaks of sending his disciples *"the Comforter"* (Jn. 14:16; 15:26; 16:17). These particular scriptures were then blatantly claimed by Islam as being the prophetical words which declared Muhammad's forthcoming.

### Alleged New Testament Scriptures heralding Muhammad's Prophetical Reign

Muhammad is known to Islam as *"the promised one."* He is purportedly the one man chosen by God to establish Islam and become the "seal" of the prophets. Islamic scholars in an effort to justify and advance the cause of Islam have knowingly corrupted the Gospel scriptures by deliberately "altering" the textual content. The Greek word for "Comforter" always appears throughout the Gospels as *"Parakletos."* It can be interpreted as "Comforter, Helper and/or Advocate." Islamic apologists declare that the word *periklytos* is what really appeared in the original Greek text. *Periklytos* when translated into the Arabic, means *ahmed* or *"worthy of praise."* This artful word substitution would then make the scripture read: *"And I will pray the Father, and he shall give you another who is worthy of praise"* (Muhammad). This passage is also translated as saying *"the one who is worthy of praise which is Muhammad whom the Father will send in my name, he shall teach you all things."* The fatal flaw to all these Islamic "proofs" lies in the fact that not one Biblical manuscript exists, where the word *Perilkytos* is found in Jn 14:16. Every variant version records the word *parakletos.*

**115**

Muslims will ignore this fact though, and adamantly refuse to accept any counterdiction to their reasonings. The two words also sound nearly alike when pronounced in the Greek language. This closeness in pronunciation can easily deceive the uneducated, as well as those whose eyes are already blinded to the light of Christ.

## Counter Arguments against *Periklytos*

Christian scholars have proved the foolishness of Islamic claims that Muhammad is the Comforter, by focusing on the context of Jesus' words as they appear in scripture. Some of their discoveries as to why Muhammad cannot possibly be the fulfillment of Jesus' Koranic prophecy are:

1. The Comforter is a Spirit (Jn. 14:16-17, 26)

   Jesus in his words to his disciples promised to send them the *"Spirit of truth."* Muhammad was a human being, composed of flesh and blood. The Holy Spirit is not a human being.

2. Jesus announced that the Holy Spirit would be with His disciples forever (Jn. 14:16)

   Muhammad was born, lived out his life and died on the 8th of June 632 A.D. He is buried in Medina. The Holy Spirit came upon the Apostles in the upper room and has never departed from the Church (Acts 2:1-4). Furthermore, Jesus declared that the Comforter would dwell with us (Jn. 14;17). Muhammad could not be and cannot be in anybody today. This prophet is not omnipotent, nor is he God.

3. The world cannot receive the Holy Spirit (Jn. 14:17).

The world did see Muhammad for he was born of flesh. The sinful men of this earth though, are ignorant of the presence of the Holy Spirit.

4. The promise (Jn. 20:22; Acts 1:5)

Jesus promised his disciples that he would send them a Comforter in *"a little while"* (Jn. 14:19). This word, *"a little while"* clearly means a quick fulfillment: *"a few-days."* Muhammad would not be born for another five hundred plus years. Jesus breathed on the disciples after his resurrection and said, *"Receive ye the Holy Ghost"*(Jn. 20:22). What would Muslims say to this passage?

5. The Disciples were required to tarry in Jerusalem (Lk 24:49, Acts 1:4, 8).

The Holy Spirit was promised by Jesus to come upon his followers in the city of Jerusalem. They were to *"receive power"* and be the Lord's witnesses *"in Jerusalem, and in all Judea, and in Sameria, and to the ends of the earth"* (Acts 1:8). This word has been and is being fulfilled by all Christians. Muhammad was born in Mecca. This "prophet" also never visited Jerusalem, nor ever became a witness to this city.

6. The work of the Holy Spirit

The Holy Spirit was sent by Jesus to give his disciples "power" to spread the Gospel Acts 1:8), to be our *Comforter, Counselor* (Jn. 14:16), and *Teacher* (Jn. 14:26). His presence on the earth is also to convict men of sin. This promised Comforter was not given so as to gain victories with carnal weapons nor lead great armies into battle. Muhammad was a warrior, who sought to

**117**

glorify himself. The Holy Spirit's purpose is to *"glorify me"* (Jesus Christ, Jn. 16:14), and reveal himself to the Christian (vs 15).

The word *Parakletos* can be interpreted as "the Comforter," and as "the one who comes along our side." It is also correct to interpret this word as meaning "advocate." The Koran denies the title of Advocate to anyone else but *Allah* (*Surahs* 2:48; 6:51;32:4; 39:44; 70; 94). Accordingly then, there is no way that Muhammad could be identified as being "the Comforter."

### "Search the Scriptures"

The scriptures truly speak of one person who is foretold: Jesus Christ. The Old Testament contains over 300 references to the Messiah, that were fulfilled in the advent of Jesus Christ. Jesus spoke to all men to, *"Search the Scriptures; for in them ye think ye have eternal life: and they are they which testify of me"* (Jn. 5:39). He challenged the Sadducees, that they erred *"not knowing the Scriptures, nor the power of God"* (Mt. 22:29). Only he knew that his actions were to be done in fulfillment of prophecy: *"Behold, we go up to Jerusalem, and all things that are written by the prophets concerning the Son of man shall be accomplished"* (Lk. 18:31-34; 24:44). It was Christ alone that could boldly declare that Moses *"wrote of me"* (Jn. 5:46). Abraham saw the day of Christ's coming and rejoiced (Jn. 8:56). The prophet spoken of in Deuteronomy 18:18 was recognized by the multitudes of Israel (Mt. 21:11). Jesus' words call out to all men, especially the children of Ishmael: *"Blessed is he, whosoever shall not be offended in me"* (Mt. 11:6).

---

1. Additional information as to the misrepresentation of Muhammad's credentials can be found in *The Islam Debate* by Josh

**118**

McDowell & John Gilchrist, or by reading, *Is Muhammad Foretold in the Bible?* by John Gilchrist.

2.   Muslims respond positively to the teaching of Old Testament types and shadows. A good comparison of Moses & Jesus Christ's similiaries and differences can be found in A.W. Pink's *Gleanings in Exodus*, "Moses a type of Christ" (75 comparisons) pgs 379-384.

3.   Muhammad confessed that the Koran was his greatest and only miracle. The Hadith though has  assembled an interesting collection of legendary feats and ridiculous wonders that have been attributed to Muhammad including:

1. The "holy Koran," a living miracle bestowed by *Allah.*
2. The "splitting of the moon" (*Sahih Al-Bukhari* Vol. 4 #831).
3. The "crying" of the date palm in the prophet's mosque
   (Ibid, Vol. 4 #783).
4. The flowing of water from the fingers of *Allah's* apostle
   (Ibid, Vol. 4 #779).
5. The "praises to *Allah*" made by the meals which Muhammad
   ate (Ibid, Vol. 4 #779).
6. The stones crying out greetings to Muhammad, when ever he
   passed them by in Mecca (ibid, Vol. 4 #779).
7. The grave rejecting the body of a Christian who had converted
   to Islam, and then re-embraced Christianity.  He could not be
   buried.  Muhammad was given credit for this "wonder"
   (Ibid, Vol. 4 #814).
8. The automatic bowing of the trees to "shade" the "prophet" as
   he answered the "call to nature" (Ibid, Vol. 4 #814).
9. Water rising in a well after it had dried up (Ibid, Vol. 4 #777).
10. A pile of harvested dates increasing after the "prophet" had
    invoked *Allah* for blessings. (ibid, Vol. 4 #780).
11. The wolf that spoke and invited men to come to Islam
    (*Fatuh-ul-Bari*, Vol. 8, pg. 23).

A study of Christ's miracles would richly benefit the Christian in witnessing to Muslims.

4.   References to Biblical Scriptures reaffirming Christ's advent can be found in: *Evidence that Demands a Verdict* by Josh McDowell, as well as *Christ in all the Scriptures* by A.M. Hodgkin

# TEN

# The Traditions of Islam

*I*slam is a faith that relies not only on the revealed word of the Koran, but on the *sunna* of the prophet. These traditions are the recollections of the words and actions of Muhammad. These narratives called hadith's are accorded by Islam, an almost equal weight of authority next to the Koran itself. They are *"the perfect expressions of the highest wisdom ever conceivable."*[1] In many instances, the hadith's define and interpret the mysterious passages of the prophet's book, contributing the details needed to practice the faith. Rules of observance are found within this anthology, as well as descriptions of Muhammad's daily activities. Battles which were fought in the early days of Islam are recounted, along with the prophet's miracles. Some of these sayings promote the merit of love and the avoidance of certain modes of behavior such as jealousy, suspicion and hatred, paralleling Christian-Judaic ethics. Other hadith's reflect the paganistic culture of the times, transmitting superstitions and a measure of the primitive beliefs of the era. The hadith's are to be followed exactly *"for that which differs from the Hadith to the extent of a hair shall be given up."*[2] The faithful Muslim then, needs a copy of the Hadith as well as a Koran in order to be assured of receiving correct divine guidance, and of living a life that is approved by *Allah.*

There are six different collections of Hadith that are judged genuine and reliable.[3] The orthodox Muslim, in order to pursue "a straight path" must be knowledgeable and obedient to all of these traditions. The Muslim scholar, Bukhari, some two hundred years

after Muhammad's death, sifted through an estimated 600,000 purported hadiths and selected 4,000 that he considered authentic.
Imam Muslim, a disciple of Bukhari, also collected another 4,000
hadiths which differed in some cases from Bukhari's assembly.
The two works by Bukhari and Muslim are the earliest assem-
blages and held in high esteem by Muslims. The hadith's that they
compiled are recognized as absolutely true. The selections in this
chapter are taken from their collections.

A few of these amazing unique revelations which came from
Muhammad's lips and are foundational beliefs of Islam that all
Muslims must accept include:

1. **Eating Onions, Garlic, and Leeks will harm
   angels**
   Jabir b. 'Abdullah reported the Apostle of *Allah* saying: *"He who eats onion and garlic and leek, should not
   approach our mosque for the angels are harmed by the
   same things as the children of Adam"* (*Sahih Muslim,*
   Vol. I, *Al-Salat* CCXI, #1147).

2. **Drinking the milk and urine of the Camel to
   regain your health**
   Anas b. Malik reported that some people belonging to
   the tribe of 'Uraina came to *Allah's* Messenger at Medina,
   but they found its climate uncongenial. So *Allah's*
   Messenger said to them; *"If you so like, you may go to
   the camels of Sadaqa and drink their milk and urine.
   They did so and were all right"* (Vol. 3, *Al-Qasama*
   DCLXIX, #4132).

3. **Mind Your Manners!**
   Anas reported that when the Prophet ate food, he
   licked his three fingers, as well as the dish, and said *"You
   do not know in what portion the blessing lies"* (*Sahih
   Muslim* Vol 3, *Al-Ashriba* DCCCXLVI, #5037).

Abbas narrated that the Prophet said, *"When you eat do not wipe your hands until you lick your fingers or have them licked by someone else"* (*Sahih Al-Bukhari,* Vol. 7 #366).

### 4. *"To Your Health"*
Narrated Abu Huraira, *Allah's* Apostle said, *"If a fly falls into the drink of any one of you, let that person dip all of it into the liquid and then throw it away. Know that there is a disease in one wing and in the other there is healing for that disease"* (*Sahih Al-Bukhari* Vol. 4, #530, Vol. 7 #673).[4]

### 5. *"Awake thou that sleepest"*
Masud narrated that a mention was made of a man who slept the whole night until morning. Muhammad remarked: *"That is a man in whose ears the devil urinated"* (*Sahih Muslim*, Vol. 1, *Al-Salat* CCLXX, #1700).

### 6. Heaven is only open on Monday and Thursday
Abu Huraira reported *Allah's* Messenger as saying: *"The gates of Paradise are not opened but on two days, Monday and Thursday and then every servant of Allah is granted pardon..."* (Vol. 4, *Al-Birr Wa's Salat-I-Wa'l-Adab* MLVII, #6223).

### 7. The Gates of Hell are locked
Abu Huraira reported *Allah's* Messenger as saying: *"When there comes the month of Ramadan, the gates of mercy are opened, and the gates of Hell are locked and the devils are chained"* (Vol. 2, *Al-Sawm* CDVI, #2361).

### 8. See the Real Thing
Abu Huraira reported *Allah's* Messenger as saying; *"He who saw me in a dream in fact saw me, for it is not*

*possible for the satan to appear in my form"* (Vol. 4, *Al-Ruya* CMXLVIII, #5635).

### 9. Spit after a bad dream
Jabir reported Allah's Messenger as saying: *"If anyone sees a dream which he does not like, he should spit on his left side"* (Vol. 4, *Al-Ruya* CMXLVII, #5620).

### 10. Yawning is from the Devil
Abu Huraira reported *Allah's* Messenger as saying: *"The yawning is from the devil. So when one of you yawns he should try to restrain it as far as it lies in his power"* (Vol. 4 *Al-Zuhd Wa Al-Raqa'lq* MCCXXVI, #7129).

### 11. Paint a Portrait and Go to Hell
Abdullah b. Mas'ud reported that the Messenger of *Allah* had said that: *"The most grievously tormented people on the Day of Resurrection would be the painters of pictures."*

Ibn Abbas heard *Allah's* Messenger say: *"All painters who make pictures would be in the fire of Hell"* (Vol. 3, *Al-Libas Wa'l-Zinah* DCCCLXXXII, #5272).[5]

### 12. Christian and Jews will be thrown into hell
Abu Burda reported Allah's Messenger as saying: *"There would come people among the Muslims on the Day of Resurrection with sins as heavy as mountains, and Allah would forgive them and He would place in their stead the Jews and Christians in Hell-Fire."* (Vol. 4, *Al-Tauba* MCXLIX, #6668).

### 13. Muhammad's father is in Hell
Anas reported: Verily, a person said: *"Messenger of Allah, where is my father?"* He said: *"(He) is in the Fire."*

123

When he turned away, he (the Holy Prophet) called him and said: *"Verily my father and, your father are in the Fire"* (Vol. 1, *Al-Imam* LXXXVI, #398).

## 14. The dead person is punished because of the weeping of his family

'Umar reported *Allah's* Apostle as saying: *"The dead is punished in the grave because of wailing on it"* (Vol. 2, *Al-Salat* CCCXXX).

## 15. Thank God for Friday

Abu Huraira reported the Apostle of *Allah* as saying: *"The best day on which the sun has risen is Friday; on it Adam was created, on it he was made to enter paradise, on it he was expelled from it. And the last hour will take place on no day other than Friday"* (Vol. 2, *Al-Salat* CCCII, #1857).

## 16. The Angels curse Women

Abu Huraira reported *Allah's* Messenger as saying: *"When a man invites his wife to his bed and she does not come, and he spends the night being angry with her, the angels curse her until morning"* (Vol. 2, *Al Nikah* DLVI-II, #3368).

## 17. Beware of Dogs and Pictures

Abu Talba reported *Allah's* Apostle having said: *"Angels do not enter a house in which there is a dog or a picture"* (Vol. 3, *Al-Libas Wa'l-Zinah* DCCCXLII, #5022).

## 18. Never Drink Water while Standing

Abu Huraira reported *Allah's* Messenger as saying: *"None of you should drink while standing; if anyone forgets, he must vomit"* (Vol. 3, *Al-Ashriba* DCCCXLII, #5022).

### 19. Drink *ZamZam* Water on your Feet

Ibn' Abbas reported: *"I served water from ZamZam to Allah's Messenger, and he drank while standing"* (Vol. 3, *Al-Ashriba* DCCCXLIII, #5023).[6]

### 20. The Motivation for Building Mosques

Hadrat Uthman said; "I heard *Allah's* Messenger as saying: *'He who builds a mosque for Allah, Allah would build for him a house in Paradise like it' "* (Vol. 4, *Al-Zuhd Wa Al* Raqa'Iq MCCXIX, #7109).[7]

### 21. Heaven is only for Muslims

It is narrated on the authority of 'Umar b. Khattab...that the Messenger of *Allah* said to him, *"Go announce to the people that none but believers shall enter Paradise"* (Vol. 1, *Al-Imam* XLIX, #209).[8]

### 22. Where is your Koran?

Ibn Umar said that the Messenger of *Allah* said: *"Do not take the Koran on a journey with you, for I am afraid lest it should fall into the hands of the enemy. The enemy may seize it and may quarrel with you over it"* (Vol. 3, *Al-Imara* DCCLXXVII, #4609).

### 23. Turn Your Body Opposite the Qibla when performing Nature's Call

Abu Ayyub reported that the Apostle of *Allah* said, *"Whenever you go to the desert neither turn your face nor turn your back towards the Qibla* (the direction of Mecca) *but face towards the east or the west."* Ayyub said: *"When we came to Syria we found that the latrines already built there were facing towards the Qibla. We turned our faces away from them and begged forgiveness of the Lord. He said, Yes"* (Vol. 1, *Al-Taharah* CIV, #507).[9]

### 24. The Call for Prayer creates a Howling Wind

Abu Huraira reported that the Messenger of *Allah* said: *"When Satan hears the call for prayer, he turns back and breaks the wind, so as to not hear the call being made"* (Vol. 1, *Al-Salat* CLVI, #756).

### 25. Clean Your Nose!

Abu Huraira reported: the Apostle of *Allah* said *"When any one of you awakes up from sleep and performs ablutions* (washings), *he must clean his nose three times, for the devil spends the night in the interior of the nose"* (Vol. 1, *Al-Taharah* XCVII, #462).[10]

### 26. Complete the Fast on Behalf of the Dead

A'isha reported *Allah's* Messenger as saying: *"If anyone dies in a state that he had to complete some fasts* (Ramadan), *his heir must fast on his behalf"* (Vol. 2, *Al-Sawm* CDXXX, #2553).

### 27. No Jews or Christians Permitted!

Umar b. Al Khattab heard the Messenger of *Allah* say: *"I will expel the Jews and Christians from the Arabian Peninsula and will not leave any but Muslims"* (Vol. 3, *Al-Jihad* DCCXXIII, #4366).[11]

### 28. The Rocks Cry Out!

Narrated Abu Huraira: *Allah's* apostle said *"The Last Hour will not be established until you fight with the Jews, and some of them will hide behind stones. The stones will betray them saying 'O Muslim! There is a Jew hiding behind me, so kill him'"* (*Sahih Al-Bukhari*, Vol. 4, *Al-Jihad*, LII, #177).

### 29. The Vilest Name

Abu Huraira reported that the Messenger of *Allah* as saying: *"the vilest name in Allah's sight is Malik al-*

*Amlak* (the King of Kings), *for there is no king but Allah"* (*Sahih Muslim* Vol. 3, *Al-Adab* DCCCXCIV, #5339).

### 30. The Return of Jesus

Abu Huraira reported that the Messenger of *Allah* said: *"By Him in whose hand is my life, the son of Mary will soon descend among you as a just judge. He will break crosses, kill swine, abolish the tribute tax, and preach Islam"* (Vol. 1, *Al-Imam*, LXXII, #1287).[12]

---

1. Quote by Abdul H. Siddiqi, English translator of the *Sahih Muslim* Hadith, pg. ii.
2. *Mishkat-al-Masabih*, Bk. 1, pgs. 2-3.
3. The six sound traditions are those of Ismail al-Bukhari (d. 870), Muslim ibn al-Hajjaj (d. 875), Abu David (d. 888), al-Timidhi (d. 892), Ibn Maja (d. 896) and al-Nissi (d. 915).

4. The English translator of *Sahih Bukhari*, Dr. Muhammad M. Khan in trying to justify this piece of the prophet's wisdom states that medical studies by microbiologists (no references given ) have discovered certain yeast cells which live *"inside the belly of the fly."* These organisms reportedly burst open when the insect *"is dipped in a liquid"* and protrude *"through the respiratory tubules of the fly."* The content of these cells then *"is an antidote for the pathogens* (micro-organisms that cause disease) *which the fly carries"* (Vol. 7, pg. 453).

This bit of Islamic nonsense is contradicted in a new study done by Dr. Peter Grubel of St. Elizabeth's Medical Center in Boston. This scientist has proved that houseflies can pick up Heliobacter pylori bacteria from human waste and deposit it on food. This bacteria is the cause of most ulcers. Countries which have the poorest sanitation also have the highest rates of H. pylori infection. He states *"Flies are perfect disease vectors: their intestinal tracts hold about 40 million bacteria, which they regurgitate regularly; 6 million more are mired in the sticky secretions that help flies walk on ceilings"* (*Newsweek*, July 28, 1997, pg. 77).

5.    This rule includes all artists who would make pictures with pencils, color paints, and/or modern day photography.  The painting of trees, flowers, landscapes, mountains and rivers is also not desirable, nor is the carving of statues.

6.    *ZamZam* water should be taken as quickly as possible.  The hadith's recommend that a Muslim pour this tonic into the body, so as to rapidly let its healing properties be distributed throughout one's system.  There is an (alleged) great blessing in it.  Proper etiquette is to follow the prophet's example.

7.    Iraq's President Saddam Hussein has approved the design for the world's largest mosque which will be built in Bagdad.  Capable of holding 30,000 worshipers, the structure will be called the Saddam Grand Mosque.  The prayer grounds and minarets will have room for another 75,000 people.  A huge artificial lake shaped like a map of the Arab world will highlight the design.  The largest existing mosque is the King Hassan Mosque in Morocco, with a capacity for 18,000 people.  The holiest Muslim shrine, the *Ka'ba* in Mecca, Saudi Arabia can hold up to one million people in open and enclosed areas. (*Ark. Democrat-Gazette*, Dec. 10, 1997, pg. 6A).

8.    Believers are those who believe in *Allah*, stand for Islam and then struggle for its cause.

9.    In seeking to comply with this tradition; Islamic homes, hotels, businesses, sports facilities, etc., have been designed and built with the structures correctly aligned away from the *Ka'ba*. Correspondingly, Muslims may defer from purchasing real estate which have facilities that are not properly orientated away from Mecca.

Modern day problems for Muslims in following this law, include determining whether a straight line approach facing Mecca is better or one that takes into account the curvature of the earth.  This question has divided Muslims *"in very sinister ways"* according to Mahmoud Ayoub, Professor of Islamic Studies at Temple University (*Intercede*, Feb. 1995, pg. 3).

A Saudi Prince, Sultan ibn Salman al-Saud, also became the first Muslim astronaut.  He participated in the eighteenth mission of the

Shuttle Discovery in 1985. The Prince though, did not comment on how he observed Islam's religious laws while in outer space.

10. Dr. Muhammad M. Khan, again defends Muhammad's revelations with the following explanation:

> "We should believe that Satan actually stays in the upper part of one's nose, though we cannot perceive how, for this is related to the unseen world of which we know nothing except what Allah tells us through His Apostle" (Sahih al-Bukhari, Vol. 4, #516, translator's note, pg. 328).

11. The most orthodox form of Islam exists today in Arabia. No churches or synagogues are permitted in the Kingdom. Saudi Arabia has decreed that there will be no public expression of Christianity. The Minister of Information for this country Ali bin Hassan told a French newspaper (Le Figaro) in 1994, that: "The Saudi Arabian government regrets that it cannot tolerate churches within her borders, but this is a commandment from Allah" (Intercede, Sept 1994, pg. 3).

Amnesty International, a human rights group based in London, reports that the Saudi Arabian metowah (religious police), "are given free rein to raid private homes and arrest those caught praying" or participating in secret worship services and Bible studies. Rewards are offered up to $7,500 for information leading to the discovery of such illegal fellowships.

Fourteen foreign workers were detained by Saudi Arabia in the Summer of 2001 for participation in Christian gatherings. Among this group were three Ethiopian Christians who found themselves detained for six months without charges. While in this status, they were severely beaten and tortured by Saudi prison officials. The three Christians stated that "being suspended with chains, each of us were flogged 80 times with a flexible metal cable and also severely kicked and beaten with anything that came into their hands." Participants of such forbidden activities can be punished with flogging (up to 150 lashes), fines, prison sentences and deportations. The Christians involved in these activities were released after Governor Prince Abdul Majid, decided to deport them after "much pressure from several governments and international human rights organizations." www.worldnetdaily.com, Jan. 31, 2002.

Two Filipino Christians,who were involved in Bible studies and Christian prayers in the Saudi prison where they were jailed, were beheaded by the sword on May 4, 1997. Ruel Janda and Arnel Betran were convicted and executed for *"forced armed robbery."* A former cellmate Donato Lama,declared that these charges were *"false and fabricated."* Another inmate reported that the probable reason for these executions lay in the fact that these men started Bible studies in the prison. Christians are forbidden to even pray while incarcerated in Saudi jails (*Intercede*, Nov/Dec. 1997, pg.3).

Even so, the Kingdom of God continues to advance in this darkened country. *Youth with a Mission* reports that since the Desert Storm conflict, more than 3,000 Saudi Muslims have come to Christ (*Charisma*, Jan.1997, pg. 36).

12. Other hadiths cite Muhammad as saying Jesus will return; to kill the AntiChrist, rule 40 years, forbid the eating of pork, marry and have children, die and be buried next to Muhammad. The tribute tax was/is required to be paid by all non-Muslims (Those who have submitted to Islam's protection: the *dhimmis*.) There would be no need of having this tax when Jesus returns, since according to Muslim theology, he would embrace Islam, along with everyone else!

# ELEVEN

# "The Spirit of Truth"

Christians in witnessing to Muslims must be prepared to become involved in discussions of faith. One's knowledge of the Lord and of Christianity will be tested by those who are eager to comprehend more of it or are zealous to overcome it. Mission work among Muslims demands an understanding of apologetics, an art of polemics and the proclamation of dogma.

Apologetics can be defined as the formal defense of an idea or one's faith. It is a learned art whereby one has the wisdom to correctly divide the Word of God. Success comes from hours of preparation, honing one's knowledge of the faith and of the Bible ever sharper, through earnest study of the scriptures. It is the ability to turn aside all challenges, asides and arguments with the use of authoritative reasonings, logical presentations and truthful evidences. The Apostle Paul declared *"...I am set for the defense of the Gospel"* (Phil. 1:17). Paul had a great anointing to speak the Word in truth. He spoke before Roman courts, the Sanhedrin, Kings, and unruly crowds to testify and bear witness of the Christian faith. The bounty of anointed apologetics is found in conversions, or *"being cut to the heart"* (Acts. 7:54). King Agrippa heard Paul's apologia and proclaimed, *"Almost thou persuadest me to be a Christian"* (Acts 26:28). Apollos with the help of the Holy Ghost was able to mightily convince *"...the Jews and that publicly, showing by the Scriptures that Jesus was Christ."* No Christian should witness the Gospel to Muslims without a time of

**131**

preparation in prayer and studying the Word.  One cannot defend the faith and entertain doubts as to the reliability of the Bible. Otherwise, the fruit of your labors among Muslims will be endless intellectual debates, confusion and the loss of integrity as a Christian.  Seek to become skilled in the giving of your testimony. This witness, combined with a liberal salting of scriptures in your words, and the power of His presence, will cause Muslims to hear. They will become still and know that He is God (Ps. 46:10).

Hand in hand with apologetics is polemics.  This is the art of waging war with words.  It is the disabling and/or destroying of your accusers through the power of the tongue or the written word. Polemics is the offense to a good defense.  It is the knowledge to refute false charges, allegations and heresies directed at you or the Christian faith. Jesus was once approached by the chief priests and scribes and asked to comment about giving tribute to Caesar.  It was a trick question.  Yet, he was able to perceive their craftiness and give them an answer where "...*they could not take hold of his words before the people.*"  The effect of his polemic caused these Jewish leaders to marvel, and be still! (Lk. 20:20-26).  Christian, the Lord may task you to respond with the same wisdom in Arab coffee houses, in the *souk* (marketplace) or before a court of Islamic law.  Paul even "*went into the synagogue, and spake boldly for the space of three months, disputing and persuading the things concerning the kingdom of God*" (Acts 19:8).  The Lord today, is causing even some Muslim mosques to open their doors to Christians.  If you are invited to one, pray first that it is God's open door and then witness Christ, for in that hour the Holy Spirit will give you what to say! (Lk. 12:12).

A dogma is an opinion which one believes.  Theologically it represents a position or a body of doctrines that have been formally and authoritatively affirmed.  These beliefs were/are set in force through Biblical authority, major Church councils and the writings of certain "fathers of the faith."  The borders of one's faith can be clearly outlined or muddled by the use or absence of it.  Hence the use of creeds came about, to briefly clarify dogma and add to one's confession of faith. Traditional Christianity employed *"The Apostle's Creed"* to affirm its tenets:

> I believe in One God, the Father Almighty,
> Creator of heaven and earth; And in Jesus Christ,
> His only Son our Lord; Who was conceived by the
> Holy Ghost, Born of the Virgin Mary, Suffered under
> Pontius Pilate, Was crucified, died and was buried;
> He descended into hell The third day, He arose again
> from the dead; He ascended into heaven, And sitteth at
> the right hand of God the Father Almighty; From thence
> He shall come to judge, the living and the dead,
> I believe in the Holy Ghost, the holy catholic church;
> The communion of saints; the forgiveness of sins;
> The resurrection of the body and life everlasting,
> Amen.

Biblically, the Christian could proclaim Jesus' great commandment as a creed of faith, for *"on these two commandments hang all the law and the prophets."* (Mt. 22:37-40; Mk. 12:28-31; Lk. 10:27-28) *"Thou shalt love the Lord thy God with all thy heart, and with all thy soul, and with all thy mind...Thou shalt love thy neighbor as thyself."* Some Christian evangelists to Muslims have advocated using a scripture from the Gospel of John, as our great declaration of faith: *"And this is life eternal, that they might know thee the only true God, and Jesus Christ, whom thou hast sent"* (Jn. 17:3).

Islam has chosen to embrace the cry: *"There is no god but Allah and Muhammad is His messenger"* as its great declaration of faith.[1] The essence of Islam's doctrine has remained the same since its inception. Changes to that doctrine will not be tolerated. Islam is a rigid faith that remains inflexible. In Islam, the Koran and hadiths give inspiration for the formation and interpretation of dogma's, coupled with opinions of religious leaders. Muslims have used creeds to a lesser degree in outlining their beliefs.[2]

When witnessing and evangelizing Muslims, major points of division between the two faiths will become evident. Most Muslims will point these conflicts out to you. Responding to their charges will take the Father's Love in you; a thorough knowledge of the Word and a complete trust that *"the Spirit of truth...will guide you into all truth."* Pray that Ishmael's spiritual eyes will be open and that Muslims *"...shall know the truth, and the truth shall make* (them) *free."*

## The Bible Is Charged By Muslims as Being Corrupt

The first charge against Christianity is that the Scriptures we possess, have "grave defects." Muslims believe that the present text of the Bible, is but a shadow of the original, having been knowingly altered and falsified by Christian believers. The Koran accuses Christians of *"hiding the truth in the Book and passing over much"* (S. 5:15, The Table). The latter reference to *"passing over much"* could possibly be a denouncement against Christians for abandoning Mosaic Laws and sacrifices. The Koran indicts Christians for these grievous acts in numerous passages: *"O People of the Scripture! Why confound ye truth with falsehood and knowingly conceal the truth"* (S. 3:71, The Imran's). The accusation of this *ayat* is typical of other Koranic incriminations.

Muslims also believe that apart from the Koran, there exists only three other revelatory works which have been wholly preserved by God. These are the *Tawrat* (Torah), the *Zabur* (Psalms) and the *Injil* (Gospels of Jesus). They are not included in the Islamic canon and are mostly ignored. Muslims have had a hard time accepting the fact that Jesus did not author a gospel, but four of his disciples did. The New Testament also contains the letters of Jesus' disciples, which in Islamic eyes corrupts the words that

Jesus spoke and amends his truth with man's opinions. The Koran is thought to be pure as no other writings have been allowed to become a part of it.

Christians and Jews possess a wealth of evidence, to refute these allegations. The original manuscripts to the Bible are missing, yet unlike the Koran, thousands of variant copies have been preserved. These "proofs" are to be found in the great libraries and museums of the world. The major "works" of scripture, the Codex *Vaticanus* (325 AD) and the Codex *Siniticus* (350 AD) date within 250 years of their composition. In addition, numerous lectionaries and other early writings by "Church Fathers" are on record, which quote large portions of scriptures without discrepancies. Historical, archaeological, and personal eyewitness accounts exist which confirm the integrity and authenticity of the Bible.[3] The discovery of the Dead Sea Scrolls, which date from the first century before Christ confirmed that the text of the Old Testament is essentially the same as to what we possess today.

The burden of proof rests with Islam, to contradict the mountain of evidence that Christianity holds. If Christians have tampered with the Word, Muslims need to demonstrate to us, where it occurred. If we have corrupted our scriptures, then Islam needs to bring forth the original uncorrupted texts. Christians should ask Muslims these questions: *"Who changed the scriptures?"* And then, *"Which translation?"* A greater challenge, might be the query, *"Cannot God protect His Word?"* *"Yes!"* The answer is obvious. God can and does! If the Creator was unable to do this for the Bible, then why would He do it for the Koran?

## The Integrity of the Bible demonstrated through the Koran

Interesting enough, passages are found in the Koran which prove that the Bible comes from God:

*And verily We gave unto Moses, the Scripture, and We caused a train of messengers to follow after him* (S. 2:87, The Cow).

*And We caused Jesus son of Mary to follow in their footsteps (the Prophets), confirming that which was revealed before him, and We bestowed upon him the Gospel wherein is guidance and a light, confirming that which was revealed before it in the Torah a guidance and admonition; unto those who ward off evil. Let the People of the Gospel judge by that which Allah has revealed therein* (S. 5:46-47, The Table).

The Koran also reveals that the Bible has direction, guidance and light:

*...even as He has revealed the Torah and the Gospel, afore time for a guidance to mankind* (S. 3:3, The Imrans)

*Lo! We did reveal the Torah, wherein is guidance and a light* (S. 5:44, The Table).

*Then when the anger of Moses abated, he took up the tablets and in their inscription, there was guidance and mercy for all those who fear the Lord* (S. 7:154, The Heights).

*And We verily gave Moses the guidance, and We caused the children of Israel to inherit the Scripture. A guide and a reminder for men of understanding*
(S. 40:53-54, The Moon)

The Koran also instructs Muslims to believe the Bible!

*Say: We believe in Allah and that which is revealed unto us and that which was revealed unto Abraham and*

136

*Ishmael and Isaac and Jacob and the tribes, and that
which was vouchsafed unto Moses and Jesus and the
Prophets from their Lord* (S. 3:85).

*And argue not with the People of the scripture unless it be
in a way that is better...Say we believe in that which has
been revealed unto us and revealed unto you* (S. 29:46,
The Spider).

## The Gospel of Barnabas

Muslims will often speak of the true witness of the gospel of
Barnabas. This apocryphal writing is widely distributed today
throughout Islamic lands. It is declared to be the only genuine
gospel truly compatible with the Koran. It prophesies the future
coming of Muhammad, and charges that Jesus is not the true Son
of God. This false gospel crucifies Judas instead of Christ, who is
safely taken away by God. The teachings of Paul are strongly
refuted by this "Barnabas," who ends his "gospel" with these
words: *"Others preach, and yet preach that Jesus is the Son of God
among whom is Paul deceived..."*

This "gospel's" origin and text betrays its falsity. It was reput-
edly "discovered" by a Fra Marino, "a monk" who was a "close"
friend of Pope Sixtus (1585-90). The man supposedly found this
book in the Pope's library, when His Holiness fell asleep. The
monk wishing to keep himself occupied, looked for something to
read. The first book he found was this forbidden "gospel." He hid
this prize in the sleeve of his robe and when the pope awoke, bid
good-by. Fra Marino then allegedly became a Muslim after reading it. This "finder" claimed that this gospel was none other than
a translation of an earlier original Arabic document which had been
written some 600 years after Jesus' death and then suppressed by
the church. No one though has ever seen an original Arabic manuscript, nor is there any reason for scholars to think that one exists.

This "forbidden gospel" reportedly passed through many hands. The earliest reliable records trace it in the early 1700's to J.E. Cramer, a counselor to the King of Prussia. He, in turn presented the manuscript in 1713 to Prince Eugene of Savoy. The Prince donated this writing to the Austrian library in Vienna, where it remains today. The Gospel of Barnabas was translated into the English in 1709 by Lonsdale and Laura Ragg, who declared it to be the work of an apostate from Christianity, written sometime between the thirteenth and sixteenth century. George Sale, translator of the Koran into English also labeled this gospel a forgery, in 1735.

Scholars have denounced the gospel of Barnabas as a medieval work of fiction. A complete Italian manuscript exists; which is though to be a copy of the original Spanish text, of which only fragments remain. Ragg noted that the paper on which this gospel was written was of a coarse cotton composition, and bore a sixteenth century Italian watermark. The handwriting, upon examination proved to be of a style used in Italy during the sixteenth century as well. This opinion was supported by other noted Italian authorities. Parts of this "gospel" contain quotes from Dante's Divine Comedy which was written in the thirteenth century. Customs which were common in fifteenth century and not practiced in first century Israel, are also found within its text. When Jesus demonstrates his power over the Temple guards, they roll upon the ground. The author of the "gospel" uses the expression like "*casks of wood when they are washed to refill wine*" (Bar. 152). In Jesus' era, wine was stored in wineskins or earthen jars. Wooden barrels were not even invented until centuries later. A geographical unfamiliarity of the writer with the Holy Land is also indicated. Jesus, for instance, embarks on a ship and sails to Nazareth, whereupon a great storm on the sea occurs. Nazareth is an inland city. It is not a seaport on the Lake of Galilee (Bar. 20).

It is thought that the author of this hoax, possibly was a fifteenth century Spanish Muslim who deliberately wrote this false gospel as an act of revenge against Christians for reoccupying his homeland. He may have been Fra Marino or the translator Mustafa de Aranda. If the man used a "pen name," he could have been one and the same person.

The book strengthens Muslim claims that Muhammad is foretold in the Bible. In one instance, Jesus tells his apostles that newly created Adam immediately sees in the sky *"a writing that shone like the sun, which said 'There is only one God and Muhammad is the messenger of God"* (Bar 39). The Savior also announces to his disciples that Ishmael was taken up to the mountain by Abraham to be sacrificed, and not Isaac (Bar. 43-44). Jesus in addition declares, *"Cursed be every one who shall insert into my sayings that I am the son of God"* (Bar. 53).

Numerous Biblical and Koranic contradictions exist within its 222 chapters, such as:

1. Jesus is born during the reign of Pilate (Bar. 3)

2. The list of the twelve disciples of Jesus includes Barnabas (Bar. 14).

3. 10,000 pigs perish when a man is delivered of 6,666 demons (Bar. 21)

4. Jesus declares that he is not worthy to even untie Muhammad's shoes (Bar. 42).

5. The Lord is betrayed for 30 pieces of gold (Bar. 214).

6. Judas is substituted for Jesus on the cross (Bar. 216-217).

Koranic discrepancies include:

1. The gospel of Barnabas repeatedly calls Muhammad the Messiah. This is a title the Koran gives to Jesus. Muhammad is always *"the messenger of God."*

2. The angels will all die on the day of Judgment. Only God will be left alive (Bar. 53). The Koran does not say this (Surah 69:15-17, The Reality).

3. Muhammad will be in hell: *"Every one, be he who he may, must go into hell, And what shall I say? I tell you that even into this shall come the messenger of God"* (Bar. 136).

4. All Muslims will go to hell: *"Then shall the messenger of God say: ' O Lord, there are of the faithful who have been in hell 70,000 years. Where O Lord, is thy mercy?'"* (Bar. 136-137).

Obviously this "gospel" is a fraudulent concoction. Even Cyril Glasse, author of *The Concise Encyclopedia of Islam* dismisses this work as being apocryphal. Every Christian who desires to witness to Muslims should become aware of this false gospel and seek to know some of its weaknesses.[4]

## The Final Warning

The last chapter of the Bible is inscribed with a strong admonition which all Christians should point out to Muslims:

*For I testify unto every man that heareth the words of the prophecy of this book, If any man shall add unto these things, God shall add unto him the plagues that are written in this book: and if any man shall take away from the words of the book of this prophecy, God shall take away his*

*part out of the book of life, and out of the holy city, and from
the things which are written in this book* (Rev. 22:18-19).

It was recorded that the great evangelist Charles Spurgeon was
once asked if he could defend the Bible. Indignantly, he replied
these words: *"Defend the Bible? I would as soon think of defending a lion! Let it out! It can take care of itself!"* [5]

Perhaps a testimony from a missionary to Egypt might illuminate Brother Spurgeon's comments. The minister reports that:

> *While I was waiting for a train, a Muslim approached me
> and in a low voice asked for a Bible. I had one in my bag,
> and quickly gave it to him. He took it, and looked up
> towards the sky and said, 'Thanks be to Thee O Lord, for
> sending me this Bible. 'He then kissed it and said 'I have
> lived all my life in sin, and have been a great man in
> doing evil. But a year ago, a man like you gave me
> Gospel according to John. I laughed at him for giving me
> such a book, told myself that it would do me no good and
> put it in my pocket. One day while was sitting along I
> took it out and begin to read it from the beginning. I
> found it very interesting and went on reading until I fin-
> ished it. Then I read it again and again. I asked
> Christians about the things I did not understand, gave up
> the bad things I used to do, and became a new man. I
> believe in Christ that He is my Savior, because He loved
> sinners, and I always speak with my Muslim brethren
> about Christ, so that they call me in our village, the
> preacher of Christ.'* [6]

### Muslims Reject the Trinity of God

The greatest sin for a Muslim is to be guilty of *"shirk"* It is an
atrocity, an abomination which *Allah* can never forgive. *Shirk* is
the denial of *Allah's* oneness. It is an unpardonable transgression

to add to God's person or to associate anyone else to be equal with Him. Muslims vehemently object to the Christian doctrine of the Trinity. They accuse Christians of being polytheists:

*O People of the Scripture! Do not exaggerate in your religion nor utter aught concerning Allah save the truth. The Messiah, Jesus son of Mary, was only a messenger of Allah and His word which He conveyed unto Mary, and a spirit from Him. So believe in Allah and His messengers, and say not "three." Cease! It is better for you! Allah is One God* (S. 4:171, Women).

*They surely disbelieve who say: Lo! Allah is the third of three; when there is no God save the one God. If they desist not from so saying a painful doom will fall on those of them who disbelieve* (S. 5:73, The Table).

*And when Allah said: O Jesus, son of Mary! Did thou say unto mankind: take me and my mother for two gods beside Allah! He said: Be glorified! It was not mine to utter that to which I had no right.*(S. 5:116).

Muslims mistakenly believe that the Christian Trinity is composed of God, the Virgin Mary and Jesus. In Islamic eyes, they believe and teach that Christians advocate a triune relationship of three gods. Hence, whenever they hear Christians speaking about the trinity of God, Muslims think we are promoting the idea of the Creator having a physical relationship with Mary to procreate Jesus. This idea repels Muslims. Christians, for once could also rightfully agree with their accusers. This concept is blasphemy! Mary, the mother of Jesus has never had a part in this relationship, despite the honors and "titles" given to her by the formal Church.

The doctrine of the Trinity is a gigantic stumbling block for Muslims. The Muslim does not know the reality of the Trinity, nor does he desire to probe into its mysteries. The Trinity of God is a doctrine of revelation, that the natural man cannot receive. It is a Holy Spirit directed illumination, where man can understand that there are three divine essences present in our God: Father, Son and Holy Spirit, all co-eternal and co-equal.

How then does one speak of such things, which are the heart and soul of Christianity? Jesus told us that we are to be *"wise as serpents and as harmless as doves."* Therefore, wisdom might advise the Christian, to first speak about other things to Islamic believers. The Trinity is a concept which must be received by faith. It is a truth that is revealed to those who are spiritually alive. Even so, the Christian must not be hesitant in proclaiming the very essence of our faith. One must not speak of these divine mysteries, from emotion, but from the knowledge that the Holy Spirit has given you, through study and wisdom. We are stewards of the mysteries of God (I Cor. 4:1). Tell the Muslim that the Christians truly believe in One God. The first of all commandments is to acknowledge Him. Draw their attention to these scriptures:

*I am the LORD thy God, which have brought thee out of the land of Egypt out of the house of bondage. Thou shalt have no other gods before me* (Ex. 20:2-3).

*Unto thee it was shown, that thou mightest know that the LORD he is God; there is none else beside him* (Deut. 4:35).

*Thus saith the LORD the King over Israel, and his Redeemer the LORD of hosts; I am the first, and I am the last; and beside me there is no God* (Isa. 44:6).

Inform your Muslim friends that Christians do not accept the idea of three gods. Christians are not polytheists. Jesus was quite clear in affirming the oneness of God. *"The first of all the commandments is, Hear O Israel: the Lord our God is one Lord"* (Mk. 12:29). Paul speaks about this truth in his Epistles as well: *"...We know that an idol is nothing in the world, and that there is none other God but one"* (I Cor. 8:4). The word trinity, is not found in the Bible, yet the doctrine is inherent throughout the scriptures. The following examples illustrate this truth:

## The Name of God

The very first verse of the Bible declares the Trinity of God. *"In the beginning God created the heaven and the earth."* The Hebrew name which is used for God in this passage is *Elohim.* It is a plural name that suggests God exists as three persons in one. This name is coupled with the singular verb for created: *bara.* The revelation of God as to His triune nature begins here in Genesis, with a plural noun and a singular verb. Evidence of a trinity; is again found in the same book, where God employs a plural pronoun to speak of Himself: *"Let us make man in our image, after our likeness..."* (Gen. 1:26). The next verse though declares the unity of God: *"So God created man in his own image, in the image of God created he him"* (vs. 27).

Another "proof" is found in Deuteronomy. *"Hear, O Israel, Jehovah our Elohim is one Jehovah"* (Deu. 6:4). This scripture declares the doctrine of the Trinity about as powerfully and clearly as it can be stated: the existence of a plurality of persons (*Elohim*) in one God (*Jehovah*). This oneness and unity of the Trinity is perfectly shown through this passage. There is one other detail in the same text, too important to overlook. The Hebrew word that is translated "one" in Deuteronomy 6:4 is *echad.* It denotes primacy as well as compound unity! *Echad* is also found in Genesis 2:5 where Adam and Eve became *"one flesh".* The Jewish people used another word for "one," meaning an absolute unity, thus "one only" or "one alone" —*yachid.* This word though, is not used in the passage of Deuteronomy 6:4.

A clear and distinct passage of the mystery of the Trinity is presented in Isaiah. *"Come near unto me, hear this: I have not spo-*

ken in secret from the beginning; from the time that it was, there am I; and now the Lord God and his Spirit, hath sent me" (Isa. 48:16). Other Old Testament texts where evidences of the Trinity may be found are: Genesis 3:22; 11:6-7; Isaiah 6:8; 9:6-7 and Isaiah 63:7-14.

## The Trinity in the New Testament

The New Testament strongly emphasizes the triune nature of God. The three persons of the Godhead can be observed uniting in many mighty works. Christians should share these examples with inquiring Muslims.

### The Incarnation of Jesus

*And the angel answered and said unto her, The Holy Ghost shall come upon thee, and the power of the Highest shall overshadow thee: therefore also that holy thing which shall be born of thee shall be called the Son of God* (Lk. 1:35).

The complete involvement of the triune God is seen in this mighty act.

### The Baptism of Jesus

*Now when all the people were baptized, it came to pass, that Jesus also being baptized, and praying, the heaven was opened. And the Holy Ghost descended in bodily shape like a dove upon him, and a voice came from heaven, which said, Thou are my beloved Son; in thee I am well pleased* (Lk. 3:21-22).

### The Great Commission

*"Go ye therefore, and teach all nations, baptizing them in the name of the Father and of the Son and of the Holy Ghost"*

(Mt. 28:19). Jesus himself, told the disciples to go forth and baptize the name of the Godhead. Notice that the word "name" is used, not "names." This is a direct announcement of the unity of the Trinity.

## The Witness of Stephen

One of the strongest scriptures proving that there are three distinct Persons in the Godhead is found in the Book of Acts. *"But he* (Stephen) *being full of the Holy Ghost, looked up steadfastly into heaven, and saw the glory of God, and Jesus standing on the right hand of God"* (Acts 7:55). There is no possible way to deny that there are three persons in this verse!

## Examples from Nature

The LORD God in His infinite wisdom has left impressions of His triune being in that which He has created. Paul informs us that *"...the invisible things of Him from the creation of the world are clearly seen, being understood by the things that are made, even His eternal power and Godhead; so that they are without excuse"* (Rom. 1:20). The natural world that man inhabits also, abundantly speaks of triune Godhead:

1. A man is one being, yet he is spirit, soul and body (I Thes. 5:23).

2. Time manifests itself in the past, present and future.

3. Space has length, breadth and height (or depth).

4. The Sun is light, heat, and energy.

5. Water occurs in three stages: steam, liquid and ice.

6. An egg is composed of three parts: shell, yolk and the egg white.

7. The human arm is one in three sections: the upper arm, forearm and the hand.

## Mathematical proof

The Muslim thinks that the Trinity that Christians believe in is 1+1+1=3 gods. Actually, the Godhead can be mathematically likened to $1 \times 1 \times 1=1$.

## Koranic Evidences

A form of the Trinity can be found in the Koran, despite the denials of Islam. Ask Muslims if they believe the Koran is the created or the uncreated word of God? If they say that it was created, then there was a time when their God could not speak, hence he was a mute God. If he created the Word and then spoke, he would have had to change from one state to another. This would violate their doctrine of God being immutable. If they admit that this book was uncreated, then the two things exist eternally. In affirming this fact, they are admitting to worshipping two gods: *Allah* and the Koran; his word. The same reasoning holds for the Spirit of God. If he is present eternally with *Allah,* this becomes the unpardonable sin or *shirk,* where another being is associated with God. If God created His Spirit at some date in the eternal past, then there was a time that existed where God was dead! He had no Spirit. Muslims then have three gods: *Allah,* The Word of God, and the Spirit of God, but they are separated. Islam exists without the means to get these three gods together into a unity of One. The venerable John of Damascus in his writings accused the Muslims of mutilating God. This in truth, is what they have done.

## A Mystery of Love

The Trinity of God is a divine mystery, which much be accepted in faith. It is the unified relationship of One God with three unique manifestations of His Presence. The bond of Love holds these Beings together in a Perfect Union. Christians should rejoice that they serve a loving Father, a Son who took on human form and a Comforter who reproves the world of sin, of righteousness and of judgment (Jn. 16:5-11). The Muslim can only speak of a unknowable sterile god who is distant from all his needs.

When witnessing to Muslims, speak of how you believe in One God, who exists with the Word (Jesus--the Logos) that was and is eternal, and of His Spirit which was and is eternally present with Him. Do not use the word *"Trinity"*, or try to undo the great mysteries of the Godhead. Let God do His perfect work in their hearts, in the fullness of His time. He will!

---

1.   Attempts have been made to accommodate Muslims who have converted to Christianity with creeds which are closely familar with their past confession of *Allah*. Thereby: *"There is no god but God and Jesus is Lord."*

2.   The fundamental creed for Muslims apart from their great confession is a declaration of their faith's five pillars. More fully developed creeds such as the *Al-Ash'ari* creed were later drawn up by modern day Islamic religious leaders.

3.   It is strongly recommended that Christians should read the following books, which present an excellent defense of the Scriptures against the accusations of Islam. They are:

   *Share your faith with a Muslim* by A. Akbar Abdul-Hagg
   *The Islam Debate* by Josh McDowell and John Gilchrist
   *Many Infallible Proofs* by Henry M. Morris

4.   For more information see: James Cannon III, "The Gospel of Barnabas" *The Moslem World* Vol.XXXII #2, Apr. 1942 pgs167-178.
5.   E.W.G. Hudgell, "The Bible and the Koran Contrasted" *The Missionary Review of the World*, Jan. 1938, pg. 27.
6.   Ibid.

# TWELVE

# The Son of God

**M**uslims revere the person of Jesus. He is the mighty prophet *Isa,* born of a virgin, who performed miracles and spoke the word of God. The Koran honors him for his ability to heal and raise the dead, declaring that he is to be exalted both in this world and in the world to come. Jesus is spoken of as the *Masih* (Messiah), the *Kalima* (Word of God) and as *Ruh* (the Spirit of God) in *Surah* 4:171. He is identified as the *Qaul al Hagg* (Word of Truth) in *Surah* 9:34.[1] Jesus is called God's Apostle sent forth to confirm the Law (S. 61:6). The Lord is described as one *"illustrious in this world and in the next"* who is *"brought near unto God"* (S. 3:45). He is a *"sign unto the worlds"* (S. 21:91). Jesus is also acknowledged in the Koran to be sinless, and among the righteous (S. 3:46, 19:19).

Despite these numerous accolades, Muslims regard Jesus as being inferior to Muhammad. Christ is only a prophet, one of many who point the way to Muhammad, the culmination of all prophets. Moreover, the Koran vehemently denies the divinity and Son-ship of Jesus. To speak of such a thing, is to invoke blasphemy. Muhammad's revelation states that *Allah* created Jesus out of dust (S. 3:59). The Koran also declares *"It befits not the Majesty of Allah that He should take unto Himself a son"* (S. 19:35). Those that say, *"God is the Messiah, the son of Mary"* are unbelievers (S. 5:17). When such infidels (Christians), declare that God has taken upon Himself a son, the Koran proclaims that they *"Utter a disastrous thing."* These statements risk the very wrath of God being sent forth (S. 19:88-92). The Koran further places a curse on all who proclaim Jesus as Lord: *"...the Christians say: The Messiah is the son of God, Allah confound them, how perverse are they"*(S. 9:30). The essence of Islam's doctrine is found in an *Surah* entitled The Unity: *"Say: He is Allah, the One! Allah, the eternal Besought of all! He begetteth not, nor was begotten. And there is none comparable unto Him"* (S. 112).

John, the Apostle, six hundred years before Muhammad's words foresaw the birthplace of this Islamic theology and others like it: the pit of hell. He does not mince any words with this doctrine of devils. *"Who is a liar but he that denieth that Jesus is the Christ? He is antichrist that denieth the Father and the Son. Whoever denieth the son, the same hath not the Father: but he that acknowledgeth the son hath the Father also"* (I Jn. 2:22-23).

## The Nature of Christ

Jesus' divinity is revealed through scripture, and is central to the Christian faith. The Biblical prophecies spoken before his Incarnation and fulfilled prove that He is indeed God. The Gospels highlight His authority over man, disease, devils, death, nature and sin. The Father God's own words, *"This is my beloved Son, in whom I am well pleased, hear ye him,"* attest to His majesty. The Savior's own testimony speaks the truth: *"I came forth from the father"* (Jn. 16:28). He accepted worship from men, and was without sin. The claims of his disciples also bear forth a collective witness to this truth. John speaks of *"That which was from the beginning, which we have heard, which we have seen with our eyes, which we have looked upon, and our hands have handled, of the Word of life"* (I Jn. 1:1).

Christ possesses all five attributes that are uniquely divine. He is eternal (Jn. 1:15; 8:58;17:5, 24; Heb. 1:11-13), omnipresent (Jn. 3:13; Mt. 18:20; 28:20; Eph. 1:23); omniscient (Jn. 16:30; 21:17; Mt. 24:24-27; Jn. 4:29; 6:70-71); omnipotent (Jn. 5:19; Isa. 9:6;

Mt.28:18; Heb.1:3; Rev.1:8) and immutable (Heb. 1:12; 13:8). He is Immanuel: God with us!

## The Testimony of the Koran

The need may arise in witnessing Christ to Muslims, to draw their attention to their own Koran. Point out to them, the miracle of Jesus' virgin birth and then ask: *"Who do they think is Jesus' real father?"* (S. 3:47; 19:20). *"What qualities would that give him?"* The Koran also credits Jesus with the ability to create. He is pictured fashioning birds out of clay and then breathing life into them (S. 3:49; 5:110). Creation is the property of God alone. Man is not able to create life from clay. Ask Muslims, how Jesus could do such works, if he was not already God in the flesh? The Koran also speaks of God in the plural: *"We breathed into her* (Mary) *our Spirit and We made her a son and her Son a sign for all peoples"* (S. 21:91). Question Muslims as to who this plural God is. Ask them "To what effect did the Spirit, have upon Mary and Jesus?" or "What kind of sign is Jesus?"

These passages pose difficulties for Muslims. Some will give fanciful interpretations, while others will be puzzled. Perhaps they will start to wonder who Jesus really is. Realize though, that if you chose to use the Koran as your witness, then you are electing to descend down to the Muslim's level of revelation, an extremely dark place with only flashes of a faint light present.

## The Word of God

The best way for a Muslim to come to Christ, and to recognize Jesus as God, is to direct him or her to read the Bible. The Word will bear much fruit with the Muslim, if it can enter into his or her heart, in the same manner that spring rains soak the soil: warmly, softly and repeatedly. The following testimony from a missionary to the Ivory Coast illustrates the soul-stirring power of the Word of God:

One day, while I was working in our flower garden on our mission station, I looked up and here was this boy about 14-years old asking,

*"Mademoiselle* (Miss)*, Can you show me how I might become a Christian?"*
I replied, *"Why yes, come into the house."*

His name was Lakika, and the conversation that followed went something like this:

I asked, *"Why do you want to become a Christian?"*
Lakika replied, *"I got the loan of a Bible from one of your Christians, and I read, and I read, and I read, and I saw that Jesus Christ is the Son of God."*
*"You are a Muslim are you not?"*
*"Yes."*
*"Do you know what this is going to cost you?"*
*"Yes, I know. My father is a very strong Muslim. He is a teacher of the Koran and has made the pilgrimage to Mecca. I know I must be obedient to my parents, but in this one thing, I must be obedient to God."*

I then proceeded to give him the Gospel from the beginning to the end. He listened very carefully. When I was finished I said to him,

*"Did you understand?"*
*"I understood very well."*
*"When do you want to become a Christian?"*
*"I want to become a Christian right now, that is why I have come."*

We both knelt down on the floor and Lakika prayed a prayer that the Father in heaven heard and the angels in heaven rejoiced to hear; the sinner's prayer. When he had

finished, I prayed for him and encouraged him to read and
to come each day for a Bible study, which he did. One
day, when he found the place to read so quickly, I said,

*"Lakika, how did you find that so quickly?"*
He answered, *"I have been reading this and it is all so
precious."* [2]

Many Muslims though reject the authority of the Bible. They
refuse to read the Word, and thus are condemned to live in darkness without the light of life. [3] Other Islamic believers would gladly hear the Word of God, but are prevented from doing so, by
restrictions and limitations. Many cannot read, and thus unques-
tionably accept what the mullah speaks as truth. Islam fears the
Bible, and numerous Islamic countries have banned its importation
and use. Jesus, though as sovereign Lord, is able to overcome
these obstacles of man. He is actively demonstrating his great love
and mercy for Ishmael, by appearing in person to many Muslims,
thus convincing them, that He is indeed their Savior and Lord.

Reports are surfacing throughout the Islamic world of supernatural appearances by the risen Savior and of His divine words
being spoken into the heart of man. The light of Jesus' presence is
indeed shining out to Muslims. Two testimonies prove that Jesus
is unilaterally calling out to Ishmael.

Christine Darg, an Evangelist to the Middle East received a
report from a Muslim student in an Arabian school in which the
young man states:

*I saw a shot of golden light coming towards us. It became
more and more bigger. At last I saw that it became a
streak of light and it came in the class and dashed on the
wall. Then it came behind the class. Just then a man
appeared with a strange long, white dress. It was something like a kandura, and had a green cloth on one side.*

**153**

*He even wore old sandals. He was so tall that he almost touched the ceiling. He looked very handsome. He was very fair and had curly hair. He brought a book with letters H. B.* (Holy Bible). *He wore a golden bangle on his head. He was very beautiful. He went around the class and touched everybody's head. The teacher was very angry with our class because we made much noise. When he came near me, I got a nice smell of rose flowers. She did not see him, but we all saw him touch her on her head. When I went home, I was thinking and thinking about this. I felt like fever. My parents asked me what had happened and I told them. They too didn't believe me like the teacher. They took me to the mosque and we met the mullah. I told him everything. He said that Isa Nabie* (Jesus) *had visited us and it is for good. So we were all happy. I know you feel it is hard to believe it, but whatever I saw is very true. He gave me all my wishes. He said, 'It is done.' I often think about this strange experience.* [4]

Margarita, a 19-year-old girl from India writes of her experience with Jesus also:

*I want to share with you what Jesus has done in my life. Six years ago, when I was taking a physics class and not doing very well I prayed, 'God would you help me.' A voice spoke in my heart, 'I am Jesus, pray in my name.' I said, "I can't, I am Muslim and I am afraid.' When I prayed to Jesus, I realized how bad I was and Jesus said, 'I will help you!' and He has. He has given me a new love. I went to a friend-- she said, 'This is all true, believe this.' But when I told my father, he became angry. He wanted me to believe in God only and not in Jesus. Later he hid my Bible. So I had nothing to help me other than a Christian friend. Then I got some Christian cassettes, and then received a Bible. Then I begin to grow! I also realized I had made mistakes. I prayed for forgiveness,*

**154**

*and again God gave me peace in my heart. Soon I want-
ed to be baptized. I was having trouble with my mother,
and could not tell her directly that I was going to be baptized, so I told her I was going to see a friend. She wanted to come with me and also my brother. Finally she let
me go. When I was baptized I had a very great joy.* [5]

### The Son of God

The divinity of Christ is a colossal stumbling block for
Muslims. The title *"Son of God"* compounds it even more, invok-
ing among Muslims, images of the Creator having a physical union
with a woman (Mary) thereby producing a son. Muslims recoil in
horror at such a thought and Christians should too. It is an abomination. The term *"Son of God"* as applied by scripture is used to
describe a spiritual and a metaphorical relationship, not a corporal
one. John the Beloved writes that Christians are now *"the sons of
God, and it doth not yet appear what we shall be: but we know that,
when he shall appear, we shall be like him; for we shall see him as
he is"* (I Jn. 3:2). John also writes in his letter *"Whosoever shall
confess that Jesus is the Son of God, God dwelleth in him, and he
in God"*(I Jn. 4:15). Jesus is the *"only begotten"* of the Father (Jn.
1:14, 18; 3:16; I Jn. 4:9).

Dr. Henry Morris, the founder and former President of
Christian Heritage College identifies five ways in which Scripture
reveals Christ's unique relationship to God:

**1. By eternal generation:** Jesus Christ is *"the image of
the invisible God, the firstborn of every creature"* (Col.
1:15). He was a Son with the Father before the world
began (Jn. 17:5, 24). The term "Son" does not mean that
Jesus was created after the Father or that He is not equal
to Him. It is a designation of submission and obedience
to the Father's will: *"Verily, verily, I say unto you, The
Son can do nothing of himself, but what he seeth the*

*father do: for whatsoever things he doeth, these also doeth the Son likewise"* (Jn. 5:19). The Father God, publicly recognized this special union when Jesus was baptized by speaking from heaven: *"Thou art my beloved Son; in thee I am well pleased"*(Lk. 3:22).

**2. By special creation:** the term *"Son of God"* is applied in scripture to those bodies which were specially formed by God outside of the normal processes of human generation. Thus the angels are *"sons of God"* by creation (Gen. 6:2; Job 1:6, 2:1; Dan. 3:25). Adam, as the first man, was sovereignly created by God (Gen. 1:27; 2:7). Jesus as the Word became flesh; the Holy Ghost coming upon Mary as well as the power of the Highest overshadowing her thus enabling her to bring forth *"the Son of God"* (Lk. 1:35).

**3. By resurrection:** Our Lord was *"the beginning, the firstborn from the dead"* (Col. 1:18). Paul informs us in his Epistle to the Romans that Jesus Christ has been *"declared to be the Son of God...by the resurrection from the dead"* (Rom. 1:4). The Apostle John identifies Him as *"Jesus Christ...the first begotten of the dead"* (Rev. 1:5).

**4. By inheritance:** A son is heir to the father's possessions in the world, so too is Christ. He *"hath been appointed heir of all things"* (Heb. 1:2). *"He that built all things is God...but Christ as a son over his own house"* Heb. 3:4, 6). Christians are "adopted"" into the family of God. Hence we too, are "sons" (Gal. 4:5).

**5. By nature:** The phrase *"son of..."* is used often as an expression of one's nature. James and John were first called *"sons of thunder"* (Mk. 3:17). Elymas the sorcerer was labeled a *"son of the devil"* (Acts 13:10). Jesus is identified as the Son of God because His very nature derives from the Father. He challenged his accusers telling them: *"Say ye of him whom the Father hath sanctified, and sent into the world, thou blasphemest; because I said, I am the Son of God? If I do not the works of my father, believe me not. But if I do, though ye believe not me, believe the works that ye may know and believe that the Father is in me, and I in him"* (Jn. 10:36-38).[6]

Patrick Cate, President of International Missions uses a simple approach with Muslims in explaining who the Son of God is. He studies the language of the people that he is witnessing to, so as to discover how many metaphorical and kinship terms are used. He then uses these expressions to form analogies which Muslims could grasp the meaning of what a *"Son of God"* is. An Egyptian, for instance is often called *"a son of the Nile."* Dr. Cate asks them, if that means *"the Nile got married and had sexual relations and produced baby people who are Egyptians or baby Nile rivers?"* [7] Of course, this question is rejected as being ridiculous. They explain to him that this is a metaphorical idiom and not a literal, biological expression. In the same way, Dr. Cate then reveals to them, that this is what the Bible is doing when it says Christ is the Son of God.

As a rule, when witnessing to Muslims for the first time, Christians should avoid entering into a conversation, which revolves solely on Jesus being the Son of God. This is not compromise but wisdom, as senseless arguments may possibly develop. Our goal as Christian witnesses to Muslims should be to develop their friendship and cultivate an interest in who Jesus really is.

The Christian would do better to reveal to Muslims, one or two of the many scriptural terms that the Bible uses to describe the majesty of Jesus Christ. He is the *"Son of man"* (Lk. 6:24); *"the Word"* (Jn. 1:1,14); *"the light of the world"* (Jn. 8:12; *"the good shepherd "* (Jn. 10:11); *"the resurrection and the life"* (Jn. 11:25) and *"the way, the truth and the life"* (Jn. 14:6). The Book of Acts can also provide a rich treasure house of proclamations of who Jesus is. Some of the gems that one can find here are: *"Lord and Messiah"* (Acts 2:36), *"Son"* (Acts 3:13), *"Holy and Righteous One"* (Acts 3:14), *"Prince of life"* (Acts 3:15), *"Prince and Savior"* (Acts 5:31), *"Lord of all"* (Acts 10:36) and *"the Christ"* (Acts 18:5).

One needs to use prudence and discernment in using this approach. Be led by the spirit of God and prayer. If the Christian witnesses Christ to the Muslim with a wrong spirit, two negative consequences may happen. You may prove your case so well, that you humiliate the Muslim. This would gain nothing for the kingdom of God. You may also inflame him or her into reciting off all two hundred or more of Muhammad's glorious titles! Christ did not call his disciples to enter into oratory contests (Acts 19:28-34).

Perhaps the answer to the problem of the Muslim accepting Jesus as the Son of God is found in the Bible. Peter developed a relationship with Christ, then recognized him as the Son of God (Mt. 16:17). Flesh and blood did not reveal this to him. The Father God sovereignly did! Later when the Lord asked if he was going away, Peter answered: *"Lord, to whom shall we go? Thou hast the words of eternal life. And we believe and are sure that thou art that Christ, the son of the living God"* (Jn. 6:68-69). The Roman centurion beheld Christ dying on the cross and knew then that, *"truly this man was the Son of God"* (Mt. 27:54; Mk. 15:39). Thomas met a resurrected Christ in person and cried out, *"My Lord and my God"*(Jn. 20:28).

Developing a relationship with Christ will bring to the Muslim a revelation of who Jesus is. Flesh and blood will not reveal it. The Father's love will do it. The Word of God will bring to the Muslim confirmation that Jesus is indeed the Son of God. The picture of the suffering Christ on the cross also calls out to Muslims to realize the truth *"For God so loved the world that he gave his only begotten Son, that whosoever believeth in him should not perish but have everlasting life"* (Jn. 3:16).

---

1.   These words are usually translated into English versions of the Koran as: *"the religion of truth"* (Arberry), *"the whole truth"* (Dawood), or as *"a statement of truth"* (Pickthall). Bezawi, a Muslim commentator states that the words *Qual-al-Hagg* may be taken as a title of Jesus Christ, i.e. **the Word of Truth** (Notes on Muhammadanism, T.P. Hughs, pg. 16). George Sale in his pioneering English translation of the Koran correctly identifies Jesus as *"the Word of Truth,"* pg. 252

2.   Personal testimony, Adeline Wilke, Regina Sask, Canada

3.   Permission to hold a "Jesus March" was given by local authorities in Khartoum, Sudan in 1999. Gospel portions of the Book of Mark in Arabic were handed out to onlookers when the believers marched by. The next day though, these Gospels were seen discarded in trash bins, and scattered about in the streets. Apparently nobody was willing to accept a holy book, that was different from the Koran. The next year, permission was again granted for believers to march. This time, copies of Evangelist/Teacher Joyce Meyers popular Word rich booklets (Help me I am: Depressed, Discouraged, Worried, Afraid, etc), in Arabic were given away. The following day observers reported not finding any books, which had been thrown away. All had been taken into homes to be read. Jesus said that we (His disciples) should be as wise as snakes and as harmless as doves. Perhaps, if the Scriptures themselves seem to be a threat, give a Word rich self help booklet by a popular Christian author to a Muslim. (Personal testimony from J.S., Cyprus)

4.   Christine Darg, *The Jesus Visions, Daystar International Inc.* P.O. Box 570 307, Orlando, Fl 32857, 1995, pg. 26

5.   Steve & Kathy Manning *Bless the Nations Ministries, Inc.* P.O. Box 411, Witt, IL 62094, Aug. 1995, pg. 21.

6.   Henry M. Morris. *Many Infallible Proofs.* Pgs. 93-97

7.   Patrick O. Cate "Gospel Communications From Within" *International Journal Of Frontier Missions,* Vol. 11 #2 Apr. 1994, pgs. 93-97.

# THIRTEEN

# "At The Cross"

The cross of Christ is Islam's greatest obstacle. Muslims reject the crucifixion of Jesus and his atoning work on the cross.[1] Christ was never crucified they argue, for God would not permit such a despicable act. Two meager verses in the Koran support this erroneous conclusion:

> And because of their saying: We have put to death the Messiah, Jesus son of Mary, Allah's messenger. They did not kill him nor did they crucify him, but they thought they did. Those who disagree about him are in doubt, and they have no knowledge save pursuit of a conjecture. They did not really kill him but Allah took him up to Himself (S. 4:157-158, Women).

Even these *ayas,* do not readily give a clear explanation of how Jesus died, so Muslims rely on two theological interpretations to make the truth "plain." One proposal advocates a substitution theory. Muslims will confess that God replaced Jesus with another person. This person was either Judas or Simon the Cyrene. Jesus was thereby rescued by God and escaped the cross. The Koran though, does not mention the existence of a proxy. The second viewpoint favors an illusion thesis. Thus, the crucifixion never took place, it was all a hoax. The Jews were simply fooled in to imagining that it had happened. This argument fails to consider that the Jews were not the only ones present at the crucifixion that day. The Roman soldiers were near the cross and so were the disciples of Jesus. Historically, evidences of Jesus' crucifixion are found in the writings of Josephus and even Tactius, an early Roman writer.

The Ahmadiyyas, a radical sect of Islam, believe that Jesus was indeed crucified, but survived the ordeal. They allege that he only fainted on the cross. Hours later though, the cool damp air of the tomb, combined with the odors of the spices therein, revived him. Their story then, has Jesus leaving Jerusalem and traveling to Kashmir, India. Here, he supposedly married, had children and died at the age of 120. This sect maintains that Jesus was buried in Srinagar, where his tomb can still be seen. The Ahmadiyyas movement is an aggressive Islamic missionary faction. It is presently active in the United States and Africa, promoting its version of "truth."

When questioned, most orthodox Muslims will point out that Jesus was a holy prophet approved by God. Thus, the Creator would not have allowed this man to suffer and die. He would have intervened and rescued this righteous man from such a shameful death. Others protest the crucifixion by arguing that a prophet of God would have been empowered to either overcome his enemies or escape from them.

Paul writes of men who become *"vain in their imaginations, and their foolish heart was darkened. Professing themselves to be wise, they became fools"* (Rom. 1:21-22).

The scriptures are quite clear that Jesus:

*...made himself of no reputation, and took upon him the form of a servant, and was made in the likeness of men: and being found in the fashion as a man, he humbled himself, and became obedient unto death, even the death of the cross* (Phil. 2:7-8).

**161**

Jesus Christ as God incarnate could have chosen to come as a great king, but came instead as a servant. He voluntarily forfeited the recognition and glory of this world. Jesus elected to humble himself thus submitting to God's perfect will. *"Father"* he prayed, *"if thou be willing, remove this cup from me: nevertheless not my will, but thine, be done"* It was for the sake of man's redemption that he endured the shame of the cross.

The Koran mentions the death of Jesus, but again this is open to interpretation: *"Peace on me the day I was born, and the day I die, and the day I shall be raised alive"* (S. 19:33, Mary). This *ayat* only informs the reader or the listener, that Jesus died, and that God will raise him up again. The Koran again fails to explain to its audience, exactly how Jesus died. Some Muslims surprisingly have come to know Jesus as their Lord by meditating on this one verse. They have found evidences of the Gospel story in this brief passage, seeing Jesus' birth, death and resurrection in it. The Spirit of God then moved on their hearts to search out and find the "plain truth" of the crucifixion in the Bible. Samuel Zwemer once related the story of how a Muslim professor from Lahore accepted Christ as his Savior, through the witness of the Koran. The man discovered through his Koranic readings that all men are sinners; that Jesus was sinless and that those who wanted to learn more about him, must read the *Injil* or Gospel.[2]

The Koran holds another key verse which may help Muslims discover the real meaning of the cross. Christians need to be aware of this passage and show it to Muslims: *"And if thou art in doubt concerning that which We reveal unto thee* (the Koran)*, then question those who read the Scripture* (the Bible) *that was before thee"* (S. 10:94, Jonah). This one *ayat*, provides a wonderful open door of light for the Muslim to leave the darkness of the Koran and seek out the true Gospel. If the Muslim reads and obeys this command, then he or she will be looking for Christians to answer their doubts. Be ready for their questions and lovingly show them our scriptures.

Emphasize the story of the crucifixion. Read to them all four Gospel accounts in context:

*And they crucified him* (Mt. 27:35).

*And it was the third hour, and they crucified him* (Mk. 15:25).

*And when they were come to the place, which is called Calvary, there they crucified him and the malefactors, one on the right hand, and the other on the left* (Lk. 23:33).

*And he bearing his cross went forth into a place called the place of a skull, which is called in the Hebrew Golgotha: Where they crucified him, and two others with him, on either side one, and Jesus in the midst* (Jn. 19:17-18).

*Then came the soldiers, and brake the legs of the first, and of the other which was crucified with him But when they came to Jesus, and saw that he was dead already, they break not his legs. But one of the soldiers with a spear pierced his side, and forthwith came there out blood and water* (Jn. 19: 32-34).

Reveal to these lost little lambs, the wonders of God's love as shown through the cross.

### The Cross of Christ

The cross of Christ represents for Christians, the essence of our faith. It is a preaching that Paul tells us, *"is to them that perish, foolishness: but unto us which are saved, it is the power of God"* (I Cor. 1:18). The cross stands before us as a sign and a wonder. Its very presence speaks to humanity of God's love (Jn. 3:16), His

**163**

faithfulness to fulfill His promises (Gen. 3:15), a new covenant (Mt. 26:26-28), man's redemption (Rom. 3:24), propitiation (I Jn. 2:2), justification (Rom. 4:25), atonement (Rom. 5:11), and victory over Satan, sin, sickness and the power of the grave (Is. 53:5; Rev. 1:18).

Despite doubts and denials by Muslims, the cross speaks to them. It whispers forgiveness and eternal life to some, and shouts to others of true peace and fellowship with the Father God. Keith Wheeler, an evangelist from Tulsa, Oklahoma was tasked by the Lord in 1988, to carry a twelve foot wooden cross. He felt these words burn in his heart:

> *Anyone can carry a cross...think about Simon of Cyrene; he carried Jesus' cross. Anyone can die on a cross...think about the two thieves on either side of Jesus. Only One, however, could die for the sins of the world...and He did that because of love. I want you to identify that message of love along the roadsides of this world where those people might never be able to come to a church or crusade.*[3]

Keith states that:

> *It has never made much sense to me how carrying wood on my shoulder can be very strategic, or even effective. I think that I've learned, or am learning, though, that God is not always looking for my great strategies plans, wisdom, or effectiveness, but my heart and my obedience. I wish that I could say that I am a bold witness for Jesus and that I love every moment of walking with the cross, but in all honesty, each time I pick up that cross and begin walking there is a humility (or is it humiliation?) that takes place that words can never describe.*[4]

## "AT THE CROSS"

The cross witnesses to Muslims, despite the hatred that Islam has for its outward image. Keith carried the cross to an Islamic nation and reported an unexpected receptiveness to it:

*What an awesome trip! From the moment we arrived, there was incredible openness and favor shown to us. While others had their luggage inspected at customs, we walked through without a single question...with a twelve-foot wooden cross! The entire time we were there we did not receive one negative word or reaction. All we heard was, **'You are welcome in Jordan and your cross is welcome here.'** We were overwhelmed at the wonderful hospitality shown to a pilgrim cross-bearer in a traditionally hostile land towards Christians.*

*To our knowledge, nothing this openly evangelistic had ever been attempted in this area of the world. After praying for a few days, I felt that God gave me a strategy. When people approached me and asked about the cross I was to answer as always, **'I bring good news! You can have peace, but only to the extent that you allow Jesus Christ the Prince of Peace to rule and reign in your hearts.'** Then I was to ask for forgiveness for all the atrocities that had been done in the name of the cross against the Arab people and explain that the cross was not an instrument of fear and cruelty against a people, but against a Man...Who forgives all of us. Since the cross was really a message of forgiveness, it brings hope and peace--if only we ask Him.*

*People would begin to ask more questions and the crowds would grow...Before long I would be preaching! Once, even, in front of the Mosque at the hour of prayer...and the people asked me to stay! As you know, I hesitate to report how many commit their lives to Jesus simply because I really don't know...only God knows what really happens in people's hearts.* ***I will say this, though, for someone to kneel at the foot of a cross in a Muslim country and say a prayer aloud is a pretty good indication that the person has truly counted the cost and wants to follow Jesus.*** *In countries like this, if one person does this publicly it is an amazing thing. On this trip, however many people were kneeling at the cross and giving their lives to Jesus!*

*So much of the church in this part of the world is in the "survival mode" because of the reality of persecution, most have strong feelings against the Muslims. As a result, there really isn't a motive to reach out to the lost. Bob and I had the privilege of speaking in some of the churches and challenging them to follow Jesus outside of the walls of the church buildings. By the end of our trip, some of the Christians were walking openly in the streets and roadsides with us and witnessing. One even led a Muslim man to Jesus!*[5]

The cross of Christ is powerful! Jesus said "*if I be lifted up from the earth, will draw all men unto me*" (Jn. 12:32). Muslims need Christ in this hour, more than ever as their Savior. The cross reaches out to them in love. We as Christians must also do the same.

### Islam Disavows the Sin Nature of Man

The question as to why Jesus died, may puzzle Muslims more than the details of his death. Islam as a religion fails to comprehend the true reason for the crucifixion of Jesus. It cannot see the need for one man to give himself as a ransom for many (Mk. 10:45). The doctrine of original sin and the fall of man, does not exist in Islamic theology. The inherent corruption of human nature is also not recognized by Islam.

Christianity accepts that man was created in the image of God, but fell due to Adam's disobedience. This initial sin brought enmity between God and man. As a result, corruption and depravity reigned over the earth and Adam's seed. The severity of this first transgression and the curse it brought could only be rectified by a divine Savior, promised by God Himself (Gen. 3:15).

Islam views the fall of man as being just a mistake, due to man's *"creative weakness"* (S. 4:28). *"We made a covenant with Adam, but he forgot, and we found no steadfastness in him"* (S. 20:115, TaHa). The Koran says that due to Satan's suggestion, Adam disobeyed God's command and went astray. The Creator though had mercy on Adam and *"relented towards him and rightly guided him"* (S. 20:122). Even so, *Allah* must have been a little confused that momentous day, for Adam is immediately told by God, that because of his sin of forgetfulness: *"Thou art forgotten this Day"* (S. 20:126). *Allah* then says to Adam that this is the reward of the transgressor (S. 20:127). This first man is left, abandoned by God. He has no hope, no promise and no reward. *Allah* also informs Adam that all his children will now be enemies one to another (S. 20:124). Then *Allah* backtracks his words and announces: *"We have honored the children of Adam...and made provision of good things for them and have preferred them above many of those whom we created..."* (S. 17:70, The Cave). Adam and his wife are exiled from heaven to earth and then promptly ignored by God, save for the comforting advice to follow his guidance whenever it is revealed (S. 7:24). The creation story as revealed by the Koran, serves as a poor foundation for the Muslim who desires to build a relationship with his God. It is just not possible.

Islam decrees that Adam's sin was due to ignorance. His penalty was an earthly deportation and disfellowship from God, but his original nature was untouched. Adam and his descendants did not have to endure a fallen nature. It was weak from the beginning.

Islam repudiates the idea of original sin.  Man sins but is not sinful.  There is no sin nature, rather all men are formed by God into a true image (Islam).  This perfect birth pattern in man, is later set aside by the cumulative effects of negative parental actions, and societal mistakes.  This is the reason why men deviate from their true nature and enter into wrong paths (sinful actions and habits).  Muhammad's own hadiths though, counteract this dictum.  One well-known saying declares that "*the newborn child is touched by the Satan and starts crying because of the touch of Satan.*"[6]  The prophet also announces in another hadith that, "*Satan runs in the body of Adam's son* (i.e. man), *as his blood circulates in it.*"[7]  Could these sayings be oblique references to the sin nature of man, and ignored by Islam?  The hadiths also reveal, that the only exceptions to this "*touch of the Satan*" are Jesus and his mother.  Kindly ask Muslims to explain this theological discrepancy!

The Muslim is very aware of sin in his religion.  There are descriptions in the hadiths of what constitutes sin and how it may be absolved.  Forgiveness of sin, in Islam comes from being obedient to the Sharia Law.  This duty to the Law also incurs for the Muslim, a liability to undergo corporal punishment.  These penalties for sin must be exacted, so that proper retributions can take effect.  The disciplines of floggings, stonings, and amputations are thought to encourage repentance since these penance's "*divert with a violent shock the soul of man.*"[8]  Redemption also comes from performance.  Muhammad declared that whoever "*performed his ablution well, his sins would come out from his body, even coming out from under his fingernails.*"[9]  If one observes the daily prayers, fasts, does good works, makes the required pilgrimage and even faithfully says the 99 names of God, then his minor sins will be appeased.  Major transgressions cannot be forgiven by the (divine) Law.  *Allah* can only erase these debts on the day of judgment.

This future great day of wrath is wholeheartedly feared by all Muslims.  Even Muhammad was concerned about it, proclaiming to his followers that there would be:

*A day when all mankind will stand before the Lord of the Worlds. The people will sweat so profusely on the Day of Resurrection that their sweat will sink seventy cubits into the earth and it will rise up till it reaches the people's mouths and ears.* [10]

Of course the pious Muslim, might pray for sickness, disease or calamity to over take him! Possessing these miseries, would bring divine benefits to the believer. Muhammad revealed that *Allah* would expiate some of his sins because of it.[11] The prophet must have needed a lot of expiating though, since it is recorded that his wife A'isha said, "*I never saw anybody suffering so much from sickness as Allah's Apostle.*"[12]

### The Heavenly Scales

Merit in heaven is also built up through the accomplishment of good deeds. If these acts are of sufficient weight, the Muslim believes that they will tip the scales of divine judgment and guarantee entrance into paradise. The Koran declares that "*Whoever has done an atom's weight of good shall meet with its reward*" (S. 99:7, The Earthquake). The Hadith records Muhammad as saying that God would create a good deed in the person's name and multiply it "*from ten to seven hundred times*" as favor.[13] Evil deeds though are said to be recorded on just a one-to-one basis with God. Muhammad thoughtfully reassured his disciples about faithfully doing these works of virtue. He said: "*There is none among you whose deeds alone would attain salvation, and entitle him to get to Paradise...Not even I.*"[14]

### The Prophet's Prayers

Now if the doing of all these works of virtue, cannot bring comfort to a sinful Muslim, one last Islamic hope remains: the prophet Muhammad. He promised his followers that if they prayed for him daily, he would on the day of judgment, intercede to God for them. *"My intercession is for the great sinners of the community."*[15] This is the great promise and hope of Islam. Muhammad though in this instance, greatly deceived himself and his followers. The prophet obviously forgot the divine word which was revealed to him in the Koran: *"Intercession is wholly in the hands of God "* (S. 39:43, The Throngs). Faithful believers of Islam are warned to guard themselves against a day of judgment when no intercession will be acceptable from one another (S. 2:48, The Cow). Christians have the security of knowing that Jesus *"is able to save them to the uttermost that come unto God by him, seeing he ever liveth to make intercession for them"*

## The Silence of Guilt

One of the best actions for a Muslim regarding sin, is to just keep quiet about it. *Allah's* messenger declared that his followers would get *"pardon for their sins, except those who publicized them"*[16] Therefore, if *Allah* had concealed the deed, it would be better for that servant to hide it away also. This new revelation of Muhammad's counters everything the LORD God has ever Biblically required his people to do.

The children of Israel were obligated to make a public sin offering, even if *"the thing be hid from the eyes of the assembly"* (Lev. 4:13). When these sins were known then they were to offer a sacrifice before the congregation. The LORD God gave further instructions for His people when the sin was known. If that person did not utter it, or reveal it *"then he shall bear the iniquity."* A trespass offering was required (Lev. 5). The great day of Atonement served as a public demonstration of the community's repentance before God (Lev. 16).

The people of Ninevah, an ungodly city, were convicted of their sins by the prophet Jonah's words. They repented to God publicly in sackcloth and ashes (Jonah 3:8-10). Christians are also told by James in his Epistle to *"Confess your faults one to another, and pray one for another, that you may be healed"* (Ja. 5:16).

## *"Though Your Sins Be as Scarlet"*

The Muslim has no real assurance that his sins are truly forgiven. Islamic Law cannot do it, neither can the performing of good deeds cover his guilt. Muhammad is inadequate to the task. Keeping silent also, will not erase the sin. Paul informs us that: *"There is none righteous, no not one"* (Rom. 3:10). *"For all have sinned, and come short of the glory of God"* (vs. 23).

Tell these "sons of Ishmael" that you have good news for them. God hates sin but loves the sinner! (Eze. 33:11). Speak to them of His promise in Isaiah: *"Come now, and let us reason together, saith the LORD: though your sins be as scarlet, they shall be as white as snow; though they be red like crimson, they shall be as wool"* (Isa. 1:18). Share with them the parable of the prodigal son. Tell them, how the father forgave his son and then restored him as well (Lk. 15:11-32). Muslims need to know that God would love to forgive and restore them to fellowship with Him. Relate to them, how Jesus forgave the thief on the cross next to him. This story impresses Muslims, because this man was a sinner under the law, and had not lived a life of doing good. The prophet Muhammad was not even born. Yet, Christ guaranteed the thief entrance into paradise (Lk. 23:39-43). He was the one man who was uniquely able to forgive sin. The way to a Muslim's heart is in making him realize that he is a sinner, who is in need of a Savior. The separation between him and the distant God, he knows can be ended, but only through the bridge of a cross. Point out to the Muslim, the words of Paul in his letter to Timothy: *"For there is one God, and one mediator between God and men, the man Jesus Christ"* (I Tim. 2:5). Muhammad was only able to pray that he would be forgiven. Speak to them of John the Baptist's declaration of Jesus: *"Behold the Lamb of God, which taketh away the sin of the world"* (Jn. 1:29). Comfort them with the Apostle John's message: *"If we confess our sins, he is faithful and just to forgive us our sins, and to cleanse us from all unrighteousness"* (I Jn. 1:9).

### *"Come unto me... and I will give you rest"*

A young Egyptian Muslim experienced the joy of Christ's forgiveness by first being exposed to the Word of God. A death of a family friend who happened to be Christian helped Abdul in his own journey towards the Kingdom of God. He happened to be in the home comforting the grieving family, when the pastor of the Evangelical Church came by to visit. The minister then started reading portions of the Gospel of Matthew to the family. Abdul a faithful Muslim was horrified, but in spite of his desire not to hear, he listened to the pastor's readings anyway. *"The words are wonderful,"* he thought. This taste, quickened Abdul to search out and find this forbidden Gospel. He was successful and soon possessed a Bible. During the next two years Abdul read this "Book" through three times, but always in secret. The result of this, in his own words: *"I became much concerned about my own soul. I felt my guilt before God and conviction of sin. I could neither sleep nor work at school. I could not ask anybody lest my father should hear."*

Abdul then decided to find forgiveness for his sins through the Islamic faith. He began to read the Koran and pray the Muslim prayers with a new fervor. He abandoned reading the Bible. Abdul's conviction that he was a sinner remained, despite all his ritual performances of prayers and holy readings. As time passed, Abdul's condition only grew worse. He could not find relief, no matter what he did. The young man then dared to ask a Muslim friend. *"How can I be saved from my sins?"* The man replied, *"Have you become a Christian? Be careful, unless those infidels lead you astray from the right way."* When, Abdul heard this answer, he kept quiet for a long time.

Another season came, and Abdul found himself again, being driven to ask the same question to those around him. One older man queried him: *"What sins have you committed?"* The young student told his interrogator his offenses. *"These are nothing,"* he replied. *"Don't bother yourself, only say, 'There is no god but God, and Muhammad is the Apostle of God,' and you will be safe."* Abdul dutifully followed this advice for two weeks but remained unsatisfied. He then returned to his "mentor": and told him that he could not rest as no change had taken place in his life. The man inquired exactly what did he mean by this statement. The young man replied that he was still living in sin and could not get rid of it. The older Muslim was astonished and said: *"Nobody can stop sinning, save the Prophets. Only say what I told you about before, and God will forgive you your sins."*

Abdul then answered: *"I want to get rid of my habits, which cause me weariness and trouble. I want to have rest, and I know there is a connection between sin and weariness of soul."* The "mentor" became very angry and told him to depart with these words: *"You are a Christian, you are an infidel, leave me at once, before you convert me to become an infidel like yourself."* The young student was shocked at the older Muslim's reaction and explained that he really was a Muslim, but just wanted to know the doctrines of his religion. Abdul then, thanked his friend and left, saying inwardly to himself: *"What is the use of a religion which will neither save me from my sins in this world nor give me the assurance of eternal life in the world to come?"*

This heated conversation though, led the young man to begin to read the Bible again. He then asked God to lead him to the true religion. One Saturday morning Abdul relates:

> *I took my Bible and went away into a solitary place. I made up my mind that I would find rest for my troubled soul or die in that lonely place. At length I opened my Bible to* Matthew 11:28. *"Come unto me all ye that labor*

**173**

*and are heavy laden, and I will give you rest." I prayed*
*saying, 'Jesus, if you will give me this promised rest, I will*
*follow You at any cost.'*

*It was about midnight when the burden of sin on my heart*
*suddenly rolled away. I felt that Heaven had come down*
*to earth, and my heart was filled with His rest and peace.*
*Speaking to the Lord, I said: 'Jesus, You have now proved*
*to me that You are the son of God, yes God Himself, for*
*no one can forgive sins but God only. You have granted*
*me forgiveness of sin, and given me this wonderful rest. I*
*can now say with Thomas, 'My Lord and my God.' Lord,*
*you know that I have never attended any Christian serv-*
*ice. I promise to go to church tomorrow, and confess that*
*Jesus is my personal Savior.*

Abdul then begged Jesus to make him an evangelist so that he
might tell others of the love that the Lord had given to him. Two
years later Abdul was baptized and took the name of Marcus Abd-
el-Masih (Mark, the bondslave of Christ). The Lord then gloriously fulfilled his prayer and allowed Marcus to become an evangelist, as well as a Pastor of the Evangelical Church in Egypt.[17]

### Islam Denies the Atonement of Christ

Islam fails to comprehend the need for an atonement for
humanity. Such a concept is foreign to Muslims, since mankind in
their eyes, does not need a Savior. The act of submission to God
or becoming a Muslim is sufficient. Islam also rejects the idea that
God required an atonement, since He is able to forgive without limitations (except *shirk*). The eyes of Muslims are blinded to the
necessity of Christ's death on the cross.

The atonement of Christ is necessary for two reasons: God's
holiness and man's sinfulness. God is a holy divine Being. His
righteousness calls for the punishment of the sinner, but His grace

provided a plan for the sinner's pardon: the sacrifice of His son at Calvary. Christ died for our sins. Paul writes: *"For he hath made him to be sin for us, who knew no sin: that we might be made the righteousness of God in him"* (II Cor. 5:21). Jesus suffered spiritually and physically for our sins (Gal. 3:13; I Pet. 2:24). Through this act of divine obedience, Christ became mans' eternal justifier (Rom. 5:9), propitiation (Rom. 3:25; I Jn. 2:2), substitute (I Cor. 15:3; I Pet. 2:24) Redeemer (Mt. 20:28; Jn. 17:9; Eph. 5:25; Heb. 9:12) and Reconciler (Rom. 5:10; Col. 1:20).

The Christian's challenge is to help inquiring Muslims understand why Jesus had to suffer and die on the cross. Christians need to be "comfortable" (familiar) with the atonement of Christ. Hence, a thorough knowledge of the Word of God is needed to properly share with Muslims the beauty of God's redeeming plan. Speak to Muslims that the atonement was God's idea, not mans, to remedy sin. Man sinned but God redeemed. The old covenant of the Law could not absolve it. A new covenant was necessary (Jer. 31:31-34; Mt. 26:26-30). Illustrate for Muslims, the miracle story of the scarlet cord of redemption found throughout the Old Testament. Start with the coats of skins that God made to clothe Adam and Even, then Abel's first sacrifice (Gen. 3:21; 4:3-4). Tell them the true meaning of the Passover Lamb (Ex. 12:12; Jn. 1:29; Rev. 5:12; 13:8). Explain to them why a blood sacrifice was needed by God to pay the penalty of sin: *"For the life of the flesh is in the blood: and I have given it to you upon the altar to make an atonement or your souls: for it is the blood that maketh an atonement for the soul"* (Lev. 17:11; Heb 9:22). It was for this reason that Jesus offered himself as a ransom (I Pet. 1:19).

Ransom means to buy back for a price. The Lord paid the price for men's sin; his own precious blood (II Cor. 8:9). The idea of a blood sacrifice is familiar to Muslims. Islam observes the great festival of *Id Al-Adha*. It is the concluding ceremony of the pilgrimage to the *Ka'ba*. The feast is marked with the offering of animal sacrifices, and is observed simultaneously throughout the whole Muslim world. The meat is then distributed to the poor, in hope of gaining some merit from God. The blood sacrifices have no atoning value for Muslims. This annual feast supposedly commemorates God's miracle substitution of the ram in place of Abraham' son. *"We ransomed him with a tremendous victim"* (S. 37:102-107; The Ranks). Most Muslims believe that Ishmael was the son offered by Abraham. The Bible though clearly states that Isaac was chosen by God to be sacrificed (Gen. 22:2). The *Id Al-Adha* celebration was mandated by Muhammad, to replace the observance of the Jewish day of atonement. It was also a "feast" that the pre-Islamic idol worshiping inhabitants of Mecca formerly observed.

Christian, this festival is a door of opportunity to witness to Muslims. Declare to them, how the LORD God accepted Jesus' blood sacrifice for the sins of all men, for all time. No other blood sacrifice is ever needed. The words that Paul wrote to Timothy, speak volumes to Muslims and serves as a powerful witness to them: *"For there is one God, and one mediator between God and men, the man Christ Jesus; Who gave himself a ransom for all, to be testified in due time"* (I Tim. 2:5-6).

The sacrifice of Christ speaks to Muslims. A remarkable viewpoint to this effect was written an Afghan author in *Lights of Asia*; a book on comparative religion. Sirdar Iqbal Ali Shah, a nominal Muslim, was not far from the Kingdom of God when he penned these words:

> *The cross is the center of all revelation. Have you ever thought what the Bible would be like without the cross? Take the cross out of this book and you won't be able to recognize it. If there be no promise of the cross in the Old Testament then its laws distress men, it is a book of fatalism. If there be no cross in the New Testament, then it blazes with pitiless splendor. But put the cross back, and at once the book becomes a Gospel. Its law becomes love,*

*its shadows flee away, its destiny is the Father's House.*
*No wonder that redeemed souls put the cross at the center*
*of their experience. On that they rest confidence...To*
*reveal my sin merely would make me afraid of tomorrow.*
*I want my sin conquered; I want to get it beneath my feet.*
*The cross is the place of victory. Christ did it upon the*
*cross. I say it reverently: He could not do it but for the*
*cross. It was expedient for one man to die for the people.*
*He hath put away sin--all sin--original sin and actual sin*
*by the sacrifice of Himself. There was no other good*
*enough to pay the price of sin. He could only unlock the*
*gate of heaven and let us in. Education could not do it.*
*Social reform cannot do it. It is Christ upon the Cross who*
*discovers sin, who forgives sin, who conquers sin.* [18]

The great seventeenth century song writer, Isaac Watts, perhaps best summarizes what many Christians have already realized, in the chorus from his hymn *"At the Cross"*:

*At the cross, at the cross*
*Where I first saw the light,*
*And the burden of my heart rolled away (rolled away).*
*It was here by faith I received my sight,*
*And now I am happy all the day!*

Forgiveness of sins and acceptance of one's blood-bought salvation through the cross is an act of faith. It is a heartfelt belief that God requires and honors.

## Muslims Exclude the Resurrection of Christ

The crowning proof of Christianity is found in the resurrection of Jesus Christ from the dead. Everything else is secondary. Paul writes that *"...if Christ be not risen, then is our preaching vain, and your faith is also vain"* (I Cor. 15:14). John calls Jesus *"the first begotten of the dead"* (Rev. 1:5). Christ appeared to John on the

**177**

isle of Patmos declaring, *"I am he that liveth, and was dead; and, behold I am alive forevermore, Amen; and have the keys of hell and death"* (Rev. 1:18). The death of Christ cannot be separated from the resurrection.

Muslims believe that Jesus was taken up by God into heaven like Enoch. He will return again at some future date to prepare the way for mans judgment. Muslims though desperately need to know the message of the empty tomb. Christians serve arisen Savior, who reigns in victory. He is a glorious Savior, *"bringing many sons unto glory, to make the captain of their salvation perfect through sufferings"* (Heb. 2:10).

---

1.   It is related by the Muslim historian Waqidi, that Muhammad displayed such a hatred for the cross that he destroyed everything brought into his house which had the figure of Christ placed on it (*Notes on Muhammadanism,* T. P. Hughes, pg. 26).

2.   Samuel M. Zwemer "The Islamic World and Missions Today" *The Missionary Review of the World,* Oct. 1926, pgs 745-752.

3.   *Keith Wheeler Ministers, Inc.* June 1995, pg. 1
4.   Ibid. pg. 2.
5.   Ibid, pgs 2-3,  27 Oct. 1996.
6.   *Sahih Muslim,* Vol. 4 *Al-Fadail,* CMLXXXVIII #5837.
7.   *Sahih Bukhari,* Vol. 8 #238.
8.   Comments by Abdul Siddiqi, English translator of *Sahih Muslim* Vol. 3 *Al-Hudud* DCLXXIX. pg. 910.

9.   *Sahih Muslim,* Vol. 1 *Al-Taharah,* C #476
10.  *Sahih Bukhari,* Vol. 8 #539
11.  Ibid. Vol. 7 #544, 545
12   Ibid. Vol. 7 #549
13.  *Sahih Muslim,* Vol. 1 *Al-Iman,* LX, #235.
14.  *Sahih Muslim,* Vol. 4 *Al-Qiyama Wa'l-Janna Wa'n-nar,* MCLXVIII #6760-6770.
15.  *Sahih Bukhari,* Vol. 6 #3, 242-243; *Sahih Muslim,* Vol. 1 *Al-Salat* CLV #747; Abu Daud Sunna

16.  *Sahih Muslim* Vol. 4 *Al-Zuhd Wa Al-Raqa'ig* MCCXXV, #7124.

17.  "The Testimony of Marcus Abd-El-Masih," *The Moslem World,* Vol. XXXV, Jul. 1945, #3, pgs. 211-215.

18.  *Lights of Asia,* London, 1934. pg. 76.

# FOURTEEN

# "If Allah Wills"

Sooner or later the Muslim must come to terms with his eternal destiny. Does heaven or hell await? Only *Allah* knows, for man according to Islam is only saved as God wills.[1] One's fate is predestined by God, who appoints an angel to record the destiny of each human being while they are still in the womb. This angel writes out that person's future deeds, time of death, means of livelihood and whether he or she will be blessed or cursed in religion.[2] Thus a man may do good deeds characteristic of the inhabitants of Paradise, until only a cubit separates him from heaven, then what has been written by the angel will impose itself so that he will perform evil deeds and will enter hell. The same sentence is true for the man who exhibits evil works. This person will be thought to be on the road to hell, until the decree of the angel is implemented. Then he will start doing good deeds and enter heaven. Muhammad sovereignly declared to his disciples that *"There is none among you, but has his place assigned for him either in the Hell-fire or in Paradise and has his happy or miserable fate (in eternity) determined for him."*[3] These followers then appealed to the prophet, as to whether they should continue to perform "good deeds" or not. Muhammad counseled them to carry on with this practice *"for everybody will find it easy to do such deeds as will lead him to his destined place for which he has been created."*[4]

The Koran with all of its "divine decrees" absolutely makes clear for the Muslim, the intent of God: *"For Allah sends astray*

*whom he wills, and guides whom he wills"* (S. 35:8). This proclamation is reinforced by numerous other *ayas*, such as: *"Whom God
wills, he leaves to wander: who he wills, he places on a straight
path"* (S. 6:39) and *"God sends to stray whom he pleases, and
guides whom he pleases"* (S. 14:4; 74:31).

Thus no Muslim knows for sure what his ultimate kismet will
be.[5] The traditions speak that when *Allah* created man, he took
some gains of dust in his right hand and then threw them behind
his back and said, *"You are destined to hell-fire and I do not care."*
Then this god looks into hell and says, *"Are you full?"* Hell
answers back and replies, *"I can hold still more."*[6]

What a great difference between this travesty of God's goodness and what is written in John: *"For God so loved the world that
He gave His only begotten Son"* (Jn. 3:16). God lovingly formed
man in His own image and gave us the capability to love and be
holy. The Creator has given man a free will. As created beings, we
have a self determination to follow either good or evil. Man is the
arbiter of his own destiny. Joshua confronted the people of Israel
with these words: *"Choose you this day whom ye will serve"*
(Josh. 24:15). The people then determined to put away their
strange gods, and inclined their hearts unto the LORD God of
Israel. They elected to make a covenant that day to serve God and
obey His voice (vss. 23-24). It is God's will to create responsible
beings. Man was not made to be a machine, but formed to be
accountable, rational, decision-making creatures. The Creator as a
sovereign LORD can see the end from the beginning of all creation. Yet, this Loving Divine Being who foresees the future also
chooses not to force our right to chose. God is sovereign, but man
has the freedom to be responsible. Paul writes *"For it is God which
worketh in you both to will and to do of his good pleasure"*
(Phil. 2:13). The church body, in age's past has experimented with
the doctrines of predestination. Calvin proclaimed the election of
man and emphasized on the sovereignty of God. Paul writes that
*"...he hath chosen us in him before the foundation of the*

*world...having predestinated us unto the adoption of children by Jesus Christ to himself according to the good pleasure of his will"* (Eph. 1:4-5). Again in the Epistle to the Roman's, Paul states *"For whom he did fore know, he also did predestinate to be conformed to the image of his Son"* (Rom. 8:29-30). Yet, the call of God freely goes out to all men. It is not foreordained by the whim of God or by an angel's inscription, but by man's choice. Jesus said *"whosoever liveth and believeth in me shall never die..."* (Jn. 11:25). Paul reinforces this thought by declaring *"For whosoever shall call upon the name of the Lord shall be saved "* (Rom. 10:13). Again in Revelation, the Spirit and the bride say *"Come. And let him that heareth say Come. And let him that is athirst come. And whosoever will, let him take the water of life freely"* (Rev. 22:17).

The cumulative effect of Muhammad's revelations, has been to bestow a sense of fatalism upon his followers. The Muslim world is ruled by fatalism. Man is a slave who is created without the need to take responsibility for his actions. No one can challenge the will of God, neither can it be changed. Therefor all events, circumstances, accidents, misfortunes or blessing are dictated by *"Allah's will."* What happens in life is inevitable and must be accepted, for *"Nothing shall ever befall upon us except what Allah has ordained for us "*(S. 9:51).

Despite the sentence of fate, no Muslim need worry about spending eternity in hell. Muhammad guaranteed that the fires of hell were only for unbelievers. Thus, the Muslim despite his sinful ways can take reassurance that he will be rescued from the torments of hell. Islamic theology has determined that eternal punishment does not apply in the case of Muslims. Hell is only a temporary state similar to purgatory. Muhammad through his intercession to God will be granted on the day of Resurrection, the privilege of taking out of hell all those who have *"faith in their hearts, equal to the weight of a barley grain"* [7] Other Muslims will be released from hell because of *Allah's* mercy for their repeated acts of prostration to him in the midst of this fire. They will be admitted into heaven and be known by their *"blackened bodies"* as the *"hell-fire people."* [8]

## The Bridge Over Hell

The absurdity of Muhammad's fantasies is further reflected by his vision of a bridge that extends over the midst of hell. *As-Siret* as it is called is a bridge that all must pass over on the day of judgment. It is sharper than the edge of a sword and its way is lined with thorns to catch the wayward. The feet of the infidel will slip passing through it, and he will fall into the fires of hell. Muslims though will be sure footed, walking safely over this treacherous span into Paradise. Muhammad announced that he would be the first to arise from the dead, and would lead his followers over this bridge. They will not cross over in peace though, but in bloody warfare. The Hadith decree that Muhammad's disciples will stop and *"retaliate upon each other for the injustices done among them in the world"* [9] This little end-time engagement will cause them to be *"purified of all their sins and they will be admitted into Paradise."* [10]

## The Agonies of Hell

Hell is an awful place. It is a realm of darkness, terror and eternal torment, originally set aside for the devil and his angels (Mt. 25:41). This region is everlasting, and all consuming (Rev. 14:11; 21:8). The lost, whether heathen, Jew, Christian or Muslim, will find no redemption in hell. Scripture informs us that *"whosoever whose name was not found written in the book of life was cast into the lake of fire"* (Rev. 20:11-15). There will be no second chance to leave. The prophet will not be able to intercede to God to deliver his followers out of this final punishment, neither will they be able to escape over some mythical bridge of salvation. Hell is a place of woe for the wicked (Ps. 11:6; Isa. 65:11-12). The enemies of the cross of Christ *"whose end is destruction will be gathered here"* (Phil. 3:19).

The LORD God though does not willingly desire or want to send souls to hell. People send themselves into eternal damnation. Evil always rejects goodness. God is love. Peter writes of the Creator's wish by declaring He is *"longsuffering to us-ward, not willing that any should perish, but that all should come to repentance"* (II Pet. 3:9). God is merciful, entreating the sinner to change his ways. The reward for this obedience is eternal life.

Witness to the Muslim that it is Jesus Christ and not Muhammad, who is entitled *"the faithful witness and the first begotten of the dead "* (Rev. 1:5). Show him or her the scripture where our Lord speaks to John, and says: *"I am he that liveth, and was dead; and behold, I am alive forevermore, Amen; and have the keys of hell and of death"* (Rev. 1:18).

## The Pleasures of Paradise

*"If Allah wills,"* the faithful Muslim will enter into the realms of paradise. It is a carnal heaven however, full of sensual delights and reserved primarily for the male species. Here, the most worthy warriors of Islam will find gardens overflowing with bubbling springs, thrones encrusted with gold and diamonds and goblets full of wine placed at the ready. There will be cushions set in rows on silken carpets that are spread about, and camels at the ready (S. 88:8-17). The Koran declares that these "saints" will be attired in *"green robes of the finest silk"* with armlets of gold (S. 18:32). They will find themselves in the shade on reclining couches, served by youths who have a perpetual freshness about them (S. 36:54-55; 37:41; 44:51-57). Those who "merit" paradise will neither suffer pain nor incur intoxication from drinking *"delicious wine,"* which will flow out from heavenly rivers (S. 47:15). *Allah* will also thoughtfully provide young female companions who are perpetually virginal, to satisfy their every desire. These slave girls

will be chained in pavilions and given out by this god as rewards for their past good deeds (S. 56:8-38). Muhammad further described this heaven as being filled with domes of pearls and soil of musk. The first meal all the faithful would eat in heaven would be *"fish liver."* [11] Expanding this fantasy, the prophet declared to his eager followers that they would each see in paradise *"a pavilion made of a single hollow pearl sixty miles wide"* [12] Here, would live wives, in each corner, who would not see those in the other corners, *"and the believers will visit and enjoy them."* [13] In this fairy tale of Islamic "hadithic truth," the prophet recounts how he saw a tree in paradise so big that a rider on a camel would travel in its sake for one hundred years without passing it.[14]

The Messenger of *Allah* in a wild imaginative dream fabricated a night ascent into heaven. He, himself had doubts whether it was a dream, or figment of his fertile mind, but spoke it forth anyway (S. 17:3). Put to the test by his followers, the prophet invented a tale in which he described heaven as consisting of seven levels. Here, the Angel Gabriel who had six hundred wings welcomed him to the first level.[15] Muhammad saw Jesus in the second heaven and *Yahya* (John the Baptist) lived in the third. *Yusef* (Joseph in the O.T.), and *Idris* (Enoch) occupied the fourth, *Harun* (Aaron) the fifth, and Moses held the honor of being the keeper of the sixth heaven. Traveling above these minor prophets, Muhammad was escorted by *Ibrahim* (Abraham) into the graces of the highest and seventh heaven. Here, he was allowed to see the two hidden rivers of paradise (the Nile and Euphrates).[16] His chest was opened, and it was washed with the water of *ZamZam* and then filled with wisdom and faith.[17] Asked by his followers, if he saw God, Muhammad replied, *"He is Light; how could I see Him?"* [18]

## The True Joys of Heaven

Heaven for the Christian differs vastly from the fleshly mirages and fantasies of Muhammad. Yes, heaven is paradise, but it will be much more than sitting on clouds or playing harps. Heaven is the

**185**

Father's house, the divine home of our Creator, the LORD God (Ps. 90:17). Here, the righteous will dwell in the eternal presence of the King of kings (Rev. 22:30). They shall see His face and serve Him (vs. 4). The redeemed will also find an everlasting rest in heaven. The tabernacle of God will be with men *"and He will dwell with them, and they shall be his people"* (Rev. 21:3). There will be no more curse. *"And God shall wipe away all tears from their eyes; and there shall be no more death, neither sorrow, nor crying, neither shall there be any more pain: for the former things are passed away"* (Rev. 21:4).

## A Place of Pleasure

Heaven is truly a place of pleasure. All the delights and joys that one's heart could desire will be fulfilled (Ps. 36:8). The redeemed of the Lord will be swallowed up in joy (Isa. 35:10). The Biblical heaven that awaits the righteous far surpasses Muhammad's illusions. Paul informs us that *"Eye hath not seen, nor ear heard, neither have entered into the heart of man, the things which God hath prepared for them that love him"* (I Cor. 2:9). Yet, Christians can know what awaits us for: *"God hath revealed them unto us by his Spirit: for the Spirit searcheth all things, yea, the deep things of God"* (vs. 10). What pleasures truly await the soul that enters paradise?

There will be mansions in heaven for the Father's house has much room in it (Jn. 14:2). One can also expect to see the New Jerusalem, the Holy City where upon *"the nations of them which are saved shall walk in the light of it..."* (Rev. 21:22-24). The true heaven possesses a river of Life with waters clear as crystal. It will flow out from the throne of God and of the Lamb (Rev. 22:1). This river is emblematic of the Holy Spirit and His outflowing of blessings to the redeemed. This river will flow forever (Ps. 46:4-5). The righteous will also have unlimited access to the tree of Life and the twelve fruits it bears every month. Its leaves will give forth healing for the nations (Rev. 22:2).

## Rewards

The redeemed will be rewarded in heaven. We shall inherit all things in heaven (Rev. 21:7). The Savior will bestow crowns upon the heads of those who have overcome (Rev. 2:10), robes (Rev. 6:11), and divine recognition (Mt. 25:21). God will lovingly bestow greater abilities, more opportunities and greater efficiency upon those who have faithfully served him in life (Rev. 22:12). Our Father will also permit His children to do all that they wish to do (I Pet. 1:4).

## Freedom from Sin

Man will truly be free from the curse of sin in heaven. This holy place will not have wine-drinkers, adulterers, nor gluttons residing in its environs (I Cor. 6:9-10; Rev. 21:8). The "saints" will enter into heaven, redeemed, cleansed and possessing a new spirit (Rom. 14:17). Our selfish nature and fleshly faults will no longer operate. We will be totally centered upon God. As His children, we will no longer desire nor seek anything else. We will instead seek to be even more pleasing in His sight and able to be poured out for His sake. As servants of the LORD High God, we shall serve Him gladly and with joy (Rev. 22:3).

## Behold the Lamb

The redeemed of the Lord will see Jesus openly. Like Enoch we shall walk with God. Like Abraham, we too will know the Savior as our friend. Like John who beheld him, so shall we behold Jesus in His power and glory (Rev. 1:12-16).

## Conformed to His Image

The souls in heaven will be conformed to the image of Christ (Rom. 8:29). We will truly have the mind of Christ, thus becoming obedient to the Father's will.

## Possessing New Bodies

Like Jesus, the bodies of the saints in heaven will be transformed. Time and space will not hinder our travels. We will have abilities to move past temporal barriers (Jn. 20:19). We will enjoy food (Lk. 24:39-43). Neither will we be tired nor sick. Our resurrected bodies will be in perfect health, strong, vibrant and glorifying God eternally.

## Everlasting Joy and Eternal Life

The saved soul in heaven will be glad and rejoice in his/her salvation (Isa. 25:9). We shall worship the Creator in song (Jn.4:23-24). John heard: *"a great voice of much people in heaven saying Alleluia; Salvation and glory, and honor and power, unto the Lord our God"* (Rev. 19:1). Heaven will be our eternal home. It will be an everlasting community and communion of the saints. We will know one another and meet and make new friends. We will honor the Lamb of God together as one, saying: *"Blessing, and honor, and glory, and power, be unto him that sitteth upon the throne, and unto the Lamb forever and ever"* (Rev. 5:13).

## Preach the Word

Christian, share with Muslims, the true joys of heaven. Encourage them to embark on a Biblical study of heaven and hell. Open up the book of Revelation to them. Ask them, if they would like for their names to be written in the Book of Life. Lead them lovingly then, in a prayer to accept Jesus as their Lord and Savior. Reassure them, that they now have a "birth certificate" on file in heaven. Give them a Bible to grow with, a fellowship (church) to go to, and the heartfelt promise of your friendship and prayers.

---

1. Muslim theologians counsel that the will of *Allah* can only be known through the *"august personality"* of the prophet. Therefore

188

the faithful adherent of Islam needs to learn of Muhammad's love for humanity and his views of how man should live to be "saved." *Sahih Muslim* Vol. 1, *Al-Iman* XVII, #94. Muhammad is *"the final dispenser of the will of Allah."* His teachings and those found in the Koran supposedly embody all values which humanity needs until the day of Resurrection. Muhammad also thoughtfully observed that those who lived among the community of Jews or Christians and who had heard about him, yet denied that he was a true prophet sent by God would be *"one of the denizens of hell-Fire"* *Sahih Muslim* Vol. 1, *Al-Iman* LXXI, #284.

2. *Sahih Al-Bukhari*, Vol. 4 #549, #550.
3. Ibid. Vol. 6 #472, #473, #474.
4. Ibid. #474.
5. *Kismet*, is a Turkish word that derives from the Arabic *"qismah."* It is translated as being one's portion, lot, part or fate in life.

6. *Surah* 50:30, The Winds
7. *Sahih Al-Bukhari* Vol. 9 #601.
8. Ibid. Vol. 8, #564.
9. *Sahih Al-Bukhari* Vol. 3 #620.
10. Ibid.
11. Ibid. Vol. 4, #546; Vol. 7 #544, #545.
12. Ibid. Vol. 6, #402; Vol. 7 #549.
13. Ibid.
14. Ibid. Vol 6 #295
15. *Sahih Muslim* Vol. 6, *Al-Iman*, LXXVII, #330
16. Ibid. Vol. 6, *Al-Iman* LXXV #314.
17. *Sahih Al-Bukhari* Vol. 4, #557-558.
18. *Sahih Muslim* Vol. 1, *Al-Iman* LXXIX, #341.

# FIFTEEN

# The Hand of Fatima

ehind the rigid mask of Orthodox Islam and its formal rituals, lies another hidden aspect of this faith. This is "folk Islam," the religion and practices followed by the common everyday people. Approximately 85% of all Muslims practice some form of "popular Islam."[1] Its strength/fears come from the underlying forces of: magic, saints, love potions, the evil eye, curses, healers, fertility rites, omens, sacred groves, astrology, ghosts, and dreams. These beliefs are almost impossible to classify but generally fall into four areas: spiritualism, the occult, protection from evil, and seeking to change one's fate. The Christian in desiring to witness effectively among Islamic people groups, must seek to have a knowledge of these "strange" customs. Greater than this, the warrior in Christ must possess a Holy Ghost empowerment that will be victorious over the forces of darkness which have enslaved these souls for centuries. The disciple of Jesus must also be willing to "pass" this mantle of authority on, to indigenous believers, so that they can set even more captives free.

The average Muslim is greatly influenced and sensitized to the presence of an incorporeal world. It is a mystical realm, occupied by demons, *jinn's*, ghouls and spirit wives. The Muslim world is rife with superstitions and fears. This daily concern is reflected in the fearful conversations and protective habits. Wherever one travels in the Islamic world, one is forced to realize how great of hold, these beliefs have. Taxicabs have "baby shoes" attached to the rear bumpers and axles for "good luck." The "hand of Fatima" greets you in doorways and on automobiles. Children wear protective amulets to warn off vengeful spirits. The fear of the "evil eye," dominates the lives of many Muslims. Charms are sold to counteract this curse. Women and girls find themselves cautioned to avoid looking into mirrors, lest they inadvertently admire their bodies and incur a liability to be possessed by a spirit. Sleeping alone is also to be avoided, since Muslims believe spirits always infest a solitary place. All these unwritten rules and superstitious habits play an important part in the daily life of most Muslims. Often what passes as Islam, is really just a thin veneer of religion, poorly pasted over a solid foundation of animistic practices. The four areas that adherents to "popular Islam" delve into are:

## 1. Spiritualism
Most Muslims declare their allegiance to *Allah* daily; yet fail to realize that the faith they follow is thoroughly corrupted with spiritualistic ideas and practices. Popular Islam and its companion Animistic Islam greatly impact the purity of this religion. Historically, as Islam spread throughout the world, it adopted and incorporated into its system of beliefs other existing religious thoughts such as reincarnation and transmigration (Muhammad's night journey). This blending of religious observances and tribal superstitions into the folds of Islam has occurred gradually and informally over time. The acceptance of these foreign elements is called syncretism. Since Islam does not require a change of life, or a spiritual rebirth, many converts have brought with them, a lot of "spiritual baggage."

The Kazaks of central Asia for example, call themselves Muslims, but are really animists. They "honor" the spirits of their ancestors every week by baking a special bread dedicated to them. They believe that if the departed spirits smell the odor of this bread baking, they will be

**191**

appeased. These "Muslims" also maintain that if these dead ancestors do not smell it, then dire curses will fall upon their families. Spiritualism is rampant in Islam. Some of these traditions that have been accepted into occultic Islam include:

### The *Jinn*

Muslims as believers recognize the presence of *Jinn,* a class of beings who are lesser than the angels and made of smokeless fire. One entire chapter of the Koran is dedicated to the *Jinn.* These beings, known to the Western world as *genies* eat, drink, marry, and have sexual relations. According to Islamic theology, there are multitudes of *jinn.* They are found everywhere, but especially in open and desolate stretches of land. Some of these "spirits" are righteous while others are evil. *Allah* declares in Islam's holy book, "*I created the jinn and man that they might worship me*" (S. 51:56, The Winds). Muhammad preached to the *jinn* and some became Muslims (S. 72:1-2, The Jinn). An entire mosque in Mecca has been dedicated to these "*submitted jinn.*" This dubious honor was bestowed in recognition that there, on that very "spot" a group of *jinn* met Muhammad and pledged their allegiance to Islam.[2] The prophet once said that if a Muslim happened to see one of these *jinn* who had accepted Islam, they should pronounce a warning to it for three days. If it appeared again for a fourth time, then they were to "*kill it for it is a devil.*" The prophet though, "forgot" to leave instructions as to exactly how his faithful followers could "kill" such a disembodied spirit. This leeway leaves a lot to be desired. Sobhi Malek, a gifted minister from Egypt relates the story of a Muslim theologian who thought he had some *jinn* masquerading as students in his class. The man had them beaten and they never showed up in his class again![3]

As spirits, *jinn* are considered to be always present. They can appear as animals, beasts, monsters, or people. These creatures are also thought to favor kitchens, bathrooms, and storage spaces. The Muslim believes that if one is frightened or startled while taking a bath, it is a sure sign that a *jinn* has taken possession of one's body.[4] The noises in a loft above one's living quarters, may be naturally caused by rats, but to the family and visitors below, the scurrying's and squeakings's mean just one thing: *jinn* are haunting the house. One must immediately seek to appease such spirits, lest they turn vicious and inflict greater harm. Hence, many Muslims resort to burning incense, giving alms or leaving presents of salt, water, sugar or bread.[5] Orthodox Islam even forbids Muslims to whistle, since this practice is considered to be "*communication with the jinn.*"

## The *Qarin*
Spirits known as *qarin* are also cited in the Koran. These are familiar spirits that are thought to attach themselves to all humans at birth. There is a female *qarin* assigned to every boy born, and correspondingly a male *qarin* is appointed to hover over infant girls. Their mission is to mislead humans and draw them into the hellfire's of eternity (S. 43:36-38). On the Last day, they will all testify against the souls, which they have been given custody over (S. 50:21-31). Apparently though Islamic theology is a little muddled, or else a coven of spirits surrounds *Allah's* creation, for the Koran also notates the presence of recording angels (S. 82:11). These entities are found on the right and left of every Muslim. Their job is to inscribe every good and evil deed that the individual does while living. This record will be presented to *Allah* at the judgment. The Koran, *Allah's* "truth" also stresses that "*We have appointed into every prophet, an adversary: human devils and jinn who inspire in one another, plausi-*

*ble speech though guile. If the Lord willeth, they would not do so. Leave them alone with their devisings"* (S. 6:113, Cattle).[6] Muhammad once proclaimed that he had a familiar spirit, but this *jinn* had converted to Islam, and so would not trouble him! This *jinn* rather was to be trusted, in that it would only *"command for good."*[7]

Christian, be assured what the Muslims recognize as *jinn*, and *qarin,* are none other than tormenting spirits, sent from the pit of hell to cause fear, anguish, misery as well as unexplained sicknesses and pain (Mt. 17:15-18). Granted, in some cases, *jinn* are nothing more than products of overactive imaginations and fearful minds. The power and presence of *jinn's* and *qarins* though, need not be feared if one recognizes that it was Christ at Calvary who *"disarmed principalities and powers. He made a public spectacle of them, triumphing over them in it"* (Col. 2:15, NKJV). It was also *"for this purpose was the Son of God was manifested, that He might destroy the works of the devil"* (I Jn. 3:8). Speak to those who dread these tormenting spirits and reassure them that God *"...has delivered us from the power of darkness and translated us into the kingdom of the Son of His love"* (Col. 1:13, NKJV).

### Ghouls and "Spirit Wives"

The average Muslim fears the presence of ghouls. These beings are thought to be "female demons" who consume human beings. Belief in these creatures is widely accepted in the Arab world. Fearsome entities also exist which are popularly called "spirit wives." These are real demonic spirits to whom men marry or consort with. These diabolical spirits even give birth to spirit children. Those men who have such a "spirit wife" are in popular demand within the community. People flock to their doors so as to receive guidance and help in difficulties.

The Christian who chooses to confront these unseen powers, must be confident enough to know his/her authority in Christ and be spiritually prepared to do violence to the kingdom of darkness. To face these entities with anything less than the full power of the Spirit of God and His specific orders, would be foolishness (Acts 19:13-17).

## Signs in the Sky

The Muslim since primitive times has always found portents in the heaven's above  Shooting stars and showers of meteors caused great distress in the populace, as these events are believed to be omens of death and disaster. Muhammad sought to comfort the faithful by denying that these signs had anything to do with death. Rather, he painted an imaginative picture of God hurling these missiles after devils who were listening in on heavenly conversations. This thought also appears in the Koran. *"We have adorned the heavens with constellations, and made them beautiful for onlookers. We have guarded them from every cursed devil. Those who listen in, a bright meteor will pursue them"* (S. 15:16-18, Al-Hijr; S. 72: 8-9, The Jinn). Islamic newspapers reported in 1983 that when Neil Armstrong walked on the moon, he heard strange sounds, which he could not identify. These noises, supposedly were made by *jinn*, which inhabited that sphere.

The papers faithfully reported that Armstrong had forgotten about this incident until he visited Cairo. Here, he heard the same strange noises. The Astronaut then asked what they were, and learned that these sounds were the Muslim invitation to prayer, going forth from the mosques. The newspapers related that upon hearing this explanation, Neil Armstrong immediately converted to Islam and became a Muslim. What he had heard on the moon then was the sounds of the *jinn's* imitating the call for prayer. Neil Armstrong, nevertheless, had to publicly deny this report, in an interview with an Islamic reporter.[8] The fact that this rumor contradicted the "holy word" of the Koran did not seem to bother the faithful. Many Muslims are ignorant of the contents of the Koran. A large percentage cannot read, while others fail to understand the Arabic language.

Muhammad also instructed the faithful, to fear eclipses of the sun. They were not to be seen as portents of death, but rather respected for "*Allah frightens His devotees with them. So when you see them, make haste for the prayer.*" [9] This special "eclipse prayer" consists of arduous formal prostrations, which must be exercised during the whole period of the transition. A'isha, the young wife of the prophet said that she had never seen such long prayers prayed![10]

It is well that Muslims are so "sign" oriented. Perhaps, a true heartfelt prayer during such events would help bring them to the Lord. Jesus said that "*there shall be signs in the sun, and in the moon, and in the stars; and upon the earth...with men's heart's failing them for fear for the powers of heaven shall be shaken*" (Lk. 21:11, 25-26; Acts. 2:19). One of the "signs" of the end of the age that Muslims will be expecting, is the rising of the sun from the west instead of the east. A sure astronomical impossibility, unless "the powers of heaven" are shaken! Those that know Christ as their risen Savior should rejoice on this eventful day for "*...they shall see the Son of man coming in a cloud with power and great glory. And when these things begin to come to pass, look up and lift up your heads: for your redemption draweth nigh*" (Lk. 21:27-28).

## 2. Magic, Spells and Superstitions
Islam is a religion that appeals to the common man. Its

simple duties allow it to be readily supplemented with magical incantations, spells and superstitious beliefs. The practitioners of these arts, seek to either set aside natural laws for their benefit, or else endeavor to influence the powers of fate through manipulation of the spirit world. Some of these conspicuous customs, which are found in the Islamic world are:

### The "Evil Eye"

All Muslims universally fear the "evil eye". The Arabic word for "evil eye," *Ain*, also can be translated as "jealous." The "evil eye" is the look of a jealous person. It is the gaze of a person who has envy, or evil intentions reflected outward by the eye. This look projects an evil power over the person who is targeted. The "evil eye" is blamed throughout the Muslim world for calamities and death. Muhammad feared the "evil eye" and declared it to be a "fact." He testified that a woman once cast a lustful glance at him, and he only had time to repeat the 113th *Surah* for protection. The "look" which emitted from her eyes passed through two of his upheld fingers and hit a tree behind him, splitting it in half! Muhammad then declared for all times that the power of the "evil eye" was stronger than fate.

Injury caused by the *Ain* or "evil eye" can be brought about by admiring something not your own. This act of admiration is thought to be envious also, thus engendering evil consequences. Muslims follow traditional precautions in an effort to elude this "evil eye." A pretty baby may be dressed in rags or washed infrequently to have a bad smell. A boy may be given a girl's name and dressed in that fashion, or vice versa, so as to mislead the "evil eye." Muslims consider it proper etiquette, not to compliment or praise someone. Newborn babies are not to be admired. It is often quite acceptable in their culture to say, *"Your baby is ugly."* If in doubt, say nothing! One must also, not complement a person on their health or possessions. Remember, admiration infers that you are jealous. Many Muslims chose as well, to bring new items into the household at night so as to avoid the "evil eye."

The "evil eye" can be blocked by also following the recommendations of the Hadith. Muhammad advised that the guilty party be given a bath. This water was then to be sprinkled over the offended party. Still other Muslims, would rather secure a piece of clothing from the one who transmits the "evil eye." This item is then burnt, with the smoke allowed to pass over the one effected. Muslims are truly preoccupied with the "evil eye."

**The Hand of Fatima**
The best preventative measure against the "evil eye" that is used throughout the Islamic world is the hand of Fatima. This common good luck charm, has nothing to do with the prophet's daughter, Fatima. Rather, it is a symbol of spiritual power. The hand represents the ability to control nature and bring order out of chaos. The eye in the middle of the palm, pictures the all-seeing eye of *Allah*. The number of fingers and the thumb add up to five, a number considered "lucky" in Muslim circles. One can even find them for sale in Jerusalem, and throughout Israel complete with Hebrew characters. This protective charm is also called "the hand of Maryam." in other parts of the Mid-East.

**Spell and Curses**
Woven into Islam society are the use of spells and curses. Spells are employed by the "faithful" as sure-fire methods to insure conception, find a mate or to divorce one, gain power or inflict pain and disease on an enemy. They are not to be taken lightly. Powerful demonic forces of

darkness are unleashed. Curses are also spoken, to exact revenge and to vex one's enemies. Necromancy, sorcery and witchcraft are all accepted practices in "folk Islam."

Muhammad once announced that he was affected by a spell. The accursed items were located near a well. These items were found and buried. The prophet was then set "free" from their effects.[11] These acts of sorcery apparently happened more than once in his life. The hadiths mention another case where ropes were found with knots tied in them.[12] This circumstance caused Muhammad to receive the revelation of *Surahs* 113 and 114. These "powerful" words guaranteed a countering of all "spells" of trouble. Today, charms and jewelry containing the words of these *Surahs* are made and sold where-ever Muslims gather to shop. They are worn faithfully for protection.

Valerie with her husband, Bill, were stationed some years ago in Morocco. She had hired an older Muslim woman named Hufna to assist her with the housework. Valerie soon became dissatisfied with Hufna's services, and dismissed her. The maid as she was leaving, told Valerie, *"You will regret this."* The next day Valerie awoke to find herself afflicted with a cough in her chest and severe fatigue. She sought medical help, but the doctors were not able to diagnose her problems. The tests for mononucleosis came back negative, as well as everything else they could think of. Her "condition" continued on for months. She could not lie down and breathe. Valerie was unable to care for her family and her home, so she hired a new maid, named Zorra. The young woman heard Valerie talking about her sickness and saw her infirmities. She told her, *"You have been cursed! Do you know sometimes people pay money to a person who speaks such a curse on the one they want to get sick? Do you know that*

**199**

*you can also pay money to such a person and get well? They remove curses too."* Valerie laughed and forgot about this conversation. Weeks later, Zorra asked to borrow one of Valerie's scarfs to go home, as she had forgotten hers. Valerie gave her the scarf (She forgot that a Muslim woman does not travel outside the home with her head uncovered. The maid must have had a head covering to come to work). The next day, Valerie said *"It was the strangest thing, I awoke feeling better than I had in months."* The maid came to work smiling. Valerie knew that Zorra had something to do with this curse of ill health being broken. The sickness never returned. A few years later, Valerie and Bill accepted the Lord as their Savior. As this couple grew in the faith, they made it a point to sever in prayer any past occultic hexes, vexes and demonic curses spoken over them. Valerie and Bill are now committed Christians joyfully serving the Lord.[13]

## Superstitions and Taboos

The Islamic world abounds with superstitions and forbidden acts. Muhammad counseled families *"When the night falls (evening), stop your children from going outside, for the devils are loosed at that time."* They were also to close the entrances to their tents and homes and mention *Allah's* name, *"for Satan does not open a closed door."* [14] The prophet also advised that *"an evil omen may be in an animal, a house and a woman."* [15] An owl, which perches on a house is to be feared. It is thought to be a portent of death. A man who has just shaved must not approach a bride, or a pregnant woman, a nursing mother or one who weaning her child. They all may become barren or lose their ability to nurse. Evil consequences may be avoided if the woman enters the room of meeting and walks around the man seven times. A bride must not meet another bride. One of the two may become barren. Harm may be avoided by drawing blood from the one who is guilty and then bathing on a Friday in it. A woman who is pregnant cannot go to funerals or visit the sick so as to avoid the same fate from happening to her. It is also better not to name diseases and sicknesses, lest they be called into being.

### The *Sarukh* (the cry)

Muslims believe that if a man is murdered, the spirits, which live in his blood, will continue to cry out for vengeance. The spot where this person met up with either an accidental or violent death will become infested with his *afreet* or spirit. The area where this death occurred must be avoided since it is a place of danger to all who pass by.[16]

### 3. Protection from Evil

Muslims in fearing the presence of evil, seek protection in numerous non-Biblical ways. The color blue is thought to be auspicious to ward off the "evil eye." It is commonly painted on doorways, windows, car bumpers, boats and anything else that needs special protection. Blue is a color rarely found in the plant and animal kingdoms. It is though, the predominate color of the sky above. Blue eyes are another matter. Those persons who have been "gifted" with blue eyes had better learn to refrain from grazing at Muslims with them. They may be accused of projecting the "evil eye."

Muslims also cite the names of the prophet's family for protection. The five names are that of the prophet (*al-mustafa* "the chosen"), Ali, his son in Law (*the one with who God is pleased*), his wife "Fatmed" (*Fatima*), and their two sons Hassan and Hussain. These names are combined with the name of *Allah* so as to achieve the right magical formula and/or divine guardianship. Many Islamic families also have these "sacred" names inscribed in a verse, which is then prominently displayed, on one wall of the home. This writing serves as a form of insurance against disaster and calamity: *"I have five with which to quench the heat of pestilence-the Chosen, the Pleased, their two sons and Fatima"* [17]

## The *Kiswan*

A piece of black cloth taken from the sacred *Ka'ba* in Mecca, is also highly valued by Muslims as ensuring diving protection. This outward covering is called the *Kiswan.* It is made with silk interlaced with gold, at a cost of some $4.5 million dollars. The entire cloth also has the divine name of *Allah* patterned in black on black throughout. Every year a new covering is made and placed over the *Ka'ba.*[18] The old covering is then cut into pieces and distributed to pilgrims. The color black also has a certain sacredness about it for Muslims. It symbolizes the Absolute Oneness of God.

## Sacrifices

Sacrificial offerings are often traditionally used to gain favor with the "spirits." A cloth, which has been dipped in the blood of an animal sacrificed, is considered protective. It is also popular in some parts of the Arab world to sacrifice a white chicken and then smear its blood over a new automobile so as to ensure protection.

Mehran came to the United States from Iran. He was a young student at the University of Missouri. After residing in this country for a year, he needed a car. The young man soon found what he wanted and purchased a vehicle. He then called his father in Iran to tell him the good news. The father told him to be sure and sacrifice a chicken "for the sake of the car." Mehran though, first had to find a place where he could purchase a pure white chicken. He finally stopped at a chicken farm and bought a bird. The farmer wanted to know why he just wanted one chicken. *"Wouldn't several be better?"* Mehran told him, *"It is for a sacrifice."* The University student then put the live chicken into the car's trunk and headed home.

For the sacrifice to be accepted, the chicken had to be cut just right. Mehran also had another problem. He had no garage and curious neighbors. On one side of him lived a family that taught in the local Baptist Sunday school. His other neighbors were retired missionaries. He had to do this though, and be obedient to his father. Mehran waited until he thought these neighbors would not be looking outside. He then quickly "sacrificed" the chicken and then ran around the car as fast as he could spreading the fowl's blood over it. Mehran laughs about this now, for he has been set free in Jesus. [19] He and his wife are Christians and have a ministry outreach to Muslims. [20]

### *Zar* Rituals

The word *"zar"* means "visitor" in Arabic. Muslim women will often host special "spiritual" ceremonies, in an effort to negotiate with the spirit world. One can through this ritual, appease "spirits" and remove the cause of their anger. Special women who are thought able to reconcile the spirits are engaged. The victim who is bothered by a "spirit" gives this woman an article of her apparel. The woman who is in contact with this spirit world, then make contacts with the offended entity and determines the cause of his anger. Often a certain "gift" will satisfy this "spirit." Next morning, the sorceress tells her client, what the spirit wants: perhaps some jewelry, a new dress, a camel or an automobile. A *Zar* ritual is then held. Those who attend, dance, feast, fall into trances and sometimes engage in extra martial sex. Violent behavior also has been known to occur when the "spirits" that are sought out arrive and take possession.

These "rituals" are wholly accepted by the community, since these acts are done by "spirits" and not the possessed party. Women who demonstrate the ability to gain entry into this "spirit" world quickly find themselves recognized n the community. They are respected for their extra "powers" of communication.

## Amulets

Amulets are protective devices, worn by Muslims to ward off evil. Most are small metal cases bound to the arm or ankle, containing a *Surah* from the Koran. They are a common sight in Islamic nations, especially on children. The most effective and popular chapters are: *Surahs* 1, 6, 18, 36, 44, 55, 67 and 78. There are also favorite verses thought to ensure protection from evil such as "*God is the best protector,*" or "*They guard him by the command of God,*" and "*We guard him from every stoned devil.*"

The ink to write these "charms" is specially prepared with rose water, saffron water, or even the juice of onions. If a wearer is privileged enough, the ingredients may include *Zamzam* water or human blood! Those that write these amulets must be "holy men." Holiness comes from special diets. If the man engages his business by writing the terrible names of *Allah,* he must avoid eating meat, fish, eggs, and honey. If this person specializes in writing the more amiable names of God, then butter, curds, vinegar, and salt are to be shunned.

These amulets are not just harmless little charms or superstitious oddities. Evil spirits can use these talismans to stake their claim on people's lives. Dean Galyen, an Assemblies of God missionary to Tanzania, East Africa relates of how he was holding an outdoor evangelistic meeting in that country. He had just given an invitation for those wanting salvation. As he prayed, a woman fell to the ground and began writhing like a snake. Dean motioned for the counselors to take her behind the platform. He then followed, and prayed over the woman, rebuking the devil in Jesus' name. Dean then addressed the demon and said: *"You've had her too long. You're leaving."* The evil spirit possessing the woman replied back to him in perfect English: *"I'm not leaving."* The Tanzanian woman knew no English, but the entity within her spoke it fluently. *"I'm not leaving without the baby of the covenant,"* the evil spirit answered again. Onlookers then told him, that the woman had gone to a native amulet maker. He had performed traditional rites over her, since she was pregnant. When she gave birth, an amulet was hung around the baby's neck. Upon learning this, the missionary had the baby brought to him. He then removed the charm. Immediately, the woman was released from her demonic bondage. The curse was broken. The evil spirit had no legal right to stay. The next Sunday morning, the woman *"was gloriously baptized in the Holy Spirit."* [21]

## 4. The Role of Fate

The Muslim world besides Mecca, is full of shrines and holy places. People travel to these localities to seek blessings from dead "saints" who were supposedly Islamic "holy men." They pray that these saints will intercede to *Allah* for them. Many others congregate at shrines to seek guidance. The lack of assurance of one's eternal salvation, drives many Muslims to these sacred areas. Many feel, a journey to these places, could earn them a few extra good deeds, which just might favorably tip the scales of fate. They also endeavor to find certain "influences" and power sources, which can change their appointed destiny.

**"Saints"**

Idiots, lunatics, madmen and beggars are thought to be "saints" (*fakirs, pirs*), since their natural bodies are on earth but their mental faculties are already in paradise. Those who observe "folk Islam" hold these deranged souls in awe. It is believed that they can discern the future and see into the spiritual world.

Jesus though, set a better example for his disciples. He did not esteem the boy who was afflicted by lunacy. Rather, he rebuked the evil spirit and commanded it to come out of the child (Mt. 17:14-20; Mk. 9: 17-29; Lk. 9:37-43). Then he *"took him by the hand and lifted him up..."*, whole and restored.

**Barakah**

This Arabic word for blessing refers to the presence of an impersonal spiritual force. It is a power that is greater than one found through conventional blessings. Ordinary people do not posses it. Those living "holy" individual (*pirs*) who possess this *barakah* are thought to be "enabled" to perform miracles. If enough "power" is present, then one's sickness or barrenness can be healed. Perhaps prosperity will come, children, or protection. *Barakah* is found only in special people, unique Korans, certain tombs and in mosques where these men worshiped.

**Sharifs**

A *Sharif* (noble or honorable in Arabic) is a person who claims to be a literal descendant of Muhammad the prophet through his daughter, Fatima, and her husband, Ali. Muhammad had other daughters, but Fatima was given a special blessing by him at her wedding. Each *sharif* draws his ancestry from one of the two grandsons of the prophet: Hassan or Hussain. These persons are treated with respect in Islamic society, and sought after as a means of obtaining spiritual blessings and power.

## The Popularity of Folk Islam

The practice of the occult is a major activity in day-to-day Islam. Its popularity stems from the desires of the common people to receive immediate answers to the problems of life. God is thought to be too distant to help. The Koran also does not offer ready solutions for financial pressures and sicknesses. Folk Islam serves as an outlet, where the common masses can demonstrate their emotions and curiosity. Muslims delve in "folk Islam" to have a little fun, and to relieve stress. People who are under the daily yoke of Islam are also repressed. A pervasive spirit of control is found throughout Islamic society. Direct confrontations and arguments are discouraged. People turn to "folk Islam" to settle disputes, arguments and to exact vengeance on those who have offended them.

Tradition also encourages the practice of "folk Islam." Many of these occultic arts and superstitions are passed down from family to family and culture to culture. *"If the spell worked for mother, then surely it will be good for me."* These are generational sins, performed by a people who perish for lack of wisdom.

The greatest attraction of "popular Islam" is found in its ability to control. Spells, blessings, curses, sorceries, and witchcrafts are all pursued in an effort to achieve power. Many Muslim women enter into these arts, since they are denied a conventional education. One who demonstrates a supernatural ability to summon "spirits" and make spells, gains great respect in a male dominated society that fears what it cannot control.

## The Word of the LORD

Without the Bible, Muslims have no way of knowing how detestable these practices are to the LORD. Scripture after scripture condemns such activities. The LORD God commanded the children of Israel to *"not learn"* or *"do after the abominations"* of other nations (Deut. 18:10). He specifically forbade the use of divination and enchantments (vs. 10). Witches were not allowed to live (Ex. 22:18). Those who formed charms, consulted spirits or contacted the dead were also *"an abomination unto the LORD"* (Deut. 18:11-12). People who have familiar spirits or practice wizardry come under God's judgment as well. The Creator declares *"...there is no light in them"* (Isa. 8:19-22). Those who derive their counsel from magic spells, predictions, astrology, and stargazing will find that *"they shall not be able to deliver themselves from the power of the flame..."* (Isa. 47:12-14). The prophet Ezekiel also reveals how much God hates those who make magic charms: *"Behold, I am against your pillows wherewith ye there hunt the souls to make them fly, and I will tear them from your arms, and will let the souls go..."* (Ez. 13:18, 20-21).

"Folk Islam" is an abomination to God. Those that seek after such "powers" in reality are casting the Lord aside, and following after false gods. Muslims by entering into such "black arts" attempt to circumvent God's holy will for their lives. They believe that through the power of these practices the Creator can be coerced. "Popular Islam" is a sad legacy that emanates from a faith that declares that it worships one God. Corruption and idolatry are the true fruit of Islam. Muslims have followed the example of the children of Israel. They too have set up a false calf, and have rushed to bow down and worship it (Ex. 32:1-10).

There is great hope for Ishmael's seed though. Israel despite worshipping a false calf, had an intercessor who loved them: Moses. God heard Moses plea and extended His mercy to Israel

(Ex. 32:11-14). The LORD God will also be merciful to Ishmael's children, for they too have an intercessor who truly loves them: Jesus (Heb. 7:25).

## Those that sit in Darkness

Isaiah prophesies that *"The people that walked in darkness have seen a great light: they that dwell in the land of the shadow of death, upon them hath the light shined"* (Isa. 9:2). This word applies to not just Israel, but to *"Galilee of the nations"* (i.e. the whole world). Muslims that pursue "folk Islam" are in darkness, but Jesus as the true light of the world came to give them freedom. He is the mediator that they are so desperately searching for. It is through Jesus alone, the Father God that they yearn to know, can be approached. For in Jesus the Savior, those captives that sit in darkness will find liberty proclaimed. Those that are bound in occultic prison cells will discover the doors of salvation open wide (Isa. 61:1). Jesus came to set the captives of "folk Islam" free!

---

1.  Rich D. Love "Church Planting Among Folk Muslims" *International Journal of Frontier Missions*,Vol.II #2, Apr.1994, pg. 87.

2.  *Sahih Muslim* Vol. 1, *Al-Salat* CLXXX, #903-907.

3.  Personal testimony, Springfield MO, Aug. 1996.

4.  The Arabic word *majnun* is translated mad or lunatic in English. It literally means *"to be possessed by jinn."*

5.  Muhammad decreed that the diet of *jinn* consisted of *"dried bones and dung"* (*Sahih Al-Bukhari* Vol. 5, #200; *Sahih Muslim,* Vol. 1, *Al-Salat* CLXXX, #903).

6.  *Sahih Muslim*, Vol. 4 *Al-Salam* CMXXXV, #5557, #5559

7.  Ibid. Vol. 4 *Sifat Al-Qiyma Wa'l-Janna Wa'N-Nar* MCLXVII, #6757, #6759. Muhammad also boasted of catching *"a highly wicked jinn"* who had sought to interrupt his prayers. He seized this entity and chained it to one of the pillars in the mosque. The prophet was going to let all his followers look at it, but out of respect for King Solomon he let this creature go free (*Sahih Muslim*, Vol. 1, *Al Salat* CCII, #1104). Apparently, Muhammad "remembered" his own

revelation in the Koran, where *Allah* permitted the *jinn* to assist King Solomon in constructing his mighty works. For these purported "miracles," the Koran states that *"the House of David"* (the Jews) should *"give thanks"* (S. 34: 12-13).

No where does the Bible affirm the existence of such creatures, nor does it speak of any supernatural help outside of God, being given to Solomon. The LORD God in Jeremiah counsels His people to *"Hearken not unto the words of the prophets that prophesy unto you; they make you vain: they speak a vision of their own heart, and not out of the mouth of the LORD"* (Jer. 23:16). The Apostle Paul warns of those who *"...perish: because they received not the love of the truth, that they might be saved. And for this cause God shall send them strong delusion, that they should believe a lie"* (II Thes. 2:10-11). He further advises Christians to *"...shun profane and vain babblings: for they will increase unto more ungodliness. And their word will eat as doth a canker..."* (II Tim. 2:16-17).

8.    Sobri Malek, recorded in *Islam: Introduction and Approach* pgs 141-142.
9.    *Sahih al-Bukhari*, Vol. 2 #157, #158. During this event, the prophet also reported that *"I saw hell and one of its sides was destroying one another. That was when you saw me stepping backwards during the prayer"* (Vol. 1, #713). Muhammad apparently gave a different tale for his actions during this eclipse prayer to Abdullah bin Abbas. This man declared that the messenger of *Allah* "retreated" and then later stated that *"I was shown paradise and wanted to have a bunch of fruit from it. Had I taken it, you would have eaten from it as long as the world remains."* Ibid. Vol. 1 #715.
10.   Ibid. Vol. 2, #160.
11.   *Sahih Muslim* Vol. 3, *As-Salam* CMXVI, #5428.
12.   Muhammad also claimed that he was "bewitched" into imagining he had done a thing when in reality he had not. The prophet declared that this evil deed came *"from the people of the Scriptures"* (Jews and Christians). *Sahih Al-Bukhari* Vol. 4 #400.
13.   Personal testimony given by Valerie Devlin, Niagara Falls, NY, Mar. 1997.
14.   *Sahih Al Bukhari*, Vol. 7 #527.
15.   Ibid. #649.
16.   The LORD God in the Book of Genesis affirms this spiritual "blood cry" for justice. *"What has thou done? The voice of thy brother's blood crieth unto me from the ground"* (Gen. 4:10).

This cry though is to God, not to man. God never approves vengeance on man's part. It is His responsibility (Deut. 32:35; Ps. 94:1; Nah. 1:2; Rom. 12:19; II Thes. 1:7-8). Superstition though, requires that man stay away from these areas due to unnatural death(s) occurring in this (these) place(s). Hence an element of fear is in operation.

The Old Testament laws in Deuteronomy required that a blood sacrifice be offered to God, by the elders of the city nearest where unsolved murders occurred (Deu. 21:1-9). Kenneth McCall (*Healing the Family Tree*) and Dr. Gwen Shaw (*Redeeming the Land*) advocate spiritually cleansing the land from such violent sins through communion: *"the blood of Jesus Christ his Son cleanseth us from all sin"* (I Jn. 1:7)

17. T. Canaan, *"Tasit er-Radifeh"* (Fear Cup) *The Journal Of The Palestine Oriental Society* Vol. III #3,1923, pg. 126.
18. The covering over the *Ka'ba* weighs over 1000 pounds, and is woven annually by some 200 people (*Arkansas Democrat Gazette*, Apr. 7, 1998, pg. 7A.
19. Western culture is also replete with its own brand of superstitions and good luck practices. Christians need to eliminate from their lives such "harmless" habits as: keeping four leaf clovers, holding "lucky" rabbits feet, posting overturned horseshoes, wearing the devil's horn, kissing the Blarney stone, trusting in St. Christopher (statues and medallions in automobiles), reading horoscopes, avoiding black cats, feeling "nervous" on Friday the Thirteenth, and observing Halloween.
20. Personal testimony, Springfield MO, Aug. 1996.
21. Dean Galyen, "Broken Curse" *Mountain Movers*, Vol. 38 #9, Oct. 1996. pg. 28.

# SIXTEEN

## Setting The Captives Free

uslims who dabble in the magical arts, initiate spells, fear the "evil eye" and abide by superstitions are open to the Gospel of Christ. Their very actions demonstrate a dissatisfaction with Orthodox Islam. They are looking for something more than what their religion can give them. Only in Christ though will they find true fulfillment and peace.

Presenting Jesus to Muslims who are caught up in the darkness of "folk Islam" requires much prayer, fasting, discernment, "*agape*" love, faith and a willingness to "want to" on the part of Christians. It is not a ministry for babes, but for seasoned spiritual warriors who place their strength in Christ. This is intense front line combat, waged against the forces of darkness.

Jesus said "*the kingdom of Heaven suffers violence, and the violent take it by force.*" Ministering to Muslims who are involved in occultic practices demands a total spiritual warfare that is intent on destroying all the strongholds of the devil. Satan as the strong man has freely occupied the minds and hearts of Ishmael's progeny. He has blinded them to the Word of God, taught them to hate Christ, caused them to disown the cross, and then seduced them to go whoring after false idols composed of superstitions and spells. United States Marine Corps recruiting posters of World War II displayed a portrait of Uncle Sam which said: "*Wanted a few good*

212

*men.*" Jesus as the Captain of our Salvation is in need of a few good Jehu's, or Barak's and Deborah's in this hour as well, who are willing to enter into the strong man's house and vanquish him. The disciples of Jesus were commissioned by Him, to preach that the kingdom of Heaven was a hand. They were to demonstrate its presence by healing the sick, cleansing the lepers, raising the dead and by casting out devils (Mt. 10:7-8).

The Apostle Paul confronted Elymas "*the sorcerer,*" and being "*filled with the Holy Ghost*" called this man a "*child of the devil,*" and "*enemy of all righteousness.*" Paul prophesied to Elymas that the Lord's hand of judgment was upon him in retribution for his evil deceits and mischief's. Elymas immediately became blind "*for a season*" (Acts 13:6-11). The effects of this power encounter with God brought swift punishment to the sorcerer and caused the deputy of Paphos, Sergius Paulus to believe. The man "*when he saw what was done,*" became persuaded, for he was "*astonished at the doctrine of the Lord*" (vs. 12).

Scripture declares, "*the righteous are as bold as a lion.*" Paul was bold. He was full of the Holy Ghost and discerned that the Lord wanted to have a confrontation with the powers of darkness. Elymas learned that his powers were limited. God allows these assaults against the kingdom of Heaven to happen, to demonstrate that it is His power alone that brings forth the victory. David declares, "*Thy people shall be willing in the day of thy power*" (Ps.110:3). Power encounters make souls willing to forsake sin and embrace God. When Elijah confronted the prophets of Baal, he asked the LORD God to let the people know "*that thou art the LORD God and thou hast turned their heart back again.*" The fire then fell, and when the people saw it "*they fell on their faces: and they said, The LORD, he is the God; the LORD, he is the God*" (I Kgs. 18:39).

Muslims respect power. Their history is one of having swift victories over their enemies. Strength must be demonstrated to

Muslims, for anything else would be less than Islam. Scripture reminds us *"the kingdom of God is not in word, but in power"* (I Cor. 4:20). In evangelizing Muslims who knowingly pursue the "mystical arts," these power experiences with God must occur. When the fire of God falls in their lives, then they will readily abandon their dependence on folk Islam and cleave to Jesus.

## Power Encounters

Power encounters are direct, open confrontations of the kingdom of God against the kingdom of darkness. The Christian who attacks the devil's domain is seeking to recapture territory occupied by Satan. In waging such warfare, the Christian may be called by the Holy Spirit to go on the offensive; or assume a defensive position as Satan counter attacks. Folk Islam is the devil's territory.

It is imperative that Christians realize that we are not at war with Muslims. As believers *"we wrestle not against flesh and blood, but against principalities, against powers, against the rulers of the darkness of this world, against spiritual wickedness in high places"* (Eph. 6:12). Even so, these invisible powers will stir up real confrontations with Muslims who are swayed by their powers. This though should not be viewed with fear, but only as a greater opportunity to advance the kingdom of God. Christian, there is no easy victory. Some Muslims will believe after seeing the finger of God exposed in their lives, which others will reject what God has done (Ex. 8:19; Lk. 11:20). Even so, we must remember, *"the battle is the Lord's"* (I Sam. 17:47). It is He who will give it into our hands.

Paul and Silas successfully cast a spirit of divination out of a young woman who followed them. They had a real power encounter with the kingdom of darkness and won. This victory of God though stirred up more devils. They were accused of exceedingly troubling the city, and teaching *"customs which were not lawful to receive"* (Christianity). The two Apostles were arrested, beat, whipped and then thrown into jail. God though had other plans.

SETTING THE CAPTIVES FREE

He caused another power encounter to happen: an earthquake. These events then caused the jailer and his family to be saved (Acts 16:16-34).

## The Power of Jesus' Name

The following "reports" have been received from the "front lines." They illustrate the authority and power, which the Lord God have given to those that believe in His name. Every knee must bow to Jesus' name and "*every tongue should confess that Jesus Christ is Lord...*" This scriptural promise includes all forms of folk Islam.

## Casting off Serpents

An Ethiopian Bible student reports how God used him to miraculously demonstrate the power of Jesus' name. "Nemgistu" was standing outside a Muslim village intently telling the men sitting in front of him about Jesus. A deadly viper though was hiding in the grass. Unseen, it soon crawled up to "Nemgistu's" leg and wrapped itself around the man's limb three times. The audience was horrified. The snake then attempted to reach for his other leg, so as to bring the evangelist to the ground. "Nemgistu" simply paused in his Gospel message and ordered the snake to "*Go, in Jesus' name!*" The serpent immediately uncoiled itself and slithered back into the grass. The audience was astonished. Their interest in Jesus was now magnified. The absolute overwhelming power of His name fascinated them. They were ready to believe.[1] Power encounters against the kingdom of darkness remove the stones of unbelief from the soil of men's hearts.

## Delivered from the Power of Darkness

An Indonesian Muslim named Subawi became a Christian after much searching. He was always asking questions relating to the significance of life. The local mullah grew increasing exasperated with Subawi, and finally told him to look on the bookshelf in his office and find and answer there. Subawi discovered a Bible and found Jesus. Empowered with a new faith, he shared the "good news" with his family. Subawi's mother received the Word with joy. She immediately abandoned her superstitions, magical formulas and reliance on the village shaman. This man could see into the future, but was unable to speak about her fate after death. Even Subawi's brother believed, but his own wife opposed this new faith. She grew increasing hostile to the madness called Christianity. Then, an evil spirit moved into their home. Subawi's wife recognized it, but still refused to believe in Jesus. This spirit reeked of death. It would travel from room to room in the house, emitting a foul odor. Subawi knew when it would come in, and would rebuke it in Jesus' name. This entity would then leave. Even so, this power to cast out devils in Jesus' name did not convince his wife. She remained obstinate, until a neighbor requested healing prayer for a son who was crippled. Subawi prayed in Jesus' name and the boy was healed before their eyes. The wife was impressed, but still unwilling to change. Later, his sister came by for prayer. She had several skin growths on her face, which had become infected. The woman was in need of surgery. Subawi again prayed for healing and his sister was cured right before his wife's eyes. When this happened, the wife gloriously yielded her heart to Jesus and embraced Christianity. There is now a church in Subawi's Muslim village.[2]

## Close Encounters with God

Miracles are also power encounters. They do not always involve confrontations with the kingdom of darkness though. These divine manifestations are rather, sovereign demonstrations of the Lord's power. Muslims in seeing these heavenly proofs; may unilaterally forsake their superstitions and charms and embrace Jesus.

## Rain in the Desert

Open Doors Ministry reports how a young man walked into the Bible Society bookstore in Amman and asked for an Arabic Bible. The clerk could tell from his accent that the customer was from Saudi Arabia. He also knew that Saudi's were forbidden to possess Bibles. Anyone who owned one of these forbidden books could easily find himself accused of apostasy, and liable to execution by beheading. So the salesman asked the young man, *"Why do you want to have one?"* *"I am a Christian,"* the man replied. *"How can a Saudi be a Christian?"* the clerk asked. The Saudi then told him this testimony:

> *I heard about the Christian faith through the radio, and thought about it for a long time. I had serious doubts, but prayed to God: 'If it is true that you have a Son who died for our sins, let it rain this week.' I made it very difficult for Him, because I have never seen it rain in Riyadh in August. The following day there was a downpour. All the traffic was disrupted. Now I want to have a Bible, so I can learn more about God and His Son.*[3]

## The Gift of Tongues

A pastor from Ethiopia testifies how the miraculous power of God came upon him as he was praying. He had been preaching in Sudan and was visiting a home in one of the villages. Here, he was able to meet with a group of Muslims to share the gospel. During this time, he saw that there was a man seated in the corner of the room who had not spoken. The gathering ended, but the pastor felt he should pray. He asked for and was given permission to do so. The Spirit of God then came over him and he began to speak in other tongues. The evangelist though did not realize that he was speaking in the language of the man who was sitting in the corner. He also did not know that that man was crippled.

217

This man suddenly jumped up. He started *"walking, leaping and praising God."* He then told everyone there that this man of God had said to him in his own mother tongue: *"Jesus of Nazareth will heal you if you will stand to your feet."* The man had done so and immediately found himself perfectly healed. All the people in the house then began to worship God for this great miracle. They went outside and quickly spread the news about how God had healed this man who had been lame.

As a result, forty-five Muslims in the village accepted Jesus as their Savior. Even the iman embraced Christ. The local mosque became a meeting place for Christians, since most of the people in the village had converted to Christianity.[4] The Apostle Paul writes that *"...tongues are for a sign, not to them that believe, but to them that believe not "* (I Cor. 14:22).

### A Miraculous Catch

Omar, a missionary to the African nation of Mali, speaks of how God answered the prayer of a Muslim's heart. The man was a fisherman who earned his living on the lakes nearby. He had heard Omar teach about Jesus in his village. The missionary had gone from village to village holding "informational" meetings about the contents of the Bible. The man had attended one of these lessons and had learned that Jesus associated with fishermen.

The next time the Muslim fisherman went back onto the lake, he formed a prayer on his lips. *"Jesus, I have heard that you worked with fishermen, and that you told your disciples where to fish. They did as you said and brought in a catch so large, their nets were breaking. Lord if you are truly the Son of God, then give me a catch of fish like that"*

The man had no sooner voiced this prayer, and then his nets begin to swell and overflow with fish. He could hardly pull the creatures into his boat. He became a Christian that day, and then told the missionary about it. Omar was able to instruct this new convert in the faith.[5]

## Conquering the Hosts of Hell

The Christian who desires to be empowered of God so as to wrestle devils and win, needs to follow some simple directions. Expect the fire of God to fall when:

### 1. Prayer has first gone forth

Prayer is preparation. If the Christian desires to face devils and drive them out, then prayer to the Lord must be a priority. Strongholds of darkness cannot be pulled down with human strength or brilliance. It must take a supernatural work of God. Prayer is your order form to God, requesting assistance. Joshua was empowered to do mighty works for the Lord because he spent time before him (Ex. 33:11). Jesus knew the Father's desires because He prayed. Prayer has been called "inner fire." If we want to see the outer fire of God fall and bulwarks of folk Islam tumble, we must first seek to have this inner fire within us.

### 2. Holiness is your plea

We serve a holy God, who cannot bear sin. Christians are to be holy as He is holy. Samson lost the power of God because he preferred the pleasures of iniquity. Sin that is not dealt with in our lives will quench the presence of God from appearing in Muslim's lives. Iniquity drains the anointing.

### 3. You have afflicted your soul

Fasting demolishes the strongholds of Satan. The Lord in Isaiah declares that His chosen fast will loose the bands of wickedness, undo heavy burdens, let the oppressed go free and break ever yoke. Light shall break forth and the glory of the Lord shall be your reward (Is. 58:5-8). Fasting prepares your soul for successful encounters against the powers of darkness. Daniel "mourned" for three weeks and the *"prince of the kingdom of Persia crumbled"* (Dan. 10:2-3,13).

## 4. You discern God's time and method

The men of the tribe of Issachar were knowledgeable of the times and seasons (I Chr. 12:32). Discernment of what the Lord requires in a situation is vital. Is the Spirit of God moving you to topple idols or speak forth love? Is it time for a prayer walk or a wall-buckling Jericho march? Do you face your opponent now or in three days? Is the meeting you are going to, a trap or an open door? A sensitivity to the Spirit of God is absolutely essential when confronting the powers of darkness.

There was a time when Jesus rejected the disciple's idea of having a power encounter. He refused to call down vengeance on the Samaritan village that rejected His presence. Rather, he counseled that *"the Son of man* (did) *not come to destroy men's lives, but to save them"* (Lk. 9:56).

## 5. You possess an *agape* Love

An *agape* love is like no other love. It an be defined as love which is "stretched out." An *agape* love is a Godly love. It will persevere despite rejection, and hatred. Against the venom of all the hosts of hell, *agape* love will triumph. Jesus' loved His persecutors so much he forgave them. He loved so much that He stretched forth His arms and let them crucify Him to a cross. He loved humankind so much that He died for us all. The fire of God will fall when you minister in *agape* love.

### 6. You can lay hold of a Holy Ghost Boldness to move in Faith

Boldness will take you to the very throne room of God (Heb. 4:16). Here the Christian will "find grace to help in time of need." David courageously fought the bear and the lion before he faced Goliath. He had a cause and the Lord was with him (I Sam. 17:29, 18:14). Boldness will give you a backbone to have a fear-defying faith. You can look into the eye of any devil and he will flinch. One Islamic convert has become an effective evangelist among Muslims by bolding confronting his accusers with these words: *"You do not believe that Jesus is the Son of God. I challenge you to pray to Him and say that if you are the Son of God, hear and answer my prayer."* [6]

### 7. You have a willingness to walk in Christ's footsteps

Jesus ministered to slaves and centurions, Jews and Gentiles, lepers and tax collectors. He confronted demons and madmen, fallen women and righteous Pharisees. Our Lord traveled to Samaria and into the borders of Tyre to cast forth devils. *"He could not be hid"* (Mk. 7:24-30). He walked to the cross. The Christian who ministers to Muslims must have a willingness to love and a readiness to face persecution.

I had a dream in the midst of writing this book, that as the author of it, I would like to share:

My wife and I were in a line of people. It was no ordinary queue. The defenders of Islam were cutting heads off and I was next to feel the sword's breath. I saw the woman in front of me being beheaded. The sword that they were using was dull. She was suffering and I was afraid. Then it was my turn and as I stepped forward to the block, I was awakened by my wife who was sleeping next to me. She had heard my cries. As I awoke, this

**221**

vision still in view, I heard the voice of the Lord say, *"and they loved not their lives unto the death"*

The servant and handmaiden of the Lord in reaching out to Muslims must be willing to love *"not their lives unto the death."* When you are a willing vessel for the Lord, know this: the fire of God will fall.

### After the Fire Falls

When mighty signs and wonders happen and Muslims cry out, *"This is the Lord,"* then the Christian must:

### 1. Give the Glory to God

Publicly acknowledge before your audience that this act was of God. Give the LORD praise and tell those present, it was God who was for their deliverance, healing or salvation. Isaiah praises the Lord declaring: *"I will exalt thee, I will praise thy name; for thou hast done wonderful things"* (Isa. 25:1).

### 2. Proclaim Jesus Christ

A public demonstration of God's power may not be enough to win Muslims to Christ. Miracles and power encounters do offer heaven-sent opportunities to present the Gospel. Simon, a certain man who *"used sorcery and bewitched the people of Samaria"* believed and was baptized after *"beholding the miracles and signs which were done"* (Acts 8:4-13). Later, Simon had to repent for his wickedness of heart (vss. 22-24).

### 3. Move through the Door of Opportunity

When the fire of God falls, it is the hour to ask for a decision. The children of Israel were challenged by Joshua to *"choose you this day whom ye will serve"* (Jos 24:15). Ask Muslims to make a decision now: Jesus or Islam?

Do not hesitate; souls for the kingdom of God are in the balance. It is not the hour either, for them to halt "*between two opinions.*" Do not let them say: "*We will hear thee again of this matter*" (Acts 17:32).

### 4. Direct Them to Believers

Muslims who convert are in danger physically and spiritually. A Muslim who embraces Christianity under the laws of Islam is judged guilty of apostasy. The penalty is death, for the convert has committed treason "*within his heart*" against the Islamic "*kingdom of heaven.*" [7]

Christians who minister to these new converts must counsel them. Speak to these new believers and tell them that they may have to pay a price of suffering to walk in this newfound faith (Heb. 10:38; 11:35-40). Inform them to be wise with whom they share this "good news." Nicodemus, a Pharisee and ruler of the Jews came to Christ at night. He became a follower of Jesus but did it quietly and secretly (Jn. 3:1; 19:39).

The Christian who evangelizes these new believers also has a responsibility to not abandon these new sheep. Direct your "converts" to a place where they can meet like-minded believers and be spiritually nurtured. Realize that in many cases, local believers in Muslim lands fear new converts or shy away from accepting them. They are wary of spies and deceivers who persecute the fellowship, so a time of testing may be in store for the new believer.

### Gates of Hell Ministry

Ministering to those who follow the "tenets" of folk Islam has another facet besides confrontation. This is reaching out and

223

recovering those who are lost. Many of "folk Islam's" disciples are hurting victims and slaves of fear.

C.T. Studd, a pioneering missionary to Africa, India and China once voiced his conviction on the matter of saving souls. *"Some seek wealth and some seek fame, but as for me; give me a mission shop with in a yard of hell."* Muslims who practice these dark arts are in many cases not far from the fires of hell. The Lord though is calling in this hour, for lionhearted volunteers who are willing to pluck captives from these fires. It is a time for Christians to say, *"Here am I Lord, send me."*

Sometimes Christians expect God to show forth His power with mighty signs and wonders, when all that is needed is a little love. Muslims who are caught up in enchantments and sorcery's need to be reassured of God's love and His ever-present protection. This is mission shop work.

Tell them how Jesus spoke about the fear of the "evil eye." The Lord stated, *"when thine eye is evil, thy body also is full of darkness"* (Lk. 11:34). Christians are to *"Take heed...that the light which is in thee be not darkness"* (vs. 35). Jesus also counseled his disciples to be not afraid, but to *"fear him, which after he hath killed hath power to cast into hell..."* (Lk. 12:5). The power of God is immeasurably stronger than the forces that emanate from the evil eye. Share with your Muslim friends the beauty of God's promises for safekeeping in Psalms 91. David declares that those who make the LORD God their habitation will find that: *"There shall no evil befall thee, neither shall any plague come nigh thy dwelling."* Psalms 44 also speaks of the protection of God. The Psalms, or *Zabur*, as they are known in Islam, are accepted as revealed scriptures by Muslims.

Mission shop work is not glorious, but it is richly rewarded in heaven. A mission shop near the gates of hell is an oasis of life. It could be your home, your apartment, or just a willingness to listen to a Muslim talk. To run a mission shop ministry at the gates of hell, the Christian will need plenty of *agape* love, rivers of living water, and a hellfire extinguishing anointing from the Holy Ghost guaranteed to set captives free.

1.    "From Village to Village" *Mountain Movers*, Vol. 38 #9 Oct. 1996, pgs 16-17. ("Nemgistu's" name has been changed, for his protection)
2.    *I Just Saw Jesus,* Paul Eshleman, pgs. 118-119.
3.    *Open Doors Ministry*, Special Report 1996
4.    Reported by *Intercede,* May 1995, pg. 5; *Mountain Movers,* Oct. 1996 pg. 17; and *Herald of His Coming,* Nov. 1996, pg.11.
5.    Personal Testimony, Tegucigalpa, Honduras Feb. 1997.
6.    J. Christy Wilson Jr., "The Experience of Praying for Muslims" Muslims and Christians on the Emmaus Road, pg. 333.
7.    See *Surah* 4:89, Women *"and if they desert you, then seize them and put them to death wherever you find them"* and *Surah* 3:85, The Imrans, *"Whoso seeks a religion other than Islam, it will not be accepted of him and he will be a loser in the hereafter."* Note also *Sahih Muslim*, Vol. 3, *Al-Qasama* DCLXXIII, #4152.

# SEVENTEEN

# Hagar's Legacy

Hagar's legacy for her daughters is one of tears. Abraham's maid wept in the desert and cried tears of anger, rejection, loneliness, fear and inferiority (Gen. 21:16). Abraham, the father of her child, had cast her forth. She was destitute, homeless and in danger of death. The wails of this Egyptian slave girl echoed across the empty desert wilderness. Her son, Ishmael would also surely die before the day was ended. Was there any hope?

Hagar still weeps today in the guise of millions of Islamic women. They are the "soft target" of Islam restricted by Koranic bonds and Sharia laws. They weep for the injustices done to their lives in the name of religion. They perish, for the hope of a better future has been denied them.

Hagar's cries were speedily answered though by the God of all hope. He had heard her prayers and assured her to "*fear not.*" Ishmael would live. This *Jehovah Jirah* sent Hagar a great deliverance in the form of living waters. This same God today will not deny the tears of her descendants. Their cries will be heard and great deliverance will also be their inheritance. The well of living water is not far from their eyes, if they but reach out in prayer they will see Jesus standing near their heart, with living waters to drink.

## Women in Islamic Society

Women are seen by Islam as being created equally by *Allah,* but having a different role to fulfill in life. The male is favored though and granted superiority by this god. *"Men are in charge of women, because Allah has made one of them to excel the other and because they spend of their property to support women"* (S. 4:34, Women). The women are valued in Islamic society for being homemakers and nurturers of the family. Freedoms that other non-Islamic women have are forbidden or severely restricted. Culture and Islamic law denies women the right to drive, or leave home without a male escort. They can be freely beaten, readily divorced, and even murdered in the name of *Allah.* Education is discouraged, therefore interest and practice in the occult is common. The women of Islam desperately need the light of Christ to deliver them out of the darkness of their lives. They are the hidden key to reaching the Muslim world.

## Koranic Rights

The Koran contains a whole *Surah* entitled "Women," although only a portion of it pertains to gender rights. They can inherit property, even though the share they receive will be lesser than a man's. Women can possess their own wealth, and have the right to be supported. They can give testimony in court, but their declaration is judged by the Koran to equal half of a man's word.

*Allah* places more restrictions on this sex than blessings. Men are instructed to look upon their women as fields, which need to be cultivated. They are to go to this field, as they will (S. 2:23). The male sex is commanded to admonish, banish and even whip their women, until they become obedient (S. 4:34).[1] This "holy" book orders men to confine women who are thought guilty of *"lewdness"* in *"houses unto death"* (S. 4:15). The man can also freely take of other wives *"two, three or four"* and as many *"slave girls"* as he desires. The male is also granted permission to freely divorce his mate, if she does not meet his approval or needs.

A woman can even be denied her childhood. Pre-adolescent marriages are acceptable and commonly practiced. Brides as young as six-years old are given in marriage. One hadith speaks "glowingly" of a woman who was a grandmother by twenty-one.[2] She had been married off at the advanced age of nine and then had a daughter who also was wedded young. This child bride then presented her 21-year old mother, a granddaughter.

Girls are not cherished in Islam, but thought of as "somebody's else's wealth." [3] Money spent on a female child is considered wasted, as it will only benefit the one who marries her. Father's have been known to "trade off " their daughters in exchange for another wife. Girls are also traditionally weaned earlier and given less to eat in Muslim households, in order to allow the "honored son(s)" a greater portion.

### The Hadiths

The recorded sayings of Muhammad further encroach upon the "freedoms" of Islamic women. Here outright feelings of mistrust and hatred are voiced in the name of the prophet. Wholesale condemnations are leveled against women. Islam is consumed with sexuality. Women are blamed for being the cause of these torments. One hadith proclaims, *"When a woman goes outside of the house, the devil welcomes her."* [4] To prevent this temptation, Abassi Madan, a leader in the fundamentalist Algerian Islamic Salvation Front, recommends that a woman should be permitted to leave home only *"when she is born, when she is married, and when she goes to the cemetery."* [5] Those who do venture forth must be veiled in a *burkah* from head to foot, lest any of their body parts allure a man to sin. This is a common belief held throughout the Islamic world.

A woman missionary to Pakistan gives another explanation why Muslim men desire to keep their women hidden. It is not to deny their rights of freedom or liberation. Bonnie Stoddard reports, "*the whole feeling of keeping women behind four walls and a veil is that it is for her protection because she is so loved. It is the poor Western women whose men don't care for them.*" [6] This love argument is another common excuse, which many Muslims use to justify the veiling and hiding of women. Many Muslim women also welcome veiling, saying that this covering allows them even more freedom to move about unhindered and not be noticed.

## Sexual Harassment

Unfortunately, veiling does not protect the Muslim woman from sexual harassment. Many Muslim men chose to ignore Koranic restrictions and societal mores and seek ways to express their sexual desires. Men willingly touch, pinch and even grope women in Mid-Eastern streets and markets. Rubbing one's hands against a woman's body is another common practice that occurs in most Muslim cities. There is scarcely a woman who cannot say she has not been touched. Some men even try to put their hands inside the veil. "*If a man is caught doing this he is beaten, often badly. But if he is not caught, he will boast about his exploits in the shuk with pride, like a hunter bragging about his trophies.*"[7] Few condemn such behavior.

## Man is more Perfect

The traditions further decree that man is more perfect than woman in creation, intelligence and in religion. Muhammad once declared to a group of women: "*I have not seen any one more deficient in intelligence and religion that you. A cautious sensible man could be led astray by some of you.*" [8] These women asked the great prophet for "proof" of this truth. He mentioned a Koranic verse that *Allah* had revealed where the evidence of two women equals the witness of one man. Then, he brought in *Allah's* restriction that *"a woman can neither pray nor fast during her menses."* [9] This was evidence of their deficiency. Unfortunately, this belief has persisted for the past thirteen hundred years. This misogyny occurs throughout the sacred traditions of Islam. Women are *"like a rib."* [10] Their character is crooked and therefore, they cannot be trusted by men. The prophet additionally decreed, *"A nation which makes a woman their ruler will never succeed "*[11] The prophet for all his love (lust) of women, also freely defamed their gender: *"There is no calamity more harmful to men than women."* [12]

Circumcision is practiced throughout Islamic countries. Young boys and girls go through this passage. This rite is thought to test the manliness and courage of the boy who undergoes it. He is thereby honored by the community. The girl's circumcision is carried out in privacy, and is done to reduce her sexual desires, thus preventing illicit premarital relations. This "operation" often entails the complete removal of the female's external genital parts. It is an art is normally performed by barbers, plumbers and women *mubazziras* who specialize in these "cuttings." The results are devastating, bringing upon these girls, severe mental shock, numerous urinary/uterine infections, difficult marital relations and even death in childbirth. It is a practice though which many Muslims consider to be an indispensable prerequisite for marriage.

## Marriage Customs

The Hadith's decree that a marriage outside of Islam becomes invalidated, if either person in this relationship later converts to the faith. *"The wife is regarded as divorced and the husband has no right to keep her as a wife."* [13] If the married couple both converts, then a new marriage must be performed. Furthermore, if the woman rejects Islam, she will automatically lose the custody of the children. The man can exercise his right in this new union to prohibit the woman from caring for her child(ren) from a previous marriage. Islamic law also contradicts itself by allowing male

Muslims to marry non-believers: Christian and Jewish women. The Muslim woman cannot exercise a choice. Her marriage will be arranged. She must marry a Muslim. The Christian or Jewish woman though who marries a Muslim man, can lose custody of the children, if he observes her taking the them to church or the synagogue, feeding them unclean foods (hot-dogs, bologna, or any foods containing lard), or giving them wine.

A woman can obtain paradise if she is obedient to her husband's wishes. If she dares to disobey his wishes for an instant, *Allah* will throw her into the lowest parts of hell, except she repents. Complete obedience means that if a husband desires his wife and she is busy cooking, the food must be left to burn. [14] His pleasure is not to be denied, even for an instant. The Hadith declares that the angels will turn against the wife, if she tarries.

## Polygamy

Polygamous relationships also place additional stresses on Islamic marriages. Wives find themselves haunted by fears that their husbands might take a second wife. [15] The husband in such a relationship usually favors his new wife and ignores the other, if he can. Further aggravations occur when these customs are brought into Western countries.

The "benefits" of having a polygamous marriage are readily seen through the comments of Moustafa Djaara, a construction worker from Mali. He recently married a third wife and brought her "home" to his apartment, located in a suburb near Paris. Here, the new bride found herself greeted by Moustafa's two other pregnant wives and his nine children. Moustafa when interviewed declared that polygamy is hard for a husband. His wives fight a lot, and he has to work, besides do all the shopping. He shops because as a man, Moustafa must control all the money. Even so, he wants another wife, because his father did it, as well as his grandfather, *"So why shouldn't I? When my wife is sick and I don't have anoth-*

*er, who will care for me?"* Besides, *"One wife on her own is trouble. When there are several, they are forced to be polite and well behaved. If they misbehave, you threaten that you'll take another wife."* [16]

Dr. Muhammad Al-Masir, an academic cleric from Egypt's Al-Azhar University defends the Islamic practice of taking multiple wives. He states:

> *Some people claim that polygamy harms the rights and honor of women, although the second or third wife is also a woman! In the days of the Prophet, not even one woman remained without a husband - not a spinster, nor a widow, nor a divorcee. I ask our women and daughters not to be egotistical.* [17]

Other proponents of polygamy insist that a justification of this practice is not needed. Qatari Sheikh Walid bin Hadi rationalizes polygamy as a solution to overcome barrenness, demographic gender inequalities, and adultery and as a way to increase the birth rate. He explains that in the final analysis, every man has his own reasons. *"The Prophet said: 'Do not ask a husband why he beats his wife'...According to the same principle, 'Do not ask a husband why he takes a second wife."* [18]

This eagerness to approve of polygamous marriages is not found throughout all Muslim societies. Many of the common proverbs in Islamic countries, warn against entering into these kinds of relationships. A Malaysian bit of wisdom states *"A man who has two wives under one roof has two tigers in a cage."* Another piece of advice comes from Afghanistan: *"He who likes quarrels at home contracts two marriages."* King Solomon embraced sorrow after sorrow for engaging in this practice. Scripture records *"that his wives turned away his heart after other gods: and his heart was not perfect with the LORD his God"* (I Kgs. 11:4). Experience is a wise teacher.

232

## Honor Killings

Muslim women, especially those from the Middle East, also have to contend with the pressures of honor. Other members of the family carefully monitor their habits, dress and words. If a woman's actions cause embarrassment, then her own life will be at risk. Sometimes such violations can be trivial. A 15 year-old Jordanian girl was stoned to death by her brother. He had seen her *"walking towards a house where young boys lived alone."* [19] In another report, a 15 year old Jordanian boy strangled his 14 year-old younger sister with a telephone cord, while she was talking on the phone. The boy believed his sister was involved with a man, thus shaming the family. An autopsy revealed that she was a virgin.[20]

The nation of Jordan as well as Israel attempts to record these crimes. Jordan's official statistics reveal that such crimes lead to the death of some 25 women yearly. The U.S. State Department though estimates the annual number at about 100.[21] *The Washington Post* reports that at least 200 women and girls are killed in Turkey, each year by family members. Since these crimes often go unreported, this number is likely much higher. These crimes also occur with frequency in other Islamic nations including Egypt, Pakistan, the Palestine Authority, India and even the United States.[22] Worldwide, the United Nations documents that as many as 5,000 women and girls were murdered in the year 2000, by family members. Many of these victims were killed for the "dishonor" of having been raped or divorced.[23]

One example is found in the story of Lal Jamilla, a 16 year-old Pakistani girl from the mountain village of Kohat. She was repeatedly raped and held for two days in a squalid hotel located in the frontier town of Parachinar, not far from the Afghanistan border. A junior clerk who worked in the local Department of Agriculture had kidnapped her. When her ordeal had ended, Lal Jamilla made her way back home. Here, the elders of the village heard of her "crime" and decided that only her death would restore the tribe's honor. Lal

Jamilla was then dragged from her home and shot in front of a large crowd. [24] The man who was found guilty of this offense was temporarily kept in police custody, *"for his own protection."* [25]

## *Ird* and *Sharaf*

Muslim culture defines "honor" differently in regards to the male and female genders. Men possess a non-sexual honor, which is one's *sharaf.* This honor is flexible and can be acquired, lessened, or regained, depending on a man's behavior (bravery, hospitality, and generosity). A woman's honor or *ird* is fixed, absolute and unchangeable for life. It is a measure of her proper conduct. She is born with it, grows up with it, and must die with it. It is her duty to preserve her *ird.*

A sexual offense, or accusation, however slight can cause this *ird* to be irretrievably forfeited. Even if a woman is attacked and raped, her honor *ird* is lost forever. It is the responsibility of the woman and her parental family (father, brothers, or her father's brother) to protect her *ird* at all times. Outdoors she must be veiled, and chaperoned in order not to give offense. Indoors, the woman must be guarded within her home *(harim)*, lest any visiting male stranger cause her to glance at him and thus lose this *ird.*

A woman who has lost her *ird* has destroyed the *sharaf* (male honor) of her parent's family. According to Islamic ethics, the only way of repairing this "damage" is for her paternal family to put her to death, or for her to commit suicide.[26] A husband cannot accept responsibility, for that would give him control in this situation and thus weaken the power of her family over its members. The honor of the family must be protected, even at the cost of her own life. Safety for the woman is found in bearing sons. These men can rise up and defend her.[27]

## *Saana*

The story of "Saana," a young 18-year old bride is another sad testimony. This Muslim girl was from a small "West Bank" village under rule of the Palestine Authority. She was married to an older man who she did not love. The marriage had been arranged and "Saana" had no choice. This was to be her lifetime mate. The man though, soon tired of her as a bride. He began to beat and abuse her. Life was hell, and "Saana" could not bear the daily physical torment. Three times she fled from her husband, choosing to run back to her family's home. Each time though, that "Saana" made an appearance there, her father or one of her brothers would dutifully escort the young girl to her husband's home. Finally in desperation, "Saana" ran away again. This time she found shelter with a group of friends in the Arab town of Tulkarm. The husband though informed her family that she was missing. A search was initiated for the absent newlywed. Six hours later, they found "Saana" and physically dragged her back home.

One of her brothers though had had enough of her foolish behavior. He felt "Saana" had shamed the family by her actions. The family's honor had to be restored. This brother then killed "Saana." No one in the village protested this murder. It was accepted and the man was praised for his action. He had saved the family name. [28]

## Spiritual Standing

A Muslim woman, because of her gender will only have a faint chance of making paradise. The prophet in one of his divine revelations said *"I stood at the door of hell, and observed that the majority of its occupants were women."* [29] This particular hadith is found in three separate volumes in Bukhari's collection.[30] Muhammad also declared that *Allah* had shown him that women were consigned to hell for being ungrateful to their husbands, and for not appreciating the good deeds which were done for them.

Women are also identified as being the chief disrupters of prayer. If they, or "*a dog or ass*" happen to pass in front of "*a worshiper,*" the prayer of that supplicant is invalidated.[31] Another hadith recommends that women pray in their own homes.[32] Other hadiths grant permission for women to go to the mosque for prayer, but not at night so "*that they may not be caught in evil.*" [33]

## Second Class Citizens or Daughters of the King?

This brief overview of Muslim women can only touch some of the heartbreaks of their lives. It is true though that many Muslim men do deeply cherish their wives, and treat their children with love. The vast scope of Islam also finds women within it who have more freedoms. Overall though the self-image of Muslim women is poor. They are clearly held by men to be of lesser worth. The patriarchal society that they live in regularly condemns them.

The LORD God though has not forgotten these Hagars. Jesus, His Son is the well of living water that they need to drink of in order to live. Muslim women today are the modern day equivalent of the woman by the well. Men had rejected her, but she still boldly asked the man by the well for a drink of this living water. Jesus showed her that He was the living water. This woman then became the first missionary. She told an entire city about this man: "*Come, see a man, which told me all things I ever did: Is not this the Christ?* " Muslim women are in this position. God can use them as His messengers.

A woman missionary to the Arab nations relates that many of these Muslim women "*live lives full of fear.*" She was able to share the Christian message with some though. They were attracted to it, despite the risk. Love was the force that drew them closer. A God, who loved them, with a love that they had never known. "*Then suddenly their eyes are open to Jesus Christ, the God of love. They don't know a God of love. They only know fear. And love is such a powerful force.*" [34]

Jesus loved women with a perfect Godly love. Muslim women need to hear this good news. He never condemned or even stoned the woman caught in adultery. He let the prostitute wipe his feet with her hair. He spoke parables about women; invited children to come to him, and even had women disciples (Lk. 8:2-3). As Savior, Jesus always uplifted this gender. He never treated women as sex objects, nor did he despise them.

The woman who dared to touch Jesus' garment was healed of her disease. The Lord in the midst of the crowd felt her touch. He turned around, and upon seeing her said; *"Daughter, be of good comfort "* (Matt. 9:22). She, who others would have rejected and called unclean was freely, accepted by him, Jesus publicly honored this woman and called her a daughter. She was in his eyes, a daughter of the LORD God. This is the Gospel message that Muslim women need to hear. They may be unloved, threatened or hidden away by men on earth, but they can reach out to Jesus. He will accept, comfort and honor them as Daughters of the King of kings and Lord of lords.

---

1. *"Different Islamic scholars have given their own interpretations on wife-beating. Some rule out the breaking of bones, and stress that in no case should the beating be accompanied with* "verbal assault." *The Islamic rulings section of the Palestinian Authority's daily newspaper forbids stabbings. There is a consensus that the husband should avoid leaving bruises to his wife's body, and all scholars agree that wife-beating is the husband's last resort. Still, it is recommended when a couple finds itself on the verge of divorce: "it is better for the husband to beat his wife a little, to make her feel she was wrong, than to destroy the family through divorce."* Quotation from "Honor Murders-Why the Perps Get off Easy" by Yotam Feldner, *The Middle East Media Research Center*, www.memri.org.

2. *Sahih Al-Bukhari*, Vol. 3 #831.
3. Jan Goodwin, *Price of Honor*, pg. 44 (An examination of the state of Muslim women in the Islamic world).
4. *Sahih Muslim*, Vol. 2 *Al-Nikah DXL*, #3240.

5.  *Middle East Intelligence Digest,* Feb. 1995 pg. 5.
6.  LaDonna Witmer "Muslim Women" *WherEver* (TEAM), Spr. 1997, pgs. 4-5.
7.  *Middle East Times,* Egypt, May 3, 2002.
8.  *Sahih Al-Bukhari,* Vol. 1#301; Vol. 3 #826
9.  Ibid.
10. Ibid. Vol. 7 #113
11. Ibid. Vol. 9 #219
12. Ibid. Vol. 7 #33
13. Ibid. Vol. 7 #210
14. *Mishkat Al-Masabih*

15. Supporters of polygamy argue that this custom helps prevent many social problems such as infidelity. Supposedly this tradition, provides an acceptable remedy for men who are married to infertile wives as well as caring for women left destitute. An Egyptian woman psychiatrist Nawal al-Saadawi confided to Reuters that women spoke to her of having dreams of murdering their husbands and/or the other wife (*Middle East Times,* Cairo Jan. 4, 2002). The Koran states that a man can marry up to four wives, as long as he treats them equally. It then states that this is an impossibility.

16. "France Moves to Ban Immigrant Polygamy," *Chicago Tribune,* Jan. 28, 1996, pg. 4.
17. "The Wisdom of Polygamy: Islamic Clerics Explain the Rationale" *The Middle East Media Research Institute, Inquiry and Analysis* No. 82, Feb 8, 2002.
18. Ibid, *Al Rai* (Qatar), Jan. 5, 2002.
19. " 'Honor' Murders-Why the Perps Get Off Easy" by Yotam Feldner, *Middle East Media Research Institute.*
20. Independent Media Review Analysis, Feb. 25, 2000, www.imra.org.il.
21. *The Washington Post,* Feb. 2, 2000
22. *"Honor murders in the United States are not always severely punished. In Cleveland Ohio, two male cousins of Methal Dayem were accused of killing the 21 year old woman with seven bullets for living too much like an American. One of them had his case dismissed for lack of evidence and the other was acquitted"* (Comments by *MEMRI* citing *Chicago Tribune,* July 26, 2000)
23. *Intercede,* May/June 2002, pg. 3.
24. "Many Pakistanis question lack of rights for raped, abused women" Jason Burke, *London Observer Service,* April 20, 1999.

25. Ibid, pg. 2.

26. Islamic ethics and cultural norms dictate severe actions, when a woman's honor is thought to have been violated. Tarrad Fayiz, a Jordanian tribal leader says *"A woman is like a olive tree. When its branch catches woodworm, it has to be chopped off so that society stays clean and pure."* " 'Honor' Murders-Why the Perps Get off Easy"by Yotam Feldner *The Middle East Media Research Institute.*.

27. For additional insights on this subject see: *The Arab Mind* by Raphael Patai, Scribner's & Sons, New York, 1973.

28. "Blood and Honor" *Middle East Intelligence Digest,* Feb. 1995, pg. 4.

29. *Sahih Muslim,* Vol. 4 *Al-Riqaq* MCXL, #6596-6000.

30. *Sahih Al-Bukhari,* Vol. 2 #161, Vol. 7 #124, Vol. 8 #554.

31. *Sahih Muslim,* Vol. 1 *Al-Salat* CXCII, #1032-1034, 1038.

32. Ibid. Vol. 1 *Al-Salat* CLXXVII, #891.

33. Ibid. #888.

34. Betty Stoddard "Muslim Women" *WherEver* (TEAM), Spr. 1997, pg. 4.

# EIGHTEEN

## Daughters of the King

The daughters of Ishmael are royalty, for they descend from a princely line. Ishmael's twelve sons were princes *"according to their nations."* Yet this regal ancestry has given them little joy, and faint hope for a better future. Most of Ishmael's daughters are in captivity. Their fate is one of hardship, ignorance, and complete submission to the laws of Islam. These women desperately need to know their inheritance in Christ. They need to meet King Jesus. He "who is able" can give them a far better reward and royal heritage than what the "blessings" of Ishmael have brought.

### "Come All Who Are Heavily Laden…"

The Lord in His majesty sometimes chooses to reveal himself sovereignly to these abandoned daughters, ministering life to their wounded souls.

A young Egyptian woman named "Samir" found herself the victim of abuse from her husband's daily beatings. Her family would not take her back. Desperate, she contacted another couple in Cairo who were just acquaintances, for help. She knew they were Christians, but "Samir," a Muslim had nowhere else to go. Could they give her shelter? The couple agreed, and offered her a place until the crisis was resolved. She met them, and was pleased to learn that they had an extra apartment, which they owned. It was located directly below theirs and had been used for prayer meetings.

"Samir" moved into this sanctuary and was relived to be away from the stresses of her life. The first night as she was sitting in the living room, she saw a kingly figure appear on the wall in front of her. The apparition held a golden cup in one hand and a loaf of bread in the other. He then extended his arms to her and beckoned for her to come and drink from the cup and eat of the bread.

When this happened, "Samir" bolted from the room and ran out of the apartment. She fled up to her new friends residence and screamed for them to let her in. They opened their door and found her terrified. At first, she was unable to describe what had happened, until this couple was able to calm her. She then told what she had seen. They knew immediately that it was Jesus who had appeared unto her. He was offering her communion. They explained the vision to "Samir" and explained to her about communion and the new covenant. What she had seen was not a devil but the Lord. She was to go back and trust that He would appear to her again. The woman agreed and courageously returned. The next night, she saw the vision again. Jesus was offering from his hands communion. "Samir" partook of this miracle offering of bread and wine.

From that night on "Samir's" life was changed. She accepted Christianity and forsook Islam. "Samir" eagerly began to read the Bible and volunteered to go with her Christian friends to "witness." She became bolder and bolder in Jesus, leading many souls to salvation. Yet, she soon found herself in danger for witnessing Jesus publicly. Islamic persecutors were constantly threatening her life. Her marriage was also over. Her husband would not accept a "Christian wife." The Christian couple felt that God was calling her to leave Egypt. "Samir" also agreed. They were able to get her accepted into a Bible School in the United States. There she would be safe. "Samir" trusting in Jesus, became like Ruth, the Moabitess. She left her country for another and is now in the ministry.[1]

Jesus has promised that he will not leave us comfortless, but come unto us. In many instances like "Samir's," he is appearing to these daughters. The Lord also wants his disciples to go forth as well. He said that he would never leave nor forsake us. This ministry to the daughters of Ishmael is an open door for Christian women. Christian men cannot usually witness to Muslim women, unless it is indirectly through videos, CD's, cassettes, internet web sites, television or postal Bible courses. Open contact with a male would be far too dangerous for any Muslim woman, and perilous to any man that would dare approach these daughters. Western civilization may allow meetings with "mixed company," but this is not the case in Islamic society. Women do not socialize with men.

This "rule" may be somewhat eased in Western nations. Here in these countries it would be possible for Islamic couples to interact with the people there. The wife in many of these marriages could possibly be a woman from a non-Islamic nation (America, Britain, Germany).[2] The woman then may not be entirely Islamized, nor would the Muslim husband. In that case, husbands and wives could socially interact. Thus, one could share the Gospel couple to couple. Even so, Muslim customs usually find the women in one room talking and the men in another.

### Sharing the Good News

There are two approaches for Christian women to witness the Gospel to Islamic women. Each method is dependent on the country and community where these Muslim believers reside. Islamic women who live in Western nations have a greater familiarity with the "foreign" culture and customs and may have greater "open door" to the "good news." Those women who reside in Islamic nations are more hindered by traditions, mores and language differences. The following are simple suggestions, which others more experienced in witnessing to Muslim women have offered.

## I. Witnessing Christ in Western Nations

### 1. Be a Friend

The Christian woman, who has a burden to share the Gospel with Muslim women, must first meet them and gain their friendship. This means daring to enter into her culture, as well as offering them an open door.

Many Muslim women in Western nations are fearful. They find themselves in a foreign land, alone and without the comfort of an extended family. The customs, language and perceived freedoms of the inhabitants often lead them to stay within their own community. The Christian woman who desires to meet Muslims often has to take the first step. Go where they are and be friendly. Today, one can find Muslims just about anywhere, whether in the local shopping mall, the university or the workplace. Volunteer your time, teach English, or just "welcome them" to your neighborhood. Ask God to create divine opportunities for you to meet Muslims, and them follow up on them. A friendly voice, an understanding heart and an ability to listen without judging can give you the breakthroughs you need to form friendships.

Kathy Echols, a former missionary to Pakistan, once found an instant friend by welcoming a Muslim refugee from Bosnia into her home. *"I simply greeted her with one phrase in her language, 'Welcome to my home.' She didn't know me at all, but she threw her arms around me and said, 'I will raise my children with your children and my grandchildren with your grandchildren.' She was ...desperate for friendship."* [3] The gift of friendship can lead Muslim women to the gift of eternal life in Jesus.

### 2. Share about your life in Christ.

Muslims are not hesitant to talk about religion. Islam

243

affects their whole life, not just part of it. This is something that your can also tell your new acquaintance. Real Christianity•affects one's whole life positively. Reveal to your friend what it is to live a vibrant life in Christ. Share your testimony with her. Use plenty of details and emotions. Be descriptive. She will be listening to your words and observing your actions closely. One Turkish woman revealed the effects of this type of loving witness. She simply said, *"I feel like the shell around my heart is cracking."* [4] When sharing the Gospel, keep your words loving, living and uplifting. Do not attempt to overwhelm your listener with the Gospel or present her with a preplanned "Roman Road" conversation. Be natural and let God do the talking through you.

### 3. Use Holidays as Opportunities

Holidays like Christmas and Thanksgiving, as well as Islamic celebrations, can serve as wonderful doors to gain entrance into your Muslim's friend's life. You can use these days to open conversations, or invite your new friend to be a part of them. Celebrate your friend's birthday. Most Muslim women's birthdays are ignored. Bake her a cake. Please check first that ingredients do not contain lard. This precaution will save you much embarrassment. Present your friend with a Bible in her own language as a gift. You will have a friend for life!

Muslim's observe two major holidays. The *Id-al-Adha* or "feast of the sacrifice" is the most important event in the Islamic calendar. This feast is in commemoration of Abraham's sacrifice of the ram, which released him from offering up his son. Celebrations continue for three days and consist of family visits. *'Id-al-Fitr,* a holiday that signifies the ending of the Ramadan fast. This too is a festival, which can extend for some three days of celebrations. Special dishes are prepared and everyone wears new clothes. Gifts are exchanged. A small present of food such as a cake or a card could serve as a sign of your interest and love for her and her family.

### 4. Tell stories, recite poems and sing.

All Muslims love to hear stories and poems. It is a part of their culture. Stories, poems and songs also bypass the need to have religious discussions. Simply share of Jesus' parables, His miracles, and the majesty of the Word. These same stories can be shared with her children. Invite her to an outdoor Gospel presentation. Leave a Christian video for her to watch. Tapes of Christian worship music can also minister to Muslims as well as your own songs. Learn to play a musical instrument and then "entertain" your new friends with Gospel songs. Ask the Holy Spirit to give you a "song of the Lord" to sing for your friend.

### 5. Pray

Pray for your friend at home and ask if you can pray with her. Tell her you believe in healing and miracles. Share how God has answered your prayers. Ask her if she needs prayer for healing or restoration. Even simple acts of prayer can be effective witnesses. Praying over your children before bed or saying thanksgiving over your meals in her company communicates volumes to your friend. Ask her if she prays for her family. Informal prayers from the heart, also serve as a strong witness to Muslims.

*Laylat al-Bara'ah*, or "the Night of Record," is an important date for Muslims. Muhammad said that on this night, God would set destinies for the year to come, as well as all births and deaths. Many families stay up all night and pray. Candles and lamps are left burning. Perhaps, as a Christian you could tell your friend that you too would also be praying this night for her and her family. Then do so and ask God to move mightily in their lives.

*Laylat al-Kadr* is the holiest night for Muslims. This "night of power" is remembered every year as the night when Muhammad supposedly received his first revelation of the Koran. Many Muslims believe that this is a special time when God will give them dreams and visions. Many pray all night seeking answers to their requests. This night can offer opportunities for the Christian woman to witness to your Muslim friend. Commit to pray for her and with her if the opportunity arises.

## II. Sharing the Light of Christ with Muslim Women in Islamic Nations

Christian women who desire to share the Gospel with Islamic women in Muslim lands face difficult challenges. Trust has to be cultivated and the ever-present forces of darkness must be bound. Even so, we serve a mighty God who loves to create openings of spiritual light in areas of darkness. Often the Lord will first use dreams and visions in these women's lives to move them to seek interpretations.

"Malek" was a young maid in a hotel on the Mount of Olives in Israel. She kept having a strange reoccurring dream that troubled her. After, it happened three times, she sought out a Christian friend who lived in her community. *"What is this?"* she said. *"I keep seeing a man in white who pushes me under the water."* Alice, her friend, explained to "Malek" that this "man" in white was Jesus and that he wanted her to be baptized as a Christian believer. She told her what baptism was and shared with her the Gospel. "Malek" became an eager disciple and soon asked to be baptized, even though she knew that being a Christian could present difficulties. Not long afterward this event, she visited Alice and asked for her help. She had a friend who was sick and in bed. Alice went, but told Malek, "*You are a believer now, I want you to pray and ask Jesus to heal her.*" "Malek" boldly touched her friend with her hand and then prayed, "*Be healed in Jesus' name.*" Her friend was immediately healed of her sickness.[5]

We also have been able to effectively witness again by giving small gifts to our Muslim friends on important occasions. The Christmas tree also surprisingly attracts Muslims. We have decorated our tree with angels and our house with a simple manger scene. Then we have invited our Muslim friends over to see it. This tradition always helps open a door to witness.

Cultural and language barriers also need to be surmounted, but many women are eager to improve their English language skills. They are honored when you visit them. This approach may work for women that have some experience with Western culture, but when you find yourself among women who have a village mentality, then other difficulties arise. These women are usually uneducated, quite poor, and consumed with the basic needs of food, clothing and shelter. Spiritual matters are not important, unless sickness or marital difficulties need resolving. One then has to call on the power of God to break through the darkness surrounding their lives.

One missionary who has lived in a Muslim country for 38 years states that:

*I 've found it takes at least 150 times for a Muslim woman to hear the Word of God before she understands it. They have so much to unlearn about*

*Christianity, so many prejudices to overcome. And then there's the seclusion. It makes them suspect whenever there's repeated contact with Western women.*[6]

Muslim women are suspicious of women who come from Western countries. They have been taught since childhood that such women are immoral. Christianity also has been negatively spoken of, as being perverted and corrupted. These obstacles encourage Muslim women to enter into superficial relationships. The fear of being associated with a Westerner drives them away. A common proverb states that *"Drops of water hollow out rocks."* The witness of Christ will bring drops of living water to hollow out their stony hearts. It takes a long time to produce results, but if the same drop is applied day after day, week after week, month after month, year after year the stone will dissolve.

## Entering into the Culture

These barriers to the Gospel in Islamic lands can be somewhat overcome by presenting medical clinics, opening orphanages, and giving self-help courses, such as sewing classes or educational tutoring. These methods have in the past, helped introduce the Gospel to local women. A better entry point to the culture is found through relationships. Muslim women who have some contact with Christians can help you enter into the community. These women can testify to their more fearful sisters as to the high morality, pure love and true witness that you possess.

The primary form of "entertainment" for women in Arab Islamic countries is visiting. Many Mid-Eastern Muslim women are forbidden employment, or are highly restricted in their outside activities. Thus, they fill their time with parties and social visits. Preparations for weddings and birth celebrations also offer opportunities for visits. Groups of women gather within the confines of the home and socialize. These informal meetings can offer tremendous God-given opportunities for a Christian woman to meet other Muslim women. You can later visit with them in their homes and share Christ on a one to one basis. Once you have gained a friendship, seek to nurture it by regularly visiting your friend. Truly show an interest in her, and not just her soul. LOVE her. Expect God then to bless the time and seed that you have planted in this woman (these women).

**1. Preparation for a "visit"**
Arabs are known for their hospitality. If you have been invited to a Muslim woman's home for a visit; endeavor to spiritually plan ahead for this "event."

A. Pray that the Holy Spirit would free the heart(s) of the woman (women)

B. Lift up these women specifically in prayer. Pray for victory over the bondages and superstitions that they may be in. Cry out for deliverance.

C. Bind the forces of evil. Come against the spirits of the occult and ruling princes of darkness.

D. Read and meditate on the Word, so you can sprinkle large portions of "salt" in your conversations.

E. Commit your upcoming "visit" to the Lord and then trust Him to work. He is the LORD of the Harvest.

## 2. The Visit

### A. Relax

Experienced women missionaries who have labored in Islamic lands suggest that the Christian woman who enters into a Muslim woman's home learn to do one thing well, Relax! This visit is literally an open door. It is not the time to be nervous or cold and calculating. Enjoy the time that God has given you to be with this woman (these women). If the husband has more than one wife, avoid prejudging this relationship. Do not be concerned about language difficulties. Your smile will let her (them) know, that you feel welcomed. Usually there will be someone in the home that will know a little of your language. They may even translate for you.

### B. Listen

It has been said that God gave us two ears and one mouth as a permanent reminder that we should listen twice as much as we speak. Listen to your host, and affirm the importance of her (their) religious views. Hear her (their) heart(s). You are there to gain her (their) trust. Let the Holy Ghost open up windows of opportunity in the words you hear, to speak/sow seeds of truth.

### C. Share from the Bible

The woman (women) you are with may allow you a time to "share." Speak to them of how God meets your daily needs. Tell them stories and not theological doctrines. Share confidence and details of your life. Reveal how Jesus answered your prayers. Tell how He walked with you through the crisis times in your life. If you have been involved in the occult and delivered, confide how, you "discovered" a greater power. If an opportunity presents itself, discuss man's need to have a clean heart, God's pardon, His excellent provision and great love for all of humankind.

The "list" of subjects you can give voice to is endless. Whenever possible turn or focus on a Biblical passage where Jesus is talking or ministering to a woman. She or they will recall these events and may even pray to Jesus in the future. Remember, you are "visiting" to plant seed and not necessarily there to harvest it.

### D. Apply the Love and Power of Christ

You may have the freedom during this time of "visiting" to pray for those you are with. Perhaps someone is sick or suffering. Remember you are surrounded by lives, which are burdened by rejections, fears, insecurities and occultive spirits. Muslim women are also curious. She or they may want to see how a Westerner prays. Be alert for the Great Physician, "Dr. Jesus" to show up. You can also certainly demonstrate your love for them. The Lord may cause your "visit" to be remembered. Perhaps you may hear again from your friends during a "crisis" time, allowing you to "minister" to them and apply the love of Christ to their hearts.

### Other Islamic Lands

This "visiting" culture though is not always found in other Islamic lands. Muslim women in poorer developing countries (Africa, India, Bangladesh, Philippines, etc...) are often found laboring in the fields or shops all day, and then working after hours caring for the family. It is an exhausting regime, leading to sicknesses, and early death. As a woman, you may be able to interact with these souls in the marketplace or during community weddings and celebrations. Seek to learn their language and customs. Try and dress as near as possible to the people you are with. Once they know you and "trust" you, an acceptance into their lives will come. If you truly bear Christ's love and light, the souls you meet will grow to love you. They will see Jesus in you and desire to have what you possess: A loving relationship with Him!

### Lillian Trasher

Lillian Trasher came to Egypt as a young missionary. One night, she was called to the bedside of a poor young mother who was dying of fever. She knew after her own death that her newborn infant girl was also going to be placed near the river and left to die. This mother offered Lillian her child. The young missionary woman took this child in and soon found herself in the custody of even more unwanted and abandoned children. It was the beginning of a great work of faith, a little drop of living water hollowing out stony hearts. Some ninety years have passed now, but Lillian's work for Jesus continues to significantly impact a Muslim nation. Over 20,000 children have passed through her orphanage and school located in Assiout, Egypt. They have been loved, educated and led to Christ. The Gold Medal of Honor was awarded by Egypt to the Lillian Trasher Orphanage in appreciation for its services.[7]

God can and does use women to change lives and history. Esther, Deborah, Abigail, as well as the woman by the well in John's Gospel are some examples. Women were also given the privilege of announcing the resurrection of Jesus (Jn. 20:10-18). The Lord dearly needs Christian women who are willing to become like Lillian Trasher's and leave all behind for the sake of the Gospel. Your obedience to the Savior could reach a future Esther, or a Deborah who then would be able to raise up one day, an body of Muslim women declaring Jesus Christ as their Savior.

1. Personal testimony related by R. Matar, Cairo, Egypt.
2. *"An estimated 7,000 marriages between American women and Muslim men take place every year. Statistics now show that about 80 percent of them will end in bitter divorces."* Intercede, Sept/Oct. 2000,
3. LaDonna Witmer "Muslim Women" *WherEver* (TEAM) Spr. 1997, pg. 4.
4. Ibid, pg. 5.
5. Personal testimony, Jerusalem Israel
6. Ladonna Witmer "Muslim Women" *WherEver* (TEAM) Spr. 1997, pg. 3.
7. "A Home with some 600 Kids" *Pentecostal Evangel*, Mar. 9, 1997, pg. 21 (For more information on Lillian Trasher's life, read Beth Howell's *Lady on a Donkey*).

# NINETEEN

## "Ye Shall Find"

eter, John and the rest of the disciples were exhausted. It has been a hard fruitless night. Repeatedly they
had lowered their net into the dark waters of the
Galilee, and then drawn in nothing. All of Peter's years of
fishing could not find them a catch. Not one favorite fishing spot
on the lake was productive. Every tried and true method he had
used in the past, had failed miserably. The torches that they had lit
to attract the fish, now only reflected their drawn expressions off
the water. They were weary, soiled and hungry. Dawn was breaking and the hour was upon them to beach the boat.

Yet, a man with a familiar voice called to them from the shore:
*"Have you caught any fish?"* *"No,"* they thundered back. The
night had been in vain. This friendly stranger now spoke to them
with a voice of authority. *"Cast the net on the right side of the ship
and ye shall find."*

Peter looked at his crew, a flash of wonderment crossing his
face. He then quickly nodded his head to the rest of the disciples,
and they with a new energy, swiftly threw the net into the sea. The
water then exploded with fury. Fish of every size and description
were caught in the net. The men shouted and started to draw in the
immense catch. John though, in the midst of the excitement, suddenly knew who the stranger on the shore was. He elbowed Peter,
and said, *"It is the Lord."* The big fisherman then impulsively
jumped into the lake, in an effort to meet the man he loved. The

man was speaking again, *"Bring the fish which ye have now caught."* Peter who was in the water, now helped draw the net to the land. It was full of great fishes and did not break (Jn. 21:1-14).

This familiar story in John's Gospel, speaks of the history of Christian evangelism to Muslims. Our labors have seemed fruitless. We have toiled in darkness seeking to catch Muslims for Christ and have caught precious little. The night is nearly over though and the dawn is about to break. Are we, the church, ready to hear the voice of our Lord?

Islam has seemed to be elusive to the "nets" of the Gospel. Even so, this miracle story is prophetic. Our Lord will call His church to cast forth the net of salvation to the Muslim world, one more time. It will be a Holy Ghost unified directed effort that will result in a glorious catch of souls. It will be a miracle that no man will be able to take credit for. It will be the Lord's doing. God will answer Abraham's prayer: *"O that Ishmael might live..."* in such an astounding and astonishing way that even the patriarch would not have believed the magnitude of it. Ishmael will hear and freely come into the nets of salvation. The church though must prepare itself, to bring these souls into the Master's presence (Jn. 21:10). He will see that our net will not break.

## Christian Attitudes

The Western world and Christians have viewed Muslims with some suspicion. Sadly, it is a truth that all one needs to mention in conversation is the word *"Muslim,"* and most listeners will immediately think "terrorist." Islam is seen in these latter days as a barbarous religion. World events with their daily headlines and television spots have only asseverated this "image" problem. The past years have been filled with reports of terrorism, bombings, hostages and holy wars. Islam proclaims that it is the way of peace, but instead, it has filled the world with fear and terror. Perhaps in truth, these actions have negatively affected the attitudes of

255

Christians. Who in their right mind would want to cast a net over a pack of thrashing bloodthirsty sharks? Dynamite would do a better job, in harvesting these "fish." Except, the Lord is calling His disciples to catch live fish! Only He can turn raging sharks into harmless fish.

The actions of some 10-15% of all Muslims worldwide represent those who advocate and practice terrorism. In addition there are even greater numbers of Muslims who actively support fanatical movements. Even so, there are still many Muslims who are peaceful, loving and in need of Christ. Our attitude towards these people must change, if we are to successfully put our hands to the "net." Many Christians are lukewarm towards evangelizing Muslims. They refuse to be burdened. Some would rather go below decks and sleep, thinking: *"Perhaps if I ignore Islam, it will go away."* Others seek to adopt a *lais'sez faire'* attitude of *"Let and let live."* Then, there are those Christians who are caught up in the doldrums of mediocrity. They have signed onto the ship of convenience and self-interest. Yes, it will take a miracle to bring Muslims to Christ. It will also take a greater miracle to bring most Christians into a state where they can joyfully, and excitedly extend the "nets" of salvation to Muslims.

## The Destruction of Mecca

Muslims believe that the destruction of Mecca (the *Ka'ba*) will be one sign of many that will proclaim the end of the world.[1] The Bible repeatedly says that the terrible day of the LORD will come. God will cause men's hearts to faint. Habakkuk saw *"the tents of Cushan in affliction and the curtains of the land of Midian"* which *"did tremble"* (Hab. 3:7). Zephaniah reported that the LORD *"will utterly consume all things from off the land"* (Zeph 1:2). He will *"famish all the gods of the earth; and men shall worship him every one from his place, even all the isles of the heathen"* (2:11). The earth shall quake on this terrible day of the LORD (Mt. 24:7; Rev. 6:12-17). It is not inconceivable that God in His mercy could cause an earthquake of such gigantic proportions as to utterly swallow Mecca into the bowels of the earth forever. Billions of Islamic souls would have nowhere to turn to pray. This world-shaking event could cause men to reject the god of Muhammad and the idol of the Koran as well. This possibility could send millions of Muslims rushing into the nets of Salvation. Ishmael would embrace Christ and live.

Lest Christians rejoice prematurely as to what God might do, the Word cautions that in the days to come, God will send *"strong delusion that they should believe a lie"* (II Thes. 2:11). Many Muslims will come to know Jesus in these end times, but others though will ignore the call of the Master no matter what happens, and perish in delusion (Is. 66:4). There will come a falling away and the man of sin will be revealed (II Thes. 2 3-4).

### The Power of Love

God though may chose to ignore Mecca and just pour out His Love onto this world instead. Christians and Muslims both need the sovereign love of God in their spirits to overcome the hindering forces frustrating the spread of the Gospel. Muslims need the supernatural love of God within them to accept Christ and Christianity. A believer in Kazakhstan, a part of the former Soviet Union, relates how much love draws Muslims to Christ:

> A leading Uighur in a Muslim mosque told me, *'I want to visit Mecca and learn what Muslims really believe.'* When I saw him again a year later, I asked what he saw when he went to Mecca. He replied, *'Nothing much'* and stated weeping. I asked him, *'What is the main difference between Islam and Christianity?'* He replied, *'Islam says, "If someone hits you, hit him back three times." Christianity says, "Turn the other check." That is Love.* Now he was crying. I asked him, *'Would you like to become a Christian tonight?'* *'Yes,'* he sobbed. So I

helped him pray. We stood, held hands, and prayed. His son prayed with us, with tears of joy. Then he gave this testimony on video for his daughter: *'Today, I am a Christian. When you come back home, we can go together and tell Kazakhs about Christ.'* My friends, Muslims are reachable.'[2]

Christians also need the sovereign love of God in order to evangelize and love Muslims. Without love as a motive, the task we face is hopeless. It will profit us nothing. This love we possess must include true forgiveness and mercy.

George Otis, the founder of *High Adventure Ministries* and the *Voice of Hope Global Broadcasting Network* discovered this love in 1985. Four Hamas terrorists attacked his radio station in Southern Lebanon. Five employees of the station were killed in the raid as well as three terrorists. One terrorist was badly wounded and was captured. He was given a lengthy prison term but Otis found that in spite of this penalty his heart was utterly filled with rage. He felt that the terrorist's sentence was not adequate enough to compensate for the terrible loss of five dedicated Christian employees. Otis wanted nothing to do with the surviving terrorist. Yet as the months passed, the Lord continually pricked his heart. The thought came to Otis, that if he couldn't forgive this young man, then he had no business running his ministry. He decided to visit the man in prison. Otis brought with him an Arabic Bible and a box of cookies. What happened then was truly the hand of Jesus moving upon a man's heart. George recalls: *"I told him that despite what he had done, God required me to forgive him. That blew him away. Immediately the young man fell to his knees and asked Jesus into his heart."* [3]

The church's end-time assignment is to be ready at the Lord's word to throw the net. This "net" must be formed with cords of godly love; otherwise there will be no "catch."

## Witnessing for Christ:  Early Efforts

Christianity has thoroughly neglected evangelizing Muslims. Perhaps the defeats of the past have turned our hearts to more pleasant and profitable "fishing grounds". The great Crusade proclaimed a gospel of the sword.  Christians viewed Muslims as mortal enemies and not prodigal sons. These "outreaches" failed to win Islamic souls for Christ.  What they did do was leave a lasting legacy of bitterness and reproach from Muslims.  True missionaries to these people have been far too few.

### Francis of Assisi (1182-1226)

One of the first efforts to proclaim salvation to the Muslim came from Francis of Assisi.  This "brother" in the twelfth century traveled to Egypt with the Crusaders.  Here in the midst of battle preparations, the "saint" slipped away and conferred with the enemy.  He approached the Sultan.  This leader of the dreaded Sacreans privately heard Francis.  He then asked him to pray that God would *"reveal to him, by some miracle, which is the best religion."*  Meanwhile, the armies of the Cross were defeated at Damietta (1219).  Their bodies littered the battlefield.  Francis though was still in the camp of the "enemy." He had made by this time, an even a stronger impression on the Sultan.  Thus he was allowed safe passage back.  It was later said that the Sultan, was sufficiently moved at Francis' words and actions as to become a secret believer.  Francis later penned some words of good counsel which all Christians who desire to reveal Christ to Muslims should heed: *"Preach the Gospel at all times.  Use words if necessary."*

### Raymond Lull (1235-1315)

This martyr for Christ truly loved the Muslim people. Raymond Lull's motto was *"He that loves not, lives not."*  He was the first apostle to the Islamic world, traveling to Northern Africa. Born in Palma, Majorca, Lull was inspired to proclaim Christ to

Muslims after seeing a vision of the Lord suffering on the cross. He was a prolific writer, publishing treatises defending the Christian faith. Lull loved Jesus with a passion and desired to see all Muslims love the Lord too.

This missionary traveled to Morocco, but succeeded only in being banished from that country. He then returned to what is now Algeria in 1314, at 80 years of age. Lull did the work of an evangelist for over ten months, in secret. Then at length, Lull grew weary of being a hidden light for Jesus. He ventured forth one day into the market place of Bugia and spoke of God's judgment descending on the people, if they did not renounce Islam. His remarks started a riot. The mob seized Lull and dragged him outside of the town. Here he was stoned to death. It was June 30, 1315.

### Henry Martyn (1781-1812)

After Lull's martyrdom, five centuries of Christian inactivity passed. No Protestant missionary ventured into the lands of Islam. Henry Martyn though could not resist the still small voice of God. His one prayer to the Lord was *"to burn out for God."* Martyn prepared for his vocation by learning Sanskrit, Persian, and the Arabic language at Cambridge University. He composed tracts in Arabic. Later, Martyn translated the New Testament into the Persian, Urdu and Arabic languages. After finding religious debates with Muslims fruitless, Martyn was counseled by William Carey to reconsider the methods he was using to evangelize Muslims. The young missionary then drew up a list of seven principles, which all Christians should follow in winning Muslims to Christ.[4]

Henry Martyn did *"burn out for God."* He died of a raging fever while on a 1500-mile overland journey to Istanbul. A cruel Tarter guide who had no mercy for his illness rode him to death.

## Temple Gairdner (1873-1928)

This man of ten talents adopted Egypt as his home, and stayed there until his death. Temple Gairdner brought the Gospel to the educated Muslim. He produced Arabic musicals, dramas and poetic productions so as to bring in the harvest. Some of these dramas were miracle plays, in which Biblical stories were effectively presented on stage to reach Muslims. He wrote tracts, and books, which defended Christianity, and published a Christian magazine in Arabic. Temple Gairdner declared that his one great purpose in life was to preach Christ crucified. His heart's desire was to see Muslims come to Christ. He was a man who loved to bridge differences.

Once this missionary gave a New Testament as a gift to a Muslim. This man whose name was Mahmud, had loudly broken up Gairdner's public lecture on the crucifixion of Christ. Mahmud had attended this talk with some twenty friends, and at the opportune moment stood up and called for all true Muslims to show their abhorrence of this teaching by walking out. The hall was emptied, but Gairdner later found Mahmud and invited him to come back! He then gave Mahmud a New Testament to read. Inside of this book, Gairdner had written notes to Mahmud such as, "*I pray for you daily*" and "*Pray for those who despitefully use you.*" Six months later, Mahmud made a decision to become a Christian. He was convinced of the truth that he saw in the Word. Mahmud was also won over by love.[5]

## Samuel Zwemer (1867-1952)

Samuel Zwemer has been called the "*Apostle to Islam.*" As a young Seminary student, the Student Volunteer Movement challenged Zwemer and friend James Cantine. They desired to do a new work for Christ. Hence, they selected Arabia as the most difficult mission field that they could find. Abraham's prayer to God in Genesis 17:18 became their motto: "*O that Ishmael might live before Thee.*"

Zwemer spent twenty-three years of sacrificial service in this field. His newborn son and daughters died there. Zwemer was a gifted writer, authoring numerous studies on Islam. He found and edited: *The Moslem World*, a quarterly magazine. Muslims were Zwemer's first love. Evangelizing them, he once said is *"the Glory of the Impossible."*

## Counting the Cost

Casting forth the net of salvation to Muslims cannot be done with acknowledging the risk, that both Christian and Muslim face. Those Muslims who convert to Christianity will confront difficult and trying obstacles. The Law of Apostasy as written in the Koran commands death to all Muslims. This "divine" word says, *"if they turn back, then take them and kill them wherever you find them and chose no friend nor helper from among them"* (S. 4:89, Women). Muslims who become Christians are literally placing their lives on the line for Jesus' sake. The Koran is filled with admonitions for its followers to *"fight those of the disbelievers who are near to you and let them find harshness in you and know that Allah is with thee"* (S. 9:123, Repentance). Most Muslims converts accept this death sentence. They are willing to die for the sake of the Gospel. A greater factor, which troubles many new converts, is the loss of family members. The Muslim who embraces Christianity openly, must be prepared to face a lonely life. He or she can expect to be socially ostracized, banished, and persecuted for deciding to follow Jesus. The Muslim who becomes a Christian has in the eyes of other Muslims betrayed Islam, slandered the Koran and rejected Muhammad as a prophet. The penalties for making such a foolish choice are dishonor, disinheritance and death.

Yet Jesus declared, *"And I, if I be lifted up from the earth, will draw all men unto me."* Muslims are coming to Christ in record numbers. The nation of Bulgaria serves as one example. A large Turkish minority lives in this country. In the last few years though more than 5,000 Turks and Turkish-speaking Gypsies have come to know Christ.[6]

The net of Christ's love is stronger than the ties that bind Muslims to their family, friends and employment. Many new converts have suffered persecution, but later have testified about the privilege of suffering for Christ. The Savior has indeed warned new believers:

> *If any man come to me, and hate not his father, and mother, and wife, and children, And brethren, and sister, yea, and his own life also, he cannot be my disciple. And whosoever doth not bear his cross, and come after me, cannot be my disciple* (Lk. 14:26-27).

A Muslim who comes to Christ, must be willing to count the cost of the cross.

The laborers who are toiling to bring in this land end-time harvest for Jesus also suffer loss of family, persecution and death. David Barrett of the World Evangelization Research Center has documented records showing that over 160,000 Christians have been martyred annually for the Gospel.[7] Many other deaths have gone unreported. This is no short-term trend, but the product of a gradual increase. Jesus has told us that persecution will increase as the day draws closer for his return.

Over 300 churches have been attacked and burned in Indonesia, since 1991. Ishak Christian, a pastor, his wife and three children were burned to death inside their own church building. [8] Jesus though declared *"whosoever will save his life shall lost it: but whosoever will lose his life for my sake, the same shall save it "* (Lk. 9:24). An extremist mob of over 30,000 Muslims burned 1500 homes, in the Christian village of Shantinagar in Pakistan.[9] The inhabitants were falsely accused of desecrating the Koran. Northern Nigeria has also reported intense persecutions of

Christians.[10] Muslims have burned churches and believers there have been publicly stoned, attacked with machetes and beheaded. A Sudanese pastor Matta Boush is currently serving a thirty-year sentence for being a Christian. This man of God has led many prisoners to the Gospel and has baptized over thirty inmates. Pastor Boush believes God has commissioned him to be Christ's servant in prison.[11] Jesus has proclaimed:

> *Blessed are ye, when men shall hate you, and when they shall separate you from their company, and shall reproach you, and cast out your name as evil, for the Son of man's sake. Rejoice ye in that day, and leap for joy: for behold, your reward is great in heaven* (Lk. 6:22-23).

The greatest danger that Christians face in this age, is ignoring the command of the Lord to go forth *"into all the world and preach the Gospel to every creature"* There is a "catch" of men, waiting in the Muslim nations, if we will but throw the net of salvation over them and pull it in. Our faith prospers in areas that other religions disdain.

Samaan Ibrahim, pastors a growing work of Christ among the garbage collectors of Cairo. This group is greatly despised and marginalized in Egyptian society. Yet, as he spoke about Jesus to these "rejected ones," they became believers and then shared the faith with other members of the trade. Samaan has established a large church near the garbage village. It meets today, in a vast limestone cave near the Mokattan hills of Cairo.[12]

Jesus said, *"Blessed is that servant, whom his lord when he cometh shall find so doing"* This is the one who the Lord will reward. This disciple will see and rejoice in the catch. The servant though, who knows the Lord's will and then fails to do it *"shall be beaten with many stripes."* The danger of failing to do the Savior's will, is loss of honors, rewards, and retaining the knowledge that the souls you were tasked with saving have eternally perished.

*"For unto whomsoever much is given of him shall be much required."* Paul writes: *"Woe is unto me, if I preach not the Gospel!"*

## Throwing the Net of Salvation

### 1. Prayer and Fasting

The "net" Christians use to "catch" men is formed with cords of love. Prayer though directs where it will fall. Prayer causes the fish to hear the heart call of God to come into the net of salvation. Prayer gives the fishers of men divine energy to throw the net again, after long years without a catch. Prayer is how a good Christian fisherman prepares. Peter said, *"I go a fishing."* Christian have you prayed for a good catch of Muslims who are eager to receive Christ? Expect a net full, they are coming!

Fasting drives away devils, looses angels and calms your spirit, so you can hear the voice of the Lord in the dawn, telling you where the net must be thrown. Fasting unties nets that are tangled through anger, repairs nets that are torn by jealousy and brings unity. Esther fasted for three days and saved her nation. Fasting saves nations. Muslims will respond when whole communities, churches and people have fasted for their sake.

### 2. Preparing the Heart and Mind

This latter day Islamic harvest will be supernatural, and done by the Spirit of God. Just as the walls of communism fell, so shall the rigidity of Islam. Campus Crusade's Dr. Kim Hoon-Gon of Korea has declared, *"The Lord Jesus has the keys to open what no one can shut. I believe in the next ten years, history's greatest revival will take place."* [13]

A good fisherman prepares before casting forth his net. He knows where, when and how to fish. The net is "cleaned" and repositioned, before it is set out again. The Christian who desires to approach Muslims with the light of Christ, must also demonstrate the same readiness. Foremost, is possessing a pure heart. Jesus said, *"Blessed are the pure in heart: for they shall see God."* A person with a pure heart is without guile. Your motive for sharing Christ to Muslims is not duty or guilt, but love. Possessing a pure heart means cultivating a loving nature, a forgiving spirit and an inward genuine holiness. Peter advocates adding brotherly kindness, virtue, patience, etc. to your inner man. *"For if these things be in you, and abound, they make you that ye shall neither be barren nor, unfruitful in the knowledge of our Lord Jesus Christ"* (II Pet. 1:8). Never make a Muslim feel you are trying to convert him or her. Show them respect.

Seek to "know" Muslims. A Christian who is serious about evangelizing Muslim's should become familiar with the Koran and Hadith. Be familiar with their lifestyle and culture. Therefore, become knowledgeable of their likes and dislikes. Do not criticize Islam, but preach the Gospel instead. Avoid instructing Muslims in their faith. Often Muslims may only have a superficial knowledge of Islam. It is not the Christian's responsibility to "teach" them their beliefs, or drive them to learn Islam. The Christian should endeavor to introduce Muslims to the Bible. Try to get them to study the Word of God with you.

**3. Find Their Level**
Islam is a faith that is neither, unified nor of one accord. Christians treat it like a monolithic giant, but it is sharply divided although a common creed is shared. If you are not sure what faction is followed, ask Muslims what

"form" of Islam, they practice. Most Muslims will gladly share with you the beliefs they adhere to. These differences will affect how you witness Christ to them.

## 4. Choose the Right Method

There are wrong ways to proclaim Christ to Muslims. Standing up in the marketplace, and demeaning the prophet may look courageous, but it is not. Such displays are foolish. Your witness will only start a riot, get you killed and strengthen the faith of Muslims. Large evangelistical events labeled "Crusades" will not work either. The very word "crusade" draws up in Muslims visions of sword-welding invading armies who come to conquer and kill. Muslims are not likely to be drawn to "Gospel crusades," unless it is to stir up violence against those who attend.

Traditional methods of "fishing" do not always work with Muslims. Recognizing this, Christian churches, seminaries and Bible institutes worldwide, are developing new "fishing" methods to meet the challenge of Islam. The Evangelical Theological Seminary in Indonesia, for instance, requires students who wish to graduate to fulfill three pre-requisites. These conditions include completing all academic courses, planting at least one church and introducing a minimum of fifteen Muslims to Christ. The students of this school in following this program have in the last six years planted over 600 churches and brought more than 40,000 Muslims to Christ. Jesus is teaching Christians better ways to "fish" for Muslims.[14]

The Jesus film is having an enormous impact in the world of Islam. The Arabic version of "Jesus" is one of the most popular rental videos on the island of Bahrain.[15] Believers in Kazakhstan have set up a popular telephone story line with a Gospel message for children. When this number is called, children can hear a story of how God works in their daily lives and how they can know Jesus.[16] Even so, what works best is relationships. One on one personal evangelism. Women must witness to women, seniors to seniors, professionals, to professionals, students to students, and parents to parents.

If anything, the Christian must learn that when sharing Christ, one must be patient. Fishermen are patient workers; so must those who seek to convert Muslims. Place yourself on God's timetable. The "catch" will come "*in the fullness of time.*" J. Christy Wilson once said, "*Many missionaries in the Muslim world could be charter members of the fishermen's club consisting of those who have fished all night and taken nothing.*" [17] Dr.Patrick Cate, President of *International Missions* relates how he knew of one couple, which had no converts for the first 15 years of their ministry with Muslims. Then in the next eight years they helped plant a fellowship of 100 and enrolled over 4,500 students in a Bible correspondence course.[18] Christians possess a spiritual net that is bound with cords of love, which will not let men go. We also must have a knowing patience to wait for the morning. The Master shall then be with us in the boat and our nets will be overflowing with souls.

### "Fishing" in Kabul

Patrick Klein, founder of Asian Vision, discovered some great fishing "opportunities" in Kabul. He and another friend had traveled to Afghanistan, when a war broke out between two opposing Muslim factions. They had 110 Gospel portions in the Farsi dialect between them. They were unable to leave the city or the country for the next ten days, because of the chaos surrounding them. During this time, over 1,000 people died and some 1,500 rockets rained down on the city. Pat noticed though that in spite of all the carnage, people were very receptive to the Gospel. The Lord eagerly touched hearts in the midst of this crisis.

One man they witnessed to was a bodyguard for one of the Islamic "generals." He carried a standard AK-47 automatic rifle on him. When Pat asked this man what he believed in, the man responded with a curt reply *"Islam." "Yet, when we went into a private room, he told me that he hated Islam and the war and that Jesus and the Bible were the truth."*

Pat states that the Lord is shaking the nations as never before. *"This is"* he says, *"the greatest opportunity in history to reach people with the Gospel of Jesus Christ."* He sincerely believes *"Christians should be in war-torn areas so that they can minister to people, holding out the Word of Life to those who are dying. It is uncomfortable to go to these places, but Jesus never promised us an easy life."* This front line missionary declares that if you *"want to see God do incredible things, touching people and changing lives,"* you have to be willing to pay the price. *"The more you pay the price, the more we shall see the glorious works of God."* [19]

Peter, John and the rest of the disciples were willing to pay the price on that day long ago. It was not just that they had to fish all night to get a catch. No, they were willing to listen to the Lord's voice and follow His command obediently. They were willing to set aside their weariness and doubts and press on in faith. They had not cast away their confidence, *"which hath great recompense of reward."* Christian are you willing to pay the price or give the sacrifice that the Lord requires of you, so as to bring Him an Islamic "catch?"

## Bringing in the Net

### 1. Show Respect for your Bible
Muslims are very respectful to their "holy books." Christians as Ambassadors of Christ to the Islamic world

must be conscious of how we carry our credentials. Muslims would be shocked to see how we mark up our Bibles, exhibit tattered pages and place our Book on the floor. If we show respect for our Word and treat it with reverence, then they too will value what we possess. Make a friend of a Muslim and give them a Bible in their own language. Make sure that they are alone and not in a group. Place it in a plain paper bag, so no one else will know. Then speak to them and say: *"This book is the most precious Book, I have. If you are ever in trouble, read it and it will help you."*

## 2. Learn to Use Acceptable Words and Phrases

The Muslim may not understand who or even what you are talking about, unless you "dress" the Bible and your witness in an Islamic robe. Jesus is known generally as *Isa.* Introduce the Lord as the Word, or Savior or the *Ma'hil* (the Messiah). Delay introducing Jesus Christ as the *"Son of God"* to Muslims. The New Testament is the *Injil,* the Pentateuch is called the *Tawrat* (Torah), and the Psalms are known as the *Zabur.* Most Muslims would also identify God as *Allah* in Arabic.

## 3. Be Natural and Genuine in Sharing Your Faith

Jesus asked for us to go out and make disciples of all men. He did not ask us to become recordings or commercials. Share the light of Christ you have by using your personal testimony. Christians have a relational faith, while Muslims have a system. Follow your witness by demonstrating daily acts of Christian love and kindness. Provide multiple contacts with other Christians. Our unity and love for one another, will give forth a mighty witness to these inquiring souls. Recognize that with most Muslims, conversion is a gradual process and not an immediate decision. He must weigh it, study it and then turn his back on Islam.

This love which Christ had for the church and which Christians have for one another speaks strongly to Muslims. Rick Ridings, a missionary to the Middle-East and Europe, states that God is using the outward signs of Christianity's love, such as the communion ordinance to move Muslim hearts to His Son. He had been sharing about Christianity for months to a young Moroccan student named Ahmed, who was attending university classes in Brussels. Rick though could not observe any visible results to his efforts. Even so, he regularly invited the man to attend church with him. One Sunday, Ahmed did attend, but arrived at the service late. He had missed the praise and worship, which Rick was sure, would have attracted him into the Kingdom. The student also had failed to hear the Word. Ahmed walked into the church, just as communion was beginning. He saw the bread being broken and asked Rick about it. The missionary told him that this ordinance was for Christians only and that it was a sign of our covenant with Jesus.

The young man then abruptly declared *"I want to become a Christian right now! I confess Jesus as my Lord and Savior."* After some brief instructions, Rick then served Ahmed communion and welcomed him as a new member into the Body of Christ.[20]

Christian, make every effort to work through the local church. Your ministry can be multiplied and strengthened through the prayers and help from your fellowship. Inform your pastor, and see if he can assist you in fishing for Muslim souls. It is also helpful to find out what other Christians are doing in your area. There could be other ministries and individuals involved in the same kind of outreach.

## 4. Avoid Arguments

The Christian in declaring the Word to Muslims must always seek to keep conversations loving and Christ centered. Muslims love to argue. Phil Parshall, a lifelong minister to Muslims states *"I have never won an argument with a Muslim."* [21] It is better to try and refocus debates that are engendering contentions. Steer the conversation. Choose not to dwell on whether Muhammad was a prophet or not, but rather focus on what did he say about God, or the character of man, sin and salvation. Talk about the grace of God, divine healing, the Sermon on the Mount, or the parables of Jesus.

One method that has met with success in countering Islamic arguments and questions is to answer back with Scripture. Your detractors will not likely desire to directly refute the actual Word of God. Jesus met this challenge when He was accosted with Satan's arguments, with the words *"It is written."* The Word of God possesses a divine power and authority to silence the lips of those who would mock it. One should also recall the heritage of the servants of the LORD. Our God has promised *"No weapon that is formed against thee shall prosper; and every tongue that shall rise against thee in judgment thou shalt condemn "* (Isa. 54:17).

The Muslim also stops arguing when the power of God is demonstrated. Do not argue. Demonstrate the power of the Gospel. Heal the sick, raise the dead. If God be for you, who can be against you?

Often the witness of the Word will be disrupted by Muslims, who specifically attend Christian informational meetings to sow chaos. These hindering forces cannot always be avoided. Sometimes you will have to leave and go on to another town. Missionaries though have found success in these straits by asking their hecklers to choose one man to speak to the audience for thirty minutes about Islam and its message. In return, they must also agree to listen for the same period on the Christian message. Most Muslims have trouble speaking for five minutes about the fundamental truths and joys of Islam. Christianity though has a wonderful message of love and freedom, which many are eager to listen to. Islam does not.

Some years ago, a poll was taken of converts from Islam. They were asked what had first attracted their attention to Christ and what had brought about their conversion. Many said that it was either hearing the Bible read or reading it themselves. The LORD God affirms the power of Scripture through Isaiah. *"So shall my word be that goeth forth out of my mouth: it shall not return unto me void, but it shall accomplish that which I please, and it shall prosper in the thing whereto I sent it"* (Isa. 55:11).

### 5. Boldly Proclaim Jesus!

Christian, cast away fear and be strong in the day of the LORD. Preach the kingdom of God, and the coming Messiah. Do not preach your doubts. If you doubt what you present, your audience will see and know it. They will then believe even more the words of their prophet, in that Christians have corrupted the scriptures. No Christian should go to Muslims unprepared. Know why you believe the Bible is true and be ready to defend it. Speak of the reasons why Jesus was the Son of God, and how it was necessary for Him to pay the penalty for sin. Trust God to work, and know that as you declare the Word, His Spirit will be taking off the veils of confusion from the minds of those who listen.

Brother Andrew of *Open Door Missions* has lectured several times at the invitation of the Islamic University of

273

Gaza, on the subject of *"What is real Christianity?"* He declares, *"No evangelical has ever had that invitation."* [22] The Lord will open golden opportunities for Christians to witness to Muslims, if you but extend your faith.

Some of these God-directed opportunities exist right in our own back yard. The United States with its superior educational system is training the world. Thousands of young Islamic students are entering into our country to pursue their educational goals. *International Student Inc.* reports, *"over 250,000 foreign students from the 10/40 window are currently in the United States."* One quarter of these students originate from nations where no Christian missionary activity is allowed. Even so, statistics show that less than 30% of these students ever get invited into an American home.[23] ISI is encouraging Christians to reach out to these souls through "friendship evangelism."

If only Christians could realize the value of hospitality in witnessing. True hospitality can be defined as "the love of strangers." Many of these students are separated from their families, young, impressionable and lonely. Yet an open home and a warm welcome can change a stranger into a friend, and in doing so, open hearts to Christ. Lives that are changed can affect whole families. These families in turn, can convert entire communities, which can in time transform a nation. An open door to these "Muslim strangers" is in fact an invitation to become a missionary into these Islamic lands.

Some Christian ministries to Muslims, in the United States have even recommended that believers go a step further in these outreach activities. They advocate that Christians attend the on-campus meetings of the local Muslim Student Association. Here one could practice "presence evangelism" and learn to truly love these students.[24]

David L Ripley, the Director of SIM (Sudan Interior Missions) Training Center in Wheaton recommends that Christians identify where the neighborhood mosque is located and then make contact with the iman.[25] See if this man will let you have an opportunity to "dialogue" about Christianity and Islam. This "approach" may just put your Holy Ghost boldness to the test!

### 6. Be Constantly in Prayer

Prayer is essential at all times when witnessing to Muslims. This point cannot be over emphasized! One must not forget that you will be engaging in spiritual warfare against demonic princes and ruling nobles. You will be wrestling with principalities and powers as well as contending with wickedness in high places. Make sure you have "backup" intercessors praying, for you and your team so as to overcome the powers of darkness. Prayer pulls down the strongholds and removes chains form prisoners. Prayer is also what allows you to "walk" in the supernatural and do miracles. Prayer is what "casts forth" the net of love to envelop Muslims. Pray within your inner man as you dialogue. Pray in tongues that God would indeed open the windows of heaven to speak His Word clearly through you or your team.

### 7. Have a Godly Compassion

Christ had compassion on the multitudes. He saw their needs and felt their sufferings. Jesus sent the man who had been possessed with a legion of devils home to his friends so as to declare *"how great things the Lord hath done to thee, and hath had compassion on thee"* (Mk. 5:19).

Christians must be a people of compassion. Jude says that because of compassion, some made a difference (Jude 22). A true Christ-like love for Muslims and a compassion for their souls should be our heart's cry as we pull in the net. Overwhelming joy should be our reaction as the long-awaited "catch" comes into the net of salvation.

### 8. Be A Friend

A modern proverb states, *"One thousand friends are too few and one enemy is too many."* Both the Christian and Muslim have to overcome age-old prejudices and hostility towards each other. Hearts that desire to befriend one another cannot hold hatred and racism inside. Genuine friendship comes from a godly love and respect for one another. You admire and honor one another, despite the differences in culture, faith and thinking.

David and Jonathan had a precious friendship. Their souls were knit together. Jonathan made a covenant with David and *"loved him as he loved his own soul "* (I Sam. 18:3; 20:16-17). One was royalty and the other a shepherd, yet Jonathan gave all his personal possessions to David. They were able to come together in unity despite the hatred and anger that Jonathan's father Saul had for David. Jonathan and David refused to take offense. They elected to be friends.

Share your life with a Muslim first, before you share the Gospel. If you cannot be a friend to a Muslim, you cannot win them to Christ. Paul reveals the cost of true friendship in his letter to the Thessalonians. *"So being affectionately desirous of you, we were willing to have imparted unto you, not the gospel of God only, but also our own souls, because ye were dear unto us"* (I Thes. 2:8). Ask God to give you Muslim friends. There are thousands waiting for your gift of fellowship, waiting *"in the valley of decision: for the day of the LORD is near"* (Joel 3:14).

### Raymund Lull's Vision

Raymund Lull revealed his true thoughts for bringing Christ to Muslims, in his devotional titled, *The Book of the Lover and the Beloved.* This expression of his heart should be the purpose of all Christians who desire to bring to Jesus *"...the fish* (Muslims) *which ye have now caught."*

> *I see many knights going to the Holy Land* (the entire Muslim world today), *beyond the sea and thinking that they can acquire it by force of arms; but in the end all are destroyed before they attain that which they think to have. Wherefore it seems to me that the conquest of the Holy Land ought not to be attempted except in the way which Thou* (Jesus) *and Thine apostles acquired it, namely, by love and prayers, and the pouring out of blood and tears.* **26**

The LORD God in the Book of Psalms gives forth a precious promise to His Son, *"Ask of Me, and I will give you the nations for your inheritance and the uttermost parts of the earth for your possession"* (Ps. 2:8). Christians, we too can claim this promise for the Muslim peoples.

### Samuel Zwemer's Prayer

Some seventy-five years ago, Samuel Zwemer wrote this prayer in supplication to God for the souls of the Muslim people. I have taken the liberty of updating the population statistics and names of some of the nations in this appeal, but have let the essence of his intercession as he wrote it. I would like to complete this work with the same words of heartfelt petition. Let us pray!

## PRAYER FOR THE MUSLIM WORLD TODAY

*Almighty God, our Heavenly Father, who has made of one blood all nations, and has promised that many shall come from the East and sit down with Abraham in your Kingdom: We pray for the one and one quarter billion prodigal children in Muslim lands who are still afar off, that they may be brought near by the blood of Christ. Look upon them in pity, because they are ignorant of your truth.*

*Take away pride of intellect and blindness of heart, and reveal to them the surpassing beauty and power of your Son Jesus Christ. Convince them of their sin in rejecting the atonement of the only Savior. Give moral courage to those who love you, that they may boldly confess your name.*

*Hasten the day of perfect freedom in Turkey, Arabia, Iran and Afghanistan. Make your people willing in this new day of opportunity in China, Pakistan and Egypt. Send forth reapers where the harvest is ripe, and faithful plowmen to break furrows in lands still neglected. May the pagan tribes of Africa and Malaysia not fall a prey to Islam but be won for Christ. Bless the ministry of healing in every hospital, and the ministry of love at every mission station. May all Muslim children in mission schools be led to Christ and accept him as their personal Savior.*

*Strengthen converts, restore backsliders, and give all those who labor among Muslims the tenderness of Christ. So that bruised reeds may become pillars of his church, and smoking flax wicks burning and shining lights. Make bare your arm, O God, and show your power. All our expectation is from you.*

*Father, the hour has come; glorify your Son in the Muslim world, and fulfill through him the prayer of Abraham your friend, "O, that Ishmael might live before thee." For Jesus' sake. Amen.[27]*

---

1.   *Mishkat al-Masabih,* Bk. 23, ch. 3.
2.   *Mission Frontiers* Vol. 17 #1-2, Jan/Feb 1995, pg.33.
3.   Personal testimony, New Orleans Aug. 2001. See also *Charisma,* Vol. 22, #6, Jan. 1997, pgs. 18-19.
4.   See appendix "H" for those seven steps.
5.   "An Egyptian Convert from Islam" *Missionary Review of the World* Vol. LV #9, Sept. 1932, pgs. 493-494.
6.   "Speaking on Behalf of Muslims" *Intercede* May/June 1997, pg. 2. (Most converts to Christianity among these people are reported to be from a sovereign move of the Holy Spirit)
7.   David Barrett, "Annual Statistical Table on Global Missions: 1997" *International Bulletin of Missionary Research* Jan. 1997, pg. 25.
8.   "Indonesia" *Voice of the Martyrs* Dec. 1996, pg. 4.
9.   "Working for Peace in Pakistan" *South Asian Concern* Vol. 5 #2, Apr. 97, pgs. 1-2 (The city was burned Feb. 5-6, 1997). See also *Christianity Today* Vol. 41 #4, Apr. 7, 1997, pg. 59.
10.  I.O. Newton "Violence and Help to the Church at Poliskum" *Voice of the Martyrs* May 1995, pgs. 3,8.
11.  "News and Prayer Briefs" *Herald of His Coming* Sept. 1993, pg. 11.
12.  "Egyptian, Italian Pastors receive Pierce Award" *World Vision* Vol 40 #5 Oct/Nov 1996, pgs. 2.
13.  "A World Wide Revival of Prayer" *Intercede* Nov. 1994, pg. 5.
14.  Bill Stearns, "What in the World is God Doing?" *Discipleship Journal* Vol. 13 #6 Nov/Dec. 1993, pgs. 65-68.
15.  Paul Eshleman, *I Just Saw Jesus* The Jesus Project, Campus Crusade for Christ, 1991, pg. 40.
16.  "Call to Prayer" *Friends of Turkey* Aug/Sept. 1996, #37, pg. 3.
17.  J. Christy Wilson, "Moslem Converts" *The Moslem World* Jan 1944, pgs. 171-184.
18.  Patrick Cate, "Muslims" *International Missions* 1994, pg. 3.
19.  Patrick Klein, excerpts from *Bless the Nations Ministries,* Mar. 1997, pgs. 12-13
20.  Personal testimony given by Rick Ridings.
21.  Phil Parshall, *Beyond the Mosque,* pg. 198.

22. Brother Andrew, "The Need for Radicals" *Open Doors* Vol. 11 #9, Sept. 1996, pg. 8.

23. John W. MacVay "Ten Ways to Reach the World" *Charisma* Vol. 21 #3, Oct. 1995, pgs. 62-68; See also *Herald of His Coming* May 1997, pg. 11.

24. Contact www.internationalstudents.org for more information.

25. David L. Ripley, "Ideas for Sharing with Muslims" *Caleb Project,* SIM/Ethnic Focus Center, Wheaton, IL.

26. Kenneth Grubb, "The Passion of Raymund Lull" *Missionary Review of the World* Nov. 1937, pgs. 529-532.

27. Samuel Zwemer, "Call to Prayer", pg. 75.

# Appendices A-J

# APPENDIX A

## Islamic Articles of Faith

The true and faithful Muslim believes in the following principle articles of faith:

### 1. Belief in one God
*Allah* is one, having no partners and no equals. He is Infinite, Mighty, Merciful and ompassionate. He is the Creator and Provider. Man is unable to know Him

### 2. Sacred Scriptures
These Holy Writings include the Torah, the Psalms of David, the Gospels and the Koran. The Koran, though is the only authentic and complete book of God. It is then final revelation given to Muhammad.

### 3. The Prophets of God
Muslims believe in a number of prophets including Noah, Lot, Job and Jesus. Each nation had a warner from God. Among them all, Muhammad stands as the last messenger and the crowning glory of the foundation of prophethood.

### 4. Angels
The true believer accepts the presence of angels. They include Gabriel who brought the Koran to Muhammad. Satan is also recognized, as well as the *jinn*, capricious beings made of fire who can either do good or evil.

### 5. The Final Judgment
Large portions of the Koran reaffirm the end of the world. The dead will be judged, and those who merit *Allah's* approval will be

generously rewarded. Unbelievers, evil workers and idolaters will be cast into hell.

## 6. The Decrees of God

*Allah* is sovereign, hence all Muslims believe that He is responsible for everything that happens. He decides the fate of men and angels and is responsible for good and evil. Since this deity is wise and merciful, whatever He does must have a meaningful purpose. Man, as His creation should accept with good faith all that He does, even though one may fail to understand it fully, or deem it evil.

# NOTES

# APPENDIX B

# The Pillars of Islam

Among the specific duties set forth in the Koran and spelled out in the traditions are five essential practices that all Muslims must follow. These actions must be faithfully performed in order to gain entrance into the "gardens of paradise." They become a testimony to one's faith, but above all these "works" are needed so as to balance the scales of judgment. By "doing" these good deeds, eternal merit with God can be achieved and salvation assured.

**1. The Declaration:** *Shahada*: *"There is no god but God and Muhammad is his messenger."* This simple profession of faith contains the essence of all Islam. In it's melodious Arabic form, the words *"La Ilaha illa Allah; Muhammad rasul Assul,"* are repeated every day by all devout Muslims. This creed is included in each call to prayer. It is also found on the coins and flags of some Arab states and seen in inscriptions on buildings. The mere recital of this statement makes one a Muslim

**2. The Duty of Prayer** *Salat:* Islamic prayer is not a freeform conversation with God, but rather a highly ritualized form of worship. The Koran promises that those who pray will enter heaven. Tradition also states that each *salah* completed will ensure forgiveness of one's daily minor sins. Prayer is required five times a day but only after a cleansing ceremony has been completed. The worshipper must face Mecca and pray in Arabic.

**3. The Obligation to Fast:** *Sawm:* Once a year for a period of one month, all Muslims are required to abstain from food, drink,

285

smoking and sexual relations during the hours of daylight. This occurs during Ramadan, the ninth lunar month of the Islamic calendar. The fast is meant to test the self denial and submission of the faithful and permit the rich to experience the deprivations of the poor. Many truly seek God and find Him in dreams and visions. This time is also one of the most merriest of the year as feasting and celebrations occur during the evenings.

**4. Almsgiving:**

*Zakah:* Charity is one of the principal duties imposed by the Koran. Almsgiving is also a work of merit. The very word *zakah* means purification. The amount varies according to the different kind of properties owned, but generally is around 2 ½ % of one's income. The money is given to the poor, to travelers and to those serving the cause of Islam

**5. The Pilgrimage:**

*Hajj:* Every adult Muslim whether male or female is required to visit the *Ka'ba* in Mecca at least once during his or her life. Exemptions are permitted for the sick, the insane and women who have no husbands or other male relatives to accompany them. The pilgrimage must be made during the twelfth month of the year known as *Dhu al Hijjah.* It is widely believed that a *hajj* will guarantee entry into Paradise.

**6. The Holy War:**

*Jihad:* The "hidden pillar," the *jihad* is added as an obligation by most Muslims, but never listed officially. *Jihad* is an Arabic word meaning "to exert" or "exertion." It means to struggle on behalf of God and Islam with the pen, speech and the sword. The Kharijite sect of Islam elevated the *jihad* to a sixth pillar during the early history of Islam. There exists a wide variety of interpretations of what constitutes a *jihad.* Islamic scholars maintain that there are two: an inner *jihad* against sin and an external conflict against the enemies of Islam. One who dies in a *jihad* is guaranteed eternal life in Paradise.

# NOTES

# APPENDIX C

# The History of Muhammad's Successors

The Caliphs were the spiritual and temporal rulers of all Islam. They bore the time of *"Amir al-mu'minin"* or "Commander of the faithful." Bitter oppositions, seditions and even murders marked their reigns. A sordid legacy of the righteousness of Islam.

**1. Abu-Bakr**
The first Caliph, or deputy after Muhammad, as well as his closet friend. Abu-Baker gave his daughter A'isha (age 6) to Muhammad in marriage. As Caliph, he ruled for two years (632-634). Abu-Bakr died after eating a meal of poisoned rice.

**2. Omar**
Ruled for ten years (634-644) before being stabbed with a poisoned dagger by a Persian slave.

**3. Othman**
Married two of Muhammad's daughters and ruled for twelve years (644-656). He was stabbed to death as he was reading the Koran.

**4. Ali**
The prophet's cousin Ali, married Muhammad's daughter Fatima. He battled an army organized by the prophet's widow, A'isha and won after 13,000 Muslims had died fighting against each other. Confrontation and vengeance followed. His own supporters turned on him and in 661 A.D. assassinated Ali with a sword while he was on his way to prayer.

**5. Al-Hassan**
The son of Ali and the grandson of Muhammad, Al-Hassan ruled for five months. He accepted a gener-

ous offer to renounce his claim and stepped down. The ex-Caliph retired to his harem in Medina, where he married and divorced some one hundred and thirty Arab women. His rapid marriages and separations earned him the title of *al-Mutliq* "the Divorcer." One of his wives was hired to poison him. This she did, receiving a large sum of money for her efforts.

### 6. Al-Hussein

The brother of Al-Hassan attempted to rule. Old factions of dissent and rival claims split apart Islam. Al-Hussein sought to join rebels in Persia who were sympathetic to his claims. On route there, He and his followers were surrounded by *Sunni* Muslims and killed in battle. His head was sent as a trophy to Damascus. This incident helped create a new political movement within Islam: the *Shiate Ali* or Party of Ali; today's *Sh'ites*. This faction of Islam dedicated itself to the restoration of the hereditary Ali rule.

# NOTES

# APPENDIX D

# Islam One Faith: Many Sects

Islam declares that God is one, but unlike its confession, it is not. As a faith, it is neither unified nor in one accord. Muslims are separated into numerous sects. Of the one billion believers, 85% practice some form of folk Islam, combining the occult and animistic beliefs with Muhammad's faith. Cultural differences separate these believers too, as well as personal, geographical, linguistical and doctrinal interpretations. One famous Muslim tradition records that the prophet foresaw this happening and remarked:

> *Verily it will happen to my people even as it did to the children of Israel. The children of Israel were divided into seventy-two sects, and my people will be divided into seventy-three. Every one of these sects will go to hell, except one sect.*[1]

Ideally, the Islamic community or umma would gather together and identify the heretical groups. All deviants and rebels would be assigned to hell. Only true Muslims would be privileged to enter into paradise. In reality, schisms have separated Islam into thousands of sects and splinter groups. The principle divisions with in the body of Islam are:

---

1. *Mishkat al Misbih,* Bk. 1 Ch. 6.2

**1. Sunnism**

The majority of Muslims embrace the *Sunni* version of Islam (85-90%). Often known as the most orthodox of all the Islamic believers, they recognize the first four Caliph's as being "rightly guided" and do not attribute any special religious nor political function to the descendants of the prophet's son-in-law, Ali. The *Sunni's* follow the traditions *sunna:* well trodden paths or customs) of Muhammad, hence their name. These oral sayings or hadiths help interpret and define the Koran.

**2. Wahhabis**

This fundamentalist faction is actually a part of the *Sunni* majority, yet seeks to purge Islam of additions to the faith made later than the prophet's era. Noted for its rigid beliefs and intolerance, the *Wahhabis* demand that their own followers, as well as all other Muslims strictly observe all the religious duties of Islam or suffer flogging and death. This sect advocates man's predestination rather than salvation through good works. These fundamentalist Muslims disapprove of music, singing, laughter and clapping, but encourage the practice of polygamy. The *mutaw'ahs* or religious police come from this party of believers. The *Wahhabis* have allied themselves with the House of Sa'ud. Most of Arabia is now under their influence.

**3. Shi'ites**

Holding the same beliefs as the *Sunni* majority, the *Shi'ites* have separated themselves from their Islamic brothers over the right of succession. In their opinion, the prophet's son-in-law and cousin Ali, as well as his heirs were the legal successors to the Caliphate. Thus, Ali should have been appointed the first Caliph, and not the fourth. Hence, the head of the Islamic *umma* must be a literal descendant of the prophet. The *Shi'ites* preserve an official list of all those who should have governed Islam. This blood feud has never been resolved and has fostered hate, assassinations, and wars. The name *Shi'ite* is Arabic for "partisans." *Shi'ism* carries a strong undercurrent of sacrifice, suffering and martydom since the key figures of its theology besides the prophet and Fatima were all assassinated. The Ayatollah Khomeini and his followers came from this party.

**4. Ithna Ashariya's**

The "Twelvers" from the word *ithna'ashar* or twelve is the most important division of the *Shi'ites*. They recognize twelve imams as the descendants of Ali. The last imam was Muhammad al-Mahdi who disappeared in 878 A.D. to return and rule again one day. One hadith records Muhammad the prophet as saying, *"There is no Madhi save Jesus, the son of Mary."* The "Twelvers" believe that the imams guard and direct the destiny of the world. Pilgrimages are made to the tombs of their "saints." They wait for the return of their *al-Majid.* "Twelvers" add the name of Ali to their profession of faith, *"...and Ali is the friend of God."*

**5. Sab'iya**

The "Seveners" or *Sabiya*, restrict the number of imams to seven, but cannot seem to agree as to which seven these are. The heir to the sixth imam died before his father in 762 A.D. The rule of the prophet's succession was in doubt and various claimants arose. The number seven some feel explains this gap. It is symbolic of completion. Thus a new cycle of imams was begun. Secret doctrines and Greek philosophies influence their beliefs. Numerology affects their interpretation of the Koran. A sect of Sab'iyas once stole the sacred Black Stone in 930 A.D. and returned it in seven pieces in 951 A.D., after a ransom was paid. This faction rules Syria today.

**6. Druze**

A separated community of believers, living in Lebanon, Israel and Syria. The *Druze* are a secretive sect. They no longer accept converts. Degrees of initiation are required. They do not recognize Islamic Law, nor does Islam accept them. They are linked historically and practice common forms of worship. *Druze* living in Israel are allowed to serve in the Israel Defense Forces.

**7. Sufism**

The mystics of Islam, this sect dedicates themselves to the worship of God. Their goal is to attain a complete union with God. Divine reality is perceived by the heart, the spirit and *sira;* secrets revealed by the groups' teachers and passed on to disciples. They believe in meditation, fasting, "dancing" and the endless repetition of certain religious phases. Belief in bi-location as well as communication with plants and animals is common. *Sufis* feel that *Allah* has fixed the will of man, thus there is no difference between good and evil. The "whirling Dervishes" come from this sect.

**8. Ahmadiyya's**

The "Jehovah Witnesses" of Islam, came out of Colonial India. Their founder Mirza-Ahmad, posed as an Indian *guru* (teacher) professing to come in the spirit and power of Jesus Christ, Muhammad and Krishna. Ahmad believed that Christ did not die on the cross but came to India. Here, he lived in Kasmir until his death at the age of 120. The *Ahmadiyya's* are growing in numbers due to their strong missionary work and *da'wah* (witnessing). They are very active in Africa and the United States. The majority of the Islamic brotherhood rejects this sect.

**9. Kharijites**

The first faction of Islam "the seceders," separated from the prophet's son-in-law and then later assassinated him. Primary to their belief is the purity of conduct and doctrine. All who fail this standard are considered "infidels." They consider all but themselves, unbelievers and traitors to Islam. This group holds that the head of the Islamic community must be the most worthy Muslim, regardless of his origins. They are now know as *Ibadi* and are found in North Africa, and Oman.

**10. Bahai**

The Universalists of Islam, the *Bahai* have suffered much persecution in Iran, causing them to relocate to Haifa, Israel. They believe in humanitarianism and pacifism

294

## 11. Black Muslims

The Black Muslim movement originated in the United States through the efforts of Wallace Ford, Elijah Muhammad and Malcolm X. It was founded as a protest against white racism. This sect advocates Islamic  principles of universal brotherhood, and social justice.

The New Nation of Islam was organized in 1978 under Louis Farrakan. He organized "the Million Man March" to Washington D.C. in Oct. 1995. This movement is gradually becoming accepted into mainstream Islam. Many Afro-Americans are also embracing Islam, apart from participation in separatist Black Muslim movements.

# NOTES

# APPENDIX E

# Names Given to Muslim Men

**Muhammad:**   Named in memory and honor of the prophet of Islam. **Ahmed** and **Mahmud** are also used.

**Mustapha:**   The Elect

**Abu Bakr:**   Father-in-law, close friend of the prophet and first Caliph (632-634).

**Omar:**   Second Caliph (634-644).

**Othman:**   Third Caliph (644-656).

**Ali:**   Son-in-law and cousin of Muhammad, fourth Caliph (656-661).

**Hassan:**   Grandson of Muhammad.

**Hussein**   Grandson of Muhammad

Biblical names:   **Ibrahim** (Abraham), **Ismail, Yusuf, Yunus** (Jonah), **Musa** (Moses), **Dawud** (David), **Suleiman** (Solomon), **Yahya** (John the Baptist), **Isa** (Jesus).

Some names are compounded with **Abd** (Slave or servant) and a divine name such as **Abd al-Nasser,** "the servant of the God who gives victory." The word **din** (religion) is also used, thus **Salah ad-Din** (Saladin) meaning "integrity of religion," as well as **Jamal al-Din** or "the beauty of religion."

# Names Given to Muslim Women

| | |
|---|---|
| **Amina:** | The mother of the prophet |
| **Halima:** | Muhammad's nurse |
| **Khadija:** | Muhammad's first wife |
| **A'isha:** | The daughter of Abu Bakr, whom Muhammad married after Khadija's death. |
| **Hafsa:** | Another wife, the daughter of Omar. |
| **Zaynab:** | The name of one of Muhammad's wives, and one of his daughters. |
| **Fatima:** | A Daughter of Muhammad |
| **Rugayya:** | A Daughter of Muhammad |
| **Umm Kulthum:** | A Daughter of Muhammad |
| **Maryam:** | Mary, the mother of Jesus |
| **Hudah:** | The direction that God gives |
| **Jadila:** | The beautiful |
| **Farida:** | The pearl of great value |
| **Rashida:** | Endowed with honesty |
| **Layla:** | The night |

# NOTES

# APPENDIX F

# The Power of the Printed Page

A little old man with graying beard and kindly, smiling hazel eyes sits in a wheelchair on the veranda of a home for the aged in a near East city. His face is lined, but the lines are those of a thinker. He is talking to his Muslim neighbor-a thin, time-scarred old gentleman whose bed has been pulled out on the balcony. The first old man is telling something of his early life. A missionary friend listens while the tale is told.

*Years ago, I lived in the Holy City where I was the keeper in a large mosque. I was a devout Moslem, wearing the green turban to which I was entitled as a direct descendant of the Prophet. Five times a day when the muezzin called, I prayed with the faithful. One of my duties was to clean and fill the many ornate lamps, which hung in that mosque. I was also expected to collect the rents due from houses owned by the mosque. In these houses lived all manner of people, the better apartments being let to foreigners from whom we could demand a high rental. One of these tenants was a lady who lived alone. I wondered why she had left her far-away home to live among strangers, who, to judge by myself, loved her little.*

*One day, quite accidentally, I learned why she had come. When she gave me her rent money she handed me a small book. I suspected at once that it must be an accursed book of the*

300

*Christians, and had it not been for the precious money and the courtesy due a tenant of the holy mosque, I should have dropped the hated thing, which seemed to burn into my hand. As soon as possible I bowed politely and left the foreign lady.*

*There were other collections to be made that day, and lacking opportunity to do otherwise, I slipped the small book into my pocket. I forgot about it until later in the day when I sat alone in a shadowed corner of the great mosque. Curiosity overcame my fear and I opened the book surreptitiously.*

*Many years have gone by now, but never shall I forget my first impression of the beauty of that story. It was the Gospel according to Saint Mark, and as by some outer force I was impelled to read through the verses, which described John the Baptist, Christ's baptism, his temptation and the calling of some of the disciples. Perhaps more than all else I was impressed by the beauty and the purity of Christ's teaching and character. Suddenly I was covered with confusion. This thing, which I considered beautiful, this story, which was written in my own sacred tongue, was a despised Christian thing, a false book that they dared to set up in comparison with the holy Koran! Hastily I hid it lest I be detected.*

*Days slipped by, during which I condemned myself on the one hand and indulged my curiosity on the other. Finally I decided that there was no harm in carrying the book about with me. After all, my devotion to Islam could not be questioned. I managed to read all of the Gospel of Mark, and then, still firm in my own faith, I made bold to visit the foreign lady again and ask for other books of the same sort. I do not know what impression I made upon her, but she received me kindly and without question gave me three other Gospels.*

*In a short time I had read all four Gospels and then I secured the Book of Acts. It was not long then before I had to acknowledge that Jesus the Christ had won me as he had Paul of Tarsus, though my own conversion was much less dramatic. I was filled with a great longing to serve my Savior and Friend, who had revealed God to me in a new light-as a loving Father to whom I was precious.*

*So strong was my new faith, so compelling His plea to leave all and follow Him that I knew I must make an open declaration. The great mosque became an intolerable place; the copies of the sacred Koran, the shining lamps, the very rugs leered at me. I knew that I must turn my back on all this. My parents would disown me and disinherit me; my friends would seek to destroy me; my wife would have to do as her parents and mine decreed, and I should have to leave her and the children.*

*Weeks and months slipped by as I hesitated. My life was comfortable, even luxurious. I was loved, respected, trusted. In giving up Islam I should be giving up all security and respectability as I knew them. But while I debated about this other Prophet and compared His life to Muhammad, I knew what I must do; and at last I did it.*

*The result was all that I had anticipated, but though my suffering was great, I felt no sorrow nor regret. There were many new friends now to replace the old whom I loved with a greater love than ever and forgave wholeheartedly when they persecuted me. Penniless, I left my home city with all of its dear associations, and traveled northward. Everywhere Christians who had heard of me welcomed me, but whenever I encountered those of my old faith, they reviled me mercilessly. I was refused shelter in every Muslim home; I was shamefully cursed and ejected from restaurants and all public places where I was known.*

*For a time doubt assailed me. I wondered whether God had forgotten me. Things were strange as I traveled away from home; I did not slip easily into the new customs and religious practices. I missed my loved ones, particularly my sons, who would now grow up considering their father a renegade, an infidel, a betrayer of the faith. Perhaps these were the hardest hours of my life. But when my sorrow was deepest, when the outlook seemed blackest, God mad Himself known to me, and I was able to rise up and follow Him with renewed strength and vision.*

*Now after all these years I can testify that He has never forsaken me at any time and that He is worthy of every sacrifice made for His sake. I would not go back to the old life, with all of its security and material comfort, for all that the world has to offer. I have tried to witness for Him, to tell others of His love and beauty, and as life's shadows lengthen around me, I realize that I must work harder that no time be lost.*

Thus the fascinating tale comes to a close. Whenever he can do so, this truly converted believer reads from his "Beautiful Book" to his companions, and if we were there to see, we should note that many a face is softened that new life comes into hard, cold eyes which have seen much bitterness and disappointment, for the Prince of Peace hovers near.[1]

---

1    Mabel H. Erdman, Presbyterian Missionary, Syria. Reprinted from *The Missionary Review of the World* Oct. 1937, pgs. 482-483

# NOTES

# APPENDIX G

## "I Saw Jesus"
### by Mohammed

I was born into an orthodox Muslim family in Iran. During my childhood, I prayed five times a day. But I never really understood what I was doing, and my religion never touched my heart. As I grew, I stopped praying and participating in religious ceremonies.

Several years ago I went to India to continue my studies. At about this time, war broke out between Iran and Iraq. Many, many Iranians lost their lives, including four of my friends. I thought, *If there is a God, what is He doing while all this is going on in my country?*

During this period I became good friends with another Iranian student and we began sharing living quarters. Through this friend I came to know a Christian family in the Indian city where we were studying. Although the family often invited us to their home, they rarely discussed religion with me because they knew I was against God.

One Sunday my friend got early and went out. When he returned in the evening, I asked him were he had been. He simply said that he had gone somewhere. The next Sunday he went out again. This time he told me that he had attended church with the Christian family. *"Church?"* I shouted. *"Why should you go to church? Are you not Muslim?"* I was so disturbed that I shut myself in my room and went to bed without eating.

In September 1983, my friend asked me if I would like to go to church with him. *"Come and see the joy and love among the people. It is wonderful, really!"*

*"Why should I go to church when I never go to the mosque? Never talk to me again about church,"* I replied.

The next time I saw the Christian family, they said *"We know you are free on Sunday. Would you like to go to church with us?"*

*"No"*

*"Why not?"* they asked

*"Why do you go to church?"*

*"To worship God."*

*"I do not believe in God, so why should I go to church?"*

They asked me to go just once. Since I was bored and wanted something to do I agreed. So we attended church. When the meeting was over, the pastor of the church greeted me and asked whether I would like to come again. I just shook my head. The gesture meant neither yes nor no. But I attended church the next Sunday and the following, and the following.

One Sunday, the pastor gave me an English Bible and asked me to read it at home. I was shocked. I wanted to give it back to him and ask him to give it to someone else. I wanted to tell him I did not believe in God. But somehow I did not say anything. I took the Bible home and threw it into a corner. When I attended church again, the pastor asked me if I had read the Bible. I told him that I had not read it because my English was weak and my mother tongue was Persian.

A few weeks later, the pastor gave me a Persian Bible. Again I was shocked. How had he found a Bible in my language? But I took the Persian Bible home and put it in a corner where it began to gather dust.

During January and February 1984, I was very depressed. My country was being bombed by enemy planes and my brother was fighting at the front. I was frustrated and angry with everything and everybody. I even hit a few people and shouted at my room-mate. In my distress, I went up to the roof of my home and shouted at God, *"If You are there, why aren't You doing something about my country and all of my problems?"*

In mid-February a gospel meeting was held in a large field near my home. When I heard that people were being healed I decided to attend.

The first night I attended, I saw with my own eyes many people being healed. I could not believe all of this. I thought, *"If the doctors cannot heal these people how can it be that this man is healing them just by praying? "*

To find out the truth, I attended a second time. So many people had come that there was no place to sit down. People were standing everywhere, including many who were not able to walk, talk or hear. After preaching the Word of God, the speaker began to pray for the sick. Many people went forward and said they had been healed by God's power. I had bee closely watching a crippled man near me. He went to the front and broke his crutches, saying God had healed him. All that I saw and heard was confusing and difficult to accept.

Then in the first week of April, something happened that changed my life forever. As I was sleeping, a power began shaking me. I saw Jesus standing in the doorway of my room.

*"Mohammed! Mohammed! Mohammed! Get up! Get up!"*

I sat up, perspiring greatly. As I did, Jesus disappeared. I began to doubt if anyone had really called me. Maybe my room-mate was trying to worry me. I poked him, but he was snoring. As I slept a second time, I felt an even greater power shaking me from head to foot. Again I saw Jesus! I could see clearly His face, long hair, and beautiful robe. His eyes were powerful and piercing. The light of His presence lit the whole room.

Again Jesus called very loudly, *"Mohammed! Mohammed! Mohammed! Get up! Get up!"*

Then He disappeared again, I jumped out of bed; my whole body was shaking. I opened the door and rushed outside. It was about 4:00 in the morning. Everything was quiet and calm. Suddenly I realized that Jesus Christ was the only way to God and that I had sinned. I went up onto the roof, and there I begged Jesus to forgive my sins.

From that time, I have felt free and happy and completely born again! I no longer feel lonely or frustrated. I thank God for revealing himself to me so lovingly, even though I had been against Him.[1]

---

1.   Reprinted from *Mountain Movers*, Nov. 1990, pgs. 16-17

# NOTES

# APPENDIX H

## Seven Steps for Winning Muslims to Christ

1. Share your testimony

2. Appreciate the best in Muslims:

   a. If he or she is devout, compliment the person.
   b. If the man or woman is hospitable, praise that virtue.
   c. If the individual gives to the poor, commend their actions.
   d. If he or she cares for widows or orphans, compliment that.

3. Keep your message centered on Jesus. Do not debate, argue or criticize Muhammad or the Koran.

4. Encourage them to read and study the Bible.

5. Minister to their needs, be their friend.

6. Create a favorable atmosphere in society: pray for healing, practice medicine, start schools and educate the poor.

7. Trust the Holy Spirit to work in the life of Muslims

*Henry Martyn* (1781-1812)

# NOTES

# APPENDIX I

# The Worth of A Soul

The worth of a soul! Who can count its value? Who can appraise its worth? An immortal soul is beyond all price. In money, one soul is of more value than the wealth of the whole world. In suffering, it is better that all the people of the world should suffer all their lives on earth, if by their suffering one soul could be saved. In journeying, no foreign land is too distant or any portion of it too inaccessible, for all the people of the world to take a journey there, if by so doing one soul could be saved. There is no trouble too great, no humiliation too deep, no suffering too severe, no love too strong, no labor too hard, no expense too large, but that is worth it, if it is spent in the effort to win a soul.

Of all the creations in this world and in the world to come, the greatest, the most wonderful, the most priceless, the most enduring is a soul. God loves the soul more than all other creation. He fashioned it after His own image, and made it like unto Himself. Every soul has departed from God and gone astray, and God has brought every soul back again with a price. That price was the blood of His only begotten Son. Who took upon Himself the sin of the soul, suffered the death penalty, that the soul might be saved, cleansed, and made holy again. God loves every soul with an everlasting eternal love greater and deeper than any human love can possibly be.

Satan hates the soul. In Satan's enmity towards God, he is using all his energy, using every snare, his utmost cunning, employing every means with the one single purpose of ruining the soul of man, because Satan knows the soul is God's most cherished creation, the very apple of His eye.

A soul will never die. When this earth of ours has crumbled to dust and has passed away into the forgotten past, a soul will still be in its freshness of youth. When in the fathomless future, eternity has become hoary with age; the soul will still be young. When a million million eternities have each lived out their endless ages and have rolled by into the unthinkable past and time is no more, the soul will still be living, a conscious personal reality, endowed with perpetual youth and perpetual life.

God has said: *"He that winneth souls is wise."* If Christians would only realize the value and the immortality of a soul, and the shortness of this earthly life, they would work feverishly, unceasingly, with all their greatest energy, day after day, year after year that they might save one.

O Christians, are there souls passing your way? Are you bestirring yourself in their behalf that they may have eternal life and joy, or are you allowing them to cross your path and pass on unwarned, to an eternal death?

*W.K. Norton,*
Missionary to India (1923)

# NOTES

# GLOSSARY

**The following list contains many words and names, which appear frequently in any discussion of Islam:**

| | |
|---|---|
| **Abd** | Slave or servant, either legally or in the religious sense, thus defining an individual's relationship to God. Hence, *Abd Allah* means "the slave of God" and *Abd al-Karim* is the name of a person who is "the slave of the Most Generous." |
| **Abu** | "Father," used in many Muslim proper names such as *Abu Bakr* |
| **Ahl al-Kitab** | "*People of the Book.*" The Koran identifies Jews and Christians as such for they possess written scriptures in contrast to the heathen unbelievers. |
| **A'isha** | Muhammad's youngest wife (age 9), and most favorite. |
| **Allah** | The supreme name for God in Arabic. The word *Allah* is possibly a contraction of *al-ilah* meaning "the Divinity." *Allah* was also the title given by Muhammad's tribe to the moon god, which ruled over Mecca. Muslims revere this name and identify it as the proper and true name for God. |
| **Allah's Daughters** | The three high goddesses worshipped along with Allah, by the people in Muhammad's time. These idols were Al-Lat, the sun goddess, Al-Uzza the goddess of the morning star (Venus) and Manat, the goddess of fate. |
| **Alyasa** | The Biblical prophet Elisha, the disciple of Elijah. He is mentioned in the Koran in *Surah* 6:86. |
| **Al-Aksa** | "*The Farthest*" mosque. The name that Islam gives to the Temple Mount in Jerusalem, although its |

315

location is never mentioned in the Koran. The *Al-Aksa* Mosque is the third most important holy site in Islam, and stands atop the Temple Mount. It's silver dome distinguishes it from the Dome of the Rock or Mosque of Omar.

| | |
|---|---|
| **Al-Amin** | An early name given to the prophet Muhammad, before his revelations. It means *"the Trustworthy One."* |
| **Al-Isra** | The miraculous night journey of Muhammad (S. 17:1). |
| **Al-Masih** | "The Anointed One," a title given by the Koran for the Messiah Jesus Christ (S. 3:45). |
| **Al-Miraj** | The "ascension" of Muhammad into heaven, while on his night journey. |
| **Al-Quds** | The Arabic name for Jerusalem "the Holy," sanctified by Islam because of Muhammad's purported visit. |
| **'Awrah** | The parts of a woman's body which must be covered. They are external features or *"things to be ashamed of."* The Hadith outlines ten, including the face and the hair. Some followers of Islam, consider even a woman's hands to be 'awrah. Other parts of the Hadith proclaim that *"the woman is 'awrah, when she goes outside the house, the devil welcomes her."* Hence, women are discouraged from leaving the home. |
| **Azan** | The Muslim call to prayer. |
| **Basmalah** | This traditional prayer or saying is pronounced by Muslims many times each day as a consecration before undertaking any lawful action. It is always said before a meal, or after its completion. This Islamic prayer is the equivalent of Christianity's grace. The words *"Bismi-Llahi-r-Rahmani-r-* |

*Raham*" means "In the name of God, the Merciful, the Compassionate."

**Buraq**
The miraculous horse which the Angel Gabriel brought to Muhammad, to undertake his ascent into Heaven. The root of the word derives from *baraqa*, "to glitter."

**Caliph**
A successor, a substitute or a deputy. The Caliph's served as successors to the prophet Muhammad. They were his representatives as well as the spiritual leaders of Islam.

**Dar al-harb**
The "*abode of war.*" Those countries and territories where Islam does not prevail.

**Dar al-Islam**
The "*abode of Islam,*" a country under Islamic rule.

**Dhimma**
"Covenant" People of the covenant are non-Muslims who live in a Muslim country and have submitted to the rule of Islam. They are guaranteed rights to life, liberty and property, although certain restrictions apply.

**Fatiha**
Opening chapter of the Koran, frequently recited in prayer.

**Hadith**
The traditions of Islam. Stories and sayings from Muhammad's life and those who were near him. A source of authority for the interpretation of the Koran and Islamic law.

**Hajj**
The pilgrimage to Mecca. One of the required "pillars" of Islam. One who has undertaken this pilgrimage is called a *hajji/hajjia* upon his or her return.

**Halal**
That which is legally permitted, as opposed to *haram*, forbidden.

**Haram**
Sacred or forbidden. The two holy cities of Mecca and Medina as well as the enclosure surrounding the Dome of the Rock in Jerusalem, are sacred to Islam.

| | |
|---|---|
| **Hawari** | A term taken from the Ethiopian language, referring in the Koran to the disciples of Jesus. |
| **Hijrah** | The "migration" or emigration of Muhammad from Mecca to Yathrib (later called Medina), in 622 A.D. The beginning of the Islamic calendar whose dates are designated *anno hijrah,* A/H, in honor of the prophet's flight to safety. The word is also transliterated into the English as *hijra and hegira.* |
| **Hubal** | One of the idols worshipped in pre-Islamic Mecca. This god was set in the *Ka'ba* along with another 360 idols. The ritual casting of lots and the divining of arrows was performed in front of it. Muhammad pulled this idol down and used it as a doorstep into the *Ka'ba.* |
| **Ibn** | "Son" The term is used in such proper names as *Ibn Sa'ud.* |
| **Iblis** | This "Arabic" word derives from the Greek *diabolos* or slanderer, hence it is translated as "devil." A personal name of the evil one, otherwise known as *ash-shaytan* (from the Hebrew) and described in the Koran as "the adversary." |
| **Ibrahim** | Abraham, the father of Ishmael and Isaac. |
| **Id al Abha** | The "*feast of the sacrifice.*" The singular most important feast in slam commemorating Abraham's sacrifice of the ram, which released him from the intended sacrifice of his son. During this three-day event, communal prayers are said and an animal is sacrificed by the head of the household. |
| **Idris** | Enoch (S. 21:85). |
| **Id al-Fitr** | The festival at the conclusion of the Ramadan fasting period. |
| **Injil** | The Word of God as revealed to Jesus |

**318**

**Inshallah**

A common Muslim expression meaning *"God willing."* It indicates that all events are contingent upon the will of *Allah*.

**Isa**

The Muslim name for Jesus.

**Islam**

From the word *salam* meaning peace. Islam is also interpreted as "surrender." A follower of Islam surrenders to the will of *Allah*.

**Isma'il**

The eldest son of Abraham by Hagar. *Isma'il* is the Arabic form of Ishmael.

**Jahannam**

An Arabic loan word from the Hebrew *Gehenna*. A place of torment for the dammed; otherwise known as hell.

**Janna**

A "garden" thus a description of what paradise is like in the Koran.

**Jibril**

The archangel Gabriel, the "reported" bearer of the Koran to Muhammad.

**Jihad**

A holy war against unbelievers. A divine command to extend Islam into the *dar al-harb* (the non Islamic territories which are in disbelief). A *jihad* can be ordered to defend Islam from danger. All adult males must participate. A *jihad* cannot be undertaken against other Muslims.

**Jinn**

"Purported" invisible creatures, made from "smokeless fire." These entities possess a free will, thus they are capable of salvation or damnation. Muhammad recited the Koran at night in the desert to *jinns*. He stated that some of these spirits listened and believed in Islam. Their chiefs made allegiance to the prophet. Today, the Mosque of the Jinn is built over this location, which is in the city of Mecca. The English word "genie" derives from the Arabic *jinn*.

**Ka'ba**

*"Cube,"* Islam's holiest shrine. A large cubic stone structure covered with a black cloth located in the center of the Grand Mosque in Mecca. All Muslims orientate themselves to Mecca when at prayer. Tradition holds that this holy house (*al-bayt al-haram)* was built by Adam and restored by Abraham and Ishmael. Muhammad later helped rebuild this edifice, by setting the black stone into the corner of its wall.

**Kafir**

One who refuses to see the truth, an infidel who rejects the divine mission and revelation of the prophet Muhammad. Such an individual is ungrateful to God and is considered an atheist.

**Kahin**

A priest, a wizard or a soothsayer, akin to the Hebrew *Kohen.*

**Khitan**

Circumcision, a requirement for all male Muslims (age 13), and for many females.

**Kismet**

One's fate, portion or lot in life, as designated by *Allah's* will.

**Koran**

Literally *"the reading or the recitation."* Islam's holy book.

**Laylat al-Qadr**

The *"night of power"* or *"destiny."* The night when the Koran descended in its entirety into the soul of the prophet.

**Mahdi**

The Guided one. A messianic figure, who will appear at the end of time, to rule the world in justice and righteousness. Some Christians foresee a prophetic Islamic Anti-Christ arising from this figure (Rev. 13:11), while others see Jesus.

**Maktub**

"What is written." The sense that God has ordained what is to happen.

**Malak**

Angel, the servant and messenger of God (*malaika,* pl).

**320**

**Masihi**     A Christian, from *al-Masih,* the Messiah.

**Mawali**     Originally freed slaves; later non-Arab converts to Islam..

**Minaret**     The tower attached or beside a mosque from which the call to prayer is made. The word derives from the Arabic *manarah*, meaning lighthouse.

**Minbar**     Pulpit, a set of steps in mosques from where sermons are delivered.

**Mosque**     Muslim place of worship.

**Muezzin**     One who calls the faithful to prayer.

**Mujaddid**     The Messiah, as defined in Islamic doctrine and belief.

**Muslims**     God's chosen people, according to Islamic belief.

**Mut'a**     A form of temporary marriage for a fixed period of time, on payment to the woman. The prophet approved these relationships, especially when men went to war.

**Nabi**     Prophet. A term applied to Biblical prophets as well as to Muhammad.

**Nafs**     The soul.

**Namus**     An angel who imparted knowledge or brought revelation. The word derives from the Greek, *nomos* or law.

**Nasrani**     One from Nazareth. A term used to identify Christians.

**Nuh**     Noah.

**Qibla**     The direction that all Muslims face to pray; towards the *Ka'ba* in Mecca.

**Ramadan**

The Islamic month for fasting. Muhammad received his first revelations during this time.

**Riddah**

Apostasy from Islam. An apostate is called a *murtadd.*

**Ridwan**

The final absolute acceptance of a soul by God (S. 89:27-30).

**Ruh Allah**

A special name given in the Koran for Jesus (the *"spirit of God,"* S. 4:169)

**Salah**

Ritual prayer, one of the five pillars of Islam.

**Sawm**

Fasting, another pillar of Islam.

**Shahadah**

The Islamic confession of faith (*"There is no god but God and Muhammad is His Prophet").*

**Shaitan**

Satan, or the Devil.

**Shirk**

The most grievous sin in Islam, association of another with God (polytheism). Suggesting that God can be divided is blasphemy.

**Sunnah**

A record of sayings and activities of Muhammad.

**Surah**

A chapter of Koran. Each verse is called an *ayat* (*ayas,* pl) or sign miracle).

**Tawrat**

The Torah as revealed to Moses.

**Zabur**

The Arabic name for the Psalms of David (*Dawud).*

**Zakat**

Required alms tax (2 ½ %) of one's income. One of Islams's pillars.

# NOTES

# SELECTED BIBLIOGRAPHY

Abdul-Haqqi, Abdiyah Akbar, *Sharing Your Faith with a Muslim.* Min.: Bethany, 1980.

Accad, Fouad Elias *Building Bridges: Christianity and Islam.* Colorado Springs: NavPress, 1997.

Ali, M.. *Islam Reviewed.* Fort Meyers: Fish House, 1995.

Anderson, M. *The Trinity.* Pasadena: n.p., 1994.

Armstrong, Karen *Muhammad.* San Francisco: Harper, 1992.

Bennett, Ramon *The Wall.* Citrus Heights, CA: Shekinah, 2000.

Bergson, S.G. *The Nature of Islam.* Jerusalem: I.C.E.J., 1996.

Cragg, Kenneth *The Call of the Minaret.* New York: Oxford Univ., 1956.

_____, *Sandals at the Mosque:* Christian Presence Amid Islam. New York: Oxford Univ., 1959.

_____, *Jesus and the Muslim.* Boston: One World, 1999

Cooper, Anne *Ishmael, My Brother.* Kent: England MARC, 1993.

Darg, Christine *The Jesus Visions.* Orlando: Daystar, 1995.

Davis, David *The Rise and Fall of Islam.* Haifa, IS: Carmel Assembly, 2002.

Dretke, James P. *A Christian Approach to Muslims.* Pasdena: William Carey, 1979.

Dribble, R. F. *Mohammed.* New York: Viking, 1926.

Eshleman, Paul *I Just Saw Jesus.* Laguna: The "Jesus" Film Project, 1991.

Esposito, John L. *Islam: The Straight Path.* New York: Oxford Univ., 1991.

Garlow, James L. *A Christian's Response to Islam.* Tulsa: River Oak, 2002.

Geisler, Norman & Saleeb, Abdul, *Answering Islam.* Grand Rapids: Baker 1993.

Gichrist, John *Christ in Islam and Christianity.* Pretoria, RSA: NGSP, 1990.

Goldsmith, Martin *Islam and Christian Witness.* Brombley, Kent: OM Pub. 1991.

# SELECTED BIBLIOGRAPHY

Goodwin, Jan *Price of Honor: Muslim Women.* New York: Penguin, 1994.

Graham, Finlay M. *Sons of Ishmael: How Shall They Hear?* Nashville: Convention, 1969.

Howell, Beth P. *Lady On A Donkey.* New York: Dutton, 1960.

Hughes, T.P. *Notes On Muhammadanism.* London: Allen, 1877.

Jadeed, Iskander *How To Share The Gospel With Our Muslim Brothers?* Villach: Austria, 1991.

Kritzeck, James *Sons of Abraham: Jews, Christians and Moslems.* Baltimore: Helicon, 1965.

Lewis, Bernard *The Arabs in History.* New York: Harper, 1996.

_____, *The Middle East.* New York: Harper, 1996.

Lippman, Thomas W. *Understanding Islam.* New York: Penguin, 1990.

Livingstone, Greg *Planting Churches in Muslim Cities.* Grand Rapids: Baker, 1993.

Lofti, Nasser *Iranian Christian.* Waco: Word, 1980.

Madany, Bassam M. *The Bible and Islam.* Palos Hts.: BTGH, 1992.

Malek, Sobhi *Islam: Introduction and Approach.* Irving: I.C.I., 1992.

Mahmoody, Betty *Not without My Daughter.* New York: St. Martin's 1987.

Marsh, Charles R. *Share Your Faith With A Muslim.* Chicago: Moody, 1975.

McAll, Kenneth *Healing the Family Tree.* London: Sheldon, 1994.

McCurry, Don M., *Healing the Broken Family of Abraham.* Colorado Springs, Ministry to Muslims, 2001.

_____, *The Gospel and Islam.* Monorovia: MARC 1979.

McDowell, Josh & Gilchrist, John *The Islam Debate.* San Bernardino: Here's Life, 1983.

Mikhail, Labib *Islam, Muhammad And The Koran.* Springfield VA 1996.

Miller, William M. *A Christian's Response To Islam.* Phillipsburg: P & R, 1976.

Morey, Robert *The Islamic Invasion.* Eugene: Harvest, 1992.

Morris, Henry *Many Infallible Proofs.* El Cajon: Creation, 1990.

Neill, Stephen *A History of Christian Missions.* New York: Penguin, 1982.

Nydell, Margret *Understanding Arabs.* Yarmouth: Intercultural Press, 1987.

Otis, George Jr. *The Last Of The Giants.* New York: Chosen, 1991.

_____, *Voice of Hope.* Van Nuys, CA: High Adventure Min., 1983.

Patwick, Constance *Henry Martyn.* London: IVF, 1953

Palmer, Bernard *Understanding the Islamic Explosion.* Beaverlodge, Canada: Horizon, 1980.

Parrinder, Geoffrey *Jesus in the Quran.* New York: Oxford Univ., 1977.

Parshall, Phil *Understanding Muslims Through Their Traditions.* Grand Rapids: Baker,1995.

_____, *Beyond The Mosque.* Grand Rapids: Baker, 1985.

_____, *Bridges to Islam.* Grand Rapids: Baker, 1983.

_____, *New Paths in Muslim Evangelism.* Grand Rapids: Baker, 1980.

_____, *The Fortress & The Fire.* Bombay: Gospel Literature Service, 1975.

Patai, Raphael, *The Arab Mind.* New York: Scribner's & Sons, 1973.

Pfanier, C.G. *The Mizan-Ul-Hagg* (Balance-of-Truth). Villach, Austria: Light of Life, 1986 Reprint.

Peters, Joan *From Time Immemorial.* Chicago: JKAP, 1988.

Ragg, Laura & Lonsdale ed. & trans. *The Gospel of Barnabas.* Oxford: Clarendon, 1907.

Rasooli, Jay M. & Allen, Cady H. *Dr. Sa'eed of Iran.* Pasadena: William Carey Pub., 1957.

Roberts, Lon *Armies of the Crescent.* Jerusalem: n.p., 2002.

Saal, William J. *Reaching Muslims for Christ.* Chicago: Moody, 1991.

Sabinni, John *Islam: A Primer.* Washington D.C.: M.E.E.A., 1983.

Safa, Reza F. *Inside Islam.* Orlando: Creation, 1996.

_____, *Blood of the Sword, Blood of the Cross.* Bromley, Kent: STL, 1992.

Sangster, Thelma *The Torn Veil.* Ft. Washington: C.L.C., 1989.

Sasson, Jean P. *Princess.* New York: Morrow, 1992.

Schlink, Basilea *Allah or the God of the Bible: What is the Truth?* Basingstoke, Hants: ESM, 1987.

Schwartz, Stephen *The Two Faces of Islam.* New York: Doubleday, 2002.

Shaw, Gwen R. *Redeeming the Land.* Jasper, AR: Engeltal, 1987.

Shipler, David K. *Arab and Jews.* New York: Penguin, 1986.

Shorrosh, Anis A. *Islam Revealed.* Nashville: Nelson, 1988.

Viorst, Milton *In the Shadow of the Prophet.* New York: Doubleday, 2002.

Warrag, Ibn *Why I Am Not A Muslim.* New York: Prometheus, 1995.

_____, *The Quest for the Historical Muhammad.* New York: Prometheus, 2000.

William, John *Islam.* New York: Braziller, 1961.

Wilson, Christy *More to be Desired than Gold.* S. Hamiliton: Gordon-Conwell, 1994.

Woodberry, J. Dudley *Muslims and Christians on the Emmanus Road.* Monrovia: MARC, 1989.

Zwemer, Samuel M. *The Moslem Christ.* New York: American Tract Society, 1912.

_____, *Call To Prayer* New York: Marshall Bro., 1910.

_____, *The Moslem World* London: Student Volunteer Movement for Foreign Missions, 1907.

_____, *The Moslem Doctrine of God* New York: American Tract Society, 1905.

## Korans

Arberry, A. J., *The Koran Interpreted.* New York: Macmillan 1964.

Dawood, N. J., *The Koran.* New York: Penguin, 1993.

Pickthall, Mohammed M. *The Meaning of the Glorious Koran.* New York: Signet, 1986.

Sale, George *The Koran.* New York: A. L. Burt, 1885.

## Reference Works

Glasse, Cyril *The Concise Encyclopedia of Islam.* San Francisco: Harper, 1989.

Khan, Muhammad Muhsin *The Translation of the Meanings of Sahih Al-Bukhari.* 9 Vol., Beriut: Dar Al-Arabia, 1970.

Peeble, Bernard ed. *The Fathers of the Church.* 37 Vols. Wash. D.C.: Catholic Univ., 1970, reprint.

Siddiqi, Abdul Hamid trans. *Sahih Muslim.* Vols. 1-4, Beriut: Dar Al Arabia, 1971.

## Selected Periodicals

Abd-El-Masih, Marcus "The Testimony of Marcus Abd-El-Masih." *The Moslem World* Vol. XXXV #3, July 1945, pgs. 211-215.

Baker, Barbara "In the Shadow of Islam" *Charisma* Vol. 23, #3 Oct. 1997, pgs. 44-53, 112.

Bentley, David ed. "The Boundaries of God." Pasadena, Zwemer Institute, 1993.

Bridges, Erich "Of Jesus Mosques' and Muslim Christians" *Mission Frontiers* Vol. 19, No. 7-10, Jul-Oct. 97, pgs. 19-21.

Canaan, T. "Tasit er Radifeh" (The Cup of Fear). *The Journal of the Palestine Oriental Society,* Vol. III #3, 1923.

Cannon III, James "The Gospel of Barnabas." *The Moslem World* Vol. XXXII #2, Apr. 1942, pgs. 167-178.

Elder, E.E. "What is the Koran?" *The Missionary Review of the World* Vol. LXI #12 12/38, pgs. 578-580.

Ellington, John "A Case of Mistaken Identity? Translating the Name of Jesus in Muslim Areas." *The Bible Translator* Vol. 44, No. 4 Oct. 1993, pgs. 401-405.

Finlay, Matt "Jesus, Son of God, A Translation Problem." *The Bible Translator* Vol. 30 No. 2 Apr. 1979, pgs. 241-244.

Finney, Davida M. "The Influence of Moslem Superstitions" *The Missionary Review of the World* Vol. LX #11 11/37 pgs. 461-463.

Grubb, Kenneth G. "The Passion of Raymund Lull." *The Missionary Review of the World* Vol. LX #11 11/37, pgs. 529-531.

Hudgell, E. W. G. "The Bible and the Koran Contrasted." *The Missionary Review of the World* Vol. LXI. #12 12/38, pgs. 27-30.

Kuiper, A. and Newman, Barclay "Jesus Son of God." *The Bible Translator* Vol. 28 #4, Oct. 1977, pgs. 432-438.

Morrison, R.A. "The Patience of Unanswered Prayer." *The Moslem World* Vol. XXXV Oct. 1945 #4, pgs. 269-272.

Safa, Reza "Christ in the House of Allah." *Charisma* Vol. 22 #2, Sept. 1996, pgs. 68-70.

Tony, Peter ed. Miraculous Interventions in the Muslim World" *Open Doors* n.d., pg. 1.

Trowbridge, Stephen Van R. "Islam's Greatest Failure." *The Missionary Review of the World* Vol. XLIX #10, 10/26 pgs. 791-792.

Weerstra, Hans M. ed. "Islam." *International Journal of Frontier Missions* Vol. 11. No. 2. Apr. 1994.

# SELECTED BIBLIOGRAPHY

White, Tom ed. "Sudan." *The Voice of the Martyrs* Dec. 1996, pg. 3.

Witner, La Donna "Muslim Women." *WherEver* (TEAM), pgs. 3-6.

Zwemer, Samuel M. "The Arabic Language & Islam." *The Missionary Review of the World* Vol. XXXIII #10, Oct. 1910, pgs. 774-779.

_____, "Canon W. H. T. Gairdner of Cairo." *The Missionary Review of the World* Vol. LII #2, Feb. 1929, pgs. 91-96.

_____, "Islam's Debt to the Bible." *The Missionary Review of the World* Vol. LVIII #9 Sept. 1935, pgs. 405-407.

_____, "Francis of Assisi and Islam." *The Moslem World* Vol. XXXIX No. 4, Oct. 49, pgs. 247-251.

# NOTES

# An Appeal To Muslims

If you are a Muslim and as a result of reading this book, you find yourself desiring to become a believer in Jesus (*Isa*) Christ, you can. He is the promised *Al-Masid* who will save those who call upon him in faith. Jesus *(Isa)* really died on the cross, almost 2000 years ago in Jerusalem for your sins. God though raised Him up from the dead, so that you can have forgiveness and a new life. You can accept Him right now! Pray this prayer from your heart, out loud:

> Jesus (Isa), I confess before you that I am a sinner. I repent for my sins and I want your forgiveness. I am sorry for the hurt that I have caused to you and to other people. I renounce the sinful habits of my life and promise that I will never return to them. I ask you now to take charge of my future path.
>
> I believe you died for me that I might have eternal life. I confess that your blood was shed to cleanse away my sin. I affirm that you were raised from the dead, and that you are alive today. Jesus *(Isa),* I hereby receive you into my heart as Lord and Savior of my life. I now receive by faith, your gift of eternal life. Please write my name in the Book of Life. I thank you that you are my Savior. I will serve you faithfully, all the days of my life. Reveal to me the Father's love and help me love my fellow man.

If you have prayed this prayer, and have truthfully accepted Jesus as your Lord:

1. Welcome into the family of Christ. You are now a brother or sister in the Lord.

2. Find a Bible and read it every day.

3. Speak to God daily and pray for guidance

4. Seek out other believers in Jesus (*Isa*), or go to a Christian prayer group, fellowship or a church where the Word of God is taught.

5. Obey Christ's command and be baptized in water.

6. Joyfully share the Gospel with others.

7. Expect to be persecuted knowing that Jesus whom you now serve was also persecuted.

8. Walk in love and in forgiveness.

9. Do all things for the glory of God (I Cor. 10:31).

10. Ask God to send you His true Comforter, that you may be strengthened in your new faith. Pray that He would baptize you in the Holy Spirit with the evidence of speaking in tongues (Mk. 16:17; Acts 2:1-4; I Cor. 12:10).

11. Know that your name is recorded in Heaven in the Lamb's Book of Life (Rev. 3:5;13:8;20:12;21:27).

# Other books by Sean Black

**The Ryan Lock Series**
Lockdown
Deadlock
Gridlock
The Devil's Bounty
Lock & Load


**For kids**
Extolziby Gruff and the 39th College

# Post

## A Byron Tibor Thriller

Sean Black

For Lee

*I stand across the street from our old apartment, the exhaust fumes of the early-evening traffic and the burnished gold leaves of the late fall taking me back to the time before. It's cold. I stamp my boots on the sidewalk, trying to force warmth into my feet. A woman walking a tiny dog swaddled in a fleece sweater skirts around me. She meets my gaze, and looks away abruptly, her skull a blaze of yellow. In a city of perpetual motion, standing quietly is a suspect activity, especially when you look as I do.*

*I scare people. They see something in my eyes. At first I thought it was death, but it's not. Death is a presence, and what they see in me is an absence.*

*The light is failing. The last of the sun turns the building's stone front to a rich honey-gold for a few precious minutes as I wait it out. I tell myself I have come this far, and seen so much, that everything that has passed before me requires that I hold my position. I have to see her again. One last time.*

'Humanity won't last forever. But I don't see why we can't enjoy being human for just a little while longer.'

Nicholas Aggar

# ONE

**Lewis**

As the man in the frayed green jacket approached her counter, Shawna Day moved her right foot toward the silent alarm button grooved into the carpet directly under her cash drawer. Although he didn't appear to have a gun, and had made no effort to conceal his face with anything other than the ragged shadow of a beard, everything about him, from the head on a permanent swivel, to the hunched shoulders and the eyes that darted in every direction, screamed two words: bank robber.

With a textbook 'How may I help you today?' masking her concern, Shawna took a closer look at the man standing on the other side of the bandit screen. He was in his late twenties, although the oily blue-green fish-scale bags under his eyes made him seem older. His hair was cropped close to his skull. He turned his head slightly to the left, glancing back over his shoulder at the bank's lone security guard. Shawna glimpsed a raised red scar running in a semi-circle around the back of his skull. He was clutching a brown manila envelope. The back of his left hand was bandaged. A brown crust of dried blood had seeped through the gauze. The sight of the blood and the dirty dressing made her stomach lurch.

1

'Sir?' she prompted, her attention switching back to the envelope. It bulged at the corners. She looked for wires. There had been a bank robber in the greater Los Angeles area who had used fake bombs in a series of cash robberies.

Over the man's shoulder, she noticed the security guard, a doughy guy in his fifties who only ever spoke to the manager, and ate his lunch separately from the other members of staff, also watching her customer. His attention made her feel a little better about her own lurch of paranoia.

The man raised his head so that his eyes were level with hers. The corners of his lips turned upwards into a tight, forced smile that might have made her feel sorry for him had it not been for his eyes. The pupils were obsidian black voids. They flicked from one side of her face to the other, exploding and contracting over and over again, like the aperture of a camera shutter.

It was weird, bizarre, but it wasn't enough to press the alarm. The young man was most likely on drugs, probably PCP, the least mellow of all the street drugs. But that wasn't a matter for her. Hell, this was Santa Monica. Walk out the door and probably 75 per cent of the local population were on something: kids on Ritalin to keep them quiet; professionals on Adderall to make them more productive; housewives on Valium and Pinot Noir; boomers floating past on a gentle cloud of bud; and homeless folks, like the man facing her, who craved a little more bang for their meagre dollars.

The young man with the shutter eyes had still to speak.

'Sir,' Shawna said, a little more firmly, reminding herself that even with the kind of strength that came from just a dusting of PCP, he wouldn't be able to get through the bandit screen at her, 'there's a line. Can you tell me how I can help you today?'

The man took a deep breath and his injured left hand dropped away, leaving the right hand clutching the bulging envelope. He closed his eyes. He opened them again, with a rush of breath that whistled over even white teeth that suggested a different life in a time past. Shawna was starting to wish that he would pull a gun because what his eyes were freakier than a robbery.

A mother standing in line scolded a small boy for prodding his little sister with a chubby finger. Strapped into a stroller, the baby kicked out in frustration. The teller next to them counted out a stack of twenties for a young Asian woman. Only the security guard seemed to show any sign of interest in what was happening at window number four. Meanwhile, Shawna's leg was beginning to cramp from hovering in the unnatural position over the alarm.

Finally, the man's lips shaped to speak. He swallowed so hard she could see the bob of his Adam's apple. She smiled at him, hoping to encourage a response, something, anything.

'You're very yellow,' he said, in a perfectly quiet, even voice, as if it was the most natural statement in the world.

# TWO

At first Shawna wasn't sure she had heard him correctly. 'Excuse me?'

'I scare you. When people are scared, they turn yellow. Y'know? Like that saying about someone being a yellow belly. "That guy's yellow." Right now, you're scared.'

No, she thought, before she'd been scared. Right now she was plain old pissed off.

*What a wack job.* He wasn't a bank robber, after all. He was probably just some college kid dropout who'd thought he'd wander into the bank and try to read someone's aura. The People's Republic of Santa Monica, she thought. You had to love it. They had it all, year round. Seventy-five-degree weather, the beach, the Pacific Ocean, palm trees, vending machines for dope, and what seemed like every crazy homeless person on the west coast, all crammed into a few square miles.

'Yellow, huh?' she said. 'That's good to know. Must be because I'm a Taurus. Now, what can I do for you today?' She moved her foot away from the alarm, and reached down a hand to massage the burning at the back of her thigh.

'Forget it, okay?' he said. 'I shouldn't have said anything.' He half turned to look at the line behind him. Then, facing her again, he held up the bulging envelope. 'I need a safe deposit box. It said on the website that you still did them.'

4

'Yes, we do. Let me just get you a form. I'll need two types of ID also.'

The man stiffened. 'I don't have ID. I can pay cash, though. Twelve months up front.'

'Sir, federal regulations require us ...'

The teller next to her, a fresh-out-of-college Hispanic girl, who had been working alongside her for just a few months, shot her a sympathetic look. If you worked in a bank, you got used to people being rude to you. Even though you didn't make the rules, informing members of the public there were rules and procedures to be followed somehow made you the asshole, not them. You didn't have to like how some people acted, but you rapidly got over yourself and accepted it as part of the job. Or you looked for another, which in this economy meant you got over yourself.

Her heart beat a little faster as he reached into his jacket. 'It's real easy, lady. Take my cash. Take the envelope. Put it in a box. Give me a key and a number.'

She could hear him grinding his teeth as he spoke. She slackened a little as he produced a letter-sized envelope, opened it and thumbed through a greasy bundle of notes. 'If you'd like, I'll have the manager speak to you,' she said.

As she began to turn away, she felt the man's hand come from nowhere and grasp hers through the slot tray at the front of her counter. The bandage was gone. She could see the wound. It was a star-shaped mess of yellow pus and blood that covered the back of his hand. She hadn't even been aware of him moving it. She hadn't seen him slip it through the slot. It wasn't there and then it was. His thumb was pinching the fleshy web between her own thumb and index finger so hard that she couldn't move.

She tried to break free. His grip tightened. Now she was in pain. It stabbed all the way up her arm. She moved her foot, pressing down on the alarm button.

# THREE

The man released her hand as quickly as he had grasped it. Now she felt foolish. For obvious reasons there was no override once the alarm had been pressed. He had grabbed her, assaulted her, but it wasn't a robbery.

Their eyes met. Once more, his pupils shuttered wildly. 'Why'd you do that, huh? I wasn't going to hurt you.'

'Why'd I do what?' she asked, her nerves too jangled by this whole deal to call him 'sir'. Now they were just two people, both scared, both likely in a lot of trouble.

'You tripped the alarm,' he said.

She couldn't deny it. But how could he know? From her body position above the counter? That was how she'd been standing when he'd approached her.

Then she saw the gun, tucked into the waistband of his camo pants. Relief swept over her. He had a gun. He had grabbed her and he had a gun. In that moment she had shifted from someone looking to get an annoying customer into a world of trouble to a hyper-vigilant employee, a heroine even.

'I don't know what you're talking about, sir,' she said, her composure returning with a rush.

He began to push the letter-sized envelope stuffed with notes through the slot. 'Here, take it all. You can have whatever's left over.'

He grabbed a pen from his pants pocket, his jacket riding back down to hide the butt of the gun.

The cavalry would be on its way. Outside, she could already see traffic on Pico Boulevard clearing as the automated traffic system filtered cars within a three-block radius out of the way, holding everything beyond that with a solid wall of red lights, apart from the turn lanes, which would be kept clear for the police department.

The man scribbled an email address on the back of the bigger envelope and tried to push it through to the slot to her. 'I need you to send the box number to this email address. Nothing else. Just the number. They'll work out where it is.' The envelope was jammed halfway through. He shoved at it, the sides starting to rip. 'I'm sorry if I scared you.'

She glanced down at the email address scrawled on the front of the envelope. When she looked back up she saw two dark sedans with blacked-out windows pulling up outside. Two Santa Monica Police Department patrol cars sat across the street, and the cops were trying to corral a growing crowd of gawkers. The doors of the two sedans popped open with perfect synchronicity. She counted four men getting out. It was difficult to tell them apart, although one was slightly older and wore a suit under his body armor, while the other three were dressed in military style BDUs, their pants patterned the same as those of the man in front of her, who had now pulled out the gun.

He punched it out one-handed in the direction of the bank's security guard, who also had his weapon drawn. The four men were moving toward the door as customers scattered under desks and behind chairs or display stands, taking cover wherever they could find it. Inside the bank it was just her, the security guard and the man with the gun still on their feet. She had the bandit screen between her and the two guns but raw fear kept her feet planted where they were. It was the men who had emerged from the sedans who scared her. They moved with purpose, their features set like granite, three of them clutching assault rifles.

She watched the security guard glance over his shoulder at them as he advised the man, 'Put it down. Before anyone gets hurt.'

The man spoke: 'You'd better do what I say. They find you with that envelope and …'

She didn't move. She couldn't. Her feet felt set in concrete.

The man raised the gun so that the muzzle was no longer pointing at the security guard. He opened his mouth wide and jammed the barrel into it. His teeth clamped down on it. She watched as his index finger squeezed the trigger, the fleshy pad nearest his knuckle inching toward oblivion.

When it came, the shot made her flinch. Blood and brains spattered across the screen, inches from her face. Her hands left the envelope and flew to her face. She covered her eyes but kept them open. She heard screams but they seemed distant. A Rorschach pattern of red and grey oozed down the screen. A single fragment of white bone was embedded in the Plexiglass. She stared down the jagged ridge of bone to the man in the suit. He met her gaze. He looked from her to the body on the floor. Then his eyes settled on the envelope. Something told her that whatever was in the envelope it wasn't anything good.

# FOUR

**Graves**

Harry Graves took a knee next to the dead man. A voice in his earpiece asked, 'Is it him?' The voice belonged to Muir, the program leader. A body cam clipped to Graves's shirt relayed everything he was looking at back to the video conference room at the program's control facility, which sat six hundred miles east, in the Nevada desert next to Area 51.

'Have to wait for DNA but, yeah, it's him,' said Graves, reaching down and peeling away the combat jacket. He unbuttoned the shirt to reveal the chest. He tapped his knuckle against the left pectoral muscle. Unless rigor had set in instantly, the sound told its own story. 'You hear that?' he asked the scientist.

'Loud and clear,' said Muir.

Subcutaneous molded body armor, the ultimate in lightweight protection for the body's vital organs and completely undetectable to the naked eye. Because of the composite materials used, it didn't set off metal detectors, and a TSA agent looking at a body scan would see it without actually knowing what he was looking at. Oh, and good luck shooting someone like Lewis. Hammer a round from a .45 into his chest and it was like hitting the guy with a pellet from a BB gun. The armor ran all the way down in sections to the groin (a source of much hilarity for everyone) and

9

stopped around the top of the thighs. Only the limbs remained unprotected. The rationale was that they could be replaced with prosthetics and orthotics that would outperform normal human limb function, but major trauma to the heart or lungs, or a blood-rich area like a guy's junk, was harder to come back from.

The room darkened suddenly as the other men in Graves's response team supervised the placement of a huge black tarpaulin across the bank's glass frontage. The local cops were already shepherding customers out of the building two at a time, taking their personal details and statements. That information would be fed into various criminal and intelligence databases. It was important to establish whether Lewis had been alone and who, if any of them, he had spoken to.

The envelope had already been recovered. Shawna had been removed from the scene and was proving cooperative. Graves doubted she would be a problem but all her communications would be monitored for a period of three months and she would be placed on a watch list for non-security-cleared individuals who had been exposed to highly classified material.

'His hand?' prompted Muir.

Graves duck-walked a couple of feet and lifted Lewis's hand. He already knew what they would be looking at. So did Muir, but the guy was a scientist: he liked to see things with his own eyes.

The wound was in the shape of a star. Lewis would have sterilized his Gerber and used the locked blade to cut away the skin at the back of his hand.

'We'll change placement,' said Muir in Graves's ear.

He resisted the temptation to say, 'I told you so,' to the program leader. He had argued initially for neck rather than hand placement because it was way too easy to remove the device from the back of someone's hand. 'You want to look at what's left of his head, Professor?'

'Of course,' said Muir.

Still squatting, Graves waddled forward a few feet so the body cam took in the remains of the man's skull. Blood and brains had pooled on the floor. The facial features were intact: the subcutaneous molding that

10

covered the existing facial bone structure had held everything in place. Blood had pooled at the back of the eyes, and spilled from the mouth, nose and ears, running in thick, congealing streams down the chin and onto the neck.

'Give me a second here,' said Graves. 'Just want to check something.'

He reached under Lewis's shoulder and turned him over so he could see the back of his head. As he'd suspected. Until he'd pulled the trigger, Lewis had been one smart cookie. He'd thought stuff through. He let go, and the body slumped back to the floor.

'He really did a number on us,' he said, as much to himself as to Muir and the team of neuroscientists, tech geeks, quants, and all-round head-scoopers the good professor had assembled out there in Nevada. That was one of the things about working for Uncle Sam: you could lure in the best of the best, even in these straitened times. It wasn't just the DARPA (Defense Advanced Research Projects Agency) funding either. The private sector had all kinds of federal rules and regulations to follow. When your employer was the state, and the work was considered vital to national security, you were allowed a little more leeway. Anyone came along to ask any awkward questions, well, that was classified. Geek heaven.

The round would have passed close to the center of Lewis's brain. The angle of trajectory would likely have taken out the amygdala implant and a chunk of the parietal lobe, then passed into the temporal lobe and hit a section of the cage-like trans-cranial implant that ran all the way round to the frontal lobe, trampolining back into the brain when it hit the molded armor that wallpapered the skull. In layman's terms, Lewis hadn't so much blown his brains out as forced them to implode.

'The implant will have to be recovered,' said Muir.

Graves sighed. Why don't you come down here and scoop through the guy's freaking brains and find it then? he thought. 'I was hoping I could ship him back and you could take care of that.'

'We don't have time. If we can recover it intact, and while it still has charge, there's a chance we can run an update. If it loses power, it will take weeks, if not months, to troubleshoot.'

*Troubleshoot?* That made Graves chuckle. He could still hear the words, he just wasn't listening anymore. Terrific, he thought. Just what everyone needed. The program was a bust. A big, fat, expensive bust. Politicians and the American people liked shit that worked.

'I'll see what I can find. You want to maintain a visual?' he said.

Rice, one of the three-man team he had come in with, walked past him — he was running liaison with the civilian cops. 'Talking to yourself again, Harry?'

Graves offered him a raised middle finger.

'I have other work to attend to. Let me know as soon as you find it,' said Muir, signing off.

That was Muir. A good man at heart, no question of it, but fixated to the point where he no longer saw the bigger picture. This project did that to people. The upside was so huge, not just to the military but to the United States and therefore to the world, that even something like this was regarded by those at the center of it as a blip. Graves often wondered if this was what it had been like for those who had worked on the Manhattan Project, and those who had shepherded them. Was the only way to change the world not to think about anything beyond the next step?

At the front door, one of his men was having a heated discussion with a captain from the SMPD who wanted to access the crime scene. He was making some long speech about chains of command. Graves turned his attention to finding the goddamn needle in the haystack.

He pulled a pair of surgical gloves from his pants pocket and snapped them on. The bank staff had already been moved out of his line of sight, the cameras switched off. He could work in peace but he might have only a few minutes.

He stepped over the body. The left arm was thrown out in surrender, the fist closed tight, like a baby's. The right hand, the one that had pulled the trigger, had flopped down by his side, the gun at his feet. Lewis's eyes were open and he had that 'Who, me?' look of surprise that was so often etched on the faces of the dead. If you'd pulled the trigger, what the hell did you have to be surprised about?

12

The round had entered the soft tissue of the palate. He couldn't jam his hand through the mouth to find a tiny silver sliver.

He leaned over, his battered knees creaking as he rolled Lewis so that he was face down. The back of his head was pretty much gone. It wasn't so much a head as a mask now, which was kind of poetic under the circumstances. Although maybe that wasn't entirely fair. There had been a lot going on upstairs, probably too much, with all those billions of neurons firing like crazy, 24/7. That was how specialist Lewis had ended up like this – too much going on up top.

Usually it was the reverse. People died because they didn't think — not because they did. Harry guessed suicides were different: everything closed in on you until your whole goddamn world compressed itself into your skull. Then the only way to relieve the pressure was to flick the off switch. This had been a grab for control from a guy who didn't have any. And it had worked. Lewis had probably blown away hundreds of millions of dollars and years of work with his brains. Unless …

With the clock ticking, Graves used his fingers to scoop through the blood and brains. He should add a colander to his list of equipment. He found what he was looking for on the third attempt, a snippet of silver among the bloody grey. The metal edge of the coil caught against his middle finger. He pinched it and pulled it out.

He put it into a clear plastic sandwich bag, and tucked it into his jacket pocket. He stripped off his gloves. One of the others joined him, his assault rifle slung over his shoulder.

'Bag him and tag him for me,' said Graves.

'You got it. Where's he going?' the man asked.

'Where'd you think?' Graves prodded Lewis's left arm with the toe of his right shoe. 'You imagine what a coroner would make of him? They'd roll in one stiff and have to roll out two.'

The man smiled. 'No shit.'

Graves grimaced. 'I'll leave the wetware with you. I gotta get this little baby scanned and wired. They want to troubleshoot it, do a recall, and run an update before we got another of these on our hands.'

13

'Wetware, Harry?'

When he'd first heard the geeks using it, the term had puzzled Graves as well, until Muir had explained it to him. He'd thought it was pretty funny at first. Now, with this, and more out there like Lewis, it didn't seem quite so amusing.

'Forgetting is the most beneficial process we possess.'
Professor Bernard Williams

# FIVE

*Kunar Province, Afghanistan*

**Byron**

They came to kill me an hour before sunrise. There were three of them, silhouettes hewn in silver by a late autumn moon high above the valley.

Checked *keffiyehs* wrapped tightly around their faces left only their eyes, noses and lips visible. White trousers, greyed by the dust of the plain, fluttered in the breeze as they picked their way up the moonlit slope toward the first house. Two looked to be little more than teenagers while the third, the leader, would have been in his late twenties or early thirties — a good age in this part of the world, where four decades pretty much secured you elder status.

The younger men had AK-47s slung casually over their shoulders, barrels pointing earthwards. The leader was carrying what looked like an old Soviet Makarov semi-automatic handgun tucked into his waistband. A *pulwar*, a single-bladed curved sword, dangled from his other hip.

Somewhere in the near distance, a rhesus monkey began to chatter. It was joined by a companion, howling in solidarity. They were either greeting the dawn, pressing at the edges of the horizon, or reacting to the foreign presence, but I couldn't be sure which.

The men stopped for a moment, frozen in place. Grey-blue moonlight splashed across the edge of the *pulwar* as the leader adjusted his belt. The monkeys lapsed into silence.

Steadying the sword with his hand, the leader beckoned his two compatriots with a wave. They began to walk again, closing in on the village with each step. The gradient of the slope grew more severe, but the men maintained the same pace, unhindered by the terrain. That told me they were native to the area.

The village consisted of around two dozen houses, which had been built into the side of the hillside from traditional mud bricks. Using the slope, and the natural hollows of the hillside, the houses were stacked on top of, as well as alongside, each other. The mud bricks kept them cool during the scorching summer weather, which parched the valley below, and warm during the winter, when snow covered the peaks of the mountains that led north into Pakistan.

The arrangement of the houses and the steepness of the gradient was such that one villager could walk out of his front door directly onto the roof of his neighbor's house. Like a series of tiny two-room castles, the slope provided a natural defense against intruders. Not that the men approaching seemed worried by this. The village was completely still and everything about them, from the open display of weapons to the way they strolled languidly toward the makeshift school house perched on a rocky outcrop, suggested that they anticipated little resistance.

They were wrong. I was waiting for them.

# SIX

I had walked into the village three weeks before. At first the villagers hadn't quite known what to make of my presence. Much of that stemmed from the nature of my arrival – alone, on foot and unarmed.

My path into the village had been from the mountains to the north. On the other side lay Pakistan. Even though this was one of the remoter places on earth, it was not unusual for young men with British, French or even American accents to arrive here to take up arms.

To the villagers, my arrival was of no more than passing interest, which began to evaporate as soon as I opened my mouth and spoke to them in their own language, Pashtun. Although I spoke it with an accent that lay somewhere in the middle of the Atlantic, I was fairly fluent, with a command of regional variations. What struck me, in those first hours, as children crowded round, and I took off my boots to check my blisters, was how few questions they asked, and how easily they seemed to accept my presence. Perhaps they were simply accustomed to visitors or, more likely, they had long since realized that what you don't know can't hurt you. If I was a *jihadi*, they didn't want to know about it. If I was American and a Christian, that probably went double. What they truly wanted was to be left alone to grow their poppies on the flat plain below, and to live their lives as they had done for the past thousand years.

But a stranger's presence would change that, and even on that first day, we all knew it.

# SEVEN

The village was called Anash Kapur. It had a total population of just over a hundred. Of that hundred, twenty-two were men, thirty-four were women, and the rest were children. The children ranged in age from four babies of up to six months and a gaggle of toddlers, whose quick movement made them difficult to count. After the age of about seven, the demographic spread thinned out fairly rapidly. Child-mortality rates were high, and reaching the age of maturity made you one of the lucky ones. Not only was medical care almost non-existent, and diseases rife that had been long eradicated in the developed world, but the area was still seeded with thousands of landmines from the Russian occupation. They had been made to be especially appealing to children, a strategy that meant Afghanistan had one of the largest numbers of child amputees outside Africa. One of them was a little girl called Sasha, and she, as it happened, was the first person I ran into when I arrived.

Sasha had beautiful brown eyes, and thick, straggly black hair. As I picked my way down a shale path toward the village, she was sitting on a rock on her own, her legs dangling over the edge of a sheer drop of around thirty feet. When she saw me, she smiled. It was an expression that betrayed neither fear nor curiosity, just a warm, open smile.

I said hello to her in Pashtun and she replied. Then, as if this was a scenario that had played itself out before, she jumped to her feet, folded her remaining hand into mine and began to drag me toward the village.

Soon the rest of the children had clustered around us. Hands tugged at my clothing or simply stretched out to me through the tangle of spindly limbs and stubby fingers. Already protective, Sasha pushed the children away and shouted at one or two. One of the older boys said something about 'the little mother', which raised giggles. Slowly, the merry band began to settle, fanning out and arranging itself into less of a swarm and more of a procession, bare feet scrabbling over the worn stony path into the village. With her position as official village tour guide secured, Sasha looked up at me, as if to say, 'It's okay, I have your back,' and we moved toward an altogether less certain welcome.

The village was quiet as we approached. Down below, on the valley floor, I could make out figures in the fields, hunched over the vivid red crop. The path widened a little and the children quietened. The village houses fell away down the slope in a stepped arrangement. The highest house was also the largest. Built on one level, it enjoyed a mountain frontage of perhaps sixty feet. An elderly man with white hair and a long beard crouched outside the front door, one hand on a walking stick, staring straight ahead.

At first he didn't seem to register my presence. The older children hung back, one or two of the girls shooing away the younger ones. The excited chatter and laughter died. The elder continued to stare directly ahead. Above the mountains that lay to the east, clouds whipped across the jagged peaks. Sasha's hand felt warm and sticky in mine. I stopped, took off my rucksack and dumped it on the path at my feet. I could feel where the straps had dug into my shoulders and was aware of the pleasant sensation of lightness.

The little girl stood back from me as I walked across to join the elder. I didn't speak. It wasn't my place. Instead, I let him take his measure of me. Silence descended between us. I lowered myself into the same crouched position, parallel to him, as I followed the old man's line of sight. I would stay like this until he spoke. Until sunset, if it took that long. There was power in silence, which Americans had long since forgotten.

After ten minutes in that position, even with the days of trekking behind me, I could feel the burn at the back of my thighs, but I stayed where I was. It didn't take long for discomfort to give way to pain, then agony. I used the time to scan the terrain, mapping it in my mind as best I could, picking out routes of escape from the village and places where it would be easy to ambush someone.

A few minutes later, the elder's right hand tightened around his stick and he began to lever himself upright. He glanced at me, milky eyes sliding across my face. He hadn't been staring at the mountains to the east. He hadn't been staring at anything. He had been listening. Listening for others. This wasn't a village even the most intrepid voyager would stumble across and men like me didn't arrive alone and unarmed.

# EIGHT

As the light of that first afternoon died over the mountains, I sat at the edge of a semi-circle inside the old man's house, along with three other older men. As we talked I began to lay out the story I had developed back in Virginia. My name was Byron (a different first name was more likely to trip someone up than almost any other detail). I had been born in the Middle East to a Saudi father and an African-American mother. My parents had moved to the United States when I was young. I had been educated originally in a madrassa and later, in America, at various private schools. My father had been a devout Muslim and I had found myself returning to my religion. My spiritual journey had brought me here, via Pakistan. I was careful to say nothing about *jihad*, insurgency or anything that even hinted of politics. I allowed them to fill in the blanks for themselves. As a general rule, Western Muslims, especially the converts, talked more of a spiritual journey than of *jihad*. After all, for them, the two things were often one and the same.

The elders had listened to me with patience. They offered tea and food. After they had eaten, they smoked a hookah. They offered very little about themselves. They were here. They were farmers. That was all I needed to know.

By now it was late and the children had been shooed inside by the women. After a time, the men rose and left. The elder motioned for me to

24

follow him. We walked outside into the moonlight. He led me up a rickety wooden ladder to a terraced field. At the end was an empty shack. That would be my quarters. There was straw on the floor and several blankets already laid out. A jug of water and a bowl stood in one corner. I shook hands with the elder and he left me alone.

I washed my face, and brushed my teeth. I undressed and wrapped the blankets around myself. No one would come for me on the first night. They would wait. As far as I could tell, my story had been accepted. Nothing in the villagers' body language or manner had suggested otherwise, and I was adept at reading such things. Exhausted, I fell into a dreamless sleep.

I woke to sunshine streaming under an inch-wide gap between the bottom of the door and the sill. I poured some water from the jug into the bowl and washed. It was almost nine — late. Most of the villagers were probably long gone, in the fields below, tending their crops. I dressed quickly, pulled a mat from my backpack, knelt on it and prayed, my forehead rising and falling as I ran through the words.

A few moments after I had finished someone knocked at the door. I opened it, and there was the little girl I had met on my approach to the village. She had brought me food. I beckoned her inside. She strode past me and laid out a breakfast of bread and cheese, and what I guessed was goat's milk. She motioned for me to eat. Her manner and gestures were so adult that I couldn't help but smile. I offered her some of the food but she waved it away, then marched out, leaving me to my breakfast. I had already noticed that here the men ate first.

When I had finished eating, I went outside into sunshine. After days spent hiking through the mountains, it felt good to be at rest. I shielded my eyes and scanned the horizon, catching a glint of light from a nearby peak. They were already watching me, trying to figure out who I was and why I was there.

During the night, I had woken to find someone rummaging through my pack. It was one of the men who had sat with the village elder. I pretended to be asleep as the villager conducted a search that I had known was coming. I had already dumped any gear that might reveal my true identity about a quarter-mile back up the pass into the village. For now, though, I was happy for them to know what I'd walked in with — clothes, soap, some protein bars, a water bottle, a copy of the Koran, a prayer mat, and some propaganda pamphlets from a number of fundamentalist groups. The villagers would draw their own conclusions.

I worked alongside the villagers in the fields all morning. They showed me what to do and I did it without complaint. No one seemed surprised that I was helping. It was early in the afternoon that I became aware of two men on the eastward ridge, watching me, AK-47s slung across their backs.

The pace of work settled with the falling sun. The villagers finished, and I trudged with them back up through the stepped terraces to the village. As I reached the elder's house, I turned back toward the ridge. The men who had been watching me were gone.

The men ate first and separately from the women. The talk was of the crop, prices, and the weather, how the seasons appeared to be shifting earlier every year. It occurred to me that it was a conversation that might have taken place around a kitchen table at a farm in Iowa. No one made any mention of the two men who had been watching me from the ridge.

# NINE

By the end of the week, as far as the people of the village were concerned, I simply was. While the other children tired of me, like kids at Christmas lose interest in a new toy, Sasha followed me as much as ever, peppering me with questions.

In turn, I learned more about her. The woman I had initially taken to be her mother was an aunt. Her mother was dead. The story fell from Sasha in dribs and drabs, each chapter breaking my heart a little more but steeling my resolve to see the operation through to the end.

Sasha's mother had been born in the village, the daughter of the village elder I had met when I had first arrived. In the years before the Taliban had seized the country by the throat, she had left the village to travel to Kabul to go to school, returning only at harvest time. Then she had trained as an elementary teacher, returned to the village, married a local man and opened a small village school.

The Taliban had arrived.

I hadn't asked Sasha for the details but, from what she told me one late afternoon as she followed me from the fields, she had been spared the truth of her mother's fate. At first there had been night letters, warnings that her mother should learn her place. She had ignored the first two. The third had come in the form of four men, who had taken her while the family slept. Her body was returned the following week.

The little girl's eyes were wet as she told me the last part. It was the first time I had seen her or any of the children cry. I put my arm around her and she snuggled into me. It was perhaps the greatest moment of acceptance I had received from anyone in the village so far. She trusted me enough to show what she denied everyone else: her grief, in all its rawness.

Days passed, time slowed. The novelty of village life ebbed away, replaced by routine. The two men who had been watching me were gone.

Their absence signaled a shift. They hadn't lost interest. Their curiosity could hardly have been satiated. Neither did I think they had become more careful in their surveillance. Even if they had, I would still have known about it. That left only one option: contact with them was imminent. They were moving into the second phase of the operation.

In general, the transition from one phase, or one state of being, was the dangerous part, the part where things go wrong, taking off and landing a plane being the most obvious example. It was the same for a covert operation such as this.

I knew that I was being watched by those on my own side via satellite. But I was as alone as someone in my position could be. There would be no last-second cavalry dash if things went awry. They were operating on one simple premise that would mean either life or death: that the insurgents' curiosity would outweigh their bloodlust. With every previous contact where this group had been able to take a prisoner alive, they had done so. They understood the value of a live captive. Not only did they serve as a bargaining chip and hold valuable intelligence, a live captive offered a propaganda bonanza that few in the West understood. If things went to plan, I hoped to avoid a TV appearance and be out of the country long before they came even close to that stage. But one always had to be at peace with the knowledge that things often didn't go to plan. That was why I was used in these lone-operator situations. I wasn't braver or stronger. I was simply more accepting.

# TEN

A new morning dawned. The sun rose. The villagers ate. And then, with them, I began my day.

The crop was close to gathered as I moved slowly up the terraced steps to my new home. Sasha was waiting for me. A baby, only a few weeks old, bounced on her hip.

'Your little cousin?' I asked her in Pashtun.

She shook her head. 'My niece.'

I had been thinking of how I might get her out of the village and kept coming up blank. Once contact was made properly I would have no room for passengers. Still, there had to be a way and I had fixed on the idea of returning briefly once my objective was confirmed. It would be risky but achievable. I would attract some major shit from higher up but that was nothing new.

Sasha stared at me unblinking. 'Tell me again about America.'

'What do you want to know?' I asked her.

'Tell me about the food.'

She was quite the little cook. I had seen her making bread and stews with a flair that would have put to shame most adults. She was bright too. She could see someone perform a task once and have it down pat. I had taught her a few words of English and, while her pronunciation left a bit to be desired, she was a quick study. Outside the village she would do well.

As far as I had been able to tell, during my thirty years on the planet, life on earth was pretty much a lottery. If you were born in the West, or into a middle-class family in one of the emerging powerhouse economies, you had a shot. If you were male, all the better, although that was a weakening determinant of someone's opportunities. But be born female into a small village in Afghanistan and however bright, however capable you were, however determined, the odds were stacked almost insurmountably against you.

I crouched and told Sasha a little more of my invented life. I had already run through the story several times with her but, as with most kids, repetition seemed to be part of the enjoyment. I had been the same as a kid, homing in on a favorite story and asking my parents to read it to me over and over again.

Behind the little girl, the sun began to drop toward the mountains. They would come tonight. I could feel it. The end of the beginning of the operation was approaching. Soon I would enter the second, most dangerous, phase.

I snapped awake a little after midnight, dressed quickly in the dark and pushed open the door, stepping out onto the rough dirt threshold. There wasn't as much moonlight as I would have liked but I wasn't dictating events or their timing — not yet anyway.

If they were coming for me, I didn't want them to find me in such confined quarters. Small spaces and lots of men hyped up with adrenalin and bravado are almost invariably a bad combination.

I had already scoped out a position near to where they had been watching me. It overlooked the fields but also formed the main lower approach to the village, a simple dirt track that would take them straight up to my quarters, but I wouldn't be there when they arrived.

Moving up and to my left, I picked up the goat track. The village was silent. Doors closed. Candles extinguished. I heard people snoring as I flitted past a few houses.

The night itself was cold but not freezing. I took my time, listening for any suggestion of another person, but all was quiet.

Within an hour, I had found my position. Now all I had to do was wait.

# ELEVEN

The men who had come for me, with their guns, scuttled around the outside of the shack. They were doing so much whispering, pointing and running back and forth that I found myself doing something I hadn't anticipated. It was a reaction that many soldiers were familiar with, but one that rarely, if ever, made it into the movies where combat was always horrific and terrifying, and the protagonists were hard-eyed and lantern-jawed. I knew that war could be horrifying but combat, when you were in the middle of it, was many things besides. It could be funny — piss-your-pants, laugh-until-you-couldn't-breathe funny.

Finally, the older man, the one with the *pulwar* sword, lost patience. He pointed to one of the others, and mimed raising his foot to the wooden door.

The younger man took a run at it and hefted his boot. The door swung open, then ricocheted back into his face, leaving him sprawling on the ground. His patience exhausted, the older man wrestled the AK-47 from him and pushed his way inside, shouting in Pashtun for a man who wasn't there to get to his feet.

Whatever meagre element of surprise they might have had was spent, and the leader was angry. The others rushed inside and he pushed one out, assigning him to guard the door.

The village was awake now. I could sense eyes peering through cracks but no one left their house. They stayed put. It was a wise move because soon there was a volley of shots from inside the hut as an AK-47 let loose with the opposite of celebratory fire.

Even with shots fired, I remained relaxed. It was no accident that the construction methods used here were also good for absorbing bullets. I had even seen a mortar shell hit a thick adobe compound wall and embed without detonating.

I waited. They would no doubt interrogate the villagers but the villagers knew nothing because I hadn't told anyone I was leaving. The insurgents would grow bored and, with daylight, nervous.

When they left, I would follow. That was the plan. They would report back to the man I had come to find, or to an intermediary, in which case I would follow the intermediary. The West had become so adept at intercepting their electronic communications that the insurgents had pushed their intelligence channels back into the Stone Age.

The three men gathered in a huddle outside. Their voices carried to me on the cold wind as they argued. The elder shoved one of the others hard in the shoulder and the younger man shouted a torrent of abuse. The leader raised his sword, but for show rather than threat.

The argument was bad news. The leader of the group had lost face. In the American military an officer fuck-up prompts grumbling rather than an open show of defiance.

The leader raised his *pulwar* again. He pointed the tip toward the other houses in the village and barked orders. They started to bang on doors. When no doors opened, they kicked them wide, more carefully this time. The leader of the group tucked his *pulwar* back into the sash around his waist and marched behind the two men. They reached the village elder's compound. The door opened and the man emerged. He regarded the three armed insurgents with the same lack of surprise that had greeted my arrival. It was hard to imagine a more out-of-the-way place on the planet, yet men kept arriving. Armed men. Killers.

Even when someone had come to kill you, such meetings were often highly ritualized. Cheeks were kissed, supplications made to the Prophet, hospitality offered. This was not going to be one of those times. The leader of the group drew back his hand and slapped the elder hard across the face.

The force of the blow sent him to his knees. His wife rushed to his side and the insurgent leader kicked out at her, catching her with a boot to the head as she knelt down to tend her husband. There was more shouting. The tip of the *pulwar* was jabbed toward my shack.

'Where is he?'

The elder raised his hands, palms open, toward the insurgent leader. Even if he had known, he wasn't going to tell.

The Pashtun people in rural areas lived by the code of Pashtunwali. It revolved around ten sets of principles. The tenth commandment was *nanawatai*, the right of a person to asylum from dark forces. *Nanawatai* had saved the life of Navy SEAL Petty Officer First Class Marcus Luttrell when his team had been wiped out by Taliban fighters. It had also saved the lives of members of the Pakistan military and more than one Russian soldier. A stranger who asked for protection had to be granted it, at least until a solution could be found.

More villagers had emerged from their homes, some to watch, others to scream at the men, who were running from house to house, tearing the interiors apart in a frenzied attempt to find me. At the edge of the path into the village, the children had clustered together in a tiny knot, ushered away from the eye of the storm by their mothers. Sasha stood at the front of the little group.

An icy wind rose at my back, sweeping down the mountainside, but my gaze was fixed on Sasha. With a chill that ran all the way down my back, I realized I wasn't the only one. The insurgent leader was turning in her direction. He held the *pulwar* sword and moved it slowly from side to side, feeling its heft as he started toward her.

# TWELVE

The other children fell away as he advanced. Sasha stayed exactly where she was, through fear or, more likely, defiance. This was her valley, her village, and no one was going to intimidate her. She had more of the Pashtunwali spirit in her tiny body than the rest of the village put together. She had been the first to meet me, and I understood now that, by leading me into the village, she had invoked *nanawatai*.

Without thinking, I jumped down from the rocky outcrop I was hunkered behind and began to run. For the first time since I had arrived, I felt the tiny comms device that ran into my left ear begin to vibrate. The ops center wanted to open comms. There were no pleasantries, only a question barked into my ear, so loudly that I felt my head throb.

'Where are you going?'

'Back to the village.'

'Negative. Stay where you are. They'll likely RV with the target, whether they have you or not. Repeat. Stay where you are.'

I kept running, scrabbling across the rocky ground, racing at an angle across scattergun shale. I had lost sight of the village but could still hear people shouting at the insurgents, and piercing the din, the plaintive whine of a little girl in pain.

'Stay where you are,' the voice in my ear repeated.

I yanked out the earpiece, clicked it off and tucked it into my pocket.

I walked toward the three men with my hands raised, palms open, to make clear that I didn't have a weapon. I could see the other children grouped around Sasha. She lay on the ground, her knees pulled up to her chest, her face wet with blood, which poured from a wound that ran along her scalp. She was whimpering with pain. It was hard to listen to, but a good sign. Dead people didn't make sounds.

The insurgent leader stared at the ground. He had lost control of the situation by hitting the little girl. The villagers wouldn't forget it, and the insurgents relied on them for their day-to-day survival. The relationship between insurgents and civilians was complex. The insurgents used intimidation but were careful not to overstep the mark too frequently. An insurgency relied on the camouflage of civilian support, and if you lost that support, by striking a young girl, it was hard to win it back.

I wanted to check on the little girl but he already had the AK-47 and the Makarov pistol trained on me. From what I could see, the gash was probably not quite as bad as it looked. It would require stitches but the biggest worry was that she had suffered concussion.

I felt the prod of the gun barrel in my back. I glanced over to see a grubby exchange of money from the leader of the insurgents to the village elder. A roll of muddy notes was pressed into his palm, with a mumbled apology.

Hands reached in front of me and I felt rough fabric against my forehead. It was dragged down over my eyes and pulled tight. Hands moved to my wrists. My heart rate slowed as I let my hands be tied behind my back.

From the conversation taking place between the men, I realized that while they had been watching me for weeks there was one fact they didn't appear to have grasped.

They had no idea that I could understand every word they were saying.

They led me back up the pass. Listening to the footsteps, I could tell that the two younger men were in front, the leader behind. The leader's hand grasped the knot where my hands met and used it to guide me forwards.

They had stopped talking between themselves. From time to time, I would stumble forward and get a jab in the kidneys. They kept moving up, deeper into the mountains.

I counted every step. It helped me track the passage of time and distance and kept my mind off the little girl I had promised to keep safe and who now lay bleeding in the village.

There was no getting away from it. I felt guilty. I could have stayed where I was and allowed them to find me. I would have arrived at exactly the same point. But those weren't my orders. I was too highly valued an asset to hand myself over. In contrast, a child didn't enter into the equation. Those were the things you had to make peace with. Dead civilians were a by-product for both sides, sometimes by accident and sometimes by design. To reject that idea was to surrender the field of battle.

I tried to refocus. I had seen worse, much worse, than a young girl bleeding from the head. There had been other operations with civilian casualties, younger children, babies even, the horrors stacked on top of each other.

During my psy-ops training at Fort Bragg, I had sat alongside classmates and listened to a lecture about memory formation and trauma. The advice was simple. When bad shit happened, try not to think about it. There was even a fancy scientific term for not following this advice: potentiation. The more you recovered a memory, the more you dredged it up, the more the neurons in your brain, which fired together to create that memory, became grooved in a pattern. Long-term potentiation took place if you thought about an event too often. It was like walking into a huge storage facility, opening a unit and jamming the event, or how you remembered it, inside, then going back and rooting through it. The more you opened it, the more you rooted around, the more real it became.

Blindfolded, my captors pushing me along, I was already struggling to keep track of the passage of time and of the distance. The direction we were travelling? I'd lost sight of the sun as the mountains had closed in around us so I had no idea.

# THIRTEEN

Having encountered no one since we had left the village, my captors had begun to talk among themselves again. It was a good sign. The more comfortable they felt, the better. Less reassuring was that they were discussing who was going to kill me. The chance to kill a Westerner in cold blood was clearly a valuable opportunity. The only snag seemed to be that, having encountered no resistance, from me or anyone else, other than the villagers, they were less certain of who I was than they had been. They were sure I was American, but they believed I might be Muslim and allied in some way to their greater cause. Mostly, though, they seemed confused.

I kept my head down as I walked and tried not to give any hint that I was listening to everything that was being said. They began talking about a similar situation they'd encountered. They had captured an ISAF soldier who had wandered outside the wire of his forward operating base. He had been European. Not British, maybe Italian or French, they thought.

They had taken the man alive. He had been so scared that he had lost control of his bowels. As they talked, they seemed to find this detail amusing. They had held the soldier in an abandoned compound for several days. His capture had drawn several search parties from his base. This had provided even more sport as their comrades in arms had ambushed several more ISAF patrols, killing at least three more soldiers. In that regard, a hostage was invaluable. Even though his capture had been a stroke of luck on their part, it had cemented their reputation as specialists in this type of operation. Hence their being tasked with my detention.

They stopped suddenly. I was yanked down into a sitting position and the conversation fell away. I felt a hand on my shoulder, then the cold metal of a canteen of water pressing against my lips: another good sign. You didn't rehydrate someone you plan to kill within the next few hours, unless it was their equivalent of a final cigarette.

I could hear another voice close by now. It was male and verging on high-pitched. He was talking to the insurgent leader but ushered him away before I could catch much more than 'This is him? This is the one?'

I drank the water that was offered. It tasted good. I hadn't realized I was thirsty until it had been offered. Even in this cold, the forced march had left a trail of sweat running down my back all the way into the crack of my ass.

'You have enough?' one of the younger men asked me.

I stayed quiet. Answering in Pashtun would let them know I could understand every word they said, but answering in English would confirm their suspicions. I had decided that until they reached their destination, which I guessed wasn't too far away now, given the arrival of the other man, I would keep my own counsel and thereby keep them guessing.

Time passed. They didn't move. I wondered if we were staying there overnight. The mountains didn't lend themselves to moving after dark unless you had the benefit of night-vision goggles, and even then it was easy enough to step over a ledge.

The leader was back – alone. He hauled me to my feet and we started to walk again. The terrain grew steeper and rockier. They had moved from mountain pass to meadow and now they seemed to be climbing. I fell again, this time landing on my face. There was a harried discussion as I lay there. I felt someone untie the rope, and my hands were free. I pushed myself up, a jab from the AK-47 at my back reminding me that I was still a hostage.

The blindfold was yanked from my eyes. We must have been walking for a lot longer than I had estimated because it was light. The sudden exposure made me wince. I blinked, allowing my eyes to adjust to a flare of sunlight from a patch of snow to the left. We were higher than I had guessed, and standing on a broad ridge that tapered to a silver ribbon up ahead.

Beneath us were the slopes of the Hindu Kush. These were the mountains that had, at least for a time, shielded Bin Laden. On either side was a near-vertical drop.

Up ahead, the ridge line widened, then ended. I was pushed toward it. It seemed unlikely that they would bring me all the way up here just to push me over the edge. Then again, people in general, and religious fanatics in particular, didn't always behave in a way that was either predictable or logical.

I listened more carefully to the footsteps behind, gauging their relative positions. If they stopped walking while I continued to the edge that would be the giveaway.

As I got within ten feet I saw that what I had thought was a sheer drop was nothing of the sort: the ground fell away sharply, then evened out and two tracks curved back around the peak.

I climbed down and my captors followed. They prodded me toward the northerly path. It was about ten feet wide. Up ahead, two hard-faced men wearing black Taliban turbans stood guard outside a slit in the mountain. It was about six feet high and tapered from ten feet wide at the bottom to four at the top.

The two Taliban stepped to me, grabbing my shoulders and pushing me through the opening. I had to duck quickly to avoid hitting my head. The momentum carried me forward into a cave. It opened out to reveal a main chamber of around two hundred square feet. Passages ran off it in about half a dozen different directions. I could smell goat stew and freshly baked bread.

From the smoothness of the walls, I knew that this passageway was man-made. The air was so smoky that I coughed.

The cave was bad news. In a dark passageway with walls so thick that all contact and knowledge of my position would have been lost, I was off-radar, no satellite able to pick up my location. Perhaps that was the point. Perhaps I hadn't given the man they were looking for, the man for whom I had been live bait, enough credit. I had been relying upon live comms. Now a decision would have to be made.

To follow me into near-impregnable terrain and risk the entire operation, or to wait it out? It was no easy call. The cave systems had so many rat-runs and exit points that, short of carpet-bombing the entire mountain range, taking someone alive from within them was a near impossible task guaranteed to generate multiple special-forces casualties. Not that special forces balked at taking the risk, I knew from experience that they lived for missions like this, but there was always a political dimension. It was a call that could only be made by the President and, right now, Stars-and-Stripes-draped coffins being unloaded from the back of C-130s were not in fashion.

There was light ahead from another chamber. It seeped yellow around the edges of a piece of cloth that had been draped across it. I pushed it to one side and stepped through. Carpets had been spread on the rough stone floor. Paraffin lanterns hung from hooks on the walls. The remnants of the meal I had smelt when I walked in lay in the middle of the space.

In the center of the room there was a man. He was fat, with plump lips and eyes that twinkled above a lavish black beard. I recognized him immediately. I doubted that anyone in the Western intelligence community wouldn't have known who he was. This was the man I had come to find.

# FOURTEEN

Khazin Masori was well named. 'Khazin' translated as 'the treasurer' and, like Bin Laden, Khazin Masori was a man of wealth who had turned his back on a privileged life to wage war against the West. Unlike Bin Laden, he was, despite America's best efforts, still breathing. He was just as dangerous, though: he had directed and funded multiple operations against American interests in Afghanistan and beyond, including atrocities in Africa, Asia and Europe. He had been one of the first within the world of Islamic terror organizations to recognize the propaganda value of social media and was believed to have personally dispatched several kidnapped Westerners on camera. Not that any of it showed in his eyes as he smiled warmly, motioning for me to sit opposite him.

I wondered why I was alone with him – it was an almost unbelievable breach of security. I was three quick steps from him, close enough to dispatch him before anyone could step in.

Masori leaned forward and, as he did, I glimpsed the edge of the suicide vest that was strapped around the cleric's torso. It was standard operating procedure for someone at Masori's level to be able to guarantee his own demise if there was any risk of his falling into enemy hands. Uncharacteristically, he wasn't a man to waste time on the usual pleasantries.

'Who are you, and why are you here?' he asked in English. 'And, please, don't insult my intelligence by telling me the story you gave the people of the village.'

'It wasn't a story.'

'Everything in this world is a story, my friend.'

My job now was to buy as much time as I could. Even if the guys on my side couldn't be sure that Masori was here, my own value as an asset meant they would still be moving into position. They might not be able to penetrate the cave system to observe the situation but they would be taking up exterior positions in preparation for whatever call came.

'You know who *I* am, of course,' said Masori.

I had been briefed for this question. 'Of course. I've been waiting to meet you.'

If Masori was surprised, he didn't show it. His smile must have been cemented in place. 'You have?'

Masori was right when he said that everyone had a story. Right now I had at least three. The true story of why I was there. The story I had told the villagers. And, finally, the story that had been painstakingly prepared for Masori.

The key to engaging someone like Masori was to pinpoint what he desired most. He couldn't be tempted with anything material. He could have had that in his old life. Houses, cars, women, none of those held any allure.

No, Khazin Masori craved something far more exciting and long lasting than anything of that nature. He wanted to secure his place in history, and the way to do that was to change the world in the same irrevocable way Bin Laden had when his recruits had flown planes into the World Trade Center. You could bomb all the embassies you wanted and the Western world shrugged. Masori understood that the power of a terrorist atrocity lay not in the body count but in the imagery.

In three weeks the President of the United States was due to visit India. I had been given the details of the visit, from the main itinerary to the routes he would take, how long he would stay at each location, and his security. The plan was genuine.

I kept eye contact with Masori as I spoke. He was suspicious. A man he had never met had turned up out of the blue to hand him on a plate his best shot at murdering the leader of the Western world, and therefore taking his place alongside Bin Laden.

He didn't believe me. I knew that for certain. I wouldn't have believed the story either. That was why the boys in the back room had spent months carefully seeding the story of an American agent who had gone rogue, and who, over the past few weeks, had fallen off the intelligence services' radar. Masori might not have been aware of it, but when he started asking questions it would swiftly rise to the surface.

Having listened to me politely, he nodded. 'And these plans for his visit. You have them with you?' he asked.

I shook my head. 'They're close by. I can take your men to them but first I need to know if you're interested.'

Masori's smile was back. 'You're selling them?'

'Ten million dollars.'

The mention of money seemed to settle him a little. Now at least he had some kind of insight into a possible motive. It was beginning to make sense. Masori pressed his hands together. 'After the action has taken place and is a success. If, of course, such an action can be successful,' he said.

'No. I already took the risk in getting the details. Whether this works for you or not, I'm a dead man without access to this money.' I held Masori's gaze. 'Half up front. The rest when it's done. Whether you kill him or not is down to you. I give you the bullets. I can't be held to account for how well you use them.'

'It's a lot of money,' said Maori, rising to his feet and giving me another glimpse of his suicide belt. He smoothed down his robes. 'Allow me time to consider it.'

'The visit is in three weeks. If you're going to have everything in place, you shouldn't delay. And,' I added, 'there may be others who would be interested in what I have.'

That part was bluff. There were perhaps three or four groups or organizations with motive, funds and the know-how to use such intelligence, and two wouldn't go anywhere near it. The reality was that, just as during the Cold War, certain actions wouldn't be countenanced for fear of the scale of reprisal; the same balance existed now between the West and other regimes that could be described as anti-imperialist or *jihad*-friendly. Iran in particular knew that any involvement in something like this would almost certainly result in a nuclear strike against Tehran. Pakistan had been a hair's breath away from the same fate after 9/11. Geopolitics was in a constant state of flux but a line of equilibrium ran like a seam through most of it. That left one or two rogues such as Masori, who wanted to throw a hand grenade into the middle of the deal. The Taliban's strategy had been one of attrition aimed at the slow sapping of political will in the West to maintain a counterweight to them in Afghanistan. Masori, though, was in another league. His aim was chaos. A world ablaze – the Western world.

I stayed seated as Masori stood over me, wearing the benevolent grin with which he had greeted me. The other factor I was relying upon was his isolation. He was, after all, a man of action. Holed up in this remote region, shuttling from one location to the next, boredom had no doubt begun to set in. My appearance had probably been the most exciting thing to come his way in months.

'Give me a moment,' Masori said, and disappeared into one of the side passages that ran off the main chamber.

I sat and waited. A few moments later one of the younger men who had taken me from the village appeared and sat where Masori had. He stared at me but said nothing. I returned the compliment.

Masori would be somewhere in back, busy working his own intelligence channels to establish the veracity of my story. Minutes passed in silence, then fell away into hours. Another of Masori's men brought me food and some water. Then I needed to pee. I asked his companion and was led through the passageway to an opening at the back of the cave system. It was around three feet wide by four feet deep and seemed to be a sheer drop. I did what I had to do, then was led back to the main chamber where Masori was waiting for me.

'You will take us to these plans,' Masori said.

'Fine,' I answered.

Masori pursed his lips. 'No. Maybe it is better if I wait here.' It had been a test.

'And the money?' I asked.

'When I have the documents, and I can verify that they are genuine, you can have the first *two* million.'

'That wasn't the deal. It's five up front.'

'Three.'

We were discussing an American citizen handing over intelligence that could lead to the death of his president, and Masori was haggling like a carpet salesman in a tourist bazaar. It was a good sign, though. It meant that whatever checks he had made had confirmed the story I'd fed him.

'Four up front, six on the back end, and we have a deal,' I said, putting out my hand for Masori to shake.

He reached out and clasped both of my hands. 'My men will go with you. When they confirm the papers, I will arrange for the first payment to be made. You have an account ready?'

I tapped my temple. 'More than one. The numbers are all up here. Sure you don't want to come with me?'

Masori tugged at his beard, pensive. 'No. I trust you.'

A sound behind us. I half turned as his smile widened. His eyes twinkled even more brightly, the yellow glow from the lantern dancing across jet black pupils. I counted three sets of footsteps. His honor guard was approaching – the older man and his two younger companions.

'So I don't have to be blindfolded with my hands tied?'

'No need for that. I have something better to make sure you are a man of your word.'

Another sound from behind me. A whimper. I turned. The two bodyguards were standing behind me. They were holding something between them – a limp bundle of rags shaped like a doll.

# FIFTEEN

Fear is something you can smell. I didn't have to look at Sasha's face to see the terror in her eyes.

'Go and get what you came to give me,' Masori said. 'The child stays with me.'

'If the plans are good, I want your word that you will use them. Do you give me your word?'

His face betrayed a look of surprise at the question. He had been expecting me to ask about the little girl.

'You have my word,' said Masori.

'When I return, she comes with me.'

Masori shot me a leering smile. 'You've taken a fancy to her?'

I wanted to throw up but it was better to play along. Explaining I planned to find her a safer life would have seemed more suspicious than allowing him to think I intended to take her as a wife. 'I have plans for her, yes.

'I won't be long,' I added, motioning for one of the bodyguards to follow me. 'I take it one of your men will come with me.'

As my escort moved toward me, he was between me and Masori. I had the old Soviet pistol tucked into a cloth tie that ran around my waist.

My left elbow came up fast, smashing into the man's jaw so hard that blood spurted from his mouth as he bit clean through the tip of his tongue.

The pistol was now in my right hand. I grabbed a handful of the man's hair and yanked his head down, simultaneously bringing up a knee into his face and breaking his nose. He folded at the waist and I held him there with one hand as I brought the pistol up with the other and fired two rounds into his companion's head from a distance of less than six feet. The man slumped forward, letting go of Sasha, who screamed.

Masori stumbled backwards, his eyes fixed on me as I headed for one of the passageways. There were more shouts from within the cave system as Masori's other bodyguards scrambled to get to me. I counted six separate sets of footsteps moving towards me.

Masori's hand had slipped inside his robes to the ripcord attached to the detonator of his suicide vest. He could have pulled it and taken the girl and me with him but he hadn't. It was one thing to talk someone else into martyrdom, another to do it yourself.

I rushed past Sasha toward him. Anticipating a punch, Masori raised his hands to his face to protect himself. I shifted my weight and threw a big, wide right hook that caught him on the side of the head. His hands fell away from his face.

There was no time to remove the explosives and every chance that Masori would detonate them if I did but I had already devised a far more direct method of ensuring that he stayed alive. I grabbed his right wrist and bent it back until it snapped, then repeated the move with the left.

Two of Masori's men were getting close to the main chamber. They were both approaching from the passageway to my left. His hands were dangling uselessly at right angles to his forearms so I grabbed the back of his robe and made sure I was between him and the two men as they emerged from the narrow rock passageway.

They skidded to a halt and lowered their weapons. I raised the Makarov and shot them each through the head. My arm wrapped around Masori's windpipe, I started to drag him backwards.

Masori must have known that if I was there to kill him he'd already be dead. There was a fate worse than death, and it was where I was taking him.

He began to fumble for the cord again. I jabbed the butt of the pistol against his broken wrist. He shrieked.

I tightened my grip around his windpipe to starve him of oxygen and he began to weaken. I pulled him back still further. His feet were trying to dig into the floor.

I looked over at the little girl. 'Follow me.'

She stayed where she was, her eyes wide. She was in a state of shock, near catatonic. I shouted at her again but it did no good: her mind had closed down. An acute stress reaction had kicked in. Usually stress compelled the body into fight-or-flight mode but it could go the other way, overwhelming the nervous system to the point at which the person couldn't react at all.

I could take Masori. I could take Sasha. But I couldn't take them both. It should have been easy for me. My mission objective was extracting Masori alive. But now my feet wouldn't move. I was as frozen as Sasha was.

I could hear more of Masori's men rushing through the passageways, shouting to each other as they hurtled toward us. They were behind us, closing in from all sides.

I twisted round. It took me a second to grasp that the voices behind me were speaking English — English with American accents. Whoever was set up outside had heard the shooting and made the decision to come in and join the party. I was no longer alone.

My strength, which had barely been enough to hold Masori, kicked back in. There was nothing better in the world than being alone and hearing back-up steaming toward you, and not just any old back-up, US Special Forces, my old comrades, the best in the world.

I adjusted my balance. Masori must have weighed two hundred and twenty pounds but he felt a lot lighter all of a sudden. Perfectly gauging the pressure I needed to use with the choke hold, I hustled Masori forward and used my free hand to grab Sasha's elbow.

Three of the exfiltration team rushed past us, forming a diamond to cover my retreat with Masori and the child. I saw faces I recognized. The team leader clapped a gloved hand on my shoulder. 'Good job.'

Masori was prised from me. His broken wrists were pinned behind his back as he was dragged out of the cave system. A couple of rounds pinged off the cave wall, and the three Americans in the diamond returned fire.

I scooped the child into my arms and, for the first time, saw something apart from terror in her eyes, a flicker of recognition. My eyes narrowed to avoid the waves of dust swirling around them from the downdraught of the Sikorsky Little Bird. Somewhere in the dust and wind, time bent and split. Voices, shouts and sudden movements overlaid each other in a rush.

The team leader slashed a hand across his throat and pointed at Sasha. 'No room for her on the Bird. She stays.'

I started to argue with him. As the words tumbled from my mouth, I felt a warm, sticky spread of liquid across my chest. Sasha's eyes were open. She stared up at me, her pupils dilating. A red rose blush oozed from the center of her chest. I reached a hand down. It came away slick with blood. The team leader was screaming in my ear but the words were just fragments of sound.

I wasn't for giving her up. I fell to my knees, Sasha clutched to my chest. My head tilted back. I stared beyond the blades, beyond the mountains, and into the very heavens themselves as I held the dead child in my arms.

# SIXTEEN

The chopper flew low over the wire and landed in a wash of dust. Ground crew and medical staff emerged from the shadows, sprinting toward it, their heads low. I clambered out, my head smothered in bandages, Sasha cradled in my arms, my shirt soaked with her blood.

The six-man special-forces exfiltration team followed, faces set like granite. I reached down and brushed a strand of stray hair from Sasha's face. The others clambered past me, avoiding eye contact.

It was warmer here than up in the mountains. The sky was dark, the stars obliterated by the haze of camp lights.

Sasha's face was lily white. I laid her on the bare ground and closed her eyelids with a sweep of my hand. My fingertips left blood and dust on her face. Two army doctors and a trauma medic studied me from a distance. Even though I could feel fresh blood still leaking through the dressing covering my head wound, they didn't try to stop me.

The graveyard was quiet as I set her down. My walk had taken me through the middle of the camp. Eyes studied me all the way. The worst were those in uniform, the wire-huggers, as I thought of them; the guys who planned and replanned and visited this mess after it had all gone down, and marched around the rest of the time with their fruit-salad medals pinned to their puffed-out chests.

I was thankful that, as the country had slid further into the mire, there had been fewer and fewer of them. What the hell did they have to take credit for? The Taliban were still here. The West had never decided what the hell it wanted to be: avenger or liberator. It had proved to be both, and in being both had become neither. Finally, the IEDs, rogue Afghans and the indifference of a war-sickened people had driven the military to a strategy of drones and men like me. The bitter bounty of our righteous war? Dead little girls and two-day heroes with blackened minds and stumps for limbs that the politicians could jerk off about for as long as the homecoming parade lasted. Wrap yourself in a flag that meant jack shit, drop some dollars into a bucket, close your door, and thank the Lord it wasn't your son or daughter. That was the truth, as I saw it now. Just don't say it out loud: if there was one thing the people back home hated more than terrorists, it was some asshole holding up a mirror to them.

I kept walking, past the grunts, who had seen crazier shit than this and knew not to look at me, and the fruit-salad guys, the occasional mute local and a gaggle of NGO workers, trailing silence in my wake. Once I had set her down, I found a clear area, and set to work with an entrenching tool I had purloined from the cabin of the Little Bird.

The earth was brittle. There was no topsoil to speak of. When this smaller base had been built, the ground had been packed hard to prevent any breaching of the perimeter to plant an IED. To conserve energy, I used the blade to mark out the grave. I set to work in the center of the rectangle, digging straight down and scooping out from that hole. The field work back in the village had left me in good shape for such a task. The only time I stopped was to clear the sweat from my eyes. Progress was steady, slowed only by the care with which I piled the dug-out soil I would need to fill in the grave.

With the first foot of ground cleared, the work got a little easier. I heard footsteps close by, scuffed and deliberate, the movements of someone who knew well enough to announce their presence. I was standing in the grave by now, the ground just shy of waist height, which meant I had dug to a depth of three or so feet.

The footsteps belonged to a civilian with long hair tied back in a ponytail and a bushy salt-and-pepper beard. He looked to be in his late forties. He was dressed in boots, camo pants, and bundled up in a thick down North Face jacket.

'What was her name?' he asked, his eyes on the little girl. 'It is a girl, right? Only with all that blood …'

'Sasha,' I said. 'Her name was Sasha.'

I had seen the guy around. He wasn't special forces, but he moved in those circles, although 'flitted' was perhaps a better word. He didn't seem to talk much from what I'd seen. He was something to do with psy-ops, the guys of the future, if you listened to the brass.

'You want I can leave you alone?' he said.

I shrugged and went back to digging. He must have taken the shrug as a no because he stayed where he was. Minutes passed. The hole in the ground deepened. The ground was at shoulder level now. I glanced across. I could see the guy's ankles and the tops of his boots. There were more footsteps, in lockstep this time. I put my palms on the edge of the grave. Two grunts were carrying a child's coffin. They laid it at the feet of the guy from psy-ops, about-turned and left.

'Thought you might be able to use this,' he said.

'Appreciate it.'

'My name's Muir,' said the psy-ops guy. 'You dig any deeper, and you'll be staying down there.'

I didn't reply. If the guy hadn't been standing there, part of me felt like I could have stayed where I was, dragged the child in and pulled the earth over both of us. Muir reached out a hand and helped me up.

Between us we lifted the body into the small coffin. I wished there was something I could put in with her — a teddy bear, some jewelry, a letter. In the end, I took off my jacket, balled it up and placed it carefully under her head. I used my Gerber to ratchet the screws that secured the coffin lid. With Muir I lowered the small coffin into the grave. Muir stood, head bowed, hands clasped in front of him as I shoveled the soil on top. Then we tramped it down.

Finished, I stood back and stared at the patch of differently shaded earth. Now I was done, I felt unsure of what to do next. Part of me had hoped that, after burying the child, I would have made peace with what had happened, but I felt nothing other than I had before – grief, sorrow and anger at one more senseless act in a world full of them.

'You have kids, Sergeant?' Muir asked.

'No one calls me "Sergeant". They haven't in years.' I shook my head. 'No kids. Maybe one day. You?'

'Nope, married to my work …' Muir trailed off as he nodded toward the grave. 'You ever wonder how much of this is down to sheer bad luck?' he said.

I didn't mind listening but I didn't feel much like talking. I looked at him. 'What do you want?'

'This,' he said. 'This isn't normal. Dragging some dead kid onto the heli when it's already at full load. That's not like you. Anyone else would be shit canned.'

At last I had something to grab onto, something that made sense. The guy wasn't here to lend a sympathetic ear: he was here to tell me I'd screwed up, gotten too involved. For the first time since the Taliban kidnap party had shown up, the world seemed to have settled back on its axis. They didn't give a fuck about me. They gave a fuck that I could do the job without embarrassing them or displaying emotion. *Git 'er done, son, and shut the fuck up about it once you're finished.* Fine. That I could relate to.

'What you gonna do?' I said. 'Bench me? Be my guest. I'm done.'

'This isn't what you think, Byron. I'm not here to chew your ass. We value your work. We truly do.' He looked me in the eyes. 'You don't have to be done, Byron. You can do what you do best, sleep well and have a good life. We can help you. We want to help you. The only question is, will you let us?'

'What do you mean "help"?' I asked him.

I tried to step outside myself for a moment. A guy taking a dead kid on a chopper so that she could receive a proper burial: was it crazy or honorable? Okay, it was outside the usual parameters of behaviour, especially given my job, but it wasn't without some measure of humanity. What was the alternative? Leave her to the animals? At least this way she had a final resting place.

'You know what combat fatigue is?' Muir asked me.

I nodded. Half of the guys I worked with showed signs of it. Most often it crept up on you when you were back home, alone in the silence and stillness of civilian life, surrounded by regular people whose exposure to all this shit was a news item or the occasional piece on *60 Minutes*. The rotations had been so heavy in recent years that as soon as you got home, and started readjusting, it was time to head back into the mire. Rinse and repeat. Repeat it often enough, and it messed you up.

'Combat fatigue. PTSD. Call it what you like. It's the number-one problem for us now,' Muir said. 'We spend all this money training someone like you. It's like buying a Ferrari and never changing the oil. Sooner or later it's going to break down.'

I followed his gaze to the freshly dug grave. 'You want me to see a shrink?'

'There might be that component to it but we've developed something far more powerful.'

'If it's pills ...' I said. There was no way I was going to start taking drugs.

I had seen how that went. Get on them, and you might never get off. I had grown up around people who stuffed themselves full of all kinds of things. It never ended well.

'Something far more radical. A neural implant that wouldn't just make you better able to cope, it would make you feel and function at levels previously unheard off. Obviously it's classified so we couldn't discuss the precise nature of the technology now, and certainly not here,' he said, with a wave of his arms to take in the camp.

I had to stop myself laughing in the guy's face. This wasn't the first time I had heard about that kind of stuff. There had been some talk in special-ops circles about a chip or some kind of gizmo that they were putting in people's heads. It was out there, all right, but not by that much. Sitting in an airport in Frankfurt, I'd read an interview with some guy who said that, in the near future, he wanted people to plug straight into their search engine via an implant. All you'd have to do would be to think about LOL cats or some other bullshit and it popped up in your head. I knew that DARPA was working on some of this stuff, too, just like they had experimented with acid, electro-shock therapy and a bunch of other crazy shit over the years. Having the conversation was different, though. A discussion like this didn't come out of the blue.

'Think I'll pass,' I said.

Muir shrugged, took off his glasses and polished them with the bottom of his shirt. It seemed rehearsed, much like the rest of what he'd said.

'Think about it,' he said finally. He began to walk away.

'Hey,' I called after him, 'this new program have a name?'

Muir turned. He looked from me to the grave and back. 'Right now we're calling it TGFS.'

I knew how much the military loved their acronyms. 'What's it stand for?' I asked.

'The guilt-free soldier.'

# SEVENTEEN

I spent the next two days in classified debriefing sessions, going over every detail of the operation. We covered the events leading up to my abduction in good time and the field officer seemed satisfied with my version of events. The last few hours of the mission were a different story. I relayed what had happened with Masori as best I could. It wasn't enough. I was asked to go over it again and again until both men grew frustrated. At the end of the first afternoon session, Muir was waiting for me.

'How you doing, Byron?'

'I'm fine,' I told him.

'Everyone treating you okay?'

I shrugged. I wanted to head back to my quarters, grab a shower, get some chow and go visit the grave. Sasha still pulled at the corners of my mind. Her death was one part of the mission that I had no problem recalling. The memory was vivid to the point of being physically painful.

'Anything you need?' Muir prompted.

There was something. I had already made the request and been refused. 'I'd like to call home.'

'Soon as you're no longer in country, I can fix that for you.'

That was the answer I had already been given. I hadn't much liked it the first time either. I was sure it was connected to the debriefing, and that I was being punished in some way for the mission having gone so horribly wrong.

'I'm sorry, Sergeant. I know it's tough.'

It was something, I guessed. I gave Muir a curt nod of thanks.

'All talked out, huh?' Muir said, with a smile.

But I wasn't a man of few words. I was happy to talk about most subjects. That was part of what made me as effective in the field as I was. I liked people. They fascinated me — even the bad ones, sometimes especially the bad ones. It was something that few people outside special-forces operations understood. When civilians or the media, or even many people in the military, thought of special forces they connected them with direct-action operations, like those conducted by the SEALS. Leave base, kill or capture some asshole or assholes, and come home.

But Army Special Forces, where I had originally trained before taking on a special liaison role with the Agency, had been characterized by a different approach. Those men could fight, and teach others to do the same, but their skills lay in gathering intelligence in the field and forging alliances with friendly forces. Often there was no base to return to. Once you were outside the wire that was it. You lived, slept and ate with the locals. It was a different approach that required not only a different skill set but a different mentality. At the center of it lay communication, which was how you built trust. The problem now was that, since I had got back inside the wire, I wasn't sure anymore who could be trusted.

'Sergeant Tibor,' Muir said. 'We're worried about you. That was a pretty nasty head injury you took back there.'

'No shit,' I said. They had patched me up as best they could on the ground but I had already been told I was looking at one more surgical procedure at least, and I was still getting headaches that made me want to scoop out my brains.

'I want to get you checked out again,' said Muir. 'Can I walk you over there?'

'I know where it is,' I replied.

'Humor me.'

We headed across camp in silence. When we reached the triage area, Muir and I were greeted by an army surgeon who had already examined me a couple of times. He was holding a wooden clipboard with a form that he handed over for me to sign.

I glanced down at it. 'What's this?'

'Consent form for the RDF chip.'

'What?'

'New procedure, Sergeant. If you'd had one of these we could have avoided what happened back there.'

I studied the form a little more closely. The RDF chip was a bio-powered subcutaneous implant placed in the neck, which allowed constant monitoring of an operative's vital signs. It also had a GPS function, ensuring that the operative could be located via satellite anywhere in the world at any time.

'Forget it,' I said, tossing the clipboard back in the surgeon's direction.

'It's only ever employed when you're active. It's not like we're going to be counting how many times you go take a dump,' Muir said.

To be fair, mention of the chip hadn't exactly come from left field. I already knew a couple of other field agents and undercover operatives who were using the technology. Lone operatives went missing all the time, and if the worst had happened, I wanted those who knew me to have the closure offered by a body. The consent form reassured me that even if data was gathered while I wasn't active it could never be accessed, never mind used. The argument was the same you got with every additional layer of security. *If you don't have anything to hide, then what's the problem?*

'I'll pass,' I said. 'Anyway, that was probably my last time out now that I'm carrying this head injury.'

'Headaches?' said the surgeon. 'We should get you out of here ASAP and have a full set of tests done.'

'Listen, Doc, I just want to see get back Stateside. After that, you can do what the hell you like.'

'Of course,' said Muir. 'We understand.'

Another look passed between them. I turned round and walked away. This time no one followed me.

Sasha visited me in the dead hours of the morning when the camp was at its quietest. She stared at me with big brown eyes that filled with tears. It was only as they rolled down her cheeks that I saw they were blood. When I looked back at her eyes, they were black from the hemorrhage.

I forced my own eyes open and felt a shiver of vibration next to me on the pillow. My first thought was a cell phone, which didn't make sense. Cell phones weren't allowed on base.

Lying on my side, I reached underneath the pillow. There was nothing there apart from the sheet. It was then that the back of my hand brushed the side of my neck, and I felt it: a rice-grain-sized bump just under the skin.

I sat up and felt it with my fingertips. I got out of bed, threw on a jacket and headed for the shower block.

I stood side on to the mirror and studied the red welt of raised skin on my neck. I set off to find Muir.

# EIGHTEEN

Muir's face turned from scarlet to purple as I tightened my grip around his throat. Four grunts rushed forward and did their best to pull me away. One caught my left elbow in the face. The force of the blow sent him flying backwards. More men rushed in to help.

'You're going to kill him.'

Muir was staring at me, eyes wide. His mouth fell open. His eyes began to close as he started to lose consciousness. I relaxed my grip, and he collapsed to the floor, gasping for breath.

I found myself surrounded by a semicircle of military personnel. They stared at me but kept their distance.

'Why'd you do it?' I said to Muir.

Muir held up an open palm as he continued to gasp for air. 'Do what?' he said finally. His glasses had fallen off. I picked them up off the floor and handed them to him. One of the lenses was cracked, a fissure spidering out from the center.

'Put the RDF chip in.'

'What the hell are you talking about, Sergeant?'

'And why do you keep calling me "Sergeant"?'

Muir put his glasses back on, and slowly got to his feet, one hand massaging his windpipe. 'You consented to the RDF implant, Byron. Yesterday. You can talk to the surgeon if you don't believe me. I have your signature on the papers. You remember what we told you about Lewis, don't you?'

Either Muir was one hell of a liar or my brain was more scrambled than I knew. I swallowed hard and tried to think back to the conversation. All I could remember was very definitely refusing permission. The memory was clear.

My headache was back, a crushing pain that left my hands and feet tingling. Muir was looking at me like I was crazy. His face was changing color. The center of his forehead shifted from a natural skin tone to a blazing orange. A third eye opened in the middle of his head.

I blinked, suddenly less sure of myself. When I glanced back, Muir's face had returned to normal. The mess hall was silent.

*I'd signed the papers? Yesterday?*

'Listen, Byron. You've been through a lot over the past while. Let's get you through this debrief and back in shape. Forget this,' said Muir, as a couple of the men standing at the edge of the assembled audience began to drift back to their tables.

# NINETEEN

There are two keys to a successful escape and evasion, at least in the initial stages, and the second flows from the first. The first is the time between the escape and discovery of the escape. The second is distance. Time buys you distance, and distance from point of escape made it much more difficult for someone to find you. Get a hundred yards outside a wire before the alarm sounds, and you're screwed. Get fifty miles and you've made the searcher's job a whole different story. Not with an RDF chip, though.

At around ten that evening, I headed to the latrines with a scalpel filched from a medic's bag earlier in the day. I had been shown the consent form with my signature and initials. Both the surgeon and Muir, with a nurse, had told me the same story, and a lot of stuff about someone called Lewis. I had consented freely to the RDF chip being inserted in my neck. But I had no idea who Lewis was.

Fifteen minutes later, I emerged from the latrines, the shirt of my collar turned way up, covering the fresh wound on the left side of my neck. Rather than head back to my bunk, I hung a left, striding across the camp to the vehicle depot I had scoped out earlier.

Part of the camp's remit was to serve as a secure distribution center for humanitarian aid. I walked toward it, a man with a newly found sense of purpose. One of the first things I had learned on covert operations was that being overt worked better a lot of the time. Look like you belong somewhere, and you tend to blend into the background. If you're hesitant, it comes off you in waves, like the stench of rotting meat in summer.

Because the camp was considered secure, the trucks were lightly guarded. They were close to the mess hall, which also made an approach easy. It was simply a matter of walking through the open gate ringed by chain-link fencing.

You could tell the vehicles weren't military just by looking at how they were arranged. Rather than neat rows, they were all over the place. The only system I had observed was that the ones nearer the gate were those already loaded and due out at first light. By looking at the weight on the axles, I counted four that were good to go. It was possible but unlikely that they would be searched thoroughly before they left. Coming in was a different story as there would be no better way of delivering an IED into the camp than by humanitarian relief – Oklahoma bombing Taliban-style.

The tiny RDF chip I had just dug out from my neck was in my front pocket. I lifted the edge of the truck tarp and took a peek. I didn't care so much about what was being hauled as whether the cargo gave me an accessible space. There wouldn't be a full security check but, no doubt, there would be some cursory count to ensure that what left matched up with what got to the destination. Thankfully, there was no weighbridge to tip anyone off to an extra two hundred pounds in back.

I passed on the first truck full of cooking oil and settled for the second, which held bags of grain. Time was ticking away, and I couldn't be choosy. I clambered in, trying to make as little impression on the interior as a man of my size could.

There was some space nearer the cab. Even with the coughing of the diesel engine, I was pretty sure I would be able to pick up any conversation between the driver and the guard allotted to each truck.

Hunkering down, my knees touching my chest, I pulled a sack of grain back into place. I was pretty certain that it would pass casual inspection. If someone was actively looking for a stowaway I would be found, but if it was just a quick check I was in good shape.

I didn't dwell too much on what would happen if I was found. After all, it wasn't as if I was regular military, or that I was being held against my will. It had been made clear to me on several occasions that the program Muir seemed to be trying to recruit me into was voluntary. Like the Army Ranger motto, the Latin for which was *sua sponte*, you signed up 'of your own accord'.

So, if that was true, then why the hell was I sneaking out like a thief in the night? What the answer lacked in logic, it made up for in certainty. I didn't trust the people around me anymore. I needed answers to things I hadn't even been able to form into a coherent set of questions yet. I felt like I was losing my mind. The approach from Muir. The RDF chip I'd refused but that had been implanted. My signature on the consent form when I had no memory of signing it.

I must have dozed off because I woke a short time later to the sound of sleepy drivers and their guards standing around in the freezing cold as they divided up the convoy between them. A chink of half-light found its way to my eyes as the rear tarp was pulled back. As I had suspected, the check was cursory and followed swiftly by the opening and closing of cab doors.

A sea of engines rumbled and the convoy was on its way, settling for less than a minute at the gate before hitting what passed for freeway in the barren landscape. The trucks picked up speed. I listened keenly to pick up any conversation up front but either driver and guard weren't talkers or, more likely, it was just too late.

Now that they were on the road, I could find a more comfortable position. I had cut enough of a slit in the side tarpaulin to get eyes on the landscape so that I could pick out not only my own departure point but that of the tiny RDF chip. The truck slowed as the convoy began to climb a steep incline. I slashed again at the tarp, creating enough of a gap that I could stick my head out and get a better sense of the terrain. I could see the horizon rise in front of me. By the edge of the road was a ditch – as good a place as any to deposit the RDF transmitter, and the crest of the slope was as good a place as any to get out. I calculated that we were less than ten miles out from the camp but I had also worked out that, for every mile I hitched, the chances of someone figuring out I had left the facility edged ever upwards.

I pitched the transmitter as hard as I could out of the side of the truck. It arced its way the first ten feet or so toward the ditch.

The truck slowed with a lurch. I could hear the other vehicles beginning to brake. It wasn't a good sign, not when they were climbing a slope. A radio crackled in the cab. The message coming in was about a checkpoint up ahead.

Looking back to the spot where I had thrown the tracking device, I cursed my luck. Checkpoints were bad news – especially at night. Masquerading as a security measure, they were either set up to gather information to be passed on to insurgents or, more often, to shake down money. Soliciting bribes here, as in many developing nations, was an art form. Approaches were never direct and often took the form of simply keeping someone in one place until that person realized the fastest way of getting back on the road would be to offer a token of their appreciation for the work being done in holding them up.

I stuck my head back through the tarp to get a visual. The checkpoint was like none I'd seen here. The road at the top of the rise was lit like the Fourth of July, with big arc lights either side of the road illuminating what looked like four Dodge Charger police cruisers with flak-jacketed white cops leaning against their vehicles. It was a surreal sight.

I tried to shake the cobwebs out of my head. I closed my eyes for a second. When I opened them again, the lights were gone, replaced by the beams from two local Afghan police pick-ups. Not that any of it mattered. If I was still in the truck at the top of the rise, the slit I had cut in the tarp would betray me. It was now or never.

I ducked my head back inside, my blood chilled by what I was seeing. The sacks of grain were gone, replaced by dozens of dead bodies. Men, women, children lay all around me, their limbs contorted, like a scene from a concentration-camp death train. Looking down, I saw that they were behind me too. I was standing on one, my boots imprinted on a man's naked back.

The smell of death was everywhere. My stomach lurched and my mouth filled with bile. Panicked, I grabbed my Gerber and slashed at the tarp. Pushing off with my left foot, I climbed onto the edge of the truck, imagining hands clawing at my feet, trying to drag me back inside, and launched myself out onto the road, the truck still moving.

I hit the ground with a force that jarred my spine. The truck behind almost clipped me as it drove past. I rolled down into the ditch before I could be picked up by the headlights of the next vehicle in the convoy.

There was about a foot of freezing muddy water in the bottom of the ditch. The trucks were rumbling past toward the checkpoint. I shook my head, trying to clear everything I'd seen from my mind.

When the lights from the rear security vehicle had swept over the ditch, I clambered out on the other side. There was no time to dwell on the last moments before I had bailed, but I allowed myself a single backward glance up the rise. There was nothing out of the ordinary about the scene playing out, just four local cops who wanted to hold up an aid convoy until someone grew bored enough to pay them.

I plunged forward into the desert scrub. Time was short so I needed to fill it with as much distance as I could. Breaking into a run, I set a steady pace, the canopy of stars overhead guiding me south.

# TWENTY

Moving forward seemed to keep the visions at bay and allowed my mind to settle. I tried not to dwell on my decision to flee the camp. It was done now and nothing would change that. All that concerned me was getting home. If I kept that at the front of my mind, I would be fine. Escape, like most things, occurred in the mind. It was a question of attitude and determination. I had seen it at the SERE (Survival, Evasion, Resistance, Escape) course at Fort Bragg. I had been one of the last to be captured. When I was finally taken, I had also been one of the last to crack under interrogation. Everyone did, you were told up front: it was how long you lasted that mattered. As with resistance, the key to escape was to stay in the present and focus on your goal.

My goal was the city. Once there, I would be able to find people who could help me. My contacts were extensive and this was still a shadowland of a country where, for the right price, anything could be secured, including travel documents and a flight out.

My plan was to travel by night when my ambient temperature was most closely in sync with the land and I wouldn't be picked up by any drones or piloted aircraft using FLIR (forward-looking infrared) imaging. Moving at night, when the temperature was lowest, would keep me warm and I'd be less likely to suffer dehydration. At the camp I had noticed that the temperature was considerably higher than it had been in the mountains. By midday the heat was oppressive. I would find shade in daytime and rest up.

Along with the heat, the landscape had surprised me. It was drier than I had expected. A lot drier. Finding water would be the biggest challenge. I was already experiencing hunger pangs but those I could safely choose to ignore. Water was another matter. Dehydration would kill you just the same as a bullet through the heart. It wouldn't be pretty either, and it was something you could slide into without knowing it was happening. Lack of water messed with your mind so you had to be vigilant for the warning signs.

From nowhere, I felt a jab of pain in my foot. I reached down and pulled some kind of thorn from the bottom of my boot. I held it up to my face. It looked like the barb from some kind of cactus. It had gone straight through the leather. Looking around, I didn't see any kind of bush or tree or cactus that matched up. I tossed the spike, shrugged off the pain and kept moving.

Every once in a while, at irregular intervals, I would stop, listen, retake my course from the stars, using basic astral navigation, and scan the land ahead. The most I heard was the howl of a dog as I skirted a farmhouse, the livestock skittish at my approach. I doubled my pace to get clear before anyone came out to investigate what had alerted the animal.

A short distance beyond the stone buildings of the smallholding, I came upon a wadi. Miraculously, the bottom had water. Not much, but water nonetheless. Its presence explained the livestock and the smallholding. I filled one of the empty water bottles I had brought with me, dropped in a purification tablet, and jumped down into the riverbed.

I waded for a few hundred yards, got out and reset my course. I estimated that I had only an hour until dawn. I would keep walking a little past sunrise but not for long. As I moved, I scanned the horizon for somewhere to hole up.

With dawn came heat. There was no sign of shelter save a couple of trees. My piss was already running yellow – a bad sign. I sipped at the water I'd collected from the wadi. It tasted stale and brackish. I thought about doubling back to the smallholding and finding shelter there but decided against it. It would take ninety minutes, more with the heat, and I couldn't afford to lose the ground.

Ahead I could see the mountains on the far horizon. If I could survive and evade capture until nightfall, they would be within striking distance. Beyond the mountains was the city. More importantly, the mountains held water, vegetation, food and better cover.

I headed for one of the trees and sat down in its shade. My foot still stung from the spike that had pierced the leather. I pulled off my boots and massaged my feet. As I was putting them back on, I heard the buzz of a drone flying overhead.

Slowly, I got up, flattening my back against the short trunk, my head running into thorny branches. Glancing up, I caught a glimmer of white in the bright blue sky as the drone worked round in a loop.

From the brief glimpse I had just had, and its flight pattern, it was almost certainly a reconnaissance and surveillance UAV. If it had thermal imaging or another enhanced capability, I was toast. All I could do was sit tight. Drones could stay in the air a long time. If it moved away the operator, who was no doubt sitting safely back in the States, sipping an icy Diet Coke, had missed me. If it stayed, I was heading back to camp with a lot of explaining to do. What was it Masori had said to me? Everyone has a story. Mine would have to be a good one or I was looking at a world of pain.

The buzzing was fainter. I looked up through the jagged bone-dry branches and saw the drone a mile out from my position, circling in an ever-widening loop.

The tips of my fingers felt sticky. I closed my eyes, not wanting to look. I was afraid that the visions I'd had in the truck were returning, that I would open my eyes and see blood.

Not to look was almost worse. It amounted to an admission that I could no longer trust my own mind. I willed my eyes open, and raised a sticky hand.

There was momentary relief as I saw that the stickiness wasn't blood but a gooey clear sap. As the drone circled, I must have dug my fingernails into the tree bark. I brought it up to my nose and inhaled. A juniper tree. I'd seen them before on the approach to the mountains but not on the flat desert plains. As I looked at the mountains in the distance, I started to see more of them. They were dotted everywhere, along with sagebrush and thick balls of tumbleweed.

I dug out my water bottle and took a couple of long draws. Dehydration, the mind playing tricks. The buzz of the drone had died completely. I was alone again. The sun shifted ever upwards. I pulled down the sleeves of my jacket so that my arms were covered. I closed my eyes and drifted off to sleep.

I woke to Sasha standing over me. She stared at me with soft brown eyes. She was smiling. The juniper trees had multiplied since I had closed my eyes. They were all around me, packed so densely that they almost blotted out the mountains.

My mouth felt dry. I pulled out my water bottle. It was close to empty. I offered what little there was to Sasha. She took it from me, twisted off the cap, and emptied the dregs into her mouth. The water spilled red from the corners of her lips. She doubled over, clutching her stomach. The bottle fell to the ground. Blood arced in a torrent from her mouth. It pooled at my feet.

Then she was gone. There was no blood. The landscape was the same, a scattering of junipers and sagebrush with the mountains in the distance. I blinked and dug out the water bottle. It was half full. Lips cracked and gluey, I took a drink and found the sun. A wind had picked up. I could hear birdsong. That was it. I was alone. In a few hours it would be dark, and I could strike out for the mountains. My stomach rumbled, and I needed to pee. I stepped to the other side of the tree. My piss was closer to amber than yellow as the sunlight sparkled against it. I finished up and sat down on the other side, waiting for sunset.

I guided my mind away from Sasha. She was the past, I told myself. The desert was my present. One last push. One last push to the mountains.

I decided that when I reached the mountains I would keep moving. There was more vegetation, more contours in the land to conceal me. More than that, walking banished the horrors.

I remembered speaking to someone, before my talks with Muir back at the camp, about seeing things that weren't there. I wasn't sure who it had been or when they had spoken. All I could remember was the conversation or, more precisely, their side of it. They had told me that once PTSD or combat fatigue, or whatever tag you wanted to put on what people suffered from once they had seen too much, was present, it was often accompanied by hallucinations and flashbacks that appeared wholly real. They worked the same neural pathways as if the event was happening right in front of you. I would go see someone if I had to. Whatever it took, I would do it, but it would have to be on my terms, with a person I could trust, and I wasn't going to start popping pills or sign up as a government lab rat.

I covered the remainder of the ground in good time. At one point, I must have skirted close to a road because I saw headlights. I ducked behind a bushy juniper and waited until it passed, then tacked away from the road.

As the ground started to rise, another dog howled in the distance. I could pick out the outline of a stone compound. The sound cut through me and I altered course again, Gerber in hand, ready if the dog picked up my scent. Dogs here were like the insurgents, tough, mean motherfuckers who'd happily rip you limb from limb just because you were on their ground. I had seen US troops, guys who probably had a much-loved canine at home, shoot them.

The land grew rocky. I began to climb, my thighs and calves aching as I pushed on. The moon had disappeared behind a stack of clouds. The weather was changing — fast. There was a rumble of thunder in the distance followed by a flash that left my hands and feet tingling. I had moved down into a narrow canyon, hoping it was a pass that would save me having to climb.

Seconds later the rain swept in. The drops were like bullets, lashing over the bone-dry ground in sheets. Almost immediately I was soaked to the skin. I tilted my head back and stuck out my tongue. The rain felt good but water was already beginning to channel into the pass from higher ground.

Unclear of how long the canyon ran for, and with no way of knowing how I would be able to climb out without gear if it dead-ended, I doubled back. My boots slopped through the mud, and I had to take a knee as rocks gave way above me. Hair plastered to my face, I pressed on. The rain was hitting me so hard that it hurt. It helped me focus. I scrambled away from the sloping mouth of the canyon. Looking back, I saw that if I'd stayed I would have been waist deep in water by now.

Skirting round to the west, I climbed toward a narrow ridge line. The rain was shifting ground from under me, ripping out bushes and exposing tree roots. Thunder boomed and lightning forked. The ground crackled with the burst of electricity, and I was thrown backwards. I put out my hands in time to break the fall, got back to my feet and pressed on.

The ridge line was up ahead, blocked by a vertical rock face. To the east was a path that climbed upwards. I would take that, if it hadn't been washed out by the time I got there.

It was a short distance but it took me some time to cover the ground. I followed the path up toward the ridge. At one point, almost blinded by rain, I lost my footing at the very edge of a sheer drop. I grabbed for a tree branch. It held as my fingers closed around it, and I hauled myself up.

The path was being fractured by the force of the storm. I hunkered down on my hands and knees and begin to climb straight up. My hands searched for gaps in the rock.

With one final push I breached the ridge line and collapsed face down, my face painted a watery red thrown up from the rocks. I had made it.

A final clap of thunder sounded as I stared in disbelief at the city spread out before me. *No. It wasn't possible.* I blinked through the rain, certain that my mind was playing another trick on me. This time, though, I couldn't clear away what I was seeing. I tried closing my eyes and opening them again, willing my mind back to reality. It was no use.

Beneath me lay the original mirage, America's great city of the imagination, a blazing forest of light that rose from the desert – Las Vegas. I could pick out not just the Strip, but the signs on individual casinos and hotels. My mind might have been playing tricks, but I was sure there was nothing wrong with my eyesight.

There was only one thing for it. I would deal with this in the same way I had dealt with everything else that troubled or scared me. I would confront it. I got to my feet and set off down the slope, heading for the burning neon bubble as the storm folded its arms around me.

'How many people here believe in free will? Okay, that's going to change.'
Robert Sapolsky, professor of neurology and neurological sciences at Stanford University

# TWENTY-ONE

**Graves**

Harry Graves pulled up to the guardhouse at the entrance to the research facility seventy miles north of Las Vegas. Hot desert air rushed in as he lowered the driver's window to speak to one of the two private security contractors manning the gate. The procedure was so engrained in him that he barely gave it a second thought. As they chatted, the other guard checked the trunk. A camera mounted atop the guardhouse scanned the vehicle. A separate camera scanned Graves's face, lingering over his retina. That was the nature of security at the perimeter of the facility – high-tech and low key. The guards themselves were affable. They were there to run the system. Any breach was dealt with by others but very few had taken place – until a few days ago. Usually, the most they had to contend with was the occasional UFO spotter tracking back this way from the nearby Area 51. The overly persistent were dealt with by the local county sheriff's department and sent politely on their way.

It was a full mile before you reached the actual facility. Barring the guards armed with M-4s at the second checkpoint, and its remote location, the facility could have doubled as a college campus or the headquarters of a successful internet company in Silicon Valley. Four single-story white buildings, each with a footprint of forty thousand square feet, were laid out on a diamond pattern. Tucked away in the middle of the diamond, and obscured from sight by the four buildings, was the medical center.

Graves pulled into a parking space in front of the first building, grabbed his briefcase and headed inside. He signed in at the reception desk, passed another facial recognition and retinal scanner and headed for Muir's office.

Muir looked up as Graves walked in and slumped into a chair opposite. Lured away from his glittering academic career to run the program, he had been adept at energizing the team they'd assembled but he'd proved a poor administrator.

Graves dipped into his jacket pocket for his packet of Marlboros. He pulled one out and stuck it in his mouth while he rummaged for his lighter. The cigarette drew a reproachful stare from Muir.

'There's no smoking allowed in here, Harry,' Muir said.

'There's not?' he said, taking another drag. 'You think there's hope for me, Doc?' he asked Muir. 'I mean, I'm closing in on sixty here.'

Muir smiled across the table at him. 'You chain-smoke. You drink heavily. Your diet is, quite frankly …'

'Disgusting?' he offered.

'I was going to say appalling, but disgusting will do. And, yes, I'm sure that even in your condition, at this advanced state, and with your major organs in such a state of probable disrepair, we could find some way of prolonging your conscious life.'

Graves sighed. 'Scoop out my grey matter, stick it in a jar, hook me up to a computer. I bet you could,' he said. What a depressing thought. Eternal life. Hundreds of years more of this shit No, thanks. 'Think I'd rather just go out like Jimmy,' he said, finally. 'Y'know, suck on some metal.' Across the table, Muir stiffened at the mention of Lewis. Graves open-palmed an apology. 'I'm sorry, that was tactless.'

'Yes, it was,' said Muir.

This was the part of Muir's character that had come to worry Graves. He'd thought that a scientist, and especially one as driven as Muir appeared to be, would have been more capable of divorcing himself from the work. But in the last few months, ever since the Lewis incident, and then Byron, he'd been more like some over-sentimental animal-shelter volunteer. *What a mess.* Now they were almost a year behind and DARPA was seriously considering cutting the funding. It had taken all of Graves's political acumen to stop them pulling the rug out from under them entirely, while he worked on securing them some grey-funding, private money from investors who would benefit from whatever the project threw up.

DARPA, the Defense Advanced Research Projects Agency, was the largest single-entity funder of scientific research in the world, with an annual budget of around $3.2 billion. But while it sounded like a lot, and it was, the money was spread over one hell of a large surface area. If you or someone else could imagine it, then DARPA-funded scientists were working on it. Originally established in 1958 as a response to the Soviet threat, DARPA was to the Pentagon what Silicon Valley was to the rest of the country. From acid and mind-control techniques in the sixties to computing in the seventies, robotics in the eighties, and all manner of nuclear, biological and chemical warfare research throughout its life, DARPA was a decentralized smorgasbord of scientific endeavor with reach beyond military facilities into just about every top college campus. But, after exhausting wars in Afghanistan and Iraq, and with federal spending coming under more and more public scrutiny, they had to find a new way of doing things, both in the area of operations and outside it. That made the post-sapiens soldier program vital. The US couldn't give up on the Middle East but neither could it keep throwing bodies at it, or bomb anyone into submission. You still needed boots on the ground, but boots that were capable of doing a lot more. And that was where the PSSP came in: it was brilliant in its sheer simplicity.

And Graves's place in the grand scheme of things? He wasn't a scientist, that was for sure, and he continually had to ask the geekier members of the brains trust he dealt with to explain things in words of no more than four syllables so that he could explain it to the politicians and generals and keep the money flowing. Graves's great strength was that he had realized early in his career what he was good at and where he was weak. He was a fixer, someone who could navigate the myriad interests ranged across the CIA, the Pentagon and Congress, all the way up to the White House and the President herself. She had taken a surprisingly close interest in the project from its very earliest stages when Muir had been developing the new imaging technology that had opened the whole thing up.

'I'm sorry about what happened with Lewis,' he said finally.

Muir met his gaze.

'I mean it,' Graves went on. 'It was a damn shame. But maybe, y'know, with the stuff he had in that package it worked out for the best.'

'Do you think anyone would have believed him?' Muir asked.

'Some might have. People buy into all sorts of things these days,' he said, choosing his words with care. 'New World Order, UFOs, how 9/11 was a conspiracy because the CIA planted explosives under the Twin Towers, and all kinds of other stuff that may or may not be true, and that, ultimately, regular people don't give a shit about. As long as they can pay their mortgage, run two cars and afford a vacation, no one cares, and why would they? If we'd let Lewis tell someone his story, maybe that wouldn't have been a problem. But if he'd run into someone who'd worked out what he was? That would have been a major issue.'

Across the table from him, Muir bristled. '*What* he was?'

'Okay, *who* he was. That better for you?' He let a cylindrical turd of ash drop from his cigarette onto the floor. 'No matter. He's gone.'

'And what about Byron?' Muir said.

Graves shrugged. 'No sign of him. Guy's a ghost. Now, why don't you and I take a walk? Show me where it all happened.'

'I thought you'd have security do that?'

Graves threw down his cigarette butt and ground it under his shoe. 'I've read the report, watched all the footage, talked to people. But you were closer to him than anyone here. I'd like you to take me through what happened exactly.'

# TWENTY-TWO

They left the office and hung a left, heading toward the medical center. Researchers and scientists pecked at keyboards or hunched over workbenches. In comparison to previous visits, the atmosphere was somber. Graves was hardly surprised after what had happened. These were people who weren't used to life at the sharp end. They developed tools for government and the military; they didn't use them.

'As you know, we'd already done some troubleshooting on the implant you retrieved from Lewis and updated it,' said Muir.

'You figure out the problem?' Graves asked him.

Muir stopped dead. 'What do you see, Mr Graves?' he asked.

'What do you mean?'

'It's a simple question.'

Graves rocked back and forth on his heels and glanced around. 'I see a white corridor. I see doors either side. I see you standing next to me asking me some dumbass question.'

'That's not what Lewis would have seen. He was suffering from a disconnect between what we accept as reality and what he was experiencing.'

'Flashbacks?'

'After a fashion, but that term doesn't really capture what some of these men, not just the ones in the program, experience. Sometimes what they dredge up can become more vivid, more real to them than everything else.'

'Either of them tell you about this?' Graves asked.

Muir shook his head. 'Nope. That was what concerned me more than anything, especially with Byron. He'd made such a great subject because he was so open with us.'

Graves chewed it over. 'So how'd you know?'

'The fMRI scans showed some inconsistencies between what he was telling us and what may have been going on with him.'

'He was lying?'

They came to a sallyport manned by two guards. Both men looked up at the retinal scanners. The door clicked open. Graves pushed through. Muir waited until they were well clear of the sallyport before answering.

'No, he wasn't lying. Not in the way that it's commonly understood, as a deliberate untruth.'

Graves was starting to get irritated. Muir was incapable of a yes/no answer. Ask the guy what he'd had for breakfast and you were risking a half-hour seminar about Joel Garreau's work on genetically modifying human fat into pure energy.

'There was a struggle going on between his conscious and unconscious mind. "Struggle" might be too light a word. It was more like a fistfight. Knock 'em down, drag 'em out, bare-knuckle brawl. Here, I'll show you,' said Muir, opening a door.

Graves followed him into a large white room. A Plexiglass wall fronted on to an fMRI scanner. The back wall was filled with displays. Muir powered them up with a swipe of his finger.

'This is Byron's brain.'

Graves noted the time code in the bottom left-hand corner of the screen. The scan would have been taken on the day of his arrival at the facility. The image showed a three-dimensional colored model. By now, Graves could pick out the main areas, and had a basic grasp of what they did. Go much beyond that, though, and he was lost. 'What am I looking at here?' he said.

Muir swept a laser pointer over the image on the screen, picking out the tiny sliver of metal in the center. 'This is the central implant. We placed it inside the amygdala as a way of filtering emotional reactions, such as fear and guilt. The idea was that memory formation, retention and recall would be broadly unchanged but, because we were filtering emotional response, that traumatic memories would have zero impact.'

The red dot of the laser moved down. 'These are the cortical areas.' The laser moved up. 'And this, as you know, is the frontal lobe. The cortical areas come into play when a person recalls an episodic memory. The frontal lobe intervenes to tell a person that an episodic memory is just that, an event or series of events and experiences from the past.'

The red dot moved to the bottom of the screen to reveal a set of video controls. Muir clicked the play icon and color swept across the image, like a summer storm. He clicked another button and Byron Tibor's face appeared on an adjacent screen, his features held in a tight close-up. Graves could hear Muir's voice as he spoke to Tibor from somewhere out of frame.

Graves checked the time code on the fMRI scan. This was data taken a couple of days before Tibor's escape.

He heard Muir say, 'How you doing, Byron?'

There was a slight pause before Tibor replied, 'I'm fine.'

'Everyone treating you okay?'

Muir clicked the pause button and looked at Graves, who had no idea what a brief casual exchange between Tibor and Muir was supposed to tell him.

'The questions are irrelevant,' said Muir. 'It's the activity between the cortical areas and the frontal lobe that's key here.'

'You want to give me this in plain English, Doc?' Graves prompted.

'Tibor was physically present but his mind wasn't.'

'So where was he?'

'We'd planned on taking a closer look during the surgery so we can't say for sure but, judging by what we saw from the fMRI, and observed from his behavior while he was here, he was back in Afghanistan.'

'You're fucking with me! That was before he entered the program.'

'Just before he came to us,' said Muir.

'How is that even possible?'

Muir shrugged. 'Between the implant and the propranolol we were pretty certain that the original trauma was absent.'

The original trauma that Muir was referring to was what had originally brought Tibor into the program. It had taken place prior to the withdrawal of US forces from Afghanistan. Tibor had been sent in as a lone operative to establish contact with an insurgent leader called Masori. The op had gone well but there had been a number of casualties, including a young Afghani girl. Shortly after his return, Tibor had begun to demonstrate the classic symptoms of PTSD, including vivid flashbacks. It had come as a shock. He had been exposed to high-threat, high-risk environments for a long period. He was regarded by those who worked with him as a trusted pair of hands. Next thing they knew he was stepping off a helicopter with a dead girl in his arms. No one had seen it coming. One minute he had been the best of the best. The next he was spiraling out of control.

There had been a period of assessment. The facility was already up and running. Tibor was offered a chance to get his life back. He had done the smart thing and taken it. A couple of the early enrollees hadn't made it. The scientists had used them to refine the technology. By the time Lewis and Tibor had come along they were getting a handle on things. Both men had been success stories. They had returned to service, cycled through a number of covert operations without a hitch and shown no signs of instability. Then, seemingly from nowhere, Lewis had started to slip, and now Tibor had gone over the edge. The only difference was that Lewis hadn't taken anyone else with him.

Graves rubbed his face. 'Let me see where it happened.'

# TWENTY-THREE

Even with the blood and tissue long scrubbed from the floors, walls and ceiling by a specialized clean-up team, Graves couldn't help but feel a chill as he walked into the operating theater with Muir. A solitary CCTV camera mounted in the far-left corner had captured everything. Graves had reviewed it at least a half-dozen times. What he had seen was both horrifying and, not that he would admit it to a living soul, beautiful. The horror and the beauty were indivisible to him.

The footage had shown a seemingly unconscious Byron Tibor being wheeled in. The procedure was scheduled to take around six hours. His skull would be opened, the implant would be removed, updated and placed back where it had been.

The neurosurgery team flown in from Virginia had been about to begin when the monitors had gone crazy. Byron's eyes had snapped open, he had grabbed the scalpel poised over him, and plunged it into the surgeon's carotid artery. Rising up, he had killed the four other members of the team with a combination of his bare hands and the surgical instruments to hand. There was no security present to stop him. No one had anticipated that someone who had supposedly been placed under general anesthetic might be a threat. It was only later that forensic examination revealed the anesthetic had been tampered with. Tibor's ability to control his heart rate and other vital signs had fooled everyone, including the machines he was hooked up to.

In the chaos that followed he had fled. It had been a carefully calculated and planned escape.

'So?' said Graves, picking up a scalpel from a tray of instruments set out next to a heart monitor. 'He used the implant to get past security?'

Muir grimaced. 'Not his implant. Each person who works here has a small RFID implant inserted in their arm. It stands for radio frequency identification device. All the doors have coils with electricity running through them. If you're chipped, the metal coil in your implant is induced when you reach the door and it opens automatically. After he'd finished killing the medical team, Byron cut out one of their implants and used it to make his way out.'

'Smart motherfucker,' said Graves.

'Quite,' said Muir.

The official story relayed by the Department of Defense to the media was that the medical team had died when the light aircraft they were traveling in had crashed shortly after take-off. The cause was given as pilot error.

'You were the last person to speak to him?' said Graves.

Muir nodded. 'It's all in the statement I gave at the time.'

'You have anything to add?'

'No,' said Muir.

'You had lunch?'

'I'm not particularly hungry.'

'Gotta eat,' said Graves.


Muir sat in the passenger seat of Graves's car as they headed through the main gates. Neither of them had said much to the other since they'd walked out of the operating theater. Graves was turning over in his mind how he could keep this quiet and coming up blank. The routine protocols for such an event were already in play. There were people out looking for Byron

Tibor. Maybe they'd get lucky and find him before he could do any more damage or compromise the program. Graves doubted it.

About five miles from the facility, a distance that Tibor would have been able to cover in less than forty minutes, there was a truck stop. This was where they believed he had hitched a ride. They were in the process of hunting down and interviewing every single trucker that had passed through in the hours immediately after the escape.

There was a parking area, a gas station, a small motel and a diner. Graves pulled up outside the diner and they got out. Inside, they took a booth. A tired-looking Hispanic waiter brought them menus and water.

Graves stared out of the window as a big rig rolled out onto the highway. Byron Tibor could be anywhere in the country by now. The damage he could cause didn't bear thinking about.

'Tibor was full-spec wetware,' he said.

The waiter was back. They ordered, and Muir waited until he was out of earshot before he said, 'Yes, he was, but can we not use the term "wetware"?'

'Hey,' said Graves. 'I didn't come up with it.'

The term had come from the community of scientists and freaks called body-hackers. It was their term for the human beings who had implants placed inside their bodies. It was from this community, and others who called themselves trans-humanists that Muir had seized on the idea for the program. It was brilliant in its simplicity. The question Muir had asked was: why spend billions of dollars trying to create a soldier from the ground up when you could take someone who was already a high-level operator and upgrade them? Why reinvent the wheel? The human body was already the most sophisticated functioning organism on earth. All it needed was some tweaking using existing technology.

The human body was capable of unbelievable feats. The key, of course, was the mind and the ability of someone to control their own thoughts. A young mother should not be capable of lifting a full-size automobile. She wouldn't have the strength. Yet if her child was trapped under it, she could do it.

Of course, they had also augmented Tibor's physical abilities. Specially designed cochlear implants meshed with neurological transmitters not only made his hearing infinitely sharper than it had been but allowed him to screen background noise: he could, for instance, isolate the sound of a single human being's breathing in a building with a firefight raging outside.

Laser eye surgery had long been standard for special-forces operatives but artificial corneal implants had provided Tibor with 20/8 high-definition vision in all light levels. Coupled with what was best described as a thermal-imaging capability, his eyes allowed him to track the enemy even in pitch darkness and from a distance of up to a thousand meters.

A modified endoskeleton of flexible Kevlar mesh, augmented by trauma plates made of ultra-high molecular weight polyethylene, protected his existing organs from injury, making him highly resistant to conventional weaponry, up to and including small IEDs.

There had also been something that Muir had explained as a series of sensory substitutions that had required further implants. Lewis had been the first to have them. They had scared the hell out of Graves.

Their food arrived. A cheeseburger for Graves, and a salad for Muir. Graves wondered if anyone had ever ordered the salad before. 'You think he'll take a bullet like Lewis?' he asked Muir. 'Is that where we're headed with this?'

'Lewis was single. It makes a difference.'

It was a good point. Muir's team had seen Byron Tibor meeting his wife and their subsequent marriage as the ultimate endorsement of their work, even more so than the deadly abilities he had been imbued with. The relationship proved that Tibor could pass among regular people and, more importantly, that he could sustain a close personal relationship without showing any outward signs of aggression. Of course, there had been the incident with the two young men in New York, which Graves had ensured the NYPD didn't pursue, but Muir had argued that the behavior Tibor had demonstrated that night was within normal range. But perhaps they had been wrong. Perhaps what had happened to the men had merely been a harbinger of what was to come, of Tibor's inability to keep himself in check.

'Speaking of her,' Muir went on. 'Does she know about … ?' He trailed off.

'Not yet. All she knows is that he left seven days ago and that he's not been in touch since. But let me worry about her,' said Graves.

# TWENTY-FOUR

*New York City*

**Julia**

In the apartment she shared with her husband, Julia Tibor rolled over onto his side of the bed. Even though it took up almost all of their single bedroom she had purchased it so that when he was home he could sleep without his legs dangling over the end.

She dug under the duvet for his old sweatshirt, which lived there when he was gone. She bunched the soft wash-worn red cotton in her hand, brought it up to her face and breathed him in. Her smile widened. She stayed in bed, savoring one of the good mornings, which were by no means a constant. The constant was worry that she would get the call at work. Or, worse, that one of the department administrators would pull her out of teaching a seminar or class. Or that someone would be waiting for her when she returned home in the evening.

But that morning was different. He was safe. She knew it deep within her. He was safe and well and thinking of her. She closed her eyes, took another deep breath, and fell back into a state somewhere between sleep and waking.

Two years ago, the very idea that you could know when someone was thinking of you would have struck her as absurd. But meeting Byron had changed that, as it had changed so many things in her life. Not the superficial things, like her apartment, or her job, but the things that went deeper. He had stirred emotions in her that she had begun to doubt would ever exist for her. Not that she hadn't dated or had crushes on boys growing up, but meeting Byron had been different.

He was the first man with whom she had truly fallen in love. Instantly. From the very first moment she had seen him. That evening was burned onto her mind. She could recall it now with unflinching clarity.

It had been a party following a conference hosted by the Department of International Relations at Columbia University. She later found out that Byron, who had been auditing some classes at George Washington and had been invited along by one of the Columbia faculty, was a reluctant guest. He had intended to spend the evening in Hoboken visiting with an Army Ranger buddy.

But that night he had made no mention of his military service. Or much of anything else for that matter. Beyond the immediate pulse of physical attraction he was unlike almost any other man she had ever met. Although he had reason to be, he was not arrogant. He was far more genuinely engaged with other people than he was with himself. And people responded to him in kind. He could start speaking to someone and within a few minutes they would be telling him things they had barely told another living soul. That was how he was.

She was in a far corner of the room nursing a warm glass of Pinot Grigio. She glanced over the shoulder of the rather earnest young graduate student from Finland, who was doing his best to impress her with a long-winded monologue about something she could barely remember, and there he was.

She could have said that his smile had struck her first, or his height, or just how handsome he was. But none of that would have been true because everything came at her in a rush. The floor seemed to tilt alarmingly under her feet and her vision seemed to telescope so that everyone and everything else in the room faded until there was only him, a man she felt she knew but had never seen before.

The grad student from Finland kept talking until he must have noticed that she was staring straight past him. 'Of course,' he said, 'it's just a theory that I'm not sure is supported by the GDP figures from India. What do you think?'

The question snapped her back into the present. 'I need to visit the restroom,' she said, 'if you'd excuse me.'

'Of course,' he said, as she moved past him, suddenly conscious that she was wearing barely any makeup, that her long brown hair, which she hadn't washed in three days, was roughly pulled up, and she was wearing faded boot-cut blue jeans, a pair of red Converse high tops and an old black sweater. For a moment she thought about rushing back to her apartment to change — it was less than ten blocks away — but dismissed the idea as ridiculous. *What if he was gone by the time she got back? What if she never saw him again?*

She felt a breath of relief as she noticed that the man was talking to a professor she knew well — Gregory Lipshinsky, a noted expert on the Balkans. To her relief, Lipshinsky caught her eye as she approached. 'Ah, Julia, come and meet this young man.'

'I don't know if I'm all that young.'

She had a sense that she wanted to remember those words. The first words that she had heard him say. Again, the thought struck her as somehow absurd. They would chat and then he would leave or his impossibly beautiful girlfriend would make an appearance to whisk him off to dinner.

Hell, for all she knew he could be married.

Then her hand was folded in his, the ridges of his palms hard and calloused, and he was saying, 'I'm Byron, nice to meet you,' his voice deep and rich.

'Julia,' she managed, as he held her hand a second longer than someone just being polite.

'Julia here is one of our best doctoral candidates,' said Gregory.

Byron let go of her hand but held her gaze and smiled. 'Oh, yeah, what's the subject?' he asked, tilting back his glass.

She could feel heat rise to her cheeks. She never blushed and she hated herself for doing so now. She cleared her throat. 'It's about the impact on women's rights of the destabilization of the Middle East by the Bush administration and how that's continued with Obama.'

'Because it was so stable before, right?' Byron said.

Now Julia was able to catch her breath: her hackles had risen at the slightly patronizing tone in his voice. 'I'm not defending the old regimes but we've had a habit of backing countries where women don't even have the right to vote.'

Byron open-palmed an apology. 'I'm sorry. That came off kind of snarky, but I just got back from somewhere we've been doing everything we can to make life better for women and where American soldiers have paid with their lives for doing it so, like I said, I know what you're saying if you're talking about the Saudis but I get a little irritated when we always have to be the bad guys.'

Gregory touched them at the elbow. 'I have a feeling that this debate is going to run on, so if you'll excuse me ...' He was gone. Leaving them alone together.

'So you're what?' Julia said. 'State Department?'

Byron shrugged his broad shoulders. 'Something like that.'

'Military?'

'I was Rangers. Now I guess I'm kind of a semi-official liaison.'

Julia smiled. 'Oh, I know what that means, don't worry.'

'Oh, you do, do you?'

'Yeah. You're a company man.'

Byron stared down into the bottom of his wine glass. 'This wine really sucks. You know any place around here where we could find a real drink?'

# TWENTY-FIVE

They ended up in a bar just off Broadway with dark wooden tables and low lighting. Afterwards Julia was shy on the details of the conversation but could remember two broad lines that had run through the evening. The first was how much being with him made her want to share herself. She was usually cautious around people she had just met, but not with Byron. It was only later that she would realize this wasn't unique to her.

They talked for hours but Byron actually said very little about himself, and when he did he seemed almost embarrassed by what others might see as bragging. A tough public high school in Missouri. Captain of the football team. A full scholarship to Harvard or Yale or Stanford. The choices remained because, in the end, haunted by the smoke rising from the Twin Towers, he had joined the military, turning down a full ride at West Point to enlist as a regular soldier, then moving on to pass selection for the Rangers four years after he had begun basic training. And then? Circumspect. No war stories. No mention of medals or honors, merely a shrug of the shoulders and a single observation.

'Y'know what you policy wonks never factor in, Julia?' he'd asked her.

'Oh, what's that? Please do tell.'

His smile again, sending a tingle from the top of her head to her toes and making her shiver.

He took a sip of his beer. 'War might be hell, but combat? Combat's fricking awesome.' Another sip, the glass disappearing in surprisingly slender fingers, which might have belonged to a concert pianist. 'Once you get past the initial realization that someone's trying to kill you, of course, and that it's nothing personal.'

'Of course.'

And that was as much as he shared of his life story for the longest time. Then it was as if his career had ended in 2009, or at least disappeared behind a pitch-black veil.

It was back to her after that. Her life. Her upper-middle-class background. Her academic achievements, no less than his but at the same time far more easily attained.

So, that had been the first thing. Byron, man of mystery — at least partially.

But the second seam made her almost ashamed: she had had to keep reminding herself to stop staring at him. He was attractive and charismatic. But he was also, there was no other word for it, beautiful.

At first, as Byron pulled out a chair for her and waited until she was settled before he sat down, she had wondered if the drink was just that or whether he was gay. Then a hand settling on hers as he picked up their empty glasses and the way he met her gaze, his eyes slipping fractionally to her cleavage, told her otherwise.

Two drinks later she decided to preserve the magic of the evening and call it a night. He seemed a little disappointed ('Party pooper'), which thrilled her to the core.

He held open the door and they stepped back into the cold night air. The street was slick with rain. 'I'll get you a cab,' he said, stepping between two parked cars.

'I'm only eight blocks away.'

'Then I'll walk you home,' he said, stepping back onto the sidewalk as the rain misted around them.

'There's really no need,' she said, sounding half-hearted, even to herself. 'Plus, I don't want you …'

'Getting the wrong idea? Julia, I'm twenty-nine. I don't do one-night stands. Not that I ever did. I just want to make sure you get home safe so I have peace of mind. That's all.'

She shrugged. 'Damn.'

Byron laughed. 'Ma'am,' he said, hooking his arm out so she could slip hers through it.

At the end of the block they took a right onto Broadway, walked two blocks and crossed the street before hanging a left onto 111th. It was one more block down that the two kids appeared from behind a metal-gated alleyway. Hoods pulled over ball caps, shoulders hunched, chins on chests, but eyes spearing up, heads tilted like a bull's before it charges.

They stepped out directly in front of her and Byron, blocking their passage. She felt her arm slip away from Byron's but he reached out and took it back. His hand slipped into hers. 'Take it easy, okay.' He pulled her close to him. 'One's got a gun.'

All around her, the city froze.

# TWENTY-SIX

The smaller of the two kids raised his right arm, aiming the weapon straight at her. It was all she could see now, the black vortex of the barrel, the kid's finger itchy and trembling against the trigger. Then it was gone, blocked by Byron as he moved in front, his body between her and the two muggers.

She wasn't sure what she had expected to happen next. Some ninja moves, perhaps? Or for him to pull a gun of his own and shoot them? He did neither. Instead, he spoke to them, his voice calm, his tone even.

'Just be cool, fellas, okay? You want money? Here.'

She saw Byron's hand dig into his hip pocket and pull out a money clip. The kid without the gun stepped forward and snatched it.

'White bitch's purse too, nigger,' he said to Byron.

Byron half turned. 'Julia, give me your purse.'

From nowhere she felt a flare of rage at the violation. At Byron's ready surrender. At being called a bitch. Byron's hand reached out and plucked her purse from where it was tucked between her body and the crook of her arm. He tossed it to the kid, who was gleefully counting through his billfold.

'We done here?' Byron asked, the question directed at the kid with the gun.

The kid lowered his gun arm, slapped at his friend's shoulder with the back of his hand. 'We done, nigger.' They began to walk away. Not run.

But walk. With a pimp-roll swagger. The kid who'd had the gun on them had her purse in his hand and was already busy rifling it.

Julia turned to face Byron, who was watching them as they left the scene, his face entirely placid.

'You okay?' he asked her.

'Oh, yeah, I'm great. Just great.' The anger she heard in her own voice surprised her.

Byron shot her that easy grin. 'You're pissed at me for not pulling some Clint Eastwood move?'

She took a step back. 'No, he had a gun. Look, I don't know, maybe you could have … He called me a bitch.'

Byron shrugged. 'Hey, he called me a nigger. Sticks and stones.'

'You're right. Okay, you're right.'

'Here,' said Byron, a hand digging into his back pocket and coming up with a twenty-dollar bill, which he handed to her. 'Get a cab back to your place. Call whoever you have cards with and get them cancelled.'

'And what are you going to do?'

'I'll go home and do the same.' He touched her shoulder, bringing her eyes to his. 'Listen, Julia, we're here, we're breathing, no one got hurt. I lost some cash and a little pride and you lost whatever you had in your purse. It's all replaceable. Sometimes you lose. Even a big tough company man like me.'

An hour later the buzzer in Julia's apartment sounded. She was still up, wide awake and riding a big wave of post-mugging adrenalin while nursing a mug of Irish coffee that was two parts Jameson's whiskey to one part coffee. She crossed to the door and pressed the small white plastic intercom button. 'Yes?'

'It's Byron. I have your purse.'

# TWENTY-SEVEN

She was expecting that he had dug it out of a trash can, but as she placed it on the kitchen counter, she saw that everything was there. Credit cards. Cash. A discarded pair of earrings. Everything. It was exactly as it had been when Byron had taken it from her to give to their assailants.

The same couldn't be said for Byron. At first, as he walked into her apartment, with a somewhat sheepish look on his face, she thought it must have been raining because his T-shirt was wet. Then she saw that it was blood.

'You're bleeding.'

The apologetic shrug, his eyes studying her parquet floor. 'I'm fine.'

He raised his head and looked at her. It was as if he was expecting to be chastised. He held up his right hand. 'I did kinda hurt my hand, though. You got any ice?'

'Sure. Of course.' She bustled to the freezer compartment, grabbed a handful of ice cubes and wrapped them in a cloth. She handed it to him as he placed her purse carefully on the counter.

He took the ice pack with a soft 'Thank you.'

'The two guys?' she asked. 'Are they ... I mean, you didn't ...'

'Damn,' he said, a little of the cockiness she'd seen at the party seeping back into his features. 'You really are a liberal. They're both breathing, if that's what you want to know.'

He was right. Her first thought had been his welfare. The second had been about the physical condition of the two young men who had called her a bitch and mugged her.

'They might need some dental work,' he said. He tugged at his T-shirt, peeling the fabric away from his neck. 'This isn't my blood.'

It was theirs. There was a lot of it.

She felt relief that it wasn't his. There was something else too. Excitement. Violence repulsed her usually. But she couldn't deny the thrill of knowing that Byron had hurt the two men. She wasn't proud of feeling what she did but it was there.

Byron stood there, a man she hadn't even known existed until this evening. There was a stillness to him, a calm that lay at odds with what he'd done.

*They might need some dental work. There had been no smirk when he'd said it. It hadn't come off like bravado. He was simply reporting a fact. He pressed the ice pack against the knuckles of his right hand and watched her.*

'One of them had a gun,' she said. 'What if he'd shot you? I mean, you said yourself there was no real harm done – apart from to your pride.'

'Hey,' he protested, 'this wasn't about male pride. That's a low blow.' He put the ice pack on the kitchen counter, all the while holding her gaze. 'Would you mind if I used your bathroom to get cleaned up?'

His question broke the tension.

'Sure. It's over there. You'll find a couple of bath towels on the rack.'

'Thanks.'

He walked past her and into the bathroom. A few seconds later she heard the hiss of the shower. She went into the bedroom, kneeled down and pulled out a plastic storage box from under the bed. She opened it and took out an oversized blue hooded sweatshirt.

It had belonged to Richard, her last long-term relationship, the fellow grad student. They had lived together for a year. He was nice. And warm. And kind. And would most probably have passed out at the sight of a gun.

She held it to her face. She could still smell him. He had been a tender lover. Considerate. The sex had been – nice. Warm. Kind. Forgettable.

They had parted on good terms. There had been no arguments, no indiscretions, just a slow deceleration that had culminated in a very reasonable, mutual talk in which they had agreed to part ways. She had cried when he'd left with his stuff and the door had closed behind him. Her tears had been more a mark of respect for the end of something than any sense of loss or longing. She had held onto the sweatshirt for the same reason.

She walked out of the bedroom with it, and crossed to the bathroom door. The hiss of the shower had fallen away. She knocked twice.

The door opened and Byron stood there, a towel wrapped round his waist. His body was muscular but lean, wide line-backer shoulders, a broad, smooth chest tapering in a V to a slim waist. His arms and legs were more athlete than steroid-sucking gym rat.

She held out the sweatshirt.

'Thanks. Sure it'll fit me?'

'Oh, it's not one of mine. It's an old boyfriend's.'

He took it from her and looked at the front where the words 'Yale Varsity' were emblazoned in white lettering across the faded blue front. 'A Yalie, huh?'

'He was a nice guy,' she said, suddenly on the defensive.

'I'm just teasing.'

He stepped back inside the bathroom and held out a white plastic bag. The bloodied T-shirt was crumpled inside.

The door closed. She dumped the bag in the trash under the kitchen sink. A few moments later, Byron emerged in the sweatshirt. It had been baggy on Richard but it was skin tight on him, the cuffs finishing two inches short of his wrists and the hem barely reaching the top of his pants. 'Thanks for letting me get cleaned up.'

'Thanks for returning my purse.'

He jerked a thumb at the door. 'Well, it's late and I got an early flight to DC.'

'Company business?' she asked.

'There you go again with that company-man stuff,' he said, smiling.

He didn't move. She walked over to him. She took his injured hand and lifted it to her face. She softly kissed the swollen knuckles. 'Stay.'

Her head resting on Byron's chest, Julia lay awake in the darkness as the city raged on outside, sirens wailing periodically down Amsterdam Avenue or Riverside Drive. His right arm fell across her breasts as he pulled her in closer. His eyes were shut but his lips turned up into a smile.

'I wasn't lying about that flight.'

She glanced over at the red digits glowing from the alarm clock on her nightstand.

3:37 a.m.

He sat up, cradling her head as he moved. He leaned in for a kiss, his lips on hers already familiar. He brushed a stray strand of long black hair from her neck. 'I'll call you from DC. Okay?'

She looked up at him. Under other circumstances she would have taken it as a lie, a man extricating himself from a one-night stand with an easy promise. But this seemed different. Everything about Byron had been different. He had a way of subverting her expectations. He was hard to read yet completely transparent. She had never met anyone like him.

He hugged her in close, strong, muscular arms folding around her. He kissed her one last time, then got out of bed.

She propped herself up on one elbow and watched him dress. 'Can I ask you something?'

'Uh-oh,' he said, with his deep, throaty laugh. In her head it was already becoming *Byron's laugh*, in the same way that he had *Byron's smile*. She had known him under twelve hours and yet she knew this was it: they would be together. She just *knew*.

'Why did you go back to get my purse?'

He stood naked by the bed, his body caught in the shadows thrown through the window by a streetlight. 'The truth?'

'It'd better be.'

'I didn't have your address. Or a phone number. I only realized after I left you.'

'Are you bullshitting me?'

'No.' He paused. 'And what you said earlier about male pride. I guess it was a little dented. Male ego's a funny thing.'

She grabbed a pillow and threw it at him. 'I knew it.'

Byron feinted left and the pillow sailed past him. 'You wanted honest? I was honest.'

When he was dressed, complete with Yale sweatshirt, he sat on the bed and stroked her back. His hands were calloused in places, which she had noticed last night as they had made love. Whatever he did for a living, it wasn't just sitting behind a desk clicking on a mouse or tapping on a keyboard.

Before he left, he leaned in for one last kiss, and then he was gone. Julia sank back into the pillows, her eyelids growing heavy. She fell into a dreamless sleep.

She got up around eleven. Stumbling into the kitchen, she found a note from Byron. There was a date, a time, a location and some advice about what to wear, but no other details. She tried calling him, but his cell defaulted to voicemail. She would have to meet him. He had left her with no choice.

# TWENTY-EIGHT

Heart pounding, face flushed, Julia glanced at Byron and said, 'This is not my idea of a first date. Whatever happened to dinner and a movie?'

Two hundred feet below them, moonlight shimmered across black water. Her toes breached the lip of the bridge. Off in the distance she could see the lights of the Manhattan skyline, the Chrysler building lit green, the Empire State a blaze of red, white and blue.

Byron's hand reached for hers. 'Trust me. We'll go together, right?'

They were both wearing harnesses that cinched around their waists with straps running from groin to shoulder. She had worn jeans, sneakers and a hooded running top. Byron had come better prepared with waterproof pants. His T-shirt was from a charity event, a triathlon held in aid of wounded Army Rangers. On his wrist he had a digital watch that doubled up as a heart monitor. The screen flashed the reading every few seconds. She looked down at her hand clasped in his and saw it was recording eighty-five beats per minute.

A normal resting heart rate for someone in their late twenties who was in excellent physical shape. The heart rate of someone like that if they were sitting at home reading the arts section of the *New York Times*. Not the heart rate of someone, anyone, who was about to bungee jump from a bridge.

She started to edge back, her toes scrunching up. She felt his hand slip from hers and rest at her back. For the first time she was angry with him.

'I don't want to do it, okay? And I feel like I'm being pressured.'

He withdrew his hand as the safety supervisor reached down to check something, letting the couple have their argument if that was what it was going to be.

'I thought you'd enjoy it. I'm sorry. I truly am. I don't want you to do anything you don't want to.'

She felt herself soften. He seemed genuine. His face wore the expression of a man who was contrite.

'I'm sorry,' he said again.

She took another step back from the lip of the bridge, her hands on her hips and took three long, deep breaths.

'Julia,' he said. 'When I said I would never let something bad happen, I meant it. I checked all the gear twice myself before the safety guy. If I thought there was any risk I wouldn't have suggested it.'

She thought back to his heart rate. 'That why you're so calm?'

He glanced down to the watch and something flitted across his face. It worried her: it was the look of a man who had been caught out. 'You want to go to dinner?' he asked. 'We'll go.'

'No,' she found herself saying. 'I want to do this.'

He smiled and took her hand. 'Count of three, okay?' he said, as they edged back to the lip. 'And look up at the stars, not down at the water.'

Byron motioned for the waiter to let Julia taste the wine. The man poured a little into her glass. She tasted it. It was good. Better than good. It was sensational. Everything was better than good. Everything since the jump from the bridge had felt sharper, more intense. Colors. Smells. Taste. Byron.

She had decided not to spoil the moment by asking him why his heart rate never moved. For once she didn't want to be the woman who interrogated a guy she liked about everything on the second date. More selfishly, she didn't want to spoil her own mood. There was something to be said for allowing a person to reveal themselves at their own pace, and nothing about Byron had suggested a man who was evasive. He had boundaries when it came to work, but that was understandable in a government job. He wouldn't be much of a State Department or CIA worker if he spilled his guts to every girl he talked to at a party or went home with.

They had dinner and she kept the conversation away from work. She found herself gabbling on about how scared she had been standing on the bridge.

'There's only two fears we're born with, Julia. Falling and loud noises. They're hard-wired into our minds. Everything else we pick up.' He laid his fork on his plate and took a sip of wine.

'What about dying?' she asked him.

'That's abstract. It comes later.'

'So what fears do you have, Byron? And if you say something cheesy, like losing my number, you're picking up the check.'

He gave that same broad, open smile and his eyes crinkled at the edges. 'Lots of things. The only difference is that I'm too stupid to pay any attention.'

'So when did you get into all this extreme-sports stuff?' He had already told her that he also rock-climbed, parachuted, and had done open-water dives with hammerhead sharks, as well as snowboarding and para-sailing.

His head tilted up and his eyes half closed. 'Let me see. The more extreme stuff? Guess I started around the same time I got myself a motorbike as a twenty-fifth birthday present.' He smiled again. 'Quarter-life crisis?'

'So the military didn't give you a taste for it?'

The smile faded. His brow furrowed. He sat up in his chair and put down his wine glass. It didn't look so much like he was angry as suddenly depleted, spent. 'No. It didn't.'

'I'm sorry, I didn't mean to …'

His eyes met hers and she saw they were wet. 'You don't have to be sorry, Julia. And I'll tell you all about my time in the service. One day. But not tonight. The military saved me and I'll always be grateful for everything they gave me. Y'know, you see stuff and it can be hard for someone who hasn't been in that position to understand.'

# TWENTY-NINE

In contrast to the slightly bohemian chaos of her apartment, his place was, as she had expected, suitably utilitarian and well ordered — another by-product of his military career, she assumed. In the living room there was a couch, a coffee-table, and two rows of bookshelves. While he opened another bottle of wine in the kitchen area, she studied his books. Apart from some literary classics (Dickens, Flaubert, Camus, Mailer), they were mostly non-fiction. There were a lot of military memoirs, ranging from the civil war to more contemporary accounts of Afghanistan and Iraq, and a lot of heavyweight academic studies of current events in the Middle East from a range of Western and Middle Eastern authors. There was some philosophy too (Hegel, Kant, Nietzsche). An entire shelf was devoted to works on conflict resolution, and there were several volumes, some academic, others more journalistic, on counter-insurgency strategies.

He crossed to her and handed her a long-stemmed glass of red wine. He reached past her and clicked on an iPod, which nestled in a Bose docking station.

John Coltrane, *A Love Supreme*.

'Smooth,' she said, teasing.

'Shoot me. I like jazz.'

He leaned in to kiss her, softly at first, then more insistently. She opened her mouth and felt his tongue against hers. She was still floating from the earlier high. He cradled her face in his hands, then pulled her with him down onto the couch. She was lying on top of him. She could feel him harden against her stomach. She reached out to put her glass on the coffee-table as he unbuttoned her blouse and slid a hand inside, cupping her breast through her bra.

Between her legs, she was wet and hot. It had been less than a week since they'd first been together but already there was an ache, a need to have him inside her. His hands pulled at her blouse, then he took off her bra, kissing his way down her neck. They stood up and she took off his shirt. He reached down, his hand brushing against her thigh and working its way up between her legs.

With her arms around his neck, he lifted her up. Her legs wrapped around his waist. He held her tight as he took off his pants and then he was inside her, his hands on her ass. She bucked and writhed, completely lost. She came quickly, her head snapping back as he kissed her throat. He carried her through into the bedroom.

She put a hand across his chest. 'Lie down,' she said, the balance shifting from him to her.

He did as she had asked and she straddled him, feeling him go deeper inside her. Her back arched as she moved her hips. They stayed like that for a long time. Her moving on top of him. She came again and then he began to groan. He said her name as her hair fell across his face. They kissed as he came and she collapsed, her head resting against his muscular chest. Moments passed when neither of them moved, or said anything.

After a time she turned her head fractionally. Through her tangle of red hair, she could see that he was still wearing his heart monitor. The display flashed green in the darkness of the bedroom – the reading constant.

His heart rate. Eighty-five beats per minute. It hadn't moved. She felt a chill run through her. She could imagine someone might remain calm as they faced down their fear, especially someone who had been in frightening situations. But for your heart not to quicken when you made love as they had?

He followed her gaze to the glowing display. 'I wanted to wait before I told you,' he said softly. 'But I guess if we're to go on seeing each other I should do it now.'

His eyes were searching her face. Who was he? She had asked it before, in the manner of a woman wondering how a man she had met could be so perfect. Now it had taken on a more sinister edge. 'Yes,' she said, sitting up. 'I think you should.'

'Aghast the Devil stood, and felt how awful goodness was.'
John Milton, *Paradise Lost*
Scrawled on a tunnel under the Las Vegas Strip

# THIRTY

*Las Vegas*

**Byron**

The lights of the Strip fell away with the rising sun but Las Vegas remained, shabby and faded in the daylight. I kept walking, praying it would shatter as I drew closer. It didn't. It grew more real with each step I took, the shared features of the two landscapes shifting inexorably in front of me to those of the American south-west; wadis gave way to concrete run-offs, the grey-green landscape around Kabul was pushed out by the vivid desert reds and yellows; scrub and trees were replaced by palms arranged along neatly paved boulevards.

Between the malls, wedding chapels and golden arches of McDonald's, the horror returned. Sasha didn't feature: she had faded with the juniper trees. These were fresh horrors, with me in the lead role. It was as if time had fractured and a piece had fallen into the abyss. Everything around me appeared real. I could see, touch, taste, smell and hear Vegas all around me. Cars and trucks sped past on Las Vegas Boulevard, and no one looked twice. At one point I caught myself mumbling out loud. At least, my lips were moving, and I could hear my own voice. A video camera set on a tripod in the window of an electronics store caught anyone passing and threw their image onto a row of super-thin TV sets.

At first I didn't recognize myself. It was only when I caught sight of the raw wound on the side of my neck, and reached up to touch it, the image on screen matching the movement of my hand, that I realized I was looking at myself. Afghanistan or Nevada, I sure as hell looked like someone who had left somewhere in a hurry and spent the last few days trekking over open country, exposed to the elements at every turn.

My apparent invisibility suddenly made sense. I was the crazy homeless guy wearing long sleeves and a jacket in the blazing sun. My straight black hair had grown so it was touching my collar, and I was sporting a ragged, unruly shadow of a beard. My dark complexion was matted with a thin layer of grime, my hands were rough and calloused, fingernails long like claws.

Behind the screens, a store employee wearing a blue polo shirt was staring at me. I moved on. When I glanced back over my shoulder, he was talking to a customer. Up ahead was a bus stop with a bench advertising the services of a local attorney who specialized in DUI cases. I sat down and tried to gather myself. I needed a meal, fresh clothes, and a place to stay while I worked out what the hell had happened. There must be homeless shelters nearby but they would ask for some form of ID. Even if they didn't, the thought of having to speak to someone was frightening. The fear was absurd, but there it was.

A roar filled my ears. A JetBlue passenger aircraft came in low overhead. I looked over my shoulder to see a chain-link fence and a runway. Several small private jets were parked less than a hundred yards away. McCarran airport, it had to be. I had passed through it a couple of times. If I called Julia she could book me a ticket back to New York. The thought scared me more than a homeless shelter. I would have to present ID at the airport. Before that I would have to tell my wife that I didn't know how I'd got there but I was in Vegas.

There was something else too. The Hindu Kush might have faded back into the mists but I hadn't shaken off the feeling that I was on the run from someone or something. It crowded in on me at every fleeting glance or sudden noise. No, before I committed to any course of action, I had to figure out what the hell was going on. But first, I needed to get some money.

Even by the casual standards of Vegas, I was in no state to hang out in any of the casinos. I knew from my solitary visit for an international security conference that a lot of homeless people lived by skimming credits from slot machines abandoned by tourists. Someone would be playing one of the slots, was distracted by the lure of an all-you-can-eat buffet and left the machine with unplayed credits. The homeless would walk the casino floors on the lookout for them until house security threw them out. It was a bare-bones way of scraping a living but you had to achieve some base level of dress code. The way I looked now, I doubted I would even get through the doors of an off-Strip low-rent joint.

Covert special-forces training had taught me all the stuff that teenage boys obsessed over. Field work had taught me that firearms and close-combat skills mattered less than people assumed. The ability to see rather than merely look was far more important. From that starting point you could establish how other people in the same situation survived and assess the effectiveness of their behavior.

Five minutes later, I was Dumpster-diving in the alley behind the TV store. A fast-food restaurant at the end of the row provided a free meal. The TV store threw up a world of discarded cardboard. I tore off a couple of sturdy box flaps and walked back out to the street, heading for a freeway off-ramp I'd spotted when I'd walked into town. In front of the fast-food outlet there was a water fountain. I filled my bottles with clean water and continued on. No one looked at me twice. I was just another Vegas loser standing at the wrong end of the American Dream, invisible, a background actor in regular people's lives – I was grateful for the anonymity. I couldn't have picked a better identity or a better place to deploy it than this city.

Keeping busy settled me. Urban Survival 101 was proving the antidote to my mind storm. My past might have fractured but at least I had a present.

# THIRTY-ONE

'Get the fuck out of here, man. This here's my spot. Understand me? Mine!' the man screamed, as I walked toward the traffic waiting to turn at the bottom of the freeway ramp.

He had a standard-issue homeless-person dirty ball cap and full white beard. A farmer's tan covered his face, arms and lower legs. He wore sneakers, shorts, a couple of T-shirts, a jacket with the sleeves rolled up and shades, while he smoked a cigarette and held up his sign that announced his veteran status. Vietnam. His only problem was that, despite his booze-dried complexion, he was at least ten years too young to have picked up the end of the war in Vietnam, even allowing for a willing spirit and a forged birth certificate.

There was something else about him too, although I wasn't conscious of seeing it, not at first anyway, not until we were already in conversation, and what I was looking at had begun to fade. As I approached him, the guy's skull had glowed yellow. Not yellow from the sun bouncing off a windshield and shading his skin under the bill of his cap, but yellow in the very center top of his head.

Moving closer and using my size to intimidate, I spoke to him softly: 'Chill. I'm not here to take your spot.' I dug out my piece of blank cardboard. 'I'm going to head down there a ways. Pick my own spot.'

The guy tilted his head back, squinting up at me and revealing a scorpion patterned in black ink around his neck. 'You'd better not mess with me, man. I got a buddy round here who'll fuck you up good.'

I ignored the invitation to a pissing contest. 'I'm not looking for trouble. Just wanted to see if I could borrow a Sharpie or something to mark up my sign and see if you could give me a heads up on a couple of things.'

'You'd better give it back to me,' said the man, digging into his jacket and coming up with a black marker pen.

'One vet to another,' I said.

The man stuck out a weathered hand. 'Name's Chauncey.'

I shook but said nothing.

'Not got a name, huh? Got it. Where'd you serve?'

I ignored that question too. I printed out my message with the marker and handed it back to my new buddy, Chauncey. 'Thanks.'

'Just watch for the cops,' said Chauncey. 'They see you panhandling, they'll give you a ticket. I got myself three for loitering.'

'I don't plan on staying around too long. Just need to get myself some cash.'

Chauncey smiled. His lips peeled back to reveal yellow stumps of meth-ravaged teeth. 'That's what I said two years ago. I travel some but this place has a way of drawing people back.'

I was only half listening. I was too busy staring at the fading yellow patterns I could see where Chauncey's skull was.

*Yellow = fear.*

It didn't present itself as a fully formed thought, any more than touching ice made you think *ice = cold.* I was simply aware of the man's fear in the same way I was aware of a dozen other sensations, like the temperature, the cars driving past, and the smell of stale sweat and gas fumes. Most of the time sensory information didn't make it as far as crystallizing into a thought, and this was no different.

'Thanks for your help, Chauncey.'

I strode to the crosswalk and hit the button. As I stepped out onto the road, Chauncey called after me, 'Watch out for those Metro cops. They got some mean motherfuckers in Paradise City.'

I turned back. 'Paradise City? Thought this was Vegas.'

Chauncey yanked a thumb north up the Strip. 'That's Vegas. This here is Paradise. Biggest unincorporated city in the country. Same asshole cops, though.'

I went on my way into the baking heat. A homeless woman with a couple of shopping carts loaded with recyclables already had the south off-ramp staked out. She was tall, close to six feet, with long, bleached-blonde hair. I headed downstream of her, ceding ground. She stared at me and pouted with bright red lips but didn't say anything. There was no aura of color around her head. Maybe the yellow I'd seen when I was talking to Chauncey had been the sun after all.

I held up my sign and waited.

# THIRTY-TWO

Most of the people driving past kept their windows closed, their doors locked and their eyes set dead ahead. A couple of lone female drivers, who had to pull up right next to me while they waited for the turn signal to flip over, glowed yellow. When they did, I walked further down the ramp, away from them, and their fear seemed to fade. About an hour after I had begun, a pick-up truck stopped. The driver, a middle-aged guy with a greasy comb-over and a bad suit, opened the passenger door.

'I got a job for you. Pay sucks and it'll be tough but if you want the work …'

With the heat rolling up from ground, I was just happy for the chance to climb into an air-conditioned cab. 'How much and what do you need?'

'Need a pool digging out. Too narrow to get a digger in. Thirty bucks for the day. Do a good job and I'll use you the rest of the week.'

'Done,' I said, getting in.

The guy didn't introduce himself and I didn't ask. We took a right at the bottom of the off-ramp. The guy glanced in the mirror before the turn. 'That your old lady back there?'

'No,' I told him. 'I don't know who she is.'

'You speak good English,' said the guy, as he pulled an illegal U-turn on the Strip and headed south, away from the city.

My mixed heritage had left me with brown skin but decidedly Caucasian features. It confused people. Some pegged me as a light-skinned black guy, others as Middle Eastern or from Mediterranean Europe (a dark Italian), but a lot of the time people I encountered assumed I must be Hispanic. My appearance made for an interesting time back home but gave me great adaptability overseas where straight-up white guys were bad covert operators.

'I'm from the east coast,' I said.

'Huh,' said the guy, before lapsing into silence.

Getting in I had noticed the gun tucked under the driver's seat. A Glock 9mm with a ten-round clip. Concealed-carry wasn't that unusual out here, and if the guy was in the habit of picking up cheap labor, a gun wasn't the worst idea.

My new employer took the 215 beltway that looped south-east toward Henderson, taking the exit onto Windmill Lane, then picking up the Maryland parkway. He turned off into a residential street of ranch homes. He pulled the pick-up into a driveway and parked just short of a twenty-yard Dumpster that was already filled with about a foot of soil. He got out and I followed him into the back yard.

He had been as good as his word. The ground had been cleared at the surface and a rectangle marked out. The houses were no more than four feet apart. Any mechanical digger you could get through the gap would be only marginally more use than someone reverting to the pick and shovel that were lying in a nearby wheelbarrow.

'I'll leave you to it,' the guy said.

'How deep you want me to go?'

He glanced at his watch. 'It's like two now. Just keep going until I tell you to stop.'

With that, he headed back to the truck. I heard the engine start up, and the guy take off. Near the kitchen window there was a small patio set. A plan for the pool was laid out on the table, the corners weighed down by a couple of heavy-duty glass ashtrays. I took a look, running a finger over the dimensions. I looked back at the area that had been staked out. The outline was off. Whoever had drawn up the plan hadn't allowed for edging. The pool would be smaller than they wanted.

Rooting around in the backyard, I found a tape measure, moved the stakes and set to work. I gave myself a system and found my rhythm. I loosened the soil with the pick, shoveled it into the wheelbarrow and moved it into the Dumpster. Every half-hour or so, I would take a two-minute break to rehydrate as a sharp Nevada sun pounded my back.

About two hours in, as I stood in the middle of the hole I'd dug, my mind started to drift back to Sasha's grave. This time, though, she didn't come as a vision but as a memory. A more distant memory. It left a question. If the girl and the camp were in my past, what had happened to bring me here? I hadn't walked from Afghanistan to Vegas, so where had I come from?

I set back to work, scooping the soil out until there was a sizeable mound, then clambering out, filling the wheelbarrow, doing a dozen or so runs to the Dumpster and jumping back into the hole. Nothing came to mind about how I'd got there, but to feel fully in the present with no flashbacks felt like a kind of progress.

I was in the hole, digging, when I heard the pick-up pull back into the driveway. The driver's door slammed. I walked to the edge of the hole and climbed out. It was close to dark.

The guy who'd hired me stood, hands on hips. 'I ain't paying anybody else but you. Thought I made that clear.'

'What do you mean?'

'Well, there's no goddamn way that one man dug that,' he said.

I followed the man's gaze. The hole was six feet deep and covered an area twenty feet long by twelve feet wide.

'What's the deal?' he asked. 'I drop you off and you call some buddies to come help out? Thirty bucks is what we agreed.'

I didn't argue. 'That's good with me. Now, you have somewhere inside that I can get washed up?'

The guy eyed me. 'No funny business, okay? You take a shower, I'll find you something else to wear and then I'll drop you back. Don't fuck with me, you hear?'

The guy's skull burned yellow and red; a mixture of fear and anger. I saw that he was staring at a tattoo on my arm. 'That thing real?' the guy said.

I looked down at the ink. 'Yes, sir.'

The guy glanced back at the pool-sized hole in the yard. 'Goddamn, you guys must be like some kind of a machine.'

With some money, a pair of jeans, a fresh plaid shirt and my old clothes in a duffel bag, I climbed out of the truck. I should have worked slower. It had been a three-day job and I had done it in just under a day. Looking at the Dumpster full of soil as we drove away, I could see why the guy had freaked. It was a superhuman amount of work for one man to have done. My arms and back ached a little. Otherwise I felt fine.

My mind was clearing. On the drive back from the laboring job, I had begun to stitch together more recent events. I had been in New York with Julia when I'd received a call from the office in DC. They'd asked me to travel to Nevada. Somehow whatever had happened to me there had led to some kind of a temporary psychotic episode that had taken me back to Afghanistan where I had conducted a number of covert missions, including the one in which the child had died.

I had spoken to a man called Muir, back then and more recently. I had taken pills. I could picture them in the bathroom cabinet at home. But there had been something else too. A surgical procedure. An implant of some kind. I reached a hand up to the side of my neck. Had the implant been there? Had I or someone else cut it out and by doing so hastened another collapse? Every turn in the road, every piece that slotted back into the jigsaw puzzle of my past seemed only to throw up more questions.

I could call Julia. It would be the easiest way to figure out what the hell was going on. Yet something within me cautioned against it. A voice was telling me that I had to figure it out for myself first. That it would be dangerous to drag her into whatever this was.

Lost in the maze of my own thoughts, the first I knew of the Las Vegas Metro patrol car that had been slowly following me for half a block was when I noticed the red light spill over my feet. A siren wailed briefly. It was followed by a voice from the roof-mounted Tannoy system.

'Stop right there, buddy.'

# THIRTY-THREE

Fingers interlaced behind my head, I got to my knees. One patrol officer approached me from behind, while the other, gun drawn, covered his partner from behind the driver's door of the Crown Vic. At this moment, I was very firmly in the present, everything hyper-real. The wash of red from the patrol car's rollers spilled over the grey sidewalk.

I heard the clink of the cop behind me taking his cuffs from his utility belt. Judging by the guy's breathing, he was at least fifty pounds overweight and out of shape.

'Keep those hands right there,' the cop said.

'Yes, sir,' I said, a model of compliance.

The scuff of shoe leather on sidewalk told me that the cop was adjusting his position, getting ready to snap on the cuffs. The tips of my fingers began to vibrate as I felt the nickel-plated steel of the cuffs draw closer. The vibrations in my fingertips accelerated. I used them to gauge the position of the cop's hands, waiting until the very last fraction of a second to make my move.

The last thing the cop said was 'What you do to your neck?'

My fingers separated. My hands moved out to my sides in the shape of the cross. Tucking in my right arm, I launched my elbow back and up at a forty-five-degree angle. I made contact with the cop's face, splintering the cartilage in his nose.

Adjusting the angle of my feet, I sprang up on my heels, and used the forward momentum of the elbow strike to carry me round so I was facing the cop. The handcuffs dropped with a clatter onto the sidewalk. The cop fell back, arms windmilling as he tried to maintain his balance.

I needed his body mass to stay between me and his partner. I shot my left hand out and grabbed the utility belt. I centered myself, steadying the cop with my left hand as I used the right to pluck his duty gun, a Springfield 1911, from its holster. With my left hand, I spun him round so that he was facing his partner who was already lost in the moment. Rather than taking cover behind the door and radioing for an assist, the guy was too busy spluttering orders at me. I bent down to retrieve the cuffs, grabbed the cop's wrists and snapped them on so that his hands were held tightly in place behind his back.

Racking the slide, I jammed the gun under his jaw but kept my finger wrapped around the outside of the trigger guard. What happened in the next sixty seconds was what counted.

Both officers were terrified: a golden yellow color spilled out over their skulls, their bodies awash in adrenalin. The last thing I wanted was to have to hurt one. Equally, I wasn't going to risk whatever would come from sitting handcuffed in the back of a patrol car. Not until I had figured out what the hell was going on.

'Lower your duty weapon, put on the safety, and toss it into that drain. Once you've done those three things, I'll release your colleague to you, and you can get him medical attention. You have five seconds to comply, beginning now.' As I said it, I kept my tone even, and moved my finger to the trigger of the Springfield.

In five seconds, if his partner hadn't begun to do what I had requested, I would pull the trigger. Threats were only credible if you had every intention of carrying them through. I had made a reasonable request. If I had to kill the cop it would be because his partner had stalled or tried to play the hero. I would kill him, and then I would kill the partner if he drew down on me. After that I would leave. Right now, as I watched the cop hugging cover behind the door lower his duty weapon, I felt absolutely no discernible emotion whatsoever.

I heard the click of the safety and watched as the cop tossed his weapon at the slit between sidewalk and road that I had picked out for him. I listened as the weapon clattered against the edge of the drain and dropped down into the void.

Further down the Strip, I could see more red lights. Reinforcements. I took my hand away from where I was holding the cop's cuffed hands, turned and ran. Across the Strip to my right was the edge of McCarran airport with a couple of small private jets parked up; one bore Wynn Casino livery. A razor-wire-topped chain-link fence separated the airfield from the road. To my immediate left were a row of billboards and a slope that ran up to a palm-tree-dotted golf course. Up to the north was a Vegas landmark in the shape of the *Welcome to Fabulous Las Vegas* sign.

I headed for the open ground of the golf course. Vaulting the basic chain-link fence that served as a perimeter, I took off again, skirting back north, figuring that at some point they would have a chopper up and that an urban environment with lots of bodies would make for better cover.

The course was dark. I hugged the line of palm trees. I could hear more sirens wailing down the Strip. Among them, I picked up the crooning of an Elvis impersonator scraping the last few dollars of the day from the tourists having their picture taken next to the Las Vegas sign.

"Are You Lonesome Tonight?" I couldn't help but smile.

The smile evaporated an instant later as the ground directly ahead of me exploded, the force of the blast stripping a palm tree six feet away out to its roots, the trunk slicing into long strips, green fronds floating into the neon sky as the King kept crooning in the distance, and sirens pulsed out a staccato beat. Earth and spars of metal fence detonated all around me, a clod of earth hitting me between the eyes, the dirt blinding me. I swiped it away, my head pounding with a migraine blast of pain that sent me to my knees. I clutched my head, the black metal of the Springfield 1911 cold against my cheek. *To pull the trigger, to free myself from this torment?* The idea flashed through my mind.

I opened my eyes and glanced through the torn fencing. I was almost parallel to the Las Vegas sign. Elvis had stopped singing, his audience distracted. The tourists' cameras and cell phones, red lights blinking, shot video of the cops swarming the scene.

Sasha sat atop the Vegas sign, her face lit by yellow and red light, her legs dangling over the O in WELCOME. She waved at me as blood poured from her body.

I blinked, willing her away, denying her presence, and felt guilty. *Julia.* I said her name to myself, repeating it like a mantra, the pain in my head falling away with every incantation.

Before me, the ground that had been torn away was restored. The palm tree that had blown to pieces in front of me was whole, its fronds rippling gently in the slipstream of cars pushing their way down Las Vegas Boulevard. Up ahead, the golf-course fence squared off into a dead end. Two figures were climbing over from the other side. One was a broad, squat man sporting a ball cap. With him was a tall woman in cut-off jeans, with long blonde hair.

I raised the Springfield, a reflex action more than a sign of lethal intent. The two figures kept coming until they were close enough for it to click where I had seen them before. They were the two pan-handlers from the off-ramp.

I lowered the gun and took a step toward them. My foot caught a root, or whatever I was suffering from kicked back in, because I stumbled, falling onto one knee. They moved either side of me as a helicopter spotlight arced across the open ground of the fairway. They pulled me up and began to drag me to the fence they had just climbed over.

The woman's blonde hair tumbled across my shoulder. She stank of sweat and perfume. I tilted my head, catching sight of her throat and the prominent bulge of an Adam's apple.

'This way,' the man with the beard said to me, as we clambered over the fence, the spotlight zigzagging rapidly toward us.

On the other side, the ground fell away sharply to a concave concrete basin with a hole, some kind of access tunnel. A ladder led down into a storm drain. The blonde went first, shining a flashlight, picking out the corroded brown rungs of the ladder. I followed. The man with the beard came next. I felt myself begin to lose consciousness as darkness closed around us. Arms caught me. Then I blacked out.

# THIRTY-FOUR

*New York City*

**Graves**

The black sedan with tinted windows was parked across from the apartment building. Harry Graves sat in back, a frosted-glass partition separating him from the driver. He watched Julia Tibor as she walked past on her way to her apartment. She was attractive: long auburn hair, piercing blue eyes, a nice figure. Byron had done well for himself. And not just in terms of his wife's looks. She was bright, too, and plugged in, at least in broad terms, to their world. She was an east-coast liberal to the core and that had troubled Graves when he had learned of the relationship.

Relationships of any kind were a delicate area when it came to selecting participants in the program. The rule had been that the men selected had to be SSD – single, separated or divorced. Siblings were fine, as were parents, although the closeness of those relationships was carefully assessed – and Byron had scored top marks on that front because not only was he an only child but his parents were dead. Casual relationships between men like Byron and women they met were fine, as long as they remained that way.

Byron's relationship with the woman whom Harry was now watching fumble with her keys, as she juggled two bags of groceries, her handbag and

132

a stack of folders, had been different. There was no question of it being vetoed but a careful risk assessment had been carried out. Muir and Graves had sat down with him separately to talk to him about what he could and could not reveal.

It was hardly virgin territory. Anyone who worked with a certain level of security clearance, either as a civilian or in the military, knew that they had to construct a fairly robust firewall between their personal and working lives. That said, Byron wasn't just aware of certain classified information: he *was* classified information. He was a walking, talking, sentient top-secret project — with a mouth. At least, unlike Lewis, Byron actually got it. His stability had marked him out.

In the end it had been agreed that perhaps a long-term relationship, and marriage, could be of benefit. For one it gave him deeper cover. And it gave them leverage over him.

The only problem that remained was just how much the future Mrs Byron Tibor would know about her husband's past. In the end it had been fairly straightforward.

'Tell her the truth,' Harry had told him. 'Just finesse the transition part. That way if she starts to dig she's only going to find what's been there all along.'

So that was how it had gone. Graves knew that because Byron and Julia had been under pretty heavy covert surveillance during the early part of their relationship. It had been discontinued three months after they'd got hitched. The marriage hadn't seemed to impact on Byron any more than it would have on any other high-level operative. He couldn't talk about aspects of his work. He sometimes had to leave home at short notice and be away for an undetermined and occasionally extended period.

Graves knew that Julia had been aware of this because he had listened to recordings of the two of them discussing it. She had seemed to tease him about the clandestine nature of his work, assuming he was working for the CIA, but she knew enough not to ask too many questions.

In some ways, Muir had told Graves, Byron's marriage and ability to sustain such a close relationship without his spouse suspecting the truth had left the project way ahead of where it had been. They had proved that someone like Byron could be fully integrated. If he could live with a partner, he was ready for pretty much any operation. In some ways it had informed the planning of the operation to extract Masori — three or four possible scenarios had been placed in front of the folks in Washington. The upside was that, even if the mission failed, the worst-case scenario was that they lost one man rather than potentially dozens. It had appealed to the military advisors because it was a defiantly old-school special-forces operation that harked back to the days when special forces was more about using local populations and less about abseiling out of helicopters while armed to the teeth.

He got out of the car, walked up the short flight of stone steps and pressed the buzzer for the apartment. He waited.

'Hello?'

From her tone and the hesitancy of her response to the buzzer, he could tell she hadn't been expecting any visitors. That was good.

'Mrs Tibor, I'm from the State Department. I need to speak to you about your husband. May I come up, please?'

# THIRTY-FIVE

'Is he dead?' Julia Tibor asked Graves.

'We don't know.' He motioned for her to sit down and asked if she wanted anything. Some tea? A glass of water?

'No, thank you, Mr ... ?'

'Graves,' said Harry. 'Harry Graves.'

She sat, and he sat opposite her in an old wing-backed armchair. For a moment his mind settled on the morbid humor of his surname while on such a visit.

'Can you just tell me what's happened, Mr Graves?' she said.

Up close, she was even more striking. In contrast to most women who used makeup and clothes to create an image that worked better from a distance, it was only when you got within a few feet that you saw Byron had married a woman who would have been attractive in pretty much any era. He felt a twinge of regret at never having found anyone to share what passed for his life, but pushed it away. This was high stakes and he had to get his approach right.

'You know that your husband's job involves more than working as an intelligence analyst for the department?'

'He doesn't go into specifics but, yes, I had always assumed it was more than just sitting in an office.'

She seemed to be holding it together pretty well, thought Graves.

135

'I used to tease him about it.' She paused. 'I mean, I do tease him.'

'I can't go into specific details either but he was doing important work for us overseas, and during the course of that work he went missing.'

'Where? Where did he go missing?'

He'd known she would ask. That was why he'd omitted it. It was crucial that he built a bridge with her early on. That she didn't think he was keeping things from her. If he didn't establish trust with her now, it would only complicate matters further down the line. 'That I can't say.'

'He told me he was going to Nevada.'

'I can neither confirm nor deny where he was. But I can say that he was assisting us with an important matter of national security when he went missing.'

She sat a little straighter. 'What do you meant "went missing"? My keys go missing. A dog goes missing. A grown man doesn't go missing. You mean he was kidnapped? That's what you mean, Mr Graves?'

Harry folded his hands on his lap. 'No, Mrs Tibor. I mean exactly what I said. He's missing. We don't know where he is. He was on a mission, we were monitoring him, and he dropped off our radar.' At least that part wasn't entirely fabricated, he thought. 'Believe me, we're devoting every possible resource to locating him and we're all very hopeful.'

'And what should I do in the meantime?'

Harry sighed. She had to believe that he felt the weight of her husband's disappearance almost as much as she did. 'I'm going to ask three things of you. You don't have to agree to all or, indeed, any of them, but I do need to know your decision. First, it may put Byron's life at risk if this becomes public.'

She nodded. 'I understand that. I won't say anything to anyone about this unless you think it's the right thing.'

'I appreciate that. Now, additionally, if someone does have your husband it may be that they attempt to get in touch with you. We did have a case last year, unreported, of course, of a kidnapping where the hostage was made to contact his family directly as a way of his captors gathering intelligence.'

She leaned forward. 'You think he's been kidnapped? What do you mean? I don't follow.'

Harry rubbed his chin. 'The value in someone like your husband is often what he knows rather than in any ransom. In this case the kidnappers tried to use the family to glean information. I can't be any more specific but all we'd ask is that if your husband gets in touch, even to say he's safe, then you let us know immediately.'

'Of course. If he gets in touch let you know,' she repeated back.

Harry dug into his wallet for a piece of paper and a small silver wallet pen. He jotted down a cell-phone number. 'I'm contactable twenty-four/seven,' he said, handing it to her. 'I'll keep you updated if anything changes, but if you want to speak to me, please don't hesitate.'

She took the paper without a word. In truth there was no need for her to contact them if Byron surfaced. Her cell phone, apartment and work landlines and email were already being monitored on a live basis by the National Security Agency. If Byron got in touch, they needed to know whether she would tell them about it or not. If she followed instructions, she was safe.

And if she didn't, thought Graves, well, they had a contingency for that too.

# THIRTY-SIX

Graves was stepping back into the Town Car when his secure phone chirped. 'Graves,' he said.

'We have a positive ID,' said the man at the other end of the line.

Graves slammed the rear passenger door. 'You're sure?'

'Oh, it's definitely him. Hundred percent. Unless there's someone else out there who can toss a two-hundred-pound cop into the air like he's a softball.'

Graves closed his eyes and slowly exhaled. Finally, some good news. 'Okay, great. Let's get someone out there to go pick him up.'

'The sighting was yesterday. He wasn't detained, and now he's back off grid,' said the voice.

'Okay, so send in a team. Set up a secure containment area. Soak the ground with people until you locate him again.'

'Not something we can do that easily where he is. At least, not without risking a breach.'

The protocol for Byron was the same as it had been for Lewis. No media. Limited notification of law enforcement. Keep the details vague, and definitely no names. Apart from the risk of panic that would be created in the general population by telling them that someone from the program was on the loose and rogue, this entire field was, of course, still very much classified. If at all possible, it was staying that way. This was one can of worms that was not going to be opened, if it could be avoided.

'So where is he?' said Graves.

There was a pause that signaled he wasn't about to like what was coming.

'Where?' Graves prompted.

'Vegas,' said the voice. 'He made it to Las Vegas.'

Graves stopped himself cursing. Of course he had, he thought. Stay in the desert or a small town, and he'd be noticed sooner or later. But in a vast urban center, especially a goddamn freak show like Las Vegas, their job would be ten times more difficult. Not only was it easier to melt into an ever-shifting crowd, but the general level of security meant that sending in a big team of operatives to locate him was sure to attract attention and get people talking. This was a game-changer.

'Still no signal from the RDF tracker?' he asked. The signal from the subcutaneous device had died shortly after Byron's exit from the facility.

'That was the other news,' said the voice. 'It's been recovered ten miles north of the facility at the last active point of contact we had for him.'

After Graves had killed the call, he pounded a fist into the door. 'Son of a bitch.' He glanced up and saw Julia Tibor standing at the apartment window. She looked drained. She wasn't the only one, he thought. They needed a new plan, and fast. Something clean, sterile, a scalpel rather than a daisy-cutter bomb.

As the car pulled away from the curb, he started to make calls. The news wasn't good. He had the perfect individual in mind, but he came with a lot of baggage. Graves was going to use every bit of pull he had to bring him on board. And good luck containing him if he did. But who else out there was up to it? He came up blank. It was a shortlist of one, and right now the one was technically unavailable.

# THIRTY-SEVEN

*Las Vegas*

**Chauncey and Repo**

Chauncey had lived in the tunnels for a couple of years now. They were safer than the streets, and the streets were safer than the weekly rental motels. When it was so damn hot out on the Strip that the asphalt stuck to your feet, it was cool in the storm drains. At night, when the temperature dropped, it was warmer. You got more privacy too.

Metro cops didn't come down here unless they had to. Their radios couldn't push out a signal through all that concrete and rebar. Course, them not coming down here meant you had to handle your own business. Anything jumped off, no cop was going to help you. No, sirree. And people did come down: folks looking for a place to stay, or somewhere quiet to jack up or smoke crank. Kids came down too, gangs of 'em, looking to hunt people down for kicks. They'd caught Chauncey once. Only thing that had saved him was that there were so many of them around him they kept getting in each other's way: well, that and Repo. He'd come out of the darkness with that goddamn crazy sword of his, waving it around, blond wig stuck on his head, looking like Xena, Warrior Princess, if she hadn't shaved and had a bad hankering for crank.

The least Chauncey could do for Repo/Sheryl after that was to let him set up a place further back down the tunnel. They'd become friends, or as close as you could get to friends. For a crazy transvestite who liked to wave a sword, Repo was good people, real neat. His camp was something to see. It lay about two hundred yards down the pike from Chauncey's. Repo had hung a curtain across the tunnel so that could both have some privacy. You had to holler before you went beyond the curtain. Get the word from Repo, step on through, and you'd swear it was nicer than some condos. Repo had a shower bag, a king-sized bed, a shelf with books, a TV with a DVD player, a laptop computer. Place was a goddamn palace. All it needed was a bathroom 'stead of the white bucket that Repo used. He'd hooked up a clothes rail too. That was where he kept all his Sheryl dresses and his makeup. Sheryl was something. A real lady. Repo, though, he could be a mean son of a bitch if you crossed him.

That was what had shocked Chauncey about Repo heading out to help the guy with the crazy eyes. Chauncey and Repo both knew to stay out of the cops' business. The Metro cops could be mean. They were trigger happy, too. Maybe that was why Repo had decided to help the dude. The cops were on one side and they were on the other. And there had been something cool about what the dude had done. One second he was on his knees, the next he'd fucked up that one cop, taken his gun ('Taken his gun off a him like candy'), and his partner was screaming like a little girl. Dude wasn't joking either about shooting the cop. It had been some show. You saw a lot of crazy shit on the Strip, heard a lot of guys talk smack, too, about how they were gonna do this if Metro riled them, but no one did it. Not like that dude either.

They had watched him jump the fence into the golf course, figured he was heading their way. The tunnel was right there. Repo had taken off running, and Chauncey had tagged along. Chauncey had told him that it was a bad idea and the dude was going to bring them a world of trouble, but Repo wasn't listening. Before he knew it, Chauncey was jumping the fence too. By that stage, with that helicopter closing in, he was kinda committed, and they'd kinda had to help the brother out.

He was in bad shape when they'd got him down into camp. And the Metro cops had changed their minds about coming down there. They swarmed all over the tunnel. Sent dogs in too. But Repo and Chauncey and the dude were long gone. No way were the Metro cops going to find 'em – not down here. They musta run the whole length of the Strip almost. Miles and miles. Chauncey didn't know when the Metro cops had given up chasing 'em. All they knew was that when they headed back home the cops had smashed up all their shit. They'd taken a knife to Repo's shower bag, smashed his TV and all his electronics, even slashed Chauncey's bed so that the springs were showing.

Repo had stayed up, keeping watch, as Chauncey had got some sleep. The dude had crashed out too. He'd said things in his sleep. Chauncey had noticed he had a real bad wound on his neck, like someone had cut him.

Chauncey lay awake in the darkness and thought about the night that had gone. Crazy. He looked around at all his shit the cops had smashed up or dragged all over the tunnel. Dumb motherfuckers. What did they think they could do to a man who had to live underground? Life had already stripped away everything he had. Repo was the same. Chauncey figured that was why he'd created Sheryl. It was Repo's way of having another life, another shot.

He wondered what the crazy dude's story was. He was a vet, that was for sure. You could tell that from the way he'd dealt with the cops and carried the gun. Hell, you could tell it from the way the guy walked. He wasn't long out either. He was still sharp. Lean. In shape.

There was something else about him. Repo had noticed it too. When they were walking through the tunnels with no light at all, the dude had gone ahead of them. Repo had a torch but the dude had heard something, likely just tourists walking around above ground on the Strip. Repo had killed the light for a moment but the dude had kept walking like it was the middle of the day.

They had kept moving for the next three days, trying to keep to themselves as best they could. The tunnels were full of people who hated the cops but who would happily rat them out for a few bucks. It had crossed Chauncey's mind and he'd broached the subject with Repo. Repo had shot him down. He'd been burned by too many bad deals in the past.

They lay up during the day and early evening when the tunnel-dwellers moved out above ground to get food or go trawl the slots for credits. The first night they had found somewhere quiet and taken turns on guard duty. The second day, the guy had shared his name. Byron. A real black name, Chauncey had thought, though the guy was light-skinned.

By then even Repo was starting to have second thoughts. Byron was taking over, telling them where to go. Chauncey didn't like being told what to do usually, but the guy had a way about him. Kinda quiet authority thing. By the third day, he was the leader, and Repo, who hated just about everyone, was following him around like a puppy.

'This guy's our ticket,' Repo had whispered to Chauncey in the darkness, while they were supposed to be sleeping and Byron was doing what he called recon.

'Yeah, our ticket to the chair.'

Byron had come back with food. Real nice stuff. There was steak and mashed potato and broccoli and a bottle of wine. Chauncey was starting to think that maybe Repo had it right. Then things changed.

Repo and Chauncey had started going over what Byron had done to the cops. Chauncey was half Irish, so the story had grown some with each telling. Byron didn't seem to be enjoying it, though. It was like a big black cloud settled over him.

'Pow! I swear that motherfucker was going to fly into space,' Chauncey had said.

'Be quiet.' The words had come in a whisper so quiet that Chauncey didn't quite catch them.

'I was only …' Chauncey stumbled, as Byron gave him that death stare he had.

'Well, don't.'

Repo had started in on Chauncey: 'Yeah, shut the fuck up with that. We were all there.'

Chauncey felt hurt, like he was being cut out. Him and Repo had always been tight. Him and Sheryl tighter still.

Byron had asked them questions then. Stuff about how he'd arrived, what direction he was coming from when he'd seen Chauncey.

There wasn't much to tell. The lack of information seemed to piss him off. He'd had the look of a blackout drunk, piecing together all the crazy shit from the night before. All of a sudden he'd got up and announced they were going up above ground. All three of them. Worse, he was talking about how he'd seen a sports bar when he'd gone to get dinner. He wanted to have a beer.

Repo had start arguing with him. Soon as he moved, though, Repo and Chauncey fell in behind. They surfaced in an alley right behind the Strip.

Chauncey didn't like bars. They were pricey, and the booze was weak. Most of all, there were too many regular citizens.

Byron bellied up to the bar. He had a roll of money. They got the kind of looks that guys like them always did but the sight of the money changed the dynamic. Fucked-up-looking people in Vegas got 86ed. Fucked-up people with money, though?

'What can I get you, gentlemen?'

Byron ordered a soda. Repo got a goddamn Mai Tai and Chauncey got himself a boilermaker. Byron was staring at one of the screens. It must have been a light sports night because it was tuned to the news. He got the bartender to hike the volume.

Chauncey had sucked down the boilermaker and ordered another on Byron's tab. Any second he was expecting their pictures to flash up on screen. It had been only three days. They were surrounded by people, some watching the same pictures. This was all kinds of bad.

Byron was cool. He'd sipped his soda, his eyes never leaving the screen.

Nothing. No mention of them. Chauncey had another drink to celebrate. The cops would still be looking for them but Vegas had moved on. There was too much crazy shit for it not to.

They had left a while later. Chauncey and Repo were in high spirits. They could move back to their camp, or close. Byron's mood was darker. Repo tried to reassure him. 'Chill. You're good,' he said.

Byron had given him the look. 'No,' he'd said. 'I'm not. And neither are you. You need to get out of here. Split up, get out and don't come back. Get out of the country entirely if you can.'

'You're tripping,' Chauncey had said.

Byron had smiled. 'Not anymore, I'm not.'

# THIRTY-EIGHT

**Byron**

If I'd had any dreams while I was sleeping I didn't remember them, but I woke to find my hand closing around Chauncey's throat, slowly crushing his windpipe. I had the Springfield 1911 pressed so hard to his forehead that when I took it way it left a circular groove on the pockmarked skin between his eyes. As I lowered the gun, my hand was trembling. At first I put that down to nerves, the reaction of someone who had just come within a fraction of killing an innocent man. Then I remembered. The shaking wasn't an emotional response. It was sensory substitution, the reaction of the tips of my fingers to being closed around the metal stock of the gun.

I let go and shoved Chauncey away with my other hand. Behind Chauncey was Repo. He was clutching a sword, and for a moment I flashed back to the village in Afghanistan, and the three men who had come to kill me.

'I told you never to touch me when I'm sleeping. You want to wake me, shout at me or something, but keep your distance.'

Chauncey looked at me sheepishly. 'Sorry, I forgot. You really going to shoot me?'

The answer was yes. I said nothing.

'You want some coffee?' Repo asked me.

146

I sat up and surveyed the detritus of the broken-up camp. The cops had done a pretty number on the place. They'd be back too, and if not them, someone else. Chauncey and Repo weren't safe as long as I was around. I had to get out of there, and so did they.

Over the course of the past three nights I had remembered more. There had been no single epiphany. Instead it had been a slow piecing together that had accelerated as every new piece slotted back into place. I ran a hand over my skull, the magnetic sensors in my fingertips tingling as they came within range of my implants.

I looked up at my two unlikely saviors. 'You have to leave. Today.'

Repo wasn't having it. 'You said that last night, but, dude, you've said a lot of crazy shit since we saved your ass.'

Chauncey shrugged. 'You need to relax, brother. We stood in that bar and no one looked twice at us. Hell, there wasn't even nothing on the local news.'

How did I explain to them that governments ran news blackouts without sounding even crazier? 'Forget all that. There are people looking for me right now. Not local cops. Federal, government people. You helped me and that puts you both in danger.'

Mention of the government and the feds seemed to put Chauncey on edge. 'What's the government want with you?'

'It doesn't matter,' I said. 'The less you know, the better.'

Chauncey and Repo traded a look. They must have met more than one person down in the tunnels who had some sort of paranoid fantasy that the government was out to get them.

'All I know,' said Repo, taking a sip of his coffee, 'is that you are one bad-ass motherfucker. Look, man, you go ahead and split if you like. We ain't going to admit we helped you, never mind anything else.'

I studied their faces. I already knew they weren't going to leave. The tunnels were their home. They felt safe there. This was the life they had chosen. I dug into my back pocket and peeled off some twenty-dollar bills from the roll I had. 'At least take a vacation for a couple of weeks until the heat dies down.'

'We don't want your money,' said Repo.

'The hell we don't. Thanks, man,' said Chauncey, tucking the bills into the front pocket of his dirt-encrusted jeans.

# THIRTY-NINE

Harry Graves stepped past the sallyport toward a row of eight blue Arizona doors. He turned to the corrections officer. 'I can take it from here.'

The CO, a big man with a handlebar mustache, shook his head. 'No can do. Not with this guy.' The CO gave a heavy nod to the door. 'He come in. We gave him a cellie. Stone-cold lifer. Not someone who's going to go upsetting a'body. Fella hung hisseff while Eldon here was in the shower.'

Graves studied the CO. There was an air of fear to the man that you didn't get with jailers. It came off him in waves. It was the same vibe he'd had from everyone he'd mentioned the name Eldon James to. The guy scared people who usually weren't scared. It went way beyond anything rational. 'How'd you know he wasn't planning on doing that in any case? He was a lifer. You said so yourself.'

'Lifers don't go out like that, Mr Graves. They just don't,' said the CO. He sighed. 'Tell you what. I'll pretend like I'm deaf. How does that suit you?'

Graves didn't have the energy for this so he decided to let it go. 'He's coming with me. You know that, right? I mean, if he wants to. Seems kind of redundant to have a chaperone under those circumstances.'

'And if he doesn't want to accept your offer, then you're going to need me,' said the CO, tapping the industrial-size can of pepper spray on his utility belt.

Forty-five minutes later, Graves pulled out of the front parking lot. Next to him in the passenger seat was Eldon James. Graves was careful to call him Mr James or (once he had checked that it was appropriate) Eldon. At no time did he call Eldon James by the name everyone else had for him – a nickname by way of *The Simpsons*, which would have been funny if it had been applied to anyone except Eldon: Satan's Little Helper.

Eldon squirmed in his seat. In fact, the guy didn't stop moving. Not once. He reminded Graves of a hyperactive child with ADHD. He wasn't that much bigger than a child either. Graves wondered if that accounted for the number of men he had killed. You'd look at Eldon and not think anything of it. He was small, five feet seven, and skinny, maybe one hundred thirty-five at a push and with some rocks in his pockets. He had short cropped hair, and a pale verging on sickly complexion with big brown eyes. His feet and hands were big and out of proportion with the rest of him. He sure as hell didn't look like a killer whose blood lust had proved even too much for special forces. He didn't look like shit. But the files didn't lie. Satan's Little Helper had taken more lives than most active-service platoons. He had something else too: he was an expert tracker. You wanted to find someone, he was your man.

'You hungry?' Graves asked him, as they came up on a sign informing them of a truck stop a few miles ahead.

'Sure,' said Eldon. 'I could eat.'

'How'd they treat you back there?'

Eldon shrugged. 'Could have got messy if'n they'd kept me much longer. I need my space.'

Terrific, thought Graves. I got three hundred more miles alone in a car with this nut bag. He swiped at the stalk of his turn signal. 'Let's get you something to eat. Whatever you like. All on Uncle Sam's dime. Just like old times.'

'*Just* like old times?'

'I have a job for you, Eldon.'

'I guessed that already. Who is it, and what's in it for me?'

Graves took Eldon's directness as a good sign. The guy might have come off like some backwoods hillbilly but you didn't assemble his kill rate without having something about you. 'I'll bring you up to speed on the individual later. What's in it for you is your freedom.'

Eldon threw his head back and laughed. 'No deal.'

Graves leaned toward him. 'What do you mean "no deal"? You're looking at life without.'

'I want a return to active service. Ain't no life worth living if I can't do what God put me on the planet to do.'

'You mean take other people off it.'

'Never killed a body that didn't need some killing, Mr Graves. And I would include those two gentlemen I shot in Texas,' said Eldon.

'Active service, an official return to your unit, no dice, no way I could swing that. But I could keep you plenty busy. Off-the-books work. Some here, some overseas. You want time to think it over, I can drop you back at the prison.' said Graves.

'Good enough.'

When they had finished eating, Graves walked Eldon back out to the car. They sat in back. Graves pulled out his notebook computer and double-clicked on the file they'd assembled on Byron Tibor. He angled the screen away from Eldon for a second.

'This goes no further,' he said to Eldon. 'You do not discuss at any time the details of this operation. I also want to emphasize that in the initial stages you are charged with locating this individual. You have to wait for direct orders before you take any further action. If we can detain him, that's our chosen option.'

Eldon seemed a little deflated at this twist but he nodded.

Graves angled the screen back so Eldon could see it. Eldon grinned as he stared at the picture of Tibor. 'For real? Tibor?'

'I understand you served together for a time. That's why I thought you might be the right person for this particular task.'

'So what's he done so bad that you want him? I mean, the guy was a regular Boy Scout when I knew him.'

'He's gone AWOL, and he's carrying some sensitive information. Information that would threaten national security were it to be accessed by the wrong people.'

Eldon's eyes narrowed. 'Tibor? You sure?'

'We're sure,' said Graves.

'So you want this information back?' Eldon asked.

'Don't worry about that. We just want Tibor.'

Eldon turned his hands over so that his palms were facing up. 'I'll need money, a weapon.'

It was Graves's turn to smile. 'Don't worry. We're going to make sure you have everything you need.'

'You want him dead or alive?'

'You'll be issued with a full set of ROE. As I said, we'd prefer him alive, but circumstances …' Graves trailed off, letting Eldon read into the pause what he wished to. ROE stood for rules of engagement, the guidelines that set out under what circumstances lethal force could be deployed by a field operative. For a situation like this they usually offered several degrees more latitude than in standard military operations.

'Got any idea where he might be?'

Graves nodded. 'We believe he's in Las Vegas. Three days ago there was an incident involving Metro cops. We have him on an elevated watch list at all nearby airports. And we have people watching bus stations and other transport hubs as well as local hospitals. It's a little more complicated than a regular manhunt because we have a media blackout in place.'

'So what's the deal with this information he has? You think he's going to try and sell it or something?' Eldon asked.

'No, it's nothing like that. Let's just say that Tibor has had what might be best described as some kind of nervous breakdown,' said Graves, careful not to lie.

Eldon's eyes narrowed. 'I don't get it. The guy was like a rock. What makes someone like that flip out and run off with something that's classified?'

'Do everyone a favor, Eldon. You catch him. Leave the figuring out to us.'

# FORTY

*New York City*

**Julia**

They were watching her. And even if they weren't, it was safer for her to assume that they were. But as Julia woke after a fitful night's sleep it wasn't surveillance that was troubling her, it was whether Graves had been telling the truth. To be told that her husband had been killed in action would almost have been better than the state of limbo she had been plunged into.

She got up and walked from the bedroom into the living room and across to the small desk by the window. Last night she had shut down her computer and unplugged it at the wall. Byron had spoken in passing but at length about how the internet was the greatest invention ever, as far as governments, including their own, were concerned. Coming from anyone else it might have sounded like conspiracy stuff but the way he had laid it out had made complete sense.

'Just think, Julia, when George Orwell wrote *1984*, he was talking about a screen in everyone's living room that Big Brother could watch them through. And now look at what we have. Cameras and a perfect surveillance system that the government doesn't even have to pay for. Orwell would laugh his ass off if he were around now at how dumb people are.'

She had laughed when he'd said it but he hadn't joined in.

'The web was a piece of military technology first. You think they allowed civilian use without thinking it through?'

He hadn't been saying it to scare her. He had simply been stating a fact. She picked up the business card that Graves had left and turned it over in her hand. She thought about calling him but decided to wait until later. There were a few other things she wanted to know about him first.

She took a shower, dressed, grabbed her bag, the same bag Byron had rescued from the two muggers, and left the apartment. Outside it was a cool, crisp New York Saturday, the kind that featured in Woody Allen movies and romantic comedies. She stopped at the small Cypriot neighbourhood deli, forced herself to eat half a bagel, washed down with black coffee, then headed for the subway.

She rode the 1 Train all the way up to 116th Street, then walked across campus to her office. On the way she watched for someone following her but in the crush of people on the subway, even as it emptied out a little above 96th, it was next to impossible. If you wanted to follow someone, Manhattan had to be an ideal environment to do it.

She shared her office with two other academics. One was currently doing research in London and the other, Katrina, was from Ukraine and did most of her work from home, which left the small space to Julia. All the computers in the office were hooked up to a central system. Julia logged on to Katrina's computer, figuring that accessing the other, when the person had been away for several months, might flag somewhere. Logging in was straightforward.

She thought about using Google or a similar search engine but quickly decided against it. Typing in 'Byron Tibor' to Google would be bound to raise a flag somewhere and there was no way on the university system to hide your IP address, the unique identifier that told someone where the search request had originated. Instead she began to search through various news sites, looking for something, anything. After an hour, she gave up. There was no mention of Byron or anyone that resembled him. Whatever had happened, the people he worked for were making sure it would stay like that.

She dug into her purse and pulled out the number Graves had given her. Maybe he would slip up and give something away.

She punched in the cell number. Graves answered almost immediately.

'Mrs Tibor, how are you? Have you heard from your husband?'

Something about the urgency in his voice comforted her. He might know a lot more than she did right now, but she was sure he didn't know where Byron was.

'How did you know it was me?' she asked him.

'New York area code. I guessed.'

Yeah, right, she thought. 'No, I haven't heard anything. I was hoping you might have news.'

'I'm very sorry. We're making every effort but so far we've got nothing concrete,' said Graves. 'We're working hard, though, you can be assured of that. Byron's very important to us. We're leaving no stone unturned. We'll find him.'

'You're sure we can't contact the media?'

On the other end of the line, Graves almost choked. 'Not without risking his life and those of people he works alongside. You haven't spoken to anyone, have you?'

'No, Mr Graves. Listen, I just want my husband back safe.'

'You and me both. If you hear anything …'

'You'll be the first to know,' Julia lied.

# FORTY-ONE

**Graves**

Graves killed the call from Julia Tibor. Across from him, a data analyst from the NSA was looking at an analysis of the call. The analyst shrugged his shoulders. 'She's telling the truth.'

Graves sensed a little doubt. 'But?'

'There is a slight disruption to her speech.' He pointed at the screen. 'Here, and here. Where she asked about how you knew it was her. But that could just be the stress associated with this type of situation. Other than that it's all clean. She's telling the truth.'

'Sometimes I forget we're not supposed to know what we know,' said Graves.

'There is something else, though,' said the analyst.

Graves leaned toward him.

'Bunch of internet searches at a computer in her office at Columbia,' the analyst continued.

'Oh, yeah?' said Graves. He'd expected her to do some digging. It was human nature. The woman's husband was MIA while on government business, and they'd told her pretty much nothing. She was bright. She was hardly likely to stay home filing her nails and watching daytime TV. The only thing that had him worried was her going to the media, and putting Byron's disappearance into the public domain. 'What was she Googling?'

The analyst looked nervous. 'Come on, what?' Graves pressed.

'You sure she didn't know about the program, Harry?'

'What the fuck are you talking about? She can't know. No one knows.'

The analyst tapped a finger to the screen. 'Take a look at the search terms, Harry. She might not know everything, but she knows a lot.'

Graves started reading through the search terms. The analyst was right. There were terms in there that only someone who was on the inside could have known. 'What about her email? She shared any of this?'

'Haven't had time to go through each one but the analytics and hot words search were clear. Looks like he told her but she hasn't shared with anyone.'

Graves chewed it over. If she hadn't told anyone it was containable. The question he couldn't get past was why Byron would have said anything, even if she was his wife. The firewall that surrounded operatives like him was there for a reason that he would have understood. It came down to one simple thing – what you didn't know couldn't hurt you.

He had to go speak to her again. They had a flight heading back east in an hour. He put in a call and checked there was room. Then he headed out of the office at speed. Traffic would take up most of that hour. He needed to get to Julia Tibor before she did something with the information that they'd all regret.

# FORTY-TWO

*Las Vegas*

**Eldon**

They'd booked Eldon into the MGM Grand on the Strip. He checked in and went up to his room. When he got inside, the pre-programmed greeting screen was on the TV. He switched it off. He took some clothes from his bag and hung them in the closet. He took out one of three toothbrushes he carried on recon trips, brushed his teeth, making sure to leave a smear of toothpaste on the sink, and left the water running. Nothing, it seemed, said that a room was being used like a wet toothbrush. He walked back out, switching the sign to Do Not Disturb. He walked out of the main entrance, past the Golden Lion in the foyer, and hung a left.

He collected the beaten-up car he'd rented earlier that morning from a lot about a half-mile away and drove toward downtown. On Fremont, he parked a few blocks away from the motel he planned on using, and walked the rest of the way. After all that time in administrative segregation, cooped up twenty-three hours out of twenty-four, the sun and what passed for fresh air in Vegas felt good.

At times like this Eldon often thought of the story he'd heard as a kid about a guy who couldn't sleep because of the noise from a neighbor's cockerel. The wise man of the village tells him to get a dog that barks. Next time he goes back, the wise man tells him to get a donkey that brays all the time. Finally, when the guy has a goddamn orchestra of animals making a racket, the wise man tells him to get rid of them. All of a sudden, the cockerel cock-a-doodle-dooing seems like jack shit, and he can sleep. That was what life was like for Eldon. A fleabag motel seemed like a palace when you'd spent the last six months in solitary, the same way that a twelve-by-twelve cell was heaven when you'd spent days living in holes in the ground waiting for some asshole to pop his head out so you could blow it off.

Next to his room, an old lady with varicose veins was sitting outside reading a second-hand drugstore romance. She looked away as Eldon opened his door. He glanced at her as he turned the key in the lock. 'Ma'am?' he said.

She looked up from her book, the pages yellow. He could see that he scared her. For a small guy, he scared a lot of people. The only ones he didn't scare were the truly dumb ones. He reached into his wallet, pulled out five bucks and held it out to her.

When she spoke, her voice took him back. It was about an octave higher than he'd expected and she had a Southern accent. 'I'm retired, sugar,' she said. 'My daughter stays with me, though.'

Classy, thought Eldon, a little old lady who pimps her daughter. 'It's nothing like that. I just want you to make sure the residents know that if anyone so much as thinks of going into my room they're going to have a problem. Can you get the word out for me?'

She plucked the five spot from his hand, and stuffed it into her bra without a word.

'Thank you,' said Eldon, as he pushed the door open. He dumped what little gear he had, and headed straight back out. His neighbor didn't look up from her book as he walked past her and toward his beat-up car.

He drove back toward the Strip, dropped his ride and headed into New York, New York. He saw his contact sitting alone at the bar. Eldon sat next to him and ordered a beer. When it came, they took a table in the corner. The contact was a retired Metro detective called Chenko with a bad haircut and a beer gut. The company had men and women like him all over, usually former law-enforcement or retired agents, folks who were plugged in. Every city, every town, every organization with a few hundred employees had at least one. It saved a lot of time, especially in situations like this.

'You've been read in?' Eldon asked him.

Chenko answered, with a smirk, 'Everyone's real twitchy over this. What is he? One of ours who spent too much time with the rag heads and loves Allah?'

Eldon sipped his beer. It was ice cold and flavorless but it went down easy. 'What you have?'

'He had a run-in with two LVPD cops,' said Chenko, getting out his smartphone. He swiped the screen, pulling up a picture of a cop with a face like an inverted Panda, two purple-black eyes and a nose that had been taped back into place.

Eldon studied the damage. Whatever was going on in Tibor's head, he was getting soft. The Tibor he'd known would have killed both cops, ripped out the dash cam, and taken out any witnesses, civilian or not.

Chenko continued with the slide show: 'These are the two guys who helped him. Street names are Repo and Chauncey. They live down in the tunnels. Repo has a jacket, mostly drug-related. Burglary, theft, couple of assaults, soliciting. At weekends, he calls himself Sheryl.' Chenko swiped to a mugshot of Repo in a blond wig, lips pursed like Marilyn Monroe.

He moved onto the other man, Chauncey. Eldon studied the man's face. He looked like a truck driver from Indiana who'd just discovered the joys of meth.

'Chauncey's more your regular loser type. From what one of the patrol guys in that division told me, him and Sheryl have a thing. Different strokes, right?'

Eldon shrugged. He wasn't about to share that he also followed Repo's lifestyle in his down time. 'You know where I can find them?'

Chenko dug out a hotel tourist map. There were three locations circled. He flattened it out on the table. 'Here, here and here.' He jabbed a meaty finger at the Welcome to Las Vegas sign across from McCarran airport. 'This was where the two cops got jumped and where those two losers had set camp. They're lying low but I'd say they'll be back there before someone else stakes it out. Our boy will be long gone but guys like these are creatures of habit. They only move if the tunnels flood or they go to jail.'

# FORTY-THREE

The first tunnel Eldon checked was empty. In the second he came across a couple of tweakers hunched over a pipe. They'd seen Chauncey, Repo and Tibor together but they were hazy on the when part. Heavy-duty narcotics did that to people. A year ago, last week, five minutes before? They were all much of a muchness. Eldon left them to it and moved back to his ride.

Twenty minutes later he parked up next to the Welcome to Las Vegas sign. A couple of Elvis impersonators were having their picture taken with tourists. Across the street a Wynn Casino plane was rolling up, ready to go get the next whale with a couple of million and bring him back to Vegas.

Eldon waited for a break in the traffic and strolled across the street in the direction of the golf course. Ahead of him was a concrete ramp with high walls that shielded it from view. At the bottom it split into two tunnels. Chenko had already told him that Repo and Chauncey were usually camped out on the one closest to the road. Eldon hugged the opposite wall. He could already hear the echo of someone moving around in the right-hand tunnel. He drew his weapon.

He ran straight into the mouth of the tunnel, coming on Chauncey within seconds. He faced him and barked orders: 'Police. Hands behind your head, asshole.'

Chauncey looked at him with tired, yellow eyes. 'You got ID?'

Eldon advanced on him, grabbed his shoulder and spun him round so that he was facing the tunnel wall. He brought a knee up hard between Chauncey's legs. Chauncey groaned, slumping forward. Eldon grabbed his hands and used Plasticuffs to tie them behind his back, cinching them tight enough to cut off the flow of blood.

There was a banshee scream from further down the tunnel. Eldon pivoted round in time to see Sheryl/Repo rushing toward him with a curved samurai sword. Eldon shot him in the face, figuring that Chauncey would have the same information as his boyfriend. Red-tipped fingers flew to what was left of Repo's face as blood spattered the blond fringe of the wig he was wearing. Eldon finished him with a shot to the chest. That was a shame: Repo's outfit, an off-the-shoulder cocktail dress with diamanté edging around the neckline, was pretty damn cute.

Chauncey was crying now. Eldon crossed to the body, and checked for a pulse. He didn't have much time. Even with a suppressor, the tunnel was like a concrete amplifier complete with reverb pedal. He would take Chauncey with him, and find somewhere quiet they could talk.

Squatting down, he didn't see who rushed at him from the darkness. One second he was hunched over a dead transvestite, the next he was kissing the blood-spattered concrete, his weapon prised from his fingers.

Eldon was wiry, and a hell of a lot stronger than people assumed. He was good at wriggling out of situations. Not this time. He was pinned good. A thumb jammed into his vagus nerve, which lay next to the hyoid bone at the triangle of his jaw and neck, the jolt of pain making sure he couldn't struggle. A hand fished in his pocket. One of his own Plasticuff bands was used to secure his hands.

He could taste blood on his lips from the man he'd just executed. Straining his neck muscles, he twisted his head round, scraping the skin away from the point of his chin as he stared into the eyes of the man he'd come to find.

# FORTY-FOUR

**Byron**

I pressed the Springfield into the back of Eldon's neck. 'How you been, Eldon?'

'Y'know, living the dream, same as you. Thought you'd have left already.'

'Change of plan,' I told him. 'I saw you checking in at the Grand. Decided I'd stick around. Graves send you?'

'Name, rank and serial number. That's all you're getting. Anyway, you don't want to hang around here for too long, and I'm going to be too much trouble to take with you. Just do this and be done.'

Something approaching grudging admiration welled in me. A man like Eldon didn't need an implant or any help in doing what he did. He was a stone-cold psychopath. The guy didn't have nightmares about the people he'd killed: he had wet dreams. In fact, I'd heard he kept a tally of his kills. The last two before prison had been a couple of car-jackers in Texas who'd rolled up on him while he was taking a nap in his car.

'What was your final number, Eldon?'

'One ninety-seven. Want the breakdown?'

'Not really,' I said.

'I'm gonna give it to you anyway, case you live long enough to write your memoirs. One hundred seventy men. Twenty-one women. And seven kids. Best one was a baby out in 'Stan. Boom! What a shot. Momma was holding him, thinking that I wouldn't shoot a newborn, then pop! Right through the little fucker's head and straight into her heart. Hearts and minds, Byron, that's what it's all about over there. Am I correct?'

I said nothing. I wasn't going to get drawn in.

'What you waiting for, Robo Cop?' Eldon taunted.

I pressed a knee into the base of Eldon's spine. I could see straight into the back of his head as the flow of blood pulsed and flashed a magic lantern of color. The only thing missing was yellow. Eldon wasn't scared of death, not even deep in the center of his mind at his amygdala, the emotional nerve control that filtered our deepest fears.

A police siren whooped close by. I listened hard. I heard a car stop and two doors open, closely followed by the crackle of radios and a request for more units.

Eldon looked at me. 'What now?'

I drove the butt of the Springfield into Eldon's skull, catching him on the temple. I would have shot him but that would have meant losing the few seconds I had to get out of there before the cops arrived. I turned and headed back into the darkness of the tunnel.

# FORTY-FIVE

**Julia**

Julia started as she walked into the apartment and flicked on the lights. Graves was sitting in the leather club chair next to the fireplace. It was where Byron used to sit in the evening and read.

'We need to talk, Mrs Tibor,' he said. 'And this time you need to tell me the truth.'

'What is this? You break into my home and now you want to interrogate me. Who the hell do you think you are?'

Graves's fingers tapped the arm of the chair. 'I'm the government, Mrs Tibor, and this is a matter of national security, which means that I can go where I want, and do what I like when I get there.'

Julia couldn't believe the nerve of the guy. 'The hell with you.' She about-faced and headed for the door, half expecting it to open and reveal another heavy standing there. When she opened it there was only the empty corridor and the stairs she had just climbed.

Graves called after her: 'You want to know the truth about your husband?'

Stepping back into the apartment, she pulled the door closed behind her. She stood with her back to it. 'You told me Byron was MIA. Have you found him? Is he alive?'

'Tell you what, why don't we both try something new with each other? I'll tell you the truth, but you have to do the same for me.' He waited for her response.

'Where's my husband?'

'You have any coffee?' Graves asked her.

'I can make some.'

'I'd appreciate that.'

'Is he alive?'

Graves nodded. 'As far as we know, yes.'

Julia went into the small galley kitchen and made coffee, her hands trembling as she measured the coffee beans into the grinder and poured in the water. She was scared. Scared because of who Graves was, and what he represented, and the fact that he knew she'd lied. How he knew bothered her too. She knew that the National Security Agency monitored everything that went on, every phone call, every email, but, like most people, she didn't dwell on it any more than she was conscious of being captured on security cameras whenever she took the subway or walked into a store. Part of that came from the feeling that you need worry only if you were doing something wrong. But what was wrong and who decided? Someone could tell you something, and the act of knowing, of listening to them, as much as the act of them telling you, somehow made you complicit in the eyes of the government.

She called through to Graves, 'How do you take it?'

'Black, sugar, if you have it.'

She dug around in the cupboards and managed to find some vanilla-scented sugar. She carried two mugs into the living room and handed one to Graves.

'Thank you. Perhaps I should begin and that will make your part easier.'

She nodded for him to go ahead, blowing over the lip of the mug to cool her coffee. Her eyes flitted to a framed picture of her with Byron that stood on the mantel over the fireplace. It had been taken on their wedding day. Her brother had been Byron's best man. Apart from a few of Byron's work colleagues and their wives, the guests had been her family, her friends, or people they knew as a couple.

'When Byron left you ten days ago,' Graves started, 'he traveled to Nevada to the research facility that had helped him previously. He told you about that?'

It felt so strange to be discussing this. Even when Byron had told her about the program, it had seemed surreal. It still did. Apart from anything else, he appeared completely normal. The only way anyone could guess was from the heart monitor he sometimes wore. Even then most people would have put down the reading to his special-forces training or his sheer athleticism.

'Yes, he did,' Julia said.

'Mrs Tibor, I have to be careful what I say. I can't afford to let something slip that you don't already know about. It wouldn't be good for either of us. You understand?'

She did, only too well. 'The facility was where they gave him the neural implants, which allow him to perform at levels that normal people can't. And they stopped the PTSD – or, at least, they stopped the symptoms.'

'What did he tell you about that, Mrs Tibor? You'll understand why it's important in a second.'

'He told me he saw a young girl being killed when he was on a mission in Afghanistan. He had some kind of a breakdown, nightmares, flashbacks. Someone told him about the program. He still wanted to serve his country. The program would allow him to do that. There was a risk but he couldn't go on the way he was.'

'That's correct,' said Graves. 'He say anything else about the program? About other technology?'

She gave a nervous laugh. It would sound crazy. The technology and what it allowed Byron to do seemed far-fetched yet frighteningly real.

'The implants also gave him … I don't know the word. It sounds stupid.'

'Go on,' Graves prompted.

'It was like superpowers.' She scrambled to correct herself. 'Not like flying or climbing walls, but his senses were heightened. He had night vision, he could separate out sounds, pick out two people whispering to each other in a crowded room.'

'Anything else?'

She took a sip of coffee. 'He could read minds. Not literally. But he could look at someone and tell if they were happy, or nervous, or scared. He said it was called sensory substitution. He showed me the tiny magnets in his fingertips. He could stick his hand around a corner and read the temperature of a room. I sound like a crazy person ...'

'The subcutaneous armor? He mention that?'

'Yes.' She shook her head at the thought of it. Now she had started talking she wasn't sure she could stop. It was such a relief to share this with someone, even if that someone was a person she didn't trust. 'It wasn't something I thought much about. He told me he didn't use it unless he was on active duty. He was just my husband. I mean, is ... unless you have something to tell me.'

'No, and he is missing. That part was true. But not overseas.'

She wasn't sure what to make of this. He must have read her puzzlement because he went on, 'There was a problem with one of the implants. Another operative who had undergone the same procedure started to act in a volatile manner. The medical team and the neuroscientists were about to run an update on Byron, take it out, repair it and put it back in, but Byron went haywire. Mrs Tibor, I'm not sure how to tell you say this exactly, but Byron killed four of the team and fled the facility.'

At first she didn't know how to respond. 'That's not possible.'

'We have a recording of what happened from the security camera. He killed them and then he fled. We lost contact with him in the desert to the south of the facility. Last we heard he was seen in Las Vegas where he almost killed a cop. He's still at large.'

'I don't believe it.' She said it with all sincerity. The defining characteristic of Byron was how gentle he was. 'He's not a violent person. I mean I know that when he was a Ranger he had to do things as part of his service. That was different, though. He wouldn't harm an innocent person.'

Graves put his mug of coffee on a side table. 'Perhaps he didn't see them as innocent. What was he like before he left? Had you noticed any change in his behavior?'

This was the question she had been dreading. The news Graves had just given her didn't help her answer it either. They were already convinced that Byron was dangerous, a superhuman madman on the loose. She didn't want to say anything to reinforce that impression.

'He seemed a little on edge, but he always did before he left home. It was nothing unusual.'

She hated herself for the lie. The truth was that she had seen a side to Byron before he left that had scared her. He had seemed distracted and forgetful, more so than usual. The first real sign had come about three weeks before he left. She had woken in the middle of the night to find the sheets drenched with his sweat. His body had been completely rigid, his eyes open. She had got up and called to him from across the room. He had woken up rubbing his face and seemed completely normal. 'Just a nightmare, sweetie,' he'd told her. He'd helped her change the sheets and they had gone back to bed. In the morning he was up and out before she woke. He used to go running in the early morning. When he'd come back, he'd been the sweet, normal man who loved life that she knew. She had passed it off as an aberration. People had nightmares. Why should her perfect husband be the exception? But she'd already known the answer.

Byron had told her that after the surgery, which had taken place over six months, his memory was fine. He could remember everything that had gone before. It was simply that it didn't carry the emotional weight it once had. Over time he didn't think of the girl anymore, or any of the horrific things he had witnessed. Beyond the things he could do, it was this that had made him happy to offer himself as a volunteer. They had something that could free tens of thousands of veterans, and victims of violent crime and other traumatic events, from the cages their minds had created. They wouldn't have to walk round like zombies or take pills: they could get their old lives back.

'Would you mind if I used the bathroom?' Graves asked.

'No, go right ahead.'

Graves excused himself. She was left alone with this new knowledge. She wondered whether or not to tell Graves about the other incidents that had taken place before Byron had left. She had come home one evening to find him at the window with a gun. He had pulled her inside and told her to take cover. This had gone on for an hour before she had persuaded him that everything was fine. It was only later that she'd realized he was in the midst of a full-blown flashback. There were more nightmares, more night sweats. He grew snappy and irritable. By the time he had left, for the first time in their marriage she had been glad to see him go. Then had come Graves's first visit and with it the guilt. Byron had needed her, and she hadn't known what to do. Now he was a wanted man.

Graves took a leak, and while the toilet was refilling, slid back the mirrored door of the medicine cabinet that hung over the sink. Behind a bottle of multi-vitamins, he found what he was looking for. Propranolol was a beta-blocker, used to calm nerves and free patients from anxiety. It was also believed to damp down traumatic memories. You didn't forget, you just didn't care so much. There had been a lot of disagreement among the team at the facility about its use. In the end it had been agreed to give people in the program a low dose.

Graves opened the white plastic bottle and counted out the tablets. He checked the date of issue against the number. It was as they had suspected. Tibor had stopped taking the drug weeks ago. In itself that didn't prove anything, but it didn't look like coincidence either. The question that remained was why he had stopped taking it. Graves put the container back, washed his hands and walked out.

Julia Tibor got up as he came back into the living room. 'You want some more coffee?'

He motioned for her to sit down. She did. She seemed fidgety. She was holding out on him. He didn't need sensory substitution to get that. He didn't blame her. She was protective of her husband. That was something he could use if he had to. He sat down, leaving it to her to fill the silence.

'I just feel so helpless,' she said. 'If I could talk to him maybe I could … I don't know.'

'Mrs Tibor. Julia. Is it okay if I call you Julia?'

She was glancing back at the wedding picture above the mantel. Maybe she was wishing herself back to that day.

'Julia, I want you to know that we are doing everything we can to locate Byron and to bring him home safely. This might sound impersonal but we have a lot invested in him. Not just money but hope. I think at some point he will try to contact you. When he does it's important you let us know.'

She seemed to bristle. 'I thought you'd know anyway.'

'We will, but it would be better coming from you. You don't have to cooperate with us.'

'You make it sound like a threat.'

Harry sighed. 'I guess it is. There's also your own safety to consider. The people Byron killed were trying to help him. They were people he knew.'

'Byron wouldn't hurt me,' she said. 'He loves me.'

'The man in that picture up there, he loved you. The one we're trying to find? It's not the same guy. Not even close.' He saw the seed of doubt take. That was all they needed. He crossed to the hallway. 'I'll see myself out.'

# FORTY-SIX

**Byron**

I had no good way to get home. Whatever method I chose would involve a trade-off between journey time and risk. Hopping a flight straight from McCarran to JFK, Newark or LaGuardia would minimize the time I was exposed to a few hours but it was ultra-high risk. Those would be the airports they'd be watching, McCarran in particular. I doubted I'd make it onto the plane. My other options, driving or taking the bus, were lower risk but I'd be out there for longer. People would see me on the bus, and driving I'd have to stop for gas. There was another factor too. On a bus or plane I would be ceding control. If I encountered trouble while driving, I could at least try to take evasive action straight away. So, car it was.

I stood across the street from the Silver Dollar Casino. The valet was a young Hispanic guy called Victor. I had never met Victor. I'd left that to Repo. Chauncey had been too jumpy. Repo had had the chip of ice that delineated a real hustler from someone who had to hustle to survive.

When the other valet, an older guy, collected someone's car, I made my move. I palmed the ticket and the balance of the money to Victor. He plucked the keys from the valet stand and handed them to me.

'Cherry red.'

That was all it took. The car had been left behind as collateral by someone chasing a losing streak all the way to the very bottom of the deck. Victor had picked it up from a pit boss for a couple of hundred bucks. Chauncey and Repo had been skimming the slots when they'd heard about it. The Silver Dollar tolerated skimming as long as they didn't upset any guests, left when they were asked without making a fuss, and acted as low-level intelligence-gatherers for security. It was all part of the rich ecosystem of Vegas.

I walked round the corner, hit the clicker and opened the driver's door. The interior reeked of cigarette smoke and stale fast food. The engine turned over at the second attempt. I lowered all the windows and checked the fuel gauge. Half a tank. Enough to get me clear of the city.

I pulled out into the traffic, and headed for the western edge of the beltway. I used my rearview and side mirrors to watch the vehicles around me as I made my way up to the 95. I took it north-west, retracing my earlier journey. Before I struck for home there was someone I needed to talk to.

# FORTY-SEVEN

**Julia**

Julia woke to the blinking red light of her smartphone announcing unread email on the table next to her bed. It had taken her until four in the morning to get to sleep. Her mind was caught in a loop. Graves's visit had shattered her image of the man she had married. She rolled over and grabbed her phone. No sooner had she started opening and deleting emails than the phone vibrated in her hand to signal an incoming call. It dropped onto the bed and she had to scramble to retrieve it before it defaulted to voicemail. The number was unknown. As she clicked to answer it, she closed her eyes, praying to hear Byron's voice.

'Mrs Tibor.'

It was Graves.

'Hope I didn't wake you,' he said. 'I wanted to check in, make sure you're okay.'

Making sure she was okay meant checking whether she'd heard from Byron. Her apartment had been under surveillance since the incident, she was sure: it would have been standard operating procedure. She doubted that the timing of Graves's call was coincidental. As soon as she had begun opening emails it would have pinged, alerting Graves not only to the location of the phone she was holding but to the fact that someone was using it to open emails, and was therefore awake. She had reminded herself last night about something Byron had told her a long time ago. *There's no such thing as a coincidence in my world. And even if they do happen, you can't assume that's what it is. Not if you want to stay alive. Everything is cause and effect, even when it's not.*

She swept a tangle of hair from her face and sat up. Her left leg inched over, and she felt the coldness on Byron's side of the bed. 'I'm fine, thank you.'

'I doubt that,' said Graves. 'You sleep any?'

'Some.' She was starting to resent the man's *faux*-intimacy. No matter who her husband was (*who he had been all along?*), or what he had done, it was still her life. She hadn't signed up to this. She hadn't traded off her right to privacy in order to serve her country. 'Do you have any news?'

'Not yet,' said Graves.

'Would you tell me if you did?'

She could hear him take a puff on a cigarette and exhale. It sounded like the rattle of a skeleton that had been hung in the wind.

'No,' he said. 'Probably not. This is kind of a one-way street. Sure it's frustrating for you. It's the way it works.'

There was a silence. She was waiting for Graves to ask if she'd heard anything before she reminded herself that the question was redundant. Graves would either know or he would be relying on her to tell him.

'I know that yesterday left you with a lot to take in,' he said. 'I've emailed you a secure link to something that I hope will clarify things. I warn you now, it's unpleasant, and you're not required to watch it if you don't want to.'

Julia shivered. 'What it is?'

'Video footage from the facility. Like I said, you don't have to watch it but if you do, and you find that you can't get what you've seen out of your head, there's something in the medicine cabinet that might help. About a month's supply.'

The propranolol. Graves must have checked it when he used the bathroom. *No such thing as a coincidence, Julia.* She had meant to throw the pills away but hadn't got round to it.

'Were you going to mention it, Julia?' he asked her.

'He had been acting strangely for a while,' As soon as she'd spoken the words, she regretted it. She had crossed a line. She had shared the sanctity of her relationship with Byron, and not just with anyone, a girlfriend or her mom, but with Graves.

'We'd guessed that, but I'm glad you told me yourself. It's better that it comes from you.'

Her throat tightened. She had always prided herself on her ability to keep her emotions in check, at least outwardly. 'He never threatened me. Never. He wasn't that kind of man. He would never hurt a woman.'

'Watch the link,' said Graves, and hung up.

It had taken an hour of pacing the apartment before she had worked herself up to click on the blue underlined text of the link. Graves had used cheap car-wreck psychology knowing that it would work. Even though she knew it was better not to watch, the not-knowing would gnaw away at her until she did. With the email also came a message that for security reasons the link would only remain live until midday. The email could not be forwarded; the link had to be accessed from her IP address and could only be watched once. Blink, and you'd miss it.

She sat down on the couch and full-screened the image on her laptop. She clicked the play triangle.

It was security-camera footage. That part didn't come as a surprise. Everything else about it did, starting with the date and time stamped in white lettering at the bottom right-hand corner of the screen. She recognized the date immediately – after all, who forgot the evening they'd met the man they were about to marry?

Two young men sauntered down Sixth Avenue. One was carrying the bag they had taken from Julia. He was rifling through it like it was the most natural thing in the world. He came up with Julia's cell phone and tossed it to his buddy, who slid off the back, removed the SIM chip, tossed it and put the rear casing back in place.

They turned a corner. Another camera picked them up, its framing a little tighter. They stopped suddenly. They were wary now but the cockiness was still there.

Byron entered frame left. He had his arms raised, palms up in a 'take it easy' gesture. After that everything happened really fast.

She hugged the toilet bowl and vomited until there was nothing left to come up. A yellow stalactite of bile hung from her bottom lip. Legs shaking, she got back to her feet, holding on to the edge of the porcelain sink for support. She flushed the toilet, then filled a glass tumbler with water and rinsed her mouth. She brushed her teeth and swirled some mouthwash.

She tore open the medicine cabinet, grabbed the pill bottle, and emptied one into the palm of her hand. She washed it down with the last of the water and closed the cabinet. Her head was pounding.

She cursed Graves. She cursed Byron. Most of all, she cursed herself. She had known nothing good could come from watching what he'd sent her.

Opening the link, she'd expected to see what Byron had done at the research facility. In the process, she had already rationalized what he'd done. He was sick. He hadn't been in control of himself. The body, the vessel, had done it, but the actual person wasn't present.

What Byron had done to the two muggers was different, though. He had turned up at her apartment, a fairytale figure, the proverbial knight in shining armor. He had downplayed the risk he'd taken, made a joke of the whole thing when all the while he'd just killed two men in cold blood, showing them no mercy as they had pleaded for their lives. It was one thing to discount what had happened over the past few weeks. It was something else to know that the man she had fallen in love with was a cold-blooded executioner who had deceived her.

Her cell rang. No doubt it was Graves checking up on her. She clicked the green call button.

'Julia, listen carefully. I don't have long,' said Byron.

# FORTY-EIGHT

**Graves**

'We get a location?' Graves asked. He was in the business lounge at JFK, getting ready to board a flight back to Vegas and work out what the hell had happened to Eldon James.

'Convenience store in north Vegas. He was gone by the time we got someone there. No one saw him make the call. The pay phone was outside.'

Of course they didn't, thought Graves. 'Okay, send me the audio.' He killed the call. His flight was boarding. He grabbed his bag and headed for the gate. He handed his boarding pass as the email pinged into his inbox. Along with the audio was a location on Googlemaps. It showed the store, right next to the smaller of the Vegas airports. They could cross that off the list. Whatever enhancements Byron had, they were having to deal with something far more fundamental. Before he'd entered the program, he'd been trained to the highest level. They were up against someone who knew their play book as well as anyone, and who wasn't constrained by the same rules, no matter how elastic they'd become in recent years. Add in all the things that had made Muir and the head-scoopers cream their pants – Byron's genetic profile, which included the warrior gene, his range of intelligence and existing cognitive abilities, and physical profile. It was all now working against them.

Graves started down the gangway to the plane. He popped in his earphones and listened to the audio of the call between Byron and Julia as he walked. As so often in life, the meaning lay in the pauses and hesitations. It was what Julia hadn't said that mattered. By the time he was settled in his seat, he was happier. Now they had the wife on board, it was time for a new strategy. The start of the end game was in sight.

# FORTY-NINE

**Byron**

Muir pulled his car into the parking space outside his ground-floor apartment. The security detail that had trailed him home pulled up alongside and the two private security guards escorting the scientists got out. I retreated to the bathroom, which lay at the back of Muir's small two-bed apartment.

By concentrating my hearing I could come close to being able to visualize every movement just from the audio waves that pulsed against my cochlear implants. I could break down the scrape of the key against every part of the lock, and every single step. The guards left Muir at the door. They would wait outside in their vehicle until they were relieved by a fresh two-man detail.

As I'd waited for Muir I had been struck by how bare the apartment was, how impersonal. I had wondered why Muir put in such long hours at the facility, often sleeping in a spare bed in the medical wing, and now I had my answer. Muir and his work were indivisible. He had no partner, no children. The closest he'd come to kids was the team of young scientists he had culled from the best schools in the world – and guys like me and Lewis. We were, at least in part, creatures of his imagination, his creations.

During one of our long informal chats when I had first joined the program, Muir had shared his moment of epiphany with me. He had been at home watching the South African athlete Oscar Pistorius before the athlete's fall from grace. Pistorius, whose legs had been amputated below the knee as a child, used carbon-fiber blades to run. It was argued that, rather than being at a disadvantage, technology gave him an unfair advantage. People openly speculated that in time the Olympics and the Paralympics would swap places. Regular humans would compete in the Olympics while the Paralympics would be for people who were faster, stronger and fitter.

'That was when I realized that my whole career I had been looking through the wrong end of the telescope,' Muir had told me.

I had asked him what he meant.

'It was so blindingly obvious, Byron. It had been right there in front of us all along. We didn't need to build a robot or a computer that was smarter than we were. We already had all that. It was God's gift.'

That was when I discovered that Muir was religious. As we had walked around the outside of the facility, he had continued to explain his new philosophy. 'The human body, the human mind, is an unbelievable feat of engineering, Byron. Of course, it has to be, it's been honed by tens of thousands of years of the beta-testing we call evolution. The building blocks were there. All I needed to do was to take what human beings had developed in terms of all the technology and merge them. We were part of evolution. Our consciousness was God's blessing. He'd made us capable of changing what we were.'

I'd guessed that Muir's epiphany was like that of many who had gone before him. Once he'd explained it, it seemed completely obvious, like gravity, or the Earth being round. Man could re-engineer man and in doing so would create a new species, what Muir and his researchers called a post-sapiens. That was what I was, only I didn't feel any less human. If anything I felt more human, more alive, more truly in touch with the world and everything that went on around me. I wasn't religious. I had seen too many tragedies caused by religious fundamentalism to embrace any kind of church. But in the weeks and months of surgery and rehabilitation, I had come to understand what Muir had meant when he'd said he was taking me closer to God.

Through the crack in the bathroom door, I watched Muir walk into the tiny kitchen. He was hunched over, a man with a lot on his mind. I dug out the gun, slowly opened the bathroom door, and crept silently down the short stub of corridor. I flattened myself against the wall. Muir walked back out of the kitchen. I clamped my hand over his mouth and brought up the gun.

'I'm not going to hurt you. I want to talk. The panic alarm has been disabled. If you make any kind of a move I don't like, I'll kill you. Do you understand me?'

Muir nodded his yellow head. Most of the brain activity was in the center, near his amygdala, the trace of yellow running down from there. His frontal cortex, the rational, thinking part of the brain, remained normal. The pattern told me that Muir had been more startled than terrified by my sudden appearance.

I took my hand away. 'Talk quietly. I'll kill the two men outside as well if I have to.'

Muir turned. 'I'm glad you're alive, Byron. I had a feeling you'd come back. There are a lot of things I didn't get the chance to explain.'

'I'm sorry about how it went down,' I said. 'I didn't mean to hurt anyone.'

'I know. It would be good if you'd come back to the facility with me so I could check you over properly.' He sounded sincere.

'That's not going to happen.'

'I understand. So what do you want to know?'

'There are things I was never told.'

'It wasn't my decision to withhold information from you,' said Muir.

As he said it, I noticed the flash of color in his frontal lobe. 'I know when you're lying, remember.'

'Apart from what happened at the facility, how has everything been working?'

'That's what I wanted to talk to you about. The facility stuff.'

'You remember it?' Muir asked me.

'I was back in Afghanistan for a while. That's who I thought the medical team were. *Jihadis*. I regret what happened. If there was a way I could bring them back, I would. I'd like to be able to speak to their families too, but that's not feasible right now. Could you let them know from me that I'm sorry, that I wasn't in my right mind when I took their lives?'

Muir sighed. 'At the start of the project, one of the things we had to decide was what to do about memory formation and retention. Obviously, in order to function you had to be able to remember certain things. The question for us was how much of your long-term memory we allowed you to retain.'

'And?' I said. 'You about to tell me that I'm someone else entirely?'

'No, Byron, I'm not. It was my view and that of the team that childhood and other memories, your experiences and how you relate to them over a lifetime, are what makes you human.'

'But I'm not, am I? I'm not human. I'm one step beyond human. I'm post-sapiens.'

Muir nodded. 'True. But think about what word means. We wanted this to allow for evolution, not revolution. If we had wanted to create a pure killing machine that would have been a lot easier, believe me. But we didn't. We wanted someone who was a human being plus. Faster, fitter, stronger, more perceptive in all kinds of ways, but also someone who retained grace under extreme pressure.'

'So what happened?'

'There was a problem with the original amygdala implant. It was designed to filter out certain things. We think it degraded after a time and allowed your most traumatic memory to push out everything else. For you it was what happened on that mission in Afghanistan when the young girl died. For Lewis it was something else. We hoped by updating the implant that we could take you back to where you were.'

'But you never got the chance.'

'It's not too late, Byron. You could come back with me.'

'I killed four people.'

'A version of you did. Byron 1.0 did. I'm not sure you can be held responsible any more than Lewis could be blamed for taking his own life.'

'There's something else. What is it?'

Muir sighed. 'Byron, if I lied to you, you'd know. We've already established that.'

'I didn't say you were lying, but you're holding something back.'

I lasered in on Muir's skull as his brain lit up.

'There are some things, more than some, I can't tell you,' he said. 'Not because I don't want to but because to tell you would be to place everyone involved, including myself, in danger. You only know the surface, Byron.'

Without saying anything else, Muir crossed to a small table, pulled a sheet from a pad of paper, scrawled something on it and handed it over. Of course, Muir's apartment would be rigged, at least for sound if not with video surveillance equipment. I took the paper without looking at it, folded it in two and placed it in my pocket.

Outside the apartment, I heard a car door being carefully closed. I held up my hand to silence Muir. There were two sets of footsteps outside. They were moving slowly and methodically. I could even pick out the faintest rustle of material as one man raised his arm from his side.

I got up, walked across the room and killed the light. With six long strides I was in the hallway, my body pressed flat against the wall behind the front door. Less than a second later, a key was pressed into the lock and the door began to open.

There was a rush of movement as the two guards ran through, going straight past me. Without thinking, I stepped around the door and started to run.

The apartment light snapped back on. From inside I heard Muir shout, 'No!' There was a single shot and the sound of a body hitting the floor.

I was torn. I wanted to go back and confirm that it was Muir who had been shot. The light had gone on first. That meant whoever had pulled the trigger had known what they were doing.

I ran to the end of the block, and waited. The car was less than twenty meters away. If anyone came out of the apartment I could reach it before they could get a shot off. And I still had the Springfield.

I peeked round the corner for a split second. There was no one in the guards' vehicle and no one outside. With the Springfield punched out, I moved toward the door, hugging the wall, and ducking under windows.

The apartment door was open. I could hear the crackle of radio transmissions. The two guards were inside. Muir wasn't making any kind of noise. They had called for an ambulance. There was no way of knowing if Muir was clinging on or whether he was already gone. I was already cursing the decisions I'd made. In a standard situation on foreign soil I would have killed the two guards and taken Muir with me so that I could extract the information I needed in a more stable environment without fear of interruption. My weakness had likely cost Muir his life. The morality of killing the two guards shouldn't have been a factor. They were in the way. Was Muir dead or alive? I had to know.

I stepped into the hallway. One guard was hunched over the scientist. The other was standing behind, relaying information on his radio. The guard standing over Muir had his weapon, a Glock 9mm, in his right hand.

I shot him first, firing a single round into the top of his neck. As his partner went to draw his weapon, I shot him in the head, and followed up with a second shot to the throat, which caught him as he fell. The first guard had slumped forward. I grabbed his shoulder, and pulled him back. I shot him one more time in the head for good measure.

I looked at Muir, bent down and checked his pulse. He was dead. My fingertips began to tingle. Muir must have had an RDF tracker chip too. It was no surprise. Many of the scientists at the facility had hacked their own bodies to test their emerging technologies.

I ran my hand up to the side of Muir's skull, working a hunch. Something that Muir had said hadn't gelled with what I'd seen of the scientist's brain activity. Not that my ability to interpret brain activity was in any way honed.

As my fingertips reached Muir's temple the pulsing increased. There was something inside Muir's skull. If he'd had a metal plate – say, from an accident – my fingertips would have gone haywire. This was something more delicate. It told me that whatever I was picking up was small and likely in the middle of Muir's brain.

Reaching into my pants pocket, I took out my Gerber. Removing the RDF tracker from a dead man was a hell of a lot than easier than taking out my own. I made the incision, blood oozing over my fingers, dug a nail inside the flap of skin and popped it out. I left it where it fell, ran to the bathroom, grabbed a large bath towel and ran back to Muir.

I crossed to the two dead guards, took their weapons and punched out the clips. The first was full, the second was down a round. Assuming it had been full before, the second guard's clip looked to have a round missing. He had shot Muir, and meant it.

Blood was already soaking through the towel as I lifted Muir's body. With the dead man slung over my shoulder, I jogged back to the car. Lights were on in the other apartments. Faces peeked through curtains, disappearing as soon as they saw me. I felt sure I recognized at least one, a young robotics specialist who worked at the facility. The apartment must have been used as accommodation for more than Muir.

The trunk popped open. I lowered Muir's corpse into it. It was a tight fit. I had to adjust his limbs so that he was in a fetal position. I slammed the trunk shut, got into the driver's seat, making sure to kill the headlights, and gunned the engine.

# FIFTY

Apart from a green tinge, I could see well enough without headlights. Five miles out from the apartment complex I crested a hill. Half a dozen red rollers were heading toward me. I slowed, spun the wheel and pulled the car off the highway, careful not to tap the brakes and risk being seen. The car bumped along the rough scrub desert, and came to a stop. I killed the engine, waited until the State Police vehicles had sped past, then turned and headed back onto the highway.

I drove through the night, heading south-west, skirting the Special Activities Program testing area that housed the facility. There were two more close calls. The first was at a roadblock, the second when I passed a military convoy heading north. If they were going to kill me it would be here in this desolate landscape.

As soon as she had answered, I knew I had made a mistake in calling Julia. The Julia I had spoken to wasn't the same woman I had left at home. On the surface she had seemed relieved, and happy to hear my voice. The words were there, and arranged in the right order. Everything else, though, from the hesitation, to her tone, the way her voice rose and fell, told a different story. She was scared. Scared of me.

What should have been sixty seconds that I could use to spur me on had done the opposite. If I wasn't going home to the woman I loved, someone who would understand the choices I had made and why I had made them, what was I going home for?

As I drove, I tried to push the negativity from my mind. I did my best to reframe my thoughts. If I could make it back to New York and speak to her alone, I could make her understand.

*You've lost her. She's on their side now.*

As fast as I pushed them out, the bad thoughts returned. Traffic was picking up as I drove across the state border into California. I flicked on the radio and began to search for stations. The numbers on the digital display spun round until I found a news channel.

'Tibor is believed to be armed and extremely dangerous. People are cautioned not to approach him under any circumstances. If they do see him they should contact local law enforcement.'

So much for the news blackout. The report moved on. I kept punching the button, searching for more news as the cars on the highway driving toward Los Angeles took on a more sinister hue as each second passed. What had been a stream of metal camouflage a few moments ago now seemed more akin to a river of spy drones, each truck, each SUV with the capability to pick me out from the herd. It didn't take me long to find a talk radio station where I seemed to be the main topic of conversation. They had some supposed military expert in the studio, no doubt a wire-hugger who had last seen action twenty years ago before semi-retiring to push paper around the C-ring of the Pentagon.

Listening to them discuss me, I began to piece together the spin the agency, and whoever else was involved, had put on recent events. They mentioned a DARPA-funded program based in Nevada, which was aimed at helping veterans and active military personnel overcome combat fatigue and PTSD. Neuroscience featured in the report but it was referenced in the vaguest way. The report moved on to the incident at the facility five days previously in which a participant in the program, a former Army Ranger working for the State Department had launched a pre-planned attack killing four members of staff. He had fled the facility, using his Ranger training to evade capture, before returning several days later to kill the head of the program, whom, the government was claiming, he held responsible for difficulties I continued to have in his personal life.

The script they were running was standard operating procedure. Other information that might be uncovered, such as the existence of the facility, hinted broadly at the nature of the work, thus explaining the presence of Muir and his team, but airbrushed the specifics out. If pressed to give more details they would cite national security concerns and point to just how open they had already been. Finally, they played the card that I had seen played numerous times before when the government wanted to silence or discredit someone: they told the world the target was crazy. Once that was firmly planted in the public consciousness it wouldn't matter what I said. I was tagged as a lunatic.

My mind drifted back to Julia. At least she knew the truth. I hadn't taken the decision to confide in her lightly. For a long time afterwards, I had wondered if I had done the right thing in telling her why I was the way I was. I hadn't wanted to start our life together with a lie. That had been my reasoning. But I knew that, in telling her, I had not only breached the sacred covenant of my work, I had potentially placed her in danger. Now, though, in a set of circumstances I had never foreseen, it looked like a good decision. She would be able to corroborate my story.

I also had Muir's body, complete with some kind of implant. And I had the piece of paper he had given me before he died. On the paper there had been a name and a location. It might be a trap, of course. It might just as easily lead me to my death as to my salvation. I guessed there was only one way of finding out. I pushed down the indicator and took the exit for Bakersfield.

# FIFTY-ONE

**Graves**

Half an hour to showtime. Graves paced the length of the hotel suite. Down below, on Central Park West, under a low grey sky, yellow cabs and Town Cars swarmed outside the entrance to the Plaza. He grabbed his jacket from the back of the chair, and walked out into the corridor. The two agents there swiveled to check him out as he let the door close behind him. He walked to the next-door room and knocked. Another agent opened it, hand on his service weapon. He recognized Graves and nodded for him to come in.

Julia Tibor was at the window. She seemed lost in thought.

'Julia, it's time,' said Graves. 'They're waiting.'

Finally, she turned to him. 'You're sure I'm doing the right thing?' she asked.

'It's not just the right thing. It's the only thing. We have three more people dead, including Muir, the man who was trying to help him. We're out of options, Julia. We have to find Byron, for everyone's sake.'

The footage of Byron and the two muggers had sown the seeds of doubt. The incident at Muir's apartment complex had sealed the deal. Whatever resistance Julia had had was gone. She would do what they needed her to do.

Graves reached into his jacket and pulled out a single sheet of paper. He handed it to Julia. 'Read it again if you need to. Make sure you're happy with it.'

She scanned the statement, her hands trembling a little. It had taken a lot of persuasion and arm-twisting back in Washington before Graves had got agreement on this tactical shift. In the end, Lewis and the envelope had been his trump card. In a closed session, he'd asked the chairs of the relevant congressional committees, and the President, if they would have been happy with that material being released into the public domain. That one question was all it had taken. Of course, Byron might already have put measures in place to get whatever information he had into the public domain. It could still happen. But material was judged by the source. Discredit the source, and you discredited the material. If the *New York Times* or a major network ran a story, most people assumed there was something to it. If a guy living in his parents' basement ran the same story on his YouTube channel, it was dismissed as the rant of a crank. The story could be identical, but it was the public's view of the source that counted. It was all a matter of news management.

Flashguns exploded as Julia walked out onto the stage and took a seat, flanked on one side by Graves and on the other by a spokesperson provided by the State Department. Julia stared at the ranks of media assembled in the conference room, TV cameras capturing her every movement. She would look down at the statement, printed in sixteen point font on two pages, and there would be a fresh explosion of light.

The spokesperson, a take-no-prisoners middle-aged woman, with a sharply coiffed blond bob, wearing an Ann Taylor pant suit, spoke first. Julia would read a statement and then they would take questions. Julia had already been thoroughly briefed on what to say. Any curveballs the media threw would be handled by Graves or the spokesperson.

Julia cleared her throat, and leaned forward, getting too close to the microphone as she began, so that her voice boomed out from the speakers mounted either side of the table they were sitting at.

'My name is Julia Tibor. I am here today to make an appeal to my husband, Byron, whom I love very much, to please contact the authorities and bring an end to this.'

She found herself tearing up as she spoke. The emotion was something she didn't have to fake. Every word was heartfelt. She did love Byron. She did want him to hand himself in rather than be killed.

'Byron served his country proudly. He's not a bad person. But he has problems. I've been reassured that if he surrenders of his own volition he will be given the help he so desperately needs.'

As she came to the end of her statement, a volley of questions tangled in the air. The spokesperson silenced them. 'Yes, Rick.'

Rick, a lantern-jawed news anchor Julia recognized from one of the main cable networks, got to his feet. 'Rick Santos, FNN. Mrs Tibor, had your husband ever given you any hint that he was capable of this kind of extremely violent behavior?'

Graves tried to jump in but Julia got there ahead of him. 'No, he hadn't. I've rarely seen him lose his temper.'

As she spoke, her mind flashed back to the tape of Byron attacking the two muggers. It had been so ruthless, so efficient. It hadn't been like watching a human being. It had been more like watching a machine dismantling something piece by piece.

The questions continued to come at her thick and fast. Most were batted away by the PR handler or Graves. They let her take one or two, the ones where she could offer 'a wife's insight', and 'personalize the situation'. Those has been the phrases Graves had used.

'You say that you had noticed a change in your husband's behavior prior to his going missing and these incidents?' was one question. 'Can you be more specific, Julia?'

Julia bristled at the reporter's over-familiarity as Graves gave her the nod to answer. 'My husband was showing signs of what I realize now was post-traumatic stress disorder.'

'Could you be more specific?' another reporter pressed.

This was proving harder than she had thought it would be, and she had known it would be tough. 'He seemed to be having flashbacks. He was on edge.' Every word she uttered seemed like a greater betrayal than the one that had come before. She imagined Byron watching her tell a bunch of strangers about things that should remain private between husband and wife. 'It wasn't like him. He was such a gentle, even-tempered person. A gentleman.'

*A gentleman who killed people in cold blood.* But then, even before he had confided in her, she had known that during his military career he would almost certainly have killed. He had been a Ranger, deployed in places where war raged. Anyone who married someone in the military during a time of war would have to accept that they would go to bed at night with someone who had taken life.

She was beginning to lose her composure now. As her voice cracked and tears welled in her eyes, she sensed the reporters leaning forward, the creeping zoom of the cameras as they tightened their frame so that there was only the face of a woman in distress.

Graves intervened, tapping his watch and letting them know that there was time for one more question. Almost before he had finished he was pointing at a male reporter in the front row. Something about their body language and the eye contact between the two men told Julia that this part had been carefully choreographed. When the question came she knew she was right.

'Mrs Tibor, Julia, if Byron's watching this right now, what do you want to say to him?'

Now the tears came. The PR woman handed her a tissue. Julia looked from the pack of reporters to Graves. This was wrong. The mock-concern. The idea that all these people wanted to do was help Byron. It was a lie. Whatever Byron had done, whatever he had become, Graves, Muir, DARPA, the Special Operations Group, the politicians in Washington had made him like this. If he was a monster, he was a monster of their creation, not his own.

She took her time, dabbing at the tears, and taking a sip of water. The chatter at the edge of the room fell away to silence.

'Byron, if you're listening, if you can hear me, I want you to know that whatever you've done I love you and I don't blame you. If you can hear me, my message is simple. Keep on running. These people don't want to help you, they want you dead.'

# FIFTY-TWO

'Do you know what you just did? Do you realize how much shit you're in?'

Julia sat on the end of the hotel-room bed as Graves paced the length of the room, screaming at her. The sense of unreality she had felt as her final words to the media had tumbled forth hadn't left her. She was in the present, in a hotel room in the middle of Manhattan, with the media setting up a permanent camp on the sidewalk outside, yet she was thousands of miles away. As she had told Byron to run, and not to look back, she had felt him with her, the good Byron, the human Byron, the man she had fallen in love with and married.

Graves continued to rant, spittle flying from the corners of his mouth. 'You're in a world of shit. A universe of shit!' He stopped in front of her, and jammed a chubby finger at her face. 'This is national security. You could go to prison for this.'

She looked up at Graves's bloodhound face. Byron was a murderer but Graves was ten times worse. He and his kind were just as culpable. The only difference was that Graves let someone else do his dirty work. 'Am I under arrest, Mr Graves?' she asked.

He stared at her with piggy eyes. She could hear the rattle of his breathing.

'Because if I'm not, then I'd like to go home,' she said, getting to her feet, putting an arm out in front of her to establish a distance between them.

He took a step back. 'You walk out, and you're on your own. We won't protect you.'

It was as much as Julia could do not to laugh. 'I'll take my chances.'

She walked past him to the door. She was still torn. Without Graves, without the government, she would have to face all of it by herself. The media wouldn't give her a moment's peace. They, Graves, the Agency and a dozen other federal agencies would scrutinize her every move. At least she'd had the good sense to stop speaking when she had. She had said nothing of who (what?) Byron was, or the facility, or the work that had taken place there.

For a start, it was all too out there. The public weren't ready for it. She'd come off like a crazy person. More importantly, though, it would place not just her but Byron in even greater danger. It was one thing for a mentally unstable special-forces operative to be on the run, but quite another for some kind of half man/half machine to be out there. Every weekend warrior between here and California would be on the lookout for him, and they'd be firing first and asking questions later.

'You'll take your chances?' Graves screamed back at her. He moved toward her, got right up in her face. She could smell the stale cigarette smoke on him. It made her want to gag. 'I'm not just some guy here, Mrs Tibor. This is the government. We run the country. Think about what that actually means. The name Bradley Manning mean anything to you?'

She did her best to keep cool. She wasn't unfamiliar with men like Graves. 'I'd remind you that I'm a private citizen, Mr Tibor, protected by the Constitution. I don't work for you or the United States government.'

At the mention of the Constitution, Graves's lip rolled up into a sneer. 'You're quite correct, Mrs Tibor. And I apologize for losing my temper. So, as a private citizen, why don't you exercise your constitutional right to get the fuck out of here? You're on the outside now, same as your husband. Don't expect any more help from us.'

She wasn't going to be bullied by someone like Graves. She grabbed her coat and put it on. 'There's a lot more I could have said downstairs. A lot more. You might want to keep that in mind. Helping veterans sounds very noble. I doubt the public would feel the same if they knew what this has really been about.'

She walked out into the corridor and headed for the elevator. As the adrenalin buzz wore off, she was starting to have second thoughts. More than anything now, she wanted her husband. To speak to him. To hear his voice. To be able to tell him that, even if no one else was, she was on his side. That she loved him, more than she had ever loved anyone or anything in her life.

# FIFTY-THREE

**Eldon**

Eldon lay on the bed, his head propped up on the pillows, watching the giant flat-screen TV as the hooker he had picked up on the casino floor the night before went to work between his legs. He should have been happy right now. The suite was sweet. Graves had said he could have it for the remainder of the week. His kill tally was up by two – Chauncey, the homeless guy who had helped Tibor, and Chenko, the retired cop. He was out of prison. Graves had assured him that there would be more work – as long as he stayed out of trouble. No shooting car-jackers or assholes or civilians just because he could.

He grabbed the hooker's hair, and pulled her off his dick. Her noisy slurp was distracting him from the TV, where footage of Byron's wife at the press conference played on an endless loop between pictures of Byron Tibor, Public Enemy Number One, and a bunch of other shit about his military service and PTSD sending vets over the edge. *Blah blah blah. Yada yada yada. Booooring.*

'You see this guy?' he said to the hooker, whose name was Giselle.

Giselle rubbed her chin. 'Think my jaw's locking up. You want to try something else, sweetie?'

'That guy. You see that guy?' he said, ignoring the question and jabbing a finger at the TV set.

She pushed herself up so that she was on her knees and glanced over her shoulder at the TV. The picture right now was of Tibor in dress uniform.

'Yeah,' said Giselle. 'Looks like a young Denzel only, I dunno, maybe a little bit lighter.'

'Me and him used to be like best friends.'

Giselle stared at him, glassy-eyed. She probably figured he was bullshitting her. In her profession she'd spend hours on end listening to all kinds of crazy stuff. 'Uh-huh,' she said.

Eldon pushed off the bed and headed for the can. 'We're done. You can leave.'

'You still got me on the clock for another hour, honey.'

Eldon crossed to the closet, opened it and took a long look at his gun. One short of the two hundred mark. Giselle could make it up. He was itchy for a kill, itchy to round things off: 199 seemed so wrong, and it was driving him crazy.

He glanced back at the woman as she dressed, pulling on her panties with all the grace of an offensive linesman. Nah, thought Eldon. He wanted two hundred to be special, to count for something, to be worthy of him, and Giselle wasn't that.

He shut the closet door. She put on her dress and slid past him. She would never know how close she had just come to death. The thought cheered him a little. He turned back to the TV screen. Number two hundred was right there on screen. He could wait to round up his number. It would make it all the sweeter when the time came.

# FIFTY-FOUR

**Byron**

I rolled out of Bakersfield in a two-year-old silver Ford Escape with tinted glass. Muir's body was in back, covered with a plaid blanket. I'd left the red Honda in a parking lot. I'd also jacked and then hidden two other vehicles before I left. They had been carefully chosen to ensure that they were different in make, model and color from the others.

Requesting that the public and law enforcement look out for one vehicle was a big enough ask, but alerting them to three would be a cluster-fuck guaranteed to generate thousands of false leads that would need to be chased down. The Ford I'd taken from a different location. It was the very definition of a cheap trick. But when it came to counter-surveillance and tracking, those were often the best kinds: simple, efficient and designed to cause maximum confusion.

I took the 58 east, heading for the Pacific coast. The journey would take me a little under five hours. Near Santa Margarita I picked up the 101 north. I was inching toward the ocean, closer to the edge of the continent, hoping that I would have answers when I got there.

The fuel gauge was low. I would have to stop for gas sooner rather than later. It would be risky. It was daylight. I had no credit card, which meant I couldn't just pay at the pump, shielded from prying eyes by the bulk of the SUV.

I got off the freeway and found a gas station. The place wasn't busy: a couple of cars filling up, and one truck easing round the back of the gas station to take on diesel. I was sporting sunglasses I'd found in a compartment of the Escape.

I strode into the gas station, grabbed a couple of bottles of water, and put them on the counter along with four twenty-dollar bills. The woman behind the till was middle-aged, Hispanic, with reading glasses on a silver chain. She had watched me the whole way, and was doing a bad job of trying to appear like was she engrossed in the book she was reading. *The idle curiosity of someone bored at work or something else?*

I stared at her skull, lasering in on the center of her mind. Her amygdala was going crazy.

There were other, far more obvious, signs, in her body language. Either she was in the early stages of Parkinson's or her hand was trembling with nerves as she opened the till. I glanced back outside. The two cars that had been out front were likely using cards. Unless they came in for something else, they wouldn't be a problem.

I looked at the woman. 'You recognize me?'

She shrugged, trying to come off like she didn't have a clue what I was talking about.

'It's okay. All I want is to get gas and get out of here. That's it. But if you do anything stupid, I'll have no choice but to hurt you. Do you understand me?' I told her.

She met my gaze and nodded.

'You have a phone behind that counter.' I had already seen it. It was cordless with a single handset. 'Give it to me.'

Almost dropping it as she lifted it from the charger, she did so. 'Are you the only employee here now?'

She nodded again. She was going to be compliant. Hell, what was I to her? Either the last person she saw on earth or a story she could dine out on for days if she played along.

'You have a cell phone?' I asked her.

I tensed as she bent down, praying that she wasn't going for a gun. I had the reaction time for it not to be an issue but I really didn't want to kill some random lady just because our paths had crossed. She came up with a cell phone and handed it to me.

'Okay,' I said. 'I'm going to put gas in my car. Stay next to the window where I can see you. When I'm done, I'll leave. If someone arrives while I'm still here, just be normal. I'll be out of your life in under five. If you tell anyone about this in the first hour after I leave, I will come back and I will kill you. Do you understand me?'

She nodded. As soon as I left she would tell the next person she saw. That was human nature. Humans had restricted impulse control – especially in stressful situations when their emotions overwhelmed them.

Clutching the two phones, I walked back out, jammed the pump into the gas tank and waited for it to fill. The woman was staring at me, doing her best to make sure I could see her and what she was doing.

The numbers clicked over. I stilled my breathing, allowing my mind to flatten out and the implant to do its work. Its job was to dampen my emotional response, and allow my frontal cortex to dictate the play. Fear, elation, guilt, joy: none had a part to play anymore.

No one else pulled in. The pump clicked to a stop. I had a full tank of gas.

I didn't get back into the Escape. Instead I strode back into the gas station. The woman hadn't moved. Her eyes followed me as I walked to the counter. I took out the phones and placed them in front of her.

'I took the batteries out,' I lied. 'Where's the hard drive for the security system?' I had already scoped out the cameras. It wasn't a system that hooked up to an ISDN or broadband line to send footage to a remote server. I doubted internet service was up to much out here – ridiculous in this day and age, but it was a poor community.

She pointed.

'Show me.'

I followed her into a back room. We walked past crates of beer and soda and into a small cupboard. I pulled out my Gerber and used it to unscrew the hard drive from its casing.

'I'm going to lock you in here, okay?' I said. 'Don't worry, someone will find you eventually. Give me the key.'

She fumbled in her slacks, dug out the key to the store cupboard. I took it. 'Turn round for me.' She seemed confused by this latest instruction. I placed a hand on her shoulder and guided her round, like a parent spinning a blindfolded child before a game of pin the tail on the donkey.

Five minutes later, I opened the door and walked out. There was no one outside. I started up the Escape and drove away, heading back to the freeway.

# FIFTY-FIVE

**Julia**

Julia's cell phone lay on Byron's pillow. Through the day it would ring every few minutes, and every few minutes she would answer it in case it was her husband. It never was, and she had begun to doubt it ever would be. After she had left the hotel, hunted like an animal by a baying mob of reporters all the way back to the apartment, she had been drawn to the television news, which she had always deliberately avoided when she'd thought Byron was out in the field. Finally, the not knowing had become worse than the knowing.

There was nothing to know. That didn't stop the endless cycling of the news networks. Reports were coming in from all over the country that Byron had been spotted working at a rodeo in Texas, holding up a bank in Missouri or with a young child in a car at a drive-thru fast-food joint in New Hampshire. The authorities were actively seeking three separate vehicles, which blended inexorably into one, as the news channels churned their details with those of the sightings.

Other things started to appear alongside in the bulletins. Old photographs of Byron excavated from who knew where. Byron as a child. A photograph from his high-school yearbook. Pictures from his time in the infantry and then the Rangers. People who had known him appeared on camera. All the while it drove home to Julia how little we knew of anyone and how, while some things appeared constant (his intellect, his physical prowess, his loyalty and courage), others changed (friends who spoke of him as cold, aloof, a ruthlessly efficient soldier). Like everyone, Byron was, and had been, a different person to different people at different times. It seemed that only she had seen the vulnerable side of her husband, the human side. The irony wasn't lost on her. After all, she had met him after his enrollment in the PSS Program when the implants and other technology had already been seeded. It begged a question. Had she seen the last dying embers of the human being, the hybrid reality, or a soul with machine-like capabilities that could be switched on and off as the situation and his environment demanded?

None of the reports talked about any of that. Even if some were aware of the reality of the program, it would be heavily embargoed with unspeakable penalties for a breach. The briefest of internet searches revealed the parallel world where those dismissed as cranks talked openly about the evidence that was in the public domain: the incident with the cop in Vegas; the trail of dead bodies; the program and the significance of its location near Area 51. Various theories were put forward. Some of the speculation was awkwardly close to the reality. There was talk of the MK Ultra program, of brainwashing, of robotics, of the money that DARPA had poured into neuroscience. If only they knew, she thought. If only the crackpots actually realized that the truth was almost more incredible than some of their wildest fantasies.

The phone rang again. A 212 number. New York. Not likely to be Byron. She answered. A woman's voice. Another reporter. Young, tentative, a person not used to having to make this kind of call, someone for whom the intrusion into another person's life at the most heightened of times still seemed the splintering of human decency it was.

She began with an apology, 'Mrs Tibor, I am so sorry to bother you like this.'

At first Julia didn't say anything. She had taken to hanging up but this time she didn't. She didn't answer either. The voice filled the void.

'My name's Meredith Harris. I'm a researcher for ...' She named a popular syndicated talk show, the kind that Julia would watch as a guilty pleasure if she was sick. 'Mrs Tibor, are you there?'

Something about Meredith's tone allowed Julia to answer, 'Yes, I'm listening.'

'Oh, God, I was kind of hoping you'd just hang up or, I dunno, shout at me. My boss told me that if I don't at least speak to you then I'm fired, and I really need this job, and I've only been here like two weeks, and if I get fired I'll won't get another chance, and I have loans to pay. Sorry, none of this is your problem, and I'm really sorry about your husband, and for what it's worth I believe he's a good man.'

If this was some elaborate manipulation, she was more accomplished than anyone else who had called.

'You realize this call is being monitored, don't you?' Julia said.

Silence. 'Oh, yes, I guess that with your husband ...' Meredith trailed off.

It was late, or early, depending on how you looked at it. Julia wasn't asleep, and wouldn't be able to sleep. She gave Meredith the name of a twenty-four-hour deli and told her to meet her there in a half-hour.

# FIFTY-SIX

**Eldon**

Eldon took the cell from her and killed the call as rain splattered the awning of the bodega on East 24th Street.

'It worked,' she said. 'How'd you know it would?' She brushed a strand of long blond hair from her face.

'I didn't. I played the percentages. You were pretty good.'

'Who was it you said you worked for again?' she asked.

'CNBC,' said Eldon.

'Okay, I guess that makes sense with the whole guilt-trip deal.'

He dug into his pocket for the money, handed it to 'Meredith', and watched as she disappeared into the glistening Manhattan night. He looked down at his cell: she had keyed in the address of the diner that Julia Tibor had suggested. It was always better when the location was the other person's idea. It lowered their guard.

The young woman who had played the part of the TV researcher had been a chance encounter. When she had mentioned to him that she was an actress, Eldon had done a little improvisation of his own. He had seen her crossing the street, dodging traffic. She was back in her own little bubble, happy to have cleared four hundred bucks for a few minutes' work.

He turned up his collar, and stepped out from under the awning. As she turned the corner onto Seventh Avenue, he followed her. He needed her to keep her mouth shut, and he needed that money back for other things. All he needed now, though, was an alleyway. The only snag was that Eldon didn't want some random chick as his two-hundredth kill. It would ruin the moment. It was a milestone, a carefully crafted temple of death. It deserved someone worthy at the apex. There lay the crux of it too. The person worthy of the honor would have to carry a threat to Eldon. Most of the people whose lives Eldon had taken hadn't even seen it coming, never mind had the chance to harm him. This would be different. But between now and that moment lay some work.

He was small enough that even on a deserted New York side-street he could slip along unseen. 'Meredith's' heels clacked along. She didn't hear him until he was directly behind her, his hand slipping over her mouth, his leg sweeping away hers as he dragged her kicking and trying to scream into the gap between two buildings.

He choked her out, her eyes rolling back in her head, her face set fierce with horror. He set to work, getting off on it in a way that he never could by pulling a trigger. The intimacy of the work let his spirit soar through the canyon of buildings that pressed in on them. He pulled her to her feet, supporting her as they danced, his fingers and thumbs busy working the pressure points, taking her close to death but stopping just short.

There was a moment when his fingers brushed one of her nipples and he felt his dick harden. He stopped what he was doing, troubled by his own reaction. Then he realized that the sexual charge had not been from his flesh on hers but from his flesh against the silky fabric of her bra. Reassured, he went back to work.

Ten minutes later, the money he had given her back in his possession, along with her underwear, he emerged back onto the street. He had a date with Mrs Julia Tibor, and it wouldn't do to be late.

# FIFTY-SEVEN

**Byron**

The Ford's headlights carved through the darkness, the highway switching back on itself. I lowered the windows and savored the sea-salt freshness of the Pacific, slowing as I approached the turn for Big Sur National Park. It was little more than a fire road, the ground broken and rutted. I killed the headlights. My retinal implants took over as the trees closed in on either side, and the road narrowed.

I estimated that the cabin I was looking for lay about two miles north-east. I found a gap in the trees, pulled the Ford off the road and drove into the forest. I switched off the engine, and got out. I walked back to the road, staying just inside the tree line.

As I walked I tuned into the sounds of the forest, separating out the sounds of birds and animals, adjusting my steps to minimize the noise I made as I moved. Every fifty yards or so, I would stop, allowing my senses to gather data. Between the transcranial implant and the other enhancements, I could build a three-dimensional picture of the territory.

In the distance the ocean pulsed. A breeze picked up and shook its way through the redwoods. The cabin couldn't be too far. If I had the location right, it was well screened by the trees. Grass grew in the middle of the track leading up to it. I stepped from the edge of the forest, and took a closer look at the track, searching for fresh tire marks. If someone was up ahead waiting for me, there would be more than one set – I doubted they would have approached on foot. The track was clear. It was in light use, maybe a vehicle or two traveling up or down it every few days.

Now I could see a single light ahead. A dog barked. Then another. The one thing I had forgotten: their senses were as finely tuned as mine. Judging by the timbre of the barking, one was a large animal, the other small.

I took the barking as a good sign. Any ambush party would have cleared them out or placed them in vehicles, wary that they would act as an alarm.

Staying within the tree line, I moved forwards. The trees thinned to reveal a clearing, and a single-story cabin constructed from the same redwoods that hemmed it in. The two dogs raced from the porch to me, both mutts. The larger one's eyes indicated some wolf; the other was more terrier.

I stood my ground, and avoided eye contact, allowing them to bark and draw closer. They sniffed the air. The larger dog growled. The cabin door opened. Whoever was inside had already killed the lights to avoid being silhouetted in the doorway and easier for an intruder watching from the darkness to pick out. I could see her clearly.

She was in her fifties. Her long dark hair was pulled back into a thick ropy braid. She was slim with strong, angular features and brown eyes to go with her coffee-colored skin. For some reason, my inherent sexism perhaps, I had assumed Shakti was a man.

When Muir had scrawled the name for me, I had recognized it: the people I had met at the facility had mentioned her. Shakti, as far as I could recall, was regarded as a pioneer in the area of neural implants, sensory substitution and human augmentation. Like many top research scientists she was Indian, and had been attracted to the United States after early pioneering work had drawn the attention of the academic-military-industrial complex whose members trawled the world's universities. But she had turned her back on the work, citing ethical objections. Muir and the others had taken on what she had achieved, driving through practical applications of her work. Then, at some point, she had disappeared off the radar.

Barefoot and dressed in loose, bright clothing, she stepped forward. She was looking straight at me, and I had a feeling that her picking me out in the darkness wasn't just down to the dogs. She called them to her. They responded instantly, darting back and sitting in front of her, quivering canine sentinels.

I stepped out from the tree line, hands loose at my sides. She watched me all the way, apparently more curious than fearful. It was a strange reaction from a lone woman to a man of my size stepping from the woods around her house after dark.

'Muir sent me,' I said.

'I take it you're the man everyone's looking for,' she said. Her accent held that curiously clipped British tone, a remnant of old empire that I had noticed before in Indians of a certain class.

'You'd better come in,' she said. 'Don't mind the dogs. It's nothing personal. Any kind of machine sets them off.'

I was a machine to her? At least I knew where I stood. I walked up to the porch. The larger dog growled at me but stayed put. I was relieved. I wouldn't harm an animal, regardless of what else the implant allowed me to do without my conscience troubling me.

Inside, a narrow hallway opened up into a large open-plan living room and kitchen. Off to one side a door seemed to lead into a bedroom. In one corner of the living room there was a shrine to a Hindu goddess. She was riding a lion, her many arms holding a plethora of weapons.

'Durga?' I said, with a nod to the shrine.

'Not many people would know who it was.'

'I've traveled a lot.'

'So I've heard. Please, take a seat,' Shakti said, ushering me to sit on one of a half-dozen large cushions that lay on the floor. There was no television, no couch, only the kitchen counter and units and a solitary wooden table with four seats.

I sat cross-legged. Shakti sat opposite, the dogs arranging themselves either side of her, their eyes never leaving me.

'So they killed Muir?' she asked.

'Everyone thinks I did it,' I said. 'Why don't you?'

She smiled, completely serene. I wondered if it was connected to the spirituality evidenced by the shrine, or whether it came from living here. Big Sur had been a magnet for those seeking enlightenment since before the hippie trail of the sixties. For those interested in how the human mind functioned it wasn't an altogether unnatural place to gravitate to. Julia would like it, I thought.

'Muir was Scottish,' she said. 'They have an expression about what happens to you if you drink with the devil. Muir drank with the devil.'

'And you wouldn't?' I asked.

'What they've been saying on the radio and television about the program isn't without a grain of truth. Originally we were looking for a way of dealing with PTSD and combat fatigue, especially for the most extreme cases. That was what the work on the neural implants was about. Then, of course, the Pentagon, the CIA and the others started to take an interest.'

'Because you could use the technology for something else?' I asked.

'Yes and no,' said Shakti. 'If you can control the amygdala and how it interacts with the rest of the brain then you can cure someone of PTSD but you can also dampen their response to real-time situations. You know how powerful that is more than almost anyone, Byron.'

'And the other stuff? It's not just that I'm calmer in the middle of a firefight, I'm more of everything. All my senses, my strength, my physical abilities.'

'A lot of that was old technology. Cochlear and retinal implants have been around for a while. All we did was some superfine-tuning. The big breakthrough was the transcranial work, putting it all together. I was gone by then because I saw what they were going to use it for but Muir took it on, and made it a spectacular success.'

It was my turn to smile. 'This is what you call a success?'

'You must be hungry,' she said. 'Tired? I can offer you food, shelter, somewhere to sleep. It's late. We can talk more in the morning.'

She must have noticed me staring at her because the next thing she said me was 'Having your own portable fMRI scanner must come in pretty handy. Doesn't it complicate your personal life?'

'I don't use it with my wife.'

Shakti leaned forward, intellectual curiosity getting the better of her. 'You can switch it on and off?'

I had never been sure how to explain it. The ability to lift a car, or see in the dark, or pick out a conversation across a crowded room or, for that matter, be able to see the blood and neural function in someone's mind by looking at them: none was a constant. It wasn't something I was conscious of, any more than anyone is conscious of what they can do. If you can pull out a chair for someone or lift a baby, you don't think about it: the capability is just *there* when you need it. I did my best to articulate it to Shakti.

She listened patiently. When I had finished, she said, 'Thank you. I've waited a long time to have this talk with someone. That's the only thing I really missed when I left, being able to talk to someone like you about how it felt to be as you are.'

'Maybe you should have called Muir.'

I didn't have to gauge her neural response to what I'd said. Her facial expression told me that she was shocked. 'Muir?'

'After they shot him, and I was trying to see if he was still alive.' I waved my fingers in the air. 'I picked up what I think is an implant in his brain. That was part of the reason I wanted to find you. So you could take a look.'

'You have him with you?' she said.

'In my vehicle,' I told her.

She sprang to her feet, crossed to the kitchen and plucked a knife from a block on the counter. 'Show me,' she said.

# FIFTY-EIGHT

**Julia**

Julia Tibor sat in a corner booth facing the door, a habit she had acquired from her husband. Always have a clear view of the main entrance and know where all the exits are. At first his fussiness about seating on planes and in restaurants had driven her slightly mad. Then one day he had told her a few stories. Even though there was little risk of a terrorist attack on the Upper West Side, Byron had explained that it was simply a matter of good habits becoming engrained.

So far, there was no sign of Meredith, and no phone call to explain her absence. Julia sipped at her coffee. The place was busier than she would have suspected. It was a young post-club crowd, or perhaps a post-bar, early-club crowd, of students and hipsters, along with a few shift workers having dinner at four in the morning before they headed for the bridges and tunnels to take them out of the city and home. The city shifted from hour to hour, all the while becoming something different, depending on who you were. Right now, she was ravaged with nerves and lack of sleep and beginning to get irritated at the no-show.

She dug out her cell phone and called the number. The first time it had gone to a generic computerized voicemail message. This time someone picked up. A man.

# FIFTY-NINE

**Graves**

Graves was shaken awake. He opened his eyes to see his desk, covered with papers. He felt like shit. The manhunt for Tibor was nationwide, the resources devoted to it unprecedented, and with every minute that passed they seemed to be getting further away from him rather than closer. They could have had him in Vegas if they'd gone public. But they had waited, which had cost them dear. Now they had the worst of both worlds – rampant public speculation and panic, no clear idea of where he was and, worse, no idea of what he was thinking or even what he wanted. Was he already dead in a ditch somewhere, having pulled the same trick Lewis had but without them being able to do the clean-up? Was he running? Or was he out there, plotting some kind of revenge spurred on by his wife?

Graves looked up from the hand on his shoulder to the face of a young agency tech analyst from the NSA. They had been tasked with using the direct electronic surveillance and the powerful algorithms that filtered every email and phone call in the country to gather intelligence. The more mundane task of racing the three possible escape vehicles had been kicked down to state and local law enforcement, guaranteeing, as Graves had known it would, a complete cluster-fuck.

'You have something for me?' asked the analyst.

'Call on the wife's cell phone.'

'Incoming or outgoing?'

'Out,' said the analyst.

Now Graves was wide awake. That meant they had a number they could trace, either by triangulating the position of the device receiving or doing it more directly if it was a landline. They also had a protocol in place if it was to a computer device using, say, a Skype account. Even if Byron was gone by the time they got there, they had a definite point to start from. They could establish a cordon around it and work their way in.

'She must have had a number for him,' said Graves. 'How come we didn't know about that?'

'It's not Tibor,' said the analyst. 'We didn't have a name for the cell phone but we ran a voice analysis and it came up with a match. It's an individual by the name of Eldon James.'

*Fuck.* What the hell was she calling Eldon James for? He wasn't even involved anymore. He'd been stood down after the Vegas fiasco, a boy sent to do a man's job. 'You have a recording I can listen to?'

'Right here,' said the analyst.

The more he thought about Eldon, the more he was freaking. 'Where'd she call him from? We have a team on her, right?'

'They lost her, but we do have a location. A diner on 34th Street. They're on the way there now.'

Graves was going to ask how they'd lost her but there would be time for that later, and a partial answer would be that a bright woman, such as Julia Tibor, married to someone like Byron, would have acquired a few skills of her own, as much by osmosis and close proximity to her husband as anything else. Surveillance took manpower and expertise; counter-surveillance was a good deal more straightforward, especially if the person knew they were being watched. They had much smaller RDF tracking devices now that could be injected on a crowded subway platform, but the White House lawyers would have had a shit fit if Graves had suggested using one on a civilian who hadn't yet been charged with any crime. That was something else to figure in. The President was now taking a personal interest, never a good thing for someone in Graves's position. The White House position seemed to be that they wanted this whole deal closed down as quickly as possible. They were then counting on the American public's limited attention span and the media's quick-moving news cycle to fill the grave. It would be spun as a tragedy, an American hero for whom the government had done its best but who had cracked up. Of course, Julia Tibor could blow that whole narrative to pieces and, contrary to what the internet conspiracy theorists believed, her civilian status meant they couldn't just take her out without risking major blowback.

Graves grabbed his suit jacket from the back of his chair, and jogged for the door. If he survived this he really would have to make some lifestyle changes. Two minutes later he was in a car and heading for the diner. If Eldon James got to her first, they were all screwed.

# SIXTY

**Julia**

The man at the other end of the line had asked her to meet him outside. He had also said that he didn't have much time, that he was a friend of Byron's from way back. The clock would already be ticking, he said. Their window was limited. He apologized for the initial subterfuge. He would explain his reasons in person because they might be listening. He didn't have to explain who they were to Julia. Not anymore.

He ended the call before she could ask any more questions. She paid the check, grabbed her jacket and walked outside. She could see him standing across the street. He was short, slim, with a shaved head. His hands dug into the pockets of his long overcoat. He looked like a strong breeze would carry him away. He certainly didn't look threatening. She waited for the Don't Walk sign to flip over, and started toward him.

He smiled at her, then turned and beckoned for her to follow him. She did, then stopped. Something wasn't right. She had rushed into this. He had used time as a pressure. She had no idea whether he was or wasn't a friend of Byron's. He could be anyone. She had created a lot of enemies at the press conference. That was one thing she could be sure of.

They had walked a half-block. He stared at her as she stood there.

'Up to you what you want to do,' he said. 'But I can take you to Byron. Or …'

She followed his gaze to the dark sedan pulling up outside the diner. It was followed by a second. She recognized the man getting out. It was Graves. He looked pissed. His hands were clenched into fists as he barged through the other men spilling from the two sedans.

'Up to you,' the man repeated.

# SIXTY-ONE

**Byron**

The Ford Escape rattled its way toward the cabin, Shakti in the passenger seat next to me. Even with all the windows open, the smell of death had settled into every corner of the vehicle.

'There's an old barn out back. We can do it there,' Shakti suggested.

I moved Muir into the center of the barn. Because the tools we had at our disposal were fairly primitive, and because we were looking to establish something other than cause of death, Shakti had proposed a more direct method. We would first separate Muir's head from his torso, then take the head into the kitchen.

Removing someone's head was trickier than it might have seemed. I had seen enough *jihadi* executions to know that. At least we had the advantage that the person was already dead, and less likely to squirm. I took an axe from a wooden workbench that ran along the side of the barn. 'You might want to step back,' I said to Shakti.

I lifted the axe high over Muir's head. Once I had inflicted the major trauma, Shakti would set to work with the knives to cut through the spinal column. She seemed very calm about the whole procedure. It occurred to me, not for the first time, that soldiers and scientists had more in common than others might have thought. For a start, neither could afford to be squeamish or overly sentimental when there was a job to do.

Two hours later, her kitchen sink full of blood, Shakti had located two devices. 'From what I can tell they're probably prototypes. It's fairly usual for people working in this field to use themselves as guinea pigs,' she told me.

'You think more of the research team would have had implants?' I asked her.

She shrugged. 'No way of knowing, and in any case I'm not sure what it changes if they did.'

At least I had been right about Muir. But, as Shakti had said, what did it matter? Muir hadn't demonstrated any strange behavior or the kind of problems that had affected Lewis or me. I said as much to Shakti.

'Why would he have?' she said. 'Both you and Lewis had suffered some form of emotional trauma.'

'So the technology would work fine with people who hadn't?'

'Too many factors, Byron. And Muir didn't seem to demonstrate any of the enhanced abilities that you have and Lewis had.'

'That we knew of,' I said.

I stared at the remnants of the part of Muir's skull that held his face. The mask of flesh stared back at me. She was right. What did any of it matter if Muir had had an implant too?

# SIXTY-TWO

**Graves**

There was no sign of Julia Tibor. And they couldn't issue a general alert for Eldon, not without it seeming that the whole situation was spinning out of control. They had found something, though. In an alleyway less than two blocks away, they had found a young woman beaten so badly that she was in a coma at Mount Sinai, having suffered severe brain trauma. The prognosis was that she would likely survive but that her brain had been deprived of oxygen for such a length of time that she was as good as dead. She lay in the grey zone between life and death. Graves knew it had to have been Eldon's work but he didn't know why he hadn't just killed her. Why leave her alive?

It was a question for later. Right now they had to find Eldon and, more importantly, Julia Tibor before she suffered the same fate. If she turned up dumped in an alleyway, alive or dead, Graves and the White House would face some tough questions after how she had reacted at the press conference. A situation they were aiming to contain was only getting larger.

They left it to the NYPD to talk to potential witnesses. They were focusing on the girl found in the alleyway. No mention was being made of either Julia Tibor's proximity or even the fact that she was missing. They would leave Eldon's name out of it for now too. There was already enough in the mix. With any luck, if Julia didn't surface, the media would assume she had been forced underground by their spotlight. The situation was best served by Graves saying nothing. If it came out later, they would distance themselves from Eldon, and Julia's disappearance. They wouldn't even have to lie. They had tried to help Julia Tibor. But some people just didn't want to be helped. If she had stayed on their side, she would have been safe.

# SIXTY-THREE

**Byron**

After Shakti and I had cleaned the kitchen, we sat down to talk, both of us too hyped to sleep. Shakti sat opposite me, the dogs at her feet. Even now the two animals retained a certain wariness. Outside, the wind had picked up. I could hear the groan and creak of trees that had been there long before either of us, and would likely remain long after we were both gone.

The smaller dog twitched in its sleep, and Shakti soothed it with a rub to the back of its neck. 'You're welcome to stay as long as you need, Byron. I rarely have visitors. I collect my mail in town. I doubt anyone would find you.'

'That's kind of you, but me hiding out here doesn't solve anything.'

'What does?' she asked.

'You ask good questions,' I said.

'It's not always seen as a positive thing.'

I still didn't have a clue why Muir had sent me there. I had learned a little more about the origins of the program, how it had come into being, how it had quickly departed from its original aim, but Shakti hadn't been able to offer anything that even approached a solution to my current predicament. I was a prototype gone awry, a mess to be cleaned up, which in itself would have been fine, if it hadn't been for Julia.

227

I watched the flicker of light from one of the candles. 'Mind if I ask you a question?'

'Go right ahead.'

It was something I had dwelled upon for a long time, and yet I wasn't sure if I had ever uttered the words to a single living soul. It was a question so basic as to seem absurd, not to mention self-obsessed.

I met the Indian woman's gaze. 'What am I?'

She clasped her hands together. She didn't answer at first. Her eyes betrayed someone as devoid of an answer as I was. 'I think, Byron, that it's far too early to say what you are. That probably wasn't a very helpful answer. I told you I was better at questions.'

'You really think I'm going to be around long enough to find out?' I ran my hands through my hair, feeling the pulse of my implants at the tips of my fingers. 'I'm not sure I even deserve to live.'

She stayed silent.

I told her about my journey so far. I told her about the four people at the lab, and how I had executed them in cold blood. Shakti let me talk myself out. The more I talked, the worse I felt. It wasn't proving cathartic, or therapeutic. If anything, it was leading me to the same conclusion that Lewis must have reached.

When I next looked at Shakti she was smiling at me. It was a warm, beatific smile that pissed me off. It reminded me a little of Julia, which darkened my mood further.

I would leave. Muir had sent me on a goddamn wild-goose chase. This woman, with her life in the woods, separated from society, had no more answers than anyone else did. She had already told me there was no going back, that any attempt to remove the technology inside my head would kill me. Meanwhile, there was an army out there, looking for me, and with good cause. I was a danger to society. I had killed in cold blood with no greater motive than my own survival. There was nothing noble in what I'd done. It had served no higher purpose.

I started to get to my feet. 'I'm talking in circles here. I appreciate your hospitality, but it would probably be best if I left.'

She ushered me to sit down. 'What you just told me about the people you killed. Those were hardly the words of a machine. A machine wouldn't have those thoughts. Guilt's a human trait, isn't it, Byron?'

'My feeling bad doesn't change what I did.'

'That's true but I'm not sure you can be held entirely responsible either. Byron, the politicians may have got cold feet this time, but this research, this whole field, isn't about to go away either. For one thing there's way too much money at stake when you think of all the possible applications. And there's something else, which the human part of you has to deal with.'

I looked at Shakti.

'If you die now, Byron, or somehow manage to disappear, you're leaving your wife behind with no answers. Maybe that's worthy of a little guilt too.'

Perhaps Muir hadn't sent me to Shakti for a grand answer, or a clue to unlock the situation I was in. She had given me something far more valuable. She had given me a reason to go on. Even if I couldn't rid myself of the implant, perhaps I could find a way to allow the human part of me to reassert itself. The guilt I felt now was a sign of that. When I had killed the two muggers, I had felt nothing approaching guilt. The last guilt I had felt was over the death of Sasha, although my remorse and grief at that had stemmed from what I hadn't done rather than what I had. But, however you cut it, it was still a human emotion, one that I could place alongside my love for my wife.

I asked Shakti for a paper and a pen. There was a small wooden table near the window that I hadn't noticed when I'd first walked in. I sat down and began to write. After years of pushing buttons, swiping screens and using keyboards, the physical act of writing, of making a mark on paper, seemed alien to me at first. Technology had changed humanity as much as humanity had pushed technology forward.

As the night moved toward a fresh dawn and my hand cramped, I wrote a letter to my wife. I engaged my human side. I told her how much I loved her. I told her what she meant to me, how much better she had made my life, and how lucky I was to have found her.

When I was done, I read it over, feeling closer to her as I turned the pages. Then I folded it, placed it in the envelope Shakti had given me and wrote Julia's name on the front. I hoped I lived long enough to give it to her.

My plan was a simple one: to stay alive long enough for the firestorm surrounding me to begin to die down. I would work my way slowly back across the country, traveling at night, walking if I had to, using all the evasion strategies and skills I had amassed, and drawing on only what I needed from the technology inside me. My hope was that by the time I had worked my way back, I would have achieved some kind of balance between the old and the new, the natural and the artificial parts of myself.

My plan lasted as long as it took Shakti to return in the early afternoon. She had gone to pick up some provisions and her mail. She had also returned with a newspaper. She folded it out in front of me. 'I'm sorry, Byron,' she said. 'I'm so sorry.'

My eyes flitted from my letter to Julia, on the cleaned-up kitchen counter, to the picture of my wife on the front page of that morning's *LA Times*.

# SIXTY-FOUR

The first bomb blew out the cabin windows. Glass punched through the air. I dove for the ground as fragments flew over my head. A triangular tooth of glass spun over my head before finally embedding itself into the far wall. I looked around for Shakti, the dogs, but they were nowhere to be seen. I heard the low whistle of another bomb as it descended from the heavens. I hunkered down in a corner, bowed my head and held my hands up to my face.

The ground shook as it hit. The walls of the cabin buzzed with vibration. The blast wave lifted the Indian goddess, Durga, from the lion and sent her hurtling across the room toward me, her weapon-laden arms scything through the air. The lion stayed where it was, noble and ever vigilant as Durga slammed into a wall, her head separating from her body. As fire lit the outside of the cabin, I opened my eyes. Durga's head rolled slowly toward me and came to rest a few feet away, face up.

I stared at the goddess as her features shifted, first taking on the appearance of Sasha. A few moments later, as another bomb whistled overhead, they morphed again. This time I found myself staring at Julia.

That bomb hit further away. I tore my gaze away from the tiny painted wooden head to the blackened window frame. A torn strip of curtain fluttered with the breeze from the blast. The largest redwood near the house was split straight down the length of its trunk. Sap the color of blood oozed from it, flowing in a stream down into the stump as the two pieces parted company and fell to the ground.

My heading pounding, I got to my feet. Lightning bolts danced through my skull, each one more painful than the last. I reached down and picked up the effigy's decapitated head and stuffed it into my pocket. Staggering to the blown-out window, I looked out to a scene of chaos.

Explosions raked their way up the compacted dirt driveway, reducing it to a deep trench. The trees keened with high-pitched screams as their branches were torn away from their trunks and the red sap flowed, pooling around their naked roots.

One tree still stood, its branches ripped from it. Halfway up, I noticed Muir's face, the bloodied mask that had lain on the kitchen counter, nailed to the trunk. Above that was Sasha's face. Then came the face of the gas-station attendant. Her forehead was furrowed with deep lines, her eyes staring straight at me. There were other faces too. Some I could place easily, while others were more distant and had to be clawed from my memory.

The death masks had held my attention so completely that it took me a moment to notice the silence. The air was still. The whine of incoming ordnance fell away. Instinctively, I waited, my head still splintered with pain. After the first storm of artillery came the calm. A calm almost inevitably followed by the next wave of chaos.

I turned around, looking for the Springfield. I couldn't see it. I wondered if Shakti had taken it with her as a precaution. After all, it was how Lewis had gone out.

The cabin was as it had been before the barrage. There was still no sign of Shakti or the dogs, but apart from their absence, everything was neat and untouched. I turned back to the window. My nose bumped against the glass. The landscape lay still and perfect. The redwoods soared upwards to a cathedral ceiling of needles. The trench of the driveway had been filled back in and smoothed over.

I glanced over to the shrine. The Hindu goddess stared serenely back at me, her legs astride the lion.

The pounding in my head began to recede. The hammer blows of pain were replaced by jabs. I walked over to the kitchen counter. The copy of the *LA Times* was there. My wife's face stared back at me, along with my own. That nightmare, the true nightmare, hadn't disappeared. But Shakti had left me with something approaching hope.

Next to the newspaper was a handwritten note. There was a cell-phone number on it and the words, Cal Tech. Underneath that was a set of instructions. The note was signed: *Good luck! Shakti*

# SIXTY-FIVE

I dressed in the clothes Shakti had left for me. With a ball cap pulled down low and a pair of Aviator sunglasses, I grabbed the Springfield and headed out of the cabin. She had taken the Escape, and left me the keys to her rusty old pick-up truck for the drive to Cal Tech.

I turned the key in the ignition, and set off down the driveway. I took Pacific Coast Highway North, riding the edge of the speed limit. It was still early. Traffic was light. After a time the redwoods of Big Sur fell away. The road hugged the ocean. Early-morning sunlight sparkled across the water. Out on some rocks two lone pelicans huddled, wings tucked in tight to their bodies, their necks on a swivel.

Leaving the highway, I headed north-east in a big loop that would take me back west toward San Jose. I felt my shoulders tighten as I approached the outskirts of the city. I took the 85 through Edenvale and pulled up next to the Oakridge shopping mall. I had made the first part of the journey.

I checked the time on a bank sign. I had been given a twenty-minute window. If I was delayed, even by a flat tire, I was screwed. Shakti had good friends, people willing to risk life and liberty not just for her but for me as well, but even they had limits. Both Shakti and the person I was meeting knew that the consequences of defying the federal government by helping me would be a life spent in prison. And that was a best-case scenario. Manning, Snowden – no one wanted to be next on that list.

Keeping the sunglasses and the ball cap on, I got out of the pick-up and walked to a Mercedes SUV. I opened the front passenger door and got in. The driver was a trim, well-groomed white man in his late fifties. He didn't say anything to me as I closed the door. I could see that he was gripping the wheel tight, presumably to stop his hands shaking. This type of meet was routine to someone like me but no doubt terrifying to him. The man's index finger tapped against the wheel as he pulled out into traffic. Was he scared of me or of what he was doing? Would he bail out of the vehicle any second while I was surrounded? I had no way of knowing.

We headed for the center of San Jose, passing a high school, stores and residential streets. An elderly Hispanic woman juggled two bags of groceries as she got into her car. A couple of high-school kids sloped along the street, either ducking out early or heading in late.

A dark blue sedan pulled in behind us at a stop sign. I watched it in the side mirror until the middle-aged woman behind the wheel turned off again.

Despite the German-engineered air-con working overtime, the man next to me was sweating. The show of nerves was starting to get to me. I decided to breach the silence. 'How you holding up?'

The man swallowed. His Adam's apple bobbed. 'Okay, I guess.' He nodded ahead. 'We're almost there.'

Like everything else in America, there was one set of rules for the unwashed masses, and another for those with the deepest of pockets, or those who worked for large corporations. Flying was no different. When it came to private and corporate aviation, security was fundamentally self-regulating. A law unto themselves for those who flew commercial, the TSA didn't dare intrude into the lives of the truly wealthy.

The Mercedes pulled up at a separate gatehouse from the main airport. The driver lowered the window. The security guard asked him for the plane's tail number. He ticked something off on a clipboard, the barrier rose and we were on our way. We drove the short distance to a small enclosed parking lot where I would catch a private shuttle bus to the aircraft. Not being able to drive directly to the aircraft steps was one of the few concessions to security.

'Oh, shit.'

I followed the driver's gaze to a black Town Car as we got out of the Mercedes, the shuttle bus already rounding the corner and heading for us. A man and a woman exited the Town Car. The woman, a platinum blond with tanned leathery skin, waved excitedly at my driver as her male companion strolled toward us.

'People I know,' said the driver. 'Don't worry, they're not on our flight.'

'John, why, imagine seeing you here.' The woman greeted the driver with a southern accent and a pair of air kisses. 'And who is this?' she said, taking me in from head to toe with a look that left nothing to the imagination. Her husband joined us, shaking John's hand.

Before he could stumble, I stepped in, offering them each a handshake. 'David Walker, nice to meet you.'

The woman stared at me as she shook my hand. 'Nice to meet you, Mr Walker.' She hesitated. 'Have we met?'

John was finding his feet in the new world of subterfuge. 'David lives on the east coast. He's been out briefing me on a couple of issues with one of our suppliers.'

The husband snapped his fingers. 'Lemme guess! Chinese? Have to keep an eye on those guys. Am I right?'

I smiled. 'Hundred percent.'

The shuttle bus had stopped next to us. The doors hissed open. 'I swear I've met you before somewhere,' the woman was saying.

We let the couple board first. They sat near the front. I guessed this was about as regular as those people's lives got. I had now placed John as John Gillhood, a west-coast-based tech wizard turned businessman – I'd seen him interviewed on cable TV. A piece clicked into place as I dredged up some vague memory of him having been involved in bmi or brain-machine interface technology. Few men are entirely without motive. Gillhood's interest in the area of bmi tech not only explained Shakti knowing him, but also his willingness, despite his nerves, to help me in such high-stakes, and potentially deadly, circumstances.

I guided John to a couple of seats at the back of the bus. I could feel the woman's eyes on me. It was impossible to tell whether it was good old sexual curiosity or something that would prove more problematic.

A few moments later the shuttle bus pulled up next to a light aircraft and the couple got off. The woman's eyes never left me. I had noticed that the bus driver, a Hispanic man in his fifties, who smelled of cigarette smoke and cologne, performed his duties as if everyone around him was invisible. He didn't speak; he didn't look; he merely did.

We settled ourselves into our seats on Gillhood's plane. Gillhood had already dismissed the captain and a lone member of cabin crew. If either of them recognized me, they had shown no sign. I suspected they were like the bus driver, paid not to notice things.

It was a short taxi to the runway, and we were off, barreling down the runway and into the air. Gillhood got up from his seat, headed for the tiny galley and returned a few moments later with an ice bucket, two Waterford crystal tumblers, a bottle of Johnnie Walker Blue Label, and a couple of bottles of mineral water. I waved away the whisky and watched as Gillhood poured himself a hefty measure.

'I would've asked you how come you're so freakin' calm, but Shakti already explained that part to me,' said Gillhood, as I unscrewed the plastic cap from a water bottle and took a sip. Now that we were in the air, he was chatty. He kept his voice low, his only concession to discretion, as he peppered me with questions. When my answers proved evasive, he gave me a flash of the man who had got to the point where he would be prepared to take such a risk, and have the money to do it. I wondered whether Muir had known of the connection between the wealthy entrepreneur and Shakti, and whether that explained why he had sent me in her direction.

'Did you know about any of this before Shakti got in touch?' I asked him.

'Everyone knew that DARPA was working in this area. That's hardly been a secret. I guess no one knew how far along it had come.' From the way Gillhood was staring at me, I was starting to feel like a prized zoo exhibit. 'They tend to release things into the public domain in small pieces. Their way of testing the waters of public opinion.'

'This has gone beyond that,' I said. 'They want the whole thing to go away. Me included.'

Gillhood shrugged. 'Why do you think I agreed to help?' He reached out a whisky-clumsy hand to touch my forearm. 'Do you know how important you are?'

I peered out of the window as we cleared the clouds. There really was no such thing as a free ride, and that went triple if it involved a private plane. 'Important or valuable?' I asked.

'In the world we live in, they're interchangeable.'

'Not as far as the government's concerned,' I said.

Gillhood smiled and had another sip of Scotch. 'Of course not. Someone else is usually picking up the bill.'

'You're taking a big risk by helping me.'

'I'm giving you a ride. If I'm asked I'll tell them you didn't give me an alternative. That's hardly going to be much of a stretch, given what's happened recently.'

'That why you were sweating so much back there?'

At first Gillhood didn't answer. He followed my gaze to the window as the plane hit a patch of turbulence that buffeted it violently from side to side.

'To be honest with you, when Shakti asked me to help you, I wasn't sure what to expect. You seem much more … I don't what the word is …'

'Much more human?' I offered.

Another shudder rattled the plane as the sky around us darkened.

'Yes. Although that's not perfect either. After all, the worst things that you've done, someone could say that's the human part of you. We're a strange species in that regard.'

I couldn't argue with him on that score.

238

# SIXTY-SIX

Four hours later we dropped from the clouds toward the Manhattan skyline. Banking sharply south we headed for the small private airport near New Jersey's Meadowlands. I borrowed Gillhood's tablet computer and, using the onboard Wi-Fi, worked my way quickly through a couple of national and local news channels. Although I had slipped down the running order, following yet another college campus massacre, the outlook was bleak. I was still wanted for the deaths at the facility, I was being named as the only suspect in Muir's murder, and, worst of all, Julia was still missing.

For the first time in a long time, I was grateful for the implant. If I was to find her, assuming she wasn't already dead, I would need every ounce of control I could muster. As the small plane shuddered to a halt, Gillhood unbuckled his seatbelt and stood up. 'I have a car that can take you into the city. After that ... there's a limit to how much I can help you.'

I stood up and shook his hand. 'I understand.'

# SIXTY-SEVEN

As night fell, the temperature plunged. I watched from across the street as two uniformed NYPD cops stood sentry at the entrance to my apartment building. In the lobby, I could see the doorman. The usual guy, a short Dominican man who traveled in every day from Queens was gone. The man standing there now was six feet two, two hundred pounds, white, and almost certainly military or connected in some way. Military personnel, at least those currently serving or with recent service, carried themselves differently from civilians.

I kept walking, my face turned toward the steel-grey river. Two blocks north, I crossed the street. I walked for one more block before hanging another right. The route took me behind the apartment building.

Without waiting, I ran to the wall. It was around twelve feet high. I climbed it easily, momentum taking me most of the way, brute strength doing the rest. My fingers dug into the stone, creating handholds from the previously smooth surface. My hands found the top and I pulled myself up and over. Further down the street there was an access gate for deliveries but doing things that way would leave clear evidence that I had been there.

Beneath me was a small communal garden. I jumped down. I stayed close to the wall as I ran, heading for the fire escape. Taking another run up, I made the bottom of the ladder with ease and hauled myself toward the first metal platform.

# SIXTY-EIGHT

**Graves**

The car lurched violently as it took the corner onto Amsterdam Avenue. Graves grabbed the front passenger seat to steady himself. 'It's him?' he asked, for the fourth time in as many minutes, and got the same answer as he had the previous three times.

'Affirmative.'

Storefronts whipped past in a blur as he glanced out of the window. Ahead and behind, Amsterdam was a carpet of flashing red rollers as they moved in convoy toward the apartment building on Riverside Drive. A three-block perimeter had already been established, NYPD working alongside the DHS and other federal agencies to make sure that Byron Tibor didn't slip past them.

They had already been tipped off a few hours ago that he had arrived at Teterboro on a private jet earlier in the day. It hadn't surprised them that John Gillhood, a billionaire tech entrepreneur, had facilitated it, although how he had hooked up with Byron was still a mystery. Given that Gillhood had already lawyered up and was playing the victim card, claiming coercion, it would likely remain that way for some time to come. Not that it mattered too much. The important thing was that they finally had Byron – the last live ember of the PSS Program.

Graves pressed his finger against his ear and listened in on the chatter. They had four specialist search teams moving into the apartment building. Any residents found were being evacuated on the pretext of safety. So far the story they had fed the media had stuck, and now they were close to the end, he wanted it to stay that way. There was even talk that if the situation could be resolved without public exposure, the program might possibly be reopened. Intelligence had surfaced of a parallel program being conducted by the Chinese – and they had the advantage of being a lot less considerate of public opinion than the US. There was nothing to settle a president's conscience more quickly than the idea that someone else was about to gain an edge. First things first, though. They had to recover Tibor with a minimum of fuss.

They hung another bone-juddering left onto Broadway. The comms chatter was that the evacuation was going smoothly. Most of the apartment building's residents had been accounted for. Tibor hadn't been located yet but they were picking up sound from the apartment. Teams were moving in from ground and roof level. He had nowhere to go. The decision had already been taken that even if he had taken a hostage or hostages they weren't going to wait. As soon as the building was secured they were going in. If extracting him using normal procedures failed they had special clearance to call upon the services of a SEAL demolition team to take down the whole building if necessary.

They slowed as they approached the NYPD sawhorses at the edge of the perimeter. The car nudged through the small crowd of residents huddled together in the freezing cold. Buses were on the way to take them to an evacuation center. Graves guessed that the one plus of this going down here was that the plans were in place, all ready to be deployed.

The car stopped two blocks from the apartment building and he got out. He tapped the bottom of a fresh pack of cigarettes, ripped it open, took one out and lit it. The chatter of comms continued in his ear as he walked. The teams had reached the outside of the apartment. It had gone quiet inside. Harry could hear the tension in the voices of the team leaders as they coordinated final entry and clearance.

Flashing his creds, Graves climbed the three steps into the Homeland Security Mobile Command Vehicle. He said hello to a couple of the guys and took a seat. A wall of screens relayed live feeds from the helmet cams of the various teams. Software linked to individual GPS units rearranged the images to provide a clearer overview of the live feeds.

They were in place. A six-man team was in the corridor. Across the street, snipers covered the front window of the apartment from an elevated platform. The blinds were open but there were no lights on, as Graves would have expected with Byron's night-vision capabilities.

A small charge had been placed on the apartment door. As soon as it blew, they would go in. Graves doubted that the six men would all make it out alive. There were back-up teams in place to cover Tibor taking out all six. And the SEAL demolition team was en route.

The team leader keyed his radio. 'Ready.'

Three seconds later, the charge detonated, the door flying backwards into the apartment, dust and smoke obscuring the view from the live feeds as the team moved in.

Harry stalked out of the command post. The search was ongoing but he was certain that Byron Tibor was long gone. The only thing he could be certain of was that he had been there. An inventory had shown that nothing had been taken. The appearance raised more questions than answers. Had Tibor expected to find his wife? Did he even know she was missing? Surely Gillhood would have told him.

Lighting another cigarette, Graves headed back to the car. He was dreading the next part, having to break the bad news. The last few hours had reignited fading media interest in the story, propelling it back to rolling coverage. Worse, there was a growing public sentiment of sympathy toward Tibor. All they needed now was for him to get in touch with the media, and share his side of the story, and they would be in a world of shit.

With a sigh, he flicked his half-smoked cigarette away, ground it out under his heel, opened the door and climbed into the rear passenger seat.

Beside him, Byron Tibor reached over and closed the door on them, trapping Graves inside as he pressed the muzzle of a gun into the back of his neck.

# SIXTY-NINE

**Byron**

I told the driver to get moving. He did as he was told. I took Graves's cell phone and service weapon from him as the car rolled slowly toward the perimeter. He could only watch as we drifted past dozens of blue uniforms, none giving the car a second glance, the darkened windows ensuring our privacy.

The car nudged through a gap. For a few seconds it was surrounded by a gaggle of press who had come to see the show. After a few moments we cleared it. I told the driver to head south on Riverside.

'Where's Julia?' I asked.

Graves turned to look at me. 'I don't know.'

'Take this turn up here,' I instructed the driver. We drove three more blocks. 'Okay, pull in there.'

The driver turned into an alleyway and stopped next to a couple of trash Dumpsters. I ordered him and Graves out. They gathered at the front of the car. Graves stood next to the driver. The driver's hands were shaking. 'Walk toward me,' I told the driver.

When the driver got within a few feet, I ordered him to turn around. I wrapped one arm around his neck. Realizing what was about to happen, he tried to wriggle his way out, but he was no match for me. With a sharp twist, I snapped his neck. There was a dull crack as the top of his spinal cord separated from his head.

I lifted the man up with one arm and tossed him over the lip of the Dumpster. I turned back to Graves and tossed him the keys. 'You're driving,' I told him. 'You don't know where my wife is, but you can find Eldon. He's chipped. Just like I was.'

'What the hell are you talking about? Chipped?'

I stepped toward him. I raised my left hand. My fingertips wandered to Graves's neck, stopping at a point on the right side. I holstered the gun and reached for something else.

'Speaking of which,' I said, bringing up the blade of the knife.

'I'm not chipped,' Graves protested. He jabbed a finger at his skull. 'Look, I'm not lying.'

I smiled at him. 'You think those trackers were just for the little people like me, Harry?'

Graves nodded dumbly as I pressed the blade against his skin. 'We're all the little people,' I told him, pressing down.

I reached my fingers into the pouch of skin and pinched the tiny device between his thumb and index finger. I handed it to him. He cupped it in his open palm.

'Son of a bitch,' he muttered.

I tore a strip of fabric from his shirt and pressed it against the wound. 'Don't feel bad,' I told him.

# SEVENTY

We raced down Fourth Avenue, the street numbers falling away with each block. Graves was deathly pale. I suspected it was more to do with the realization that he wasn't running the game any more than pain from the neck wound. On the screen of his smartphone I could see a red dot pulse over a map of Manhattan as it tracked Eldon's movements.

'Why'd you pick Eldon?' I asked him. 'There are dozens of trained operatives you could have used.'

'I think I'm going to throw up,' said Graves.

We were coming up on a rack of red lights that stretched for blocks. I motioned for Graves to pull over to the curb. 'Be quick, and don't do anything stupid.'

Graves opened the door, leaned out and vomited. He closed it again. 'Why'd you think we used Eldon?'

Even without an implant, I knew the look Graves had just given me. He'd used Eldon because he was a throwaway. Plus he was so out there he could have told everyone he met about the operation and no one would have believed him.

'Listen' said Graves, 'I didn't tell him to go near your wife.'

The lights flipped to green. Graves jammed his foot on the gas pedal.

'You didn't stop him either,' I said.

Graves swiped a trail of yellow saliva from his mouth with the back of his hand. He held up the other in a *mea culpa* gesture. 'True.'

'If he hurts her, I'm killing all of you,' I told him. 'Every single person in your department will be a target. Same goes for all those asshole politicians back in DC. I'll burn the goddamn place to the ground if she's been hurt.'

'She's safe. I'm sure she is,' he said.

'That what you said about Muir?'

Graves looked taken aback. 'We didn't kill Muir.'

I shook my head. 'You sorry sack of shit. They didn't tell you that either. They say it was me? It wasn't me, Harry. I've done lots of bad things recently, but Muir wasn't one of them.'

As each second passed, Graves seemed more and more confused. He must have thought he was running the show when all along someone above him was pulling the strings.

The rain was growing more intense. Heavy drops exploded against the windshield. I barely had time to react as Sasha stepped off the sidewalk in front of the car. I reached over and grabbed the steering-wheel, the car fishtailing violently across two lanes of traffic. A yellow cab blasted its horn as it drove round them.

'What the hell are you doing?' Graves shouted at me.

I ignored him. I looked out to see Sasha, her face covered with blood, walking toward us. I blinked, trying to clear my vision. I didn't have time for flashbacks or ghosts from the past. I must have looked completely distracted because Graves chose that moment to open the door, and roll out of the car.

I grabbed the wheel again, and scooted into the driver's seat. The door still open, I raised the Springfield, capturing Graves's hunched shoulders in the iron sights. Graves was running as hard as he could between the traffic as horns blared. Sasha stood perfectly still, blood pooling at her feet, as she stared at me. My index finger closed on the trigger. Graves looked back at me with that bloodhound face of his, and something passed between us. His life was mine.

I threw the gun back on the passenger seat, and picked up his cell phone from where he had abandoned it. The blip of red flashed, its position changing fractionally. I glanced back at the retreating figure of Graves, then across to Sasha. She was smiling.

I reached over, slammed the door and took off again, leaving the blood-soaked child from Anash Kapur to fade to a speck of red dust in the rearview mirror.

# SEVENTY-ONE

The red dot tracked south along the FDR. It updated its position every ten seconds. It was hard to tell whether Eldon was on foot or stuck in slow-moving traffic. As I turned on to the expressway, which ran alongside the East River, I had my answer. Traffic was gridlocked. Up ahead, near the entrance to the Brooklyn Bridge that spanned the East River, linking Manhattan to Brooklyn, lay a tide pool of red roller bar lights from NYPD and other EMS vehicles.

I grabbed the cell phone, the Springfield and Graves's Glock, and bailed out of the Town Car, clambering over and exiting via the passenger door. Weaving my way through the vehicles, I broke into a run, Graves's cell phone in one hand, his Glock in the other.

The red dot was picking up speed. With each reappearance it ghosted further and further along the bridge. I looked up to see two NYPD cruisers parked side on across the top of the ramp that led to the bridge. A baby-faced cop leaning against the back of one of the cars was the first to spot me. He pushed off the car, shouting to another couple of patrol cops and drew his weapon. I kept the Glock by my side as I ran toward the ramp.

The cop backed away as three more officers drew their guns and trained them on me. I slowed to a stop.

'Stop right there,' one of the other cops barked at me. 'Now, put down your weapon on the ground.'

I hunkered down. Behind me I could hear a couple of people getting out of their cars, no doubt hoping for a better look at the unfolding drama. Glancing over my shoulder, as I placed the Glock on the road, I saw the flicker of camera phones, red record lights flashing. One guy wearing a suit was holding up an iPad.

'Okay, move forwards. Slowly,' came the next instruction.

I took six long slow strides.

'Okay, stop there. Hands behind your head, lace your fingers. They move, you're fucking dead, asshole. You hear me?'

I complied. My eyes probed beyond the cops blocking my path. Up ahead I picked out the swooping curve of the steel cable that led to the first stone tower of the bridge. Halfway up I saw two distant figures picking their way slowly up the cable, using the auxiliary cables on either side as handrails. They had their backs to me but that didn't stop me picking out Eldon and, in front of him, my wife.

# SEVENTY-TWO

I lowered myself to my knees, eyes fixed on the two lone figures. I could make a plea to the cops arresting me, but it would do no good. They were on auto-pilot, following a procedure that allowed for no deviation. I keened my ears, picking up the chatter from inside the patrol cars that counseled extreme caution. Three cops were walking slowly toward me, two with guns drawn. I could hear more coming up from behind. From their whispers I gleaned that they were going to take me down hard. I picked out the squeak of leather as one picked his Taser out from his utility belt. The footsteps behind me stopped. I could hear the rustle of the cop's jacket as he raised his arm.

Don't do it, I thought, as I heard the nitrogen propellant charges detonate in a puff and the Taser lines start to whip through the air, the two spikes embedding themselves in the back of my neck. My eyes locked on my wife as she stumbled, one foot slipping out from underneath her and under the steel auxiliary cable.

Time slowed. I could feel the pulse of electricity moving along the wires to me. The first jolt hit, snapping hard into my neck and sending my muscles into spasm. It traveled through the tissue into the top of the spinal cord and pulsed its way along the nerve pathways into my brainstem, the part of the human mind known as the reptilian brain; the dark, base section that dragged us from the primordial swamp.

Rather than falling forward, I felt my back straighten. One by one my fingers unmeshed. I rose to my feet, arms spreading wide. My face set like granite. I felt a rush of energy course through me. A spark of blue light flew between my fingertips as I reached back, and grabbed the two wires.

The burly cop still holding the X26 Taser stared at me, his lips parting in shock as I yanked the wires hard to reel him in. Still mesmerized, his grip tightened around the Taser. By the time he let go it was too late. The Springfield drawn, I tucked the barrel under his chin. The other cops held their fire, unable to get off a clean shot without risking taking him out. I could see the flashes of yellow bubbling up inside their heads, signaling their fear.

I ripped the two spikes from my back. I prised the Taser from the cop's hand and tossed it away. He was mumbling a prayer to himself.

'Tell your colleagues to lower their weapons,' I told him.

After a couple of stammered attempts, he managed to repeat the phrase. All but two of the cops lowered their guns. Overhead, I could hear the thump of rotor blades as a chopper flitted toward us.

The snap of a single shot punched through the night sky. The round smacked dead center between the cop's eyes. His head snapped back, the top of his skull hitting my chin. Still holding him upright, my face and upper body covered with blood and brains, I looked up to see Eldon, one arm around Julia, with a gun in his hand.

'Officer down!'

A babble of expletives and panicked instructions filled the air around me. Weapons that had been lowered mere seconds ago were raised again. I held the dead cop upright to shield myself from their fire.

Glancing down I saw a tear in my jacket near my right shoulder. Eldon's bullet must have carried on through the cop's skull to punch its way into my shoulder. Because I was already covered with the cop's blood, I had no way of telling whether it had penetrated the subcutaneous armor covering my torso.

Dragging the dead man backwards, his shoes scuffing the asphalt, I retreated toward the steel cable and the edge of the bridge. To my right came the crack of another shot. I spun, drew down on the officer who had fired, and shot him. It was as perfectly executed as Eldon's had been, smacking directly through the man's forehead as he had tried to duck behind the open door of his cruiser.

I dumped the dead weight of the man's body, spun and ran for the cabling as more live rounds poured in. A bullet pinged against the metal trellis that separated the road from the suspension cable. I swung a leg over, stopped for the briefest of seconds and fired again. This time, I caught the cop in the throat.

I started the climb. The slope of the steel started gently enough that I could run. Incoming fire pinged off the steel latticework. In a few feet I would be away from its protection and the cops on the bridge would have a clear line of fire.

I tilted my head back and stared up. I could see Eldon pushing Julia ahead of him, toward the first stone tower.

I had come to a suicide guard, a ten-foot-high section of fencing aimed at stopping jumpers. As I clawed my way to the top a round slammed into the small of my back. My stomach lurched with the pain of the impact and for a second I felt like I was going to throw up. I pressed on, hauling myself over the fence, and jumping down onto the narrow foot-wide span of cable. I grabbed the auxiliary cables on either side to steady myself. Beneath my feet I could see the dark churn of the river, the faintest crest of waves lit by the NYPD helicopter as it flew around the bridge.

Sheer force of will powered me forward. I kept climbing, my feet skidding out from under me as I reached the next suicide guard. The muzzle flashes below me had stopped. I glanced down to see the regular patrol officers falling back along the bridge toward the city. A black paramilitary phalanx of bodies swept forward in their wake. There was no turning back now. This wasn't going to end well. There would be no final-reel miracle, no windswept lovers' reconciliation. All I could do now was save the woman I loved, even if that meant sacrificing myself.

What would I have sacrificed in the end anyway? I was no longer fully human, but I retained enough of my humanity to feel the kind of emotional pain that undermined the efficient operation of a machine. I was an outlier, a step on the evolutionary ladder that the world wasn't ready for yet.

The climb grew steeper with every step. Eldon and Julia were on the ladder that led up and over the cornice of the neo-Gothic stone tower. Eldon's back was exposed. I had a clear shot at him. A shot that I was sure I could make easily. But I couldn't risk spooking Julia. If she lost her balance, or Eldon grabbed her as he fell, she would fall to her death.

I pushed forward. My back throbbed. Julia and Eldon were out of sight, gone over the edge and onto the top of the tower.

Thirty seconds later, I reached the bottom of the ladder. Eldon would be waiting for me at the top. But so would Julia. The thought of her spurred me on as I grabbed the steel rung of the ladder and began the short climb.

# SEVENTY-THREE

My fingertips pulsed as they touched the top rung of the ladder. The helicopter was directly overhead, bathing me in its light. I pushed off with my feet and grabbed the stone lip. I waited for the crush of Eldon's boots or for Eldon's face to appear over the edge. I listened as hard as I could, filtering out the rush of air from the rotor blades.

Nothing.

Palms flat on the rough stone, I pushed myself up, crawling on my belly before standing up. The stone tower ran the width of the bridge. In the center the Stars and Stripes snapped tight in the wind. Eldon stood next to it, one arm around a terrified Julia, her mind burning yellow with fear. In his hand, he held a SIG Sauer 229, the barrel aimed at Julia's head.

It was only then, in that moment, that I noticed Eldon was different. Whatever emotions he was experiencing, I couldn't discern them. There was no aura, no colors that I could see. His face masked his mind. There was no fear, no terror, no anger, nothing. My mind clawed its way back to our last encounter in the tunnels, and I remembered that while he hadn't shown fear, not even when I had held his life in my hands, I had been able to see some stab of anger. Now there was nothing.

Eldon pressed the barrel of the SIG a little harder into Julia's temple. She winced with pain. 'Should have killed me back in Vegas, Tibor.'

'She's got nothing to do with this.' I looked at my wife, shivering with cold and fear in the night air. She looked away, breaking eye contact.

'Oh, I agree,' said Eldon.

'So let her go.'

'Soon as you toss that gun and anything else you have,' said Eldon.

I looked back at Julia. I had thought about this moment for a long time. It was what had sustained me. It had allowed me to do the things I had, to endure. My love for her had proved as important as any amount of the chips or implants they had crammed inside me. Finally she looked at me, the yellow aura of fear burning so brightly in the center of her mind that I could barely make out her eyes.

I lowered the gun, all the while holding Julia's gaze. 'Okay, count of three,' I said. 'I toss it, and you let her go.'

'Agreed,' said Eldon.

I counted down. At two, I watched as Eldon eased the pressure of the barrel against Julia's head, and began to lower the gun. On three, I threw the gun, like a Frisbee, over the edge of the tower.

As good as his word, Eldon shoved Julia to one side. He pivoted slightly, raised the gun again, and fired a single shot. It caught me in the chest. The force threw me backwards with a lot more punch than the previous round I had taken. For a second my feet lifted off the ground. I landed on my back, winded, my mouth opening and closing as I gasped for air. I heard Julia scream. Her reaction to my being hurt gave me comfort. There was sweetness in the thought that she cared. I tried to lift my head to look at her, but I was still too winded to manage even that.

I stayed where I was. I didn't think the shot had penetrated the thin layer of armor under my skin, but I couldn't be sure. Eldon had come prepared. Whatever ammunition he was using, it wasn't standard.

Close-quarters combat of any kind rests on the combatants' perception. Right now, Eldon must have believed he had the edge. That was fine with me. I stayed where I was, and watched as he walked toward me.

The helicopter had shifted position so that it was side on to us. The door was open, a dark figure leaning out. He held something in front of him. It took me a second to realize that what I had taken, at first glance, to be light reflecting from a rifle scope was the lens of a camera. The helicopter wasn't there to take down either me or Eldon. Nor was it there to pluck my wife to safety. It was there to capture the moment for posterity. I thought I caught sight of Gillhood but I couldn't be sure.

I watched as Eldon stopped six feet from me. The pain rolled across my chest in waves. I felt sick. The nausea came with the growing suspicion that we'd all been played by some unseen person or persons.

I rolled onto my side. I raised my arm, hand open, fingers spread wide. Eldon aimed the gun at my head. His finger was on the trigger. Beyond him, I could see Julia hunkered down next to the flag, her hair blown across her face by the wind.

I shifted focus back to Eldon's index finger as he squeezed the trigger.

# SEVENTY-FOUR

I rolled to my left as the muzzle flashed. I swept out my left leg, catching Eldon's ankles with my heel. He stumbled forward. I pushed onto my feet. Eldon recovered his balance, raised the gun again and took a step back.

Julia was behind Eldon now. She clawed at his face with her nails. He threw an elbow. It caught her flush in the face. I heard her nose crack as she fell backwards. She sat down hard, her face bloodied. I had to fight the urge to go to her, and make sure she was okay. The only way to save her was to destroy Eldon.

I threw myself toward him and took him down at the knees. Another shot rang out. I could feel the flash hot against my body. Eldon was wiry, far stronger than he looked. He caught me a stunning blow on the side of the mouth.

I drew back my fist and punched. The blow caught the side of his head. I was on top of him now, pinning him down. I grabbed his gun arm and pushed it down by his side. One by one, I peeled his fingers from the butt of the gun. It was hard work.

After what seemed like hours, but could only have been a minute at most, I had the gun. I held it like a stone, drew it back and slammed it into the side of Eldon's head. His right eye socket caved with the force of the blow. I drew my hand back again and slammed the cold metal of the gun into his face again. A third blow, this one lower down, smashed into his mouth.

I sat up, my knees pinning his arms to his sides. His eyes rolled back in his head. He sputtered a mix of blood, saliva and fragments of teeth from his mouth. I stared down at him, mesmerized by the damage I had done. Whatever fight Eldon had had was gone.

# SEVENTY-FIVE

On either side of the tower came the sound of men climbing the ladders from the suspension cables. I sat back a little and angled the gun so that it was pointed at Eldon's face.

I glanced toward Julia. I had lost sight of her features. The lips, eyes and nose I had fallen in love with were burned away by the intense yellow glow that rose like an orb from the center of her skull. I pushed it away, my mind, the human part of it, battling with whatever they had placed inside it. It flared, then dimmed. I could see her face again.

I got to my feet, and took a step toward her. There was only one way out for us, only one way off the bridge. It was risky. This time there would be no harness, and no cord to stop us hitting the water.

The fingers of her right hand fell into mine. I stared into her eyes. She was even more beautiful than I had remembered. 'Trust me. We'll go together,' I told her, the words echoing from our past.

She pulled back from me, the tips of her fingers sliding through mine until we were no longer touching. An orb of yellow flared again. I reached up and touched her face, trying to brush it away.

'Byron, you need help,' she said.

There was a scuffle of boots on metal. A helmeted head popped over the edge. Pivoting round, I aimed the Springfield and let off a warning shot. The head disappeared.

'Here, take my hand.' I reached out to her but she backed away.

'Even if I wanted to,' she said, 'I'd never survive the drop.'

'We could be together,' I told her. 'Isn't that what you want?'

'Put down the gun, Byron. Let them help you.'

I shook my head as she stared at me. Her features began to fall away again, pushed out by the yellow. She took another step back. I could still see her eyes as they welled with tears. A second later they were gone, pushed out by the color of fear.

It was then I knew for sure that the source of my wife's terror wasn't Eldon, or the drop from the top of the bridge to the black water, or even the dozens of weapons trained, unseen, below us. The source of her terror was me.

The SWAT team were breaching the top of the ladders now. I looked down to see half a dozen red dots dancing across my body, forming a perfect kill pattern.

The black-gloved hand of one of the SWAT team members clamped onto Julia's shoulder. She glanced round, startled, but as she looked at them, the yellow faded at the edges as her fear receded. The message was simple. To her they were rescuers.

She looked back at me, and mouthed two silent words of apology. 'I'm sorry.' Her eyes pleaded for my forgiveness. She was torn. I already knew the question she was struggling with. It was the same question I had confronted, with no answer. Am I a man, or something beyond a man?

Our actions define us. I was no exception. I had killed, therefore I was a killer. It was binary in its simplicity. No amount of special pleading would change that. Julia was of another world and, I now knew, she always had been. It had been foolish for us to think we could be other than who we were. She was fully human, and I was not.

I watched as a ballistic shield was thrown up in front of her, and more men swarmed between us. I fought the desire to go to her. Letting go was not part of my program. I was engineered to secure objectives, and Julia had been my objective. She had driven me on and sustained me through all of this.

But what happened when you found that the rescued didn't need rescuing? Did you forge ahead blindly, hoping to persuade them of the purity of your intent? Or did you give way to the painful realization that every drop of blood that had been spilled was for nothing? The human part of me already knew the answer.

I could still see her face as I let the gun drop from my hand. Slowly I got to my feet. I waited for the salvo of bullets to erupt. My insides turned over. The implant began to whisper to me as the human part of my mind began to retreat, overwhelmed by the torment of Julia's rejection.

I raised my arms high above my head in surrender. Behind me the Stars and Stripes wilted as the wind died. Instructions were shouted, but I could no longer pick out the words.

The Manhattan skyline glistened to my left. I took a deep breath, filling my lungs. Pushing off with my right foot, I ran for the edge of the tower. A shot caught me in the back. My torso lurched forward but I kept moving, clearing the edge of the tower, and falling, arms spread out into the cold night air.

I tumbled in free-fall through the air toward the water below. Lights glittered all around me as I tumbled through the blue-black night. Seconds passed. I hit the surface, the force of the impact knocking the air from my chest. I surrendered, and let the water take me.

# SEVENTY-SIX

*Associated Press, New York*
*The body of a man recovered from the East River yesterday,*
*following what the Department of Homeland Security, the NYPD,*
*and FBI have described as a domestic-terrorism-related incident,*
*has been identified as Harold Graves, a federal liaison official*
*working with the Defense Advanced Research Projects Agency.*
*The cause of death is believed to be multiple gunshot wounds.*

*Authorities are still seeking former special-forces veteran and*
*State Department official Byron Tibor, following an incident on*
*the Brooklyn Bridge on Monday night, which resulted in the*
*deaths of three NYPD officers. A second man, whose name has*
*not yet been released to the media, was taken into custody at the*
*scene. Tibor's wife, Julia Tibor, an associate professor at the*
*Department of International Relations at Columbia University, is*
*believed to be recovering at a private medical facility in New*
*Jersey.*

*Services for the slain NYPD officers are taking place today*
*and tomorrow.*

# SEVENTY-SEVEN

I stand across the street from our old apartment, the exhaust fumes of the early-evening traffic and the burnished gold leaves of the late fall taking me back to the time before. It's cold. I stamp my boots on the sidewalk, trying to force warmth into my feet. A woman walking a tiny dog swaddled in a fleece sweater skirts around me. In a city of perpetual motion, standing quietly, watching, is a suspect activity, especially when you look as I do.

I scare people. They see something in my eyes. At first, I thought it was death, but it's not. Death is a presence, and what they see in me isn't a presence so much as an absence.

I glance back to the apartment building. The light is failing. The last of the sunlight turns the building's stone front to a rich honey-gold for a few precious minutes as I wait it out. I tell myself that I have come this far, and seen so much, that everything that has passed before me requires that I hold my position. I have to see her again.

The traffic is building up on Riverside Drive. Beneath the car horns I can hear each engine, the individual whirr of a timing belt, the low hum of a hybrid's batteries, I can trace a single bead of water as it falls from mud flap to road. I can shift my mind so that in the building behind I can hear conversations behind closed apartment doors all the way down to the scrape of a kitchen chair as a woman gets up, or the shift from sitcom babble to a news anchor's earnest drone as her fifteen-year-old daughter changes the channel.

My eyes roam the surface of the building to a point where I can see the stone fascia not as a flat plane but as a pitted moonscape of peaks and indentations. Flaws in the stone, flecks of brown or black where the rest is grey, are sharp and clear. Every sound is crisp and fierce. Everything is dialed up so that I exist in a permanent state of hyper-reality.

Some noises take me back to a place I would rather forget. The rattle of a loose pipe as water runs through it sounds like a .50 machine gun being fired in the distance. It makes me shiver, not in fear but from a memory of my feet frozen near-solid in my boots.

Suddenly I catch sight of her as she steps out from under the canopied entrance, the liveried doorman of the building sheltering her under his umbrella as a cab pulls up. He opens the door for her. She is about to get in. But in the moment before she ducks inside, she stops and notices the solitary man studying her from across the way. Her bright blue eyes fly wide open, then narrow again, as her conscious mind overrides what she is looking straight at and she judges what she is seeing as a cruel trick. She stands there for a moment, the doorman behind her, everyone and everything frozen in place. Although there is traffic, none of it breaks her gaze. The city is lost to us, momentarily still and silent.

She ducks out of sight, the top of the umbrella shielding the space above the roof of the cab. It pulls away. The traffic begins to flow again. Pedestrians filter back into focus: a nanny pushing an old-style Silver Cross pram; an elderly couple, the man's hand touching his wife's sleeve – a vision of the life I had imagined for us.

I will a picture into my mind of her still standing on the sidewalk, the cab uptown to her office at Columbia University abandoned. But she is gone.

Did she recognize me? The flare of yellow in her mind before she ducked into the cab tells me that she did. It makes her getting into the cab all the more wrenching. I had hoped that the passage of time might have changed her view of me. It hasn't. I have the answer I came for.

I turn away from the home I had, and walk back toward the river.

# Acknowledgements

Thanks to my editor, Hazel Orme, and to Nick Castle for his terrific cover design. Thanks also to my agent Scott Miller, and his assistant, Stephanie Hoover, as well as the rest of the team at Trident in New York.

As with every book, I am immensely grateful for the support of family and friends on both sides of the Atlantic, especially Marta and Caitlin. Last but not least, thank you to my readers who make all the hard work worthwhile.

# About the Author

To research the Ryan Lock series of thrillers, Sean Black has trained as a bodyguard in the UK and Eastern Europe, spent time inside America's most dangerous Supermax prison, Pelican Bay in California, undergone desert survival training in Arizona, and ventured into the tunnels under Las Vegas. A graduate of Columbia University in New York, he also holds a Masters degree in Philosophy, Politics and Economics from Oxford University, England.

The Ryan Lock books have also been translated into Dutch, German and Russian, with a Spanish translation of the latest book in the series, The Devil's Bounty, coming in 2013. For more information visit his website: www.seanblackbooks.com

# Other books by Sean Black

**The Ryan Lock Series**
Lockdown
Deadlock
Gridlock
The Devil's Bounty
Lock & Load

**For kids**
Extolziby Gruff and the 39th College

For more information about Sean, and his work, you can go to:
www.seanblackbooks.com

Made in the USA
Coppell, TX
15 April 2020